2
CAT FACTS

CAT FACTS

THE PET PARENT'S A-to-Z
HOME CARE ENCYCLOPEDIA

Kitten to Adult, Disease & Prevention, Cat Behavior

Veterinary Care, First Aid, Holistic Medicine

AMY SHOJAI

FURRY MUSE PUBLICATIONS

4 CAT FACTS

A Furry Muse Book
Published by Furry Muse Publications
Hardcover Edition: ISBN 978-1-948366-25-0

Copyright © 2015 Amy Shojai

Illustrations and Photos © as follows & Used With Permission:

Illustrations for Declaw; Balance; Communication; Ears; Eyes; Reproduction; © Amy Shojai

Illustrations for Alphabet chapter heading and Back Cover © DepositPhotos.com

Photos (Cover & Interior) © DepositPhotos.com

All rights reserved under International and Pan-American Copyright Conventions. Published in the United States by Furry Muse Publications, an imprint of Amy Shojai, Sherman, Texas.

http://www.SHOJAI.com

Without limiting the rights under copyright reserved above, no part of this publication may be re-produced, stored in or introduced into a retrieval system, or transmitted, in any form or by any means (electronic, mechanical, photocopying, recording or otherwise), without the prior written permission of the copyright owner of this book.

PUBLISHER'S NOTE
Every effort has been made to ensure that the information contained in this book is complete and accurate. However, neither the publisher nor the author is engaged in rendering professional advice or services to the individual reader. The ideas, procedures, and suggestions contained in this book are not intended as a substitute for consulting with your pet's physician. All matters regarding your pet's health require medical supervision. Neither the author nor the publisher shall be liable or responsible for any loss or damage allegedly arising from any information or suggestion in this book. While the author has made every effort to provide accurate product names and contact information neither the publisher nor the author assumes any responsibility for errors, or for changes that occur after publications.

First Edition: December 2015
10 9 8 7 6 5 4 3 2 1

For all the cats and dogs

Who have touched my soul—

And for one special
Furry Muse
Who started it all.

Still missing you.

6
CAT FACTS

CONTENTS

Acknowledgments		9
Entries A to Z		13-514
Appendix A:	Cat Associations	516
	Cat Breeds At A Glance	518
Appendix B:	Resources	521
Appendix C:	Symptoms At A Glance: The Quick Reference Guide for Home Diagnosis	527
Index		536
About the Author		544

8
CAT FACTS

ACKNOWLEDGEMENTS

This book would not have happened without an incredible support team of friends, family and accomplished colleagues and veterinary experts. In particular, I must thank my fellow cat lovers in the Cat Writers' Association, Inc., who have offered me both professional support and friendship along the way.

CAT FACTS is the result of 25+ years of researching, loving, and writing about these unique creatures that share our hearts—and our pillows.

After more than 30 books (and counting), I'm even more grateful today for passionate cat parents. Without you, there would be no reason for my work. Wags and purrs to my Triple-A Team (Amy's Audacious Allies) for all your help sharing the word about all my books. Youse guyz rock!

I am grateful to all the cats and dogs I've met over the years who have shared my heart. Nineteen-year-old Seren-Kitty, nine-year-old Magical-Dawg and the newcomer Karma-Kat inspire me daily. Thanks be to ALL the cats: those who live in our past, our present, and our future. I hope this book helps you with all of your nine lives.

I never would have been a pet lover, a reader and now a writer if not for my fantastic parents who instilled in me a love of the written word, and never looked askance when I preferred animals to dolls. And of course, my deepest thanks to my husband Mahmoud, who continues to support my writing passion, even when he doesn't always understand it.

I love hearing from you! Please drop me a line at my blog http://AmyShojai.com or my website http://www.shojai.com where you can subscribe to my PET PEEVES newsletter (and maybe win some pet books!). Follow me on twitter @amyshojai and like me on Facebook: http://www.facebook.com/amyshojai.cabc

Amy Shojai

10
CAT FACTS

The author has taken great pains to compile the most up-to-date information currently available for cat lovers on the care of their cat; however, veterinary medicine is constantly improving. Please consult with your veterinarian on a regular basis to provide the best care for your cat.

12
CAT FACTS

13

CAT FACTS

ABSCESS An abscess is a pocket of infection. When an injury occurs, the body attempts to protect itself by sending specialized cells to attack invading substances, like bacteria. The body builds a wall to seal off and contain the invader, and in the process also traps dead cells and other liquid debris. Commonly called pus, this liquid material is the end product of the body's fight against infection. The battlefield is the abscess, a pocket of tissue that swells as it collects the pus.

Anything that breaks the integrity of the skin can cause an abscess. Foreign bodies like splinters, or even an insect bite could cause problems. Cats are quite prone to abscesses because feline skin repairs itself so quickly. When the cat's skin heals, it may actually seal in bacteria.

ABSCESS

SYMPTOMS: Painful skin swelling or draining sore usually on neck; lethargy; loss of appetite; fever
FIRST AID: Moist warm compresses applied to sore; cleaning sore with damp cloths, supportive nutrition
VET CARE: Surgical draining; antibiotics
PREVENTION: neuter/spay cats; keep indoors

The vast majority of abscesses are caused by bite wounds. Cats' mouths contain a lot of bacteria that can infect the wound. Kitty teeth, though small, can cause serious puncture wounds that plant infectious organisms deep within the tissues. Scratches are also a problem, because cats may pick up bacteria on their feet from the litter box that grows very rapidly.

Abscesses are especially common in outdoor cats and intact felines because of their aggressive encounters with other cats. Elderly cats, very young cats, and cats whose immune systems are compromised tend to have more serious reactions. Although they can occur anywhere on the body, abscesses appear around the face area most frequently, or on the feet and legs. They almost always occur just beneath the skin.

Diagnosis is usually made from symptoms, which at first may be very subtle. A bite wound or claw injury is often hidden by fur, but can be painful even before it abscesses. The affected cat may flinch or even vocalize when the owner touches the painful area.

As the infection progresses and pus begins to collect, the area swells beneath the skin. Cats may act lethargic, and may not want to eat. Abscesses generally grow outward, and the surface skin stretches and becomes quite thin. Often, the abscess will rupture, and a blood-tinged white to yellow discharge will be seen. This looks nasty, but actually makes the cat feel much better because the infection has an outlet.

The infection typically results in a fever. A temperature over 103 degrees may indicate infection has spilled into the bloodstream and spread throughout the system. Only rarely will the abscess rupture toward the inside rather than outward. If this happens and infection spills into the abdomen or other internal structures, serious life-threatening problems can develop.

Abscesses left too long without treatment can severely damage or even kill surrounding tissue, which sloughs and falls away. The resulting large skin wounds heal very slowly, if at all.

Prompt treatment will prevent such complications. Once abscesses are so that you can feel them, most veterinarians recommend opening and draining them surgically.

First aid can help speed the healing, but not all cats will allow you to treat them at home because abscesses can be very tender. You can help draw out the infection when the abscess is soft and swollen but hasn't yet begun to drain. Apply wet hot compresses (hot as you can stand), and apply to the area for two to five times daily for five minutes on and five minutes off until it cools. Once the sore opens and begins to drain, keep the area clean by rinsing with lukewarm water. You may need to soak the area first with a wet compress if the discharge has dried in the fur.

When taken to the vet for treatment, the cat is usually sedated so he cat will allow treatment. Once Kitty is comfortably sedated, the hair around the swelling is shaved and the skin is disinfected with a betadyne or novalsan solution. Then the abscess is lanced, usually with a sterile surgical blade or scalpel. The infectious material inside is flushed from the wound with a disinfectant solution.

When the wound is quite extensive, the veterinarian may stitch into place a drain tube that keeps the skin from healing too quickly, and allows the pus to continue to escape. Otherwise, the skin will simply close over the infection, and the abscess will return. Drains are left in place for two to four days, and then removed. It may be necessary for Kitty to wear an Elizabethan collar to prevent the cat undoing the veterinarian's work. The wound may be packed with disinfectant, and often an injectable antibiotic is given followed by oral antibiotics the owner gives the cat at home (see ELIZABETHAN COLLAR).

Depending on the extent of the wound and its location, the veterinarian may completely or only partially close the opening with stitches. Sometimes it's left open and kept clean while allowing the body to heal and close the wound by itself.

Luckily, cats tend to have quite a bit of "extra" skin they can move around in. Even when cats have lost large amounts of tissue, surrounding skin may stretch enough to cover the area. But Kitty's face, lower legs and feet have little surplus skin able to slide over for cosmetic repairs. Abscesses and tissue loss in these areas can cause scarring and disfigurement.

As with most medical problems, prevention is much better than allowing the condition to develop, and having to treat it. One of the best ways to prevent abscesses is to make sure the cat's skin remains healthy (see GROOMING and ALLERGIES/FLEA ALLERGY).

Preventing the bite is even better. Keep Kitty inside to stop roaming and contact with strange cats. Sterilize your cat to reduce territorial aggressiveness (see NEUTER and SPAY).

ACNE

Feline acne is not the same condition that affects people. This relatively common skin disease of the chin and lower lip is seen in cats of all ages. Acne occurs when the hair follicles become plugged.

Sebaceous glands in the skin secrete a thick, semi-liquid fatty material called sebum that coats and protects the fur, and gives Kitty's coat a healthy sheen. When hair follicles become plugged, sebum is unable to escape, creating clogged pores that are a perfect environment for bacteria to grow.

ACNE

SYMPTOMS: Blackheads and pimples on chin; red or swollen skin; itchiness or pain
HOME CARE: Apply damp heat to chin daily; cleanse twice daily with plain water or cleansers like benzoyl peroxide type solutions
HOLISTIC HELP: Crab Apple flower essence; calendula tincture or tea
VET CARE: When infected; clipping fur and cleansing; antibiotics
PREVENTION: Feed cat from non-plastic food bowls

The exact cause of feline acne remains unclear, but the most common theory is a lack of cleanliness. Most cats are particular about grooming themselves, but the chin is difficult to reach. A dampened front paw may not be sufficient to clean the dirt and accumulated oils from the skin. Cats with oily skin are more prone to acne, as are cats fed wet food which may stick to the chin. Cats that sleep with their chins resting on hard surfaces or on dirt may develop acne.

The first signs are blackheads and pimples that erupt on the chin and lower lip. They may not bother the cat at all, and are often overlooked by owners because they're hidden by the fur. But secondary bacterial infections may develop. The area can become reddened, swollen, and either itchy or painful. Severe cases of feline acne result in the chin swelling and the lip thickening. Often referred to as "fat chin," the affected cat may look like he's pouting. Never try to "squeeze out" blackheads or pustules; that can be painful for the cat, and may spread infection beneath the skin and cause deeper infections.

In many instances where the cat is not bothered by the condition, the blackheads do not require treatment. But if the area becomes infected, the recommended veterinary treatment includes gently clipping away the fur and cleansing the area with medicated preparations. With stubborn deep infections, oral and topical antibiotics may be required, or even treatment with certain human preparations like Retin-A that help normalize the skin.

Infection generally responds to twice daily cleansing with a 2.5 to five percent preparation of benzoyl peroxide, povidone-iodine (Betadyne), or chlorhexidine (Nolvasan). Oily- skinned cats may benefit from a tar and sulfa shampoo made for cats. However, scrubbing too vigorously, or using medication that is too strong can make the condition worse. Often, the acne will return once treatment is stopped.

Changing bowls to shallower dishes may help keep Kitty's chin cleaner and less prone to problems. Metal, ceramic or glass containers are more easily cleaned than plastic dishes, which seem to cause reactions in some cats. Changing the cat's bed to softer material like a blanket that's regularly washed may also help with cats that habitually prop their chins on hard surfaces. And regularly cleaning the cat's chin will help prevent recurrences of acne.

Damp heat helps open clogged pores; once a day, dip a cloth in warm water, ring it out, and place against the cat's chin until the cloth cools. Holistic veterinarians recommend applying a tincture (or tea) of the herb calendula on a cotton ball, used as a compress for five minutes each day to help speed healing. Crab apple flower essence often is recommended to stop infection when given in a dose of four drops, about four times a day (see FLOWER ESSENCE).

Some cats will require maintenance therapy of a topical medication every two to seven days for the rest of their life.

ACUPUNCTURE

Acupuncture inserts needles into the skin, and is a bioenergetic therapy based on the traditional Chinese medicine (TCM) system of life energy. Acupuncture is considered a holistic therapy but has become a mainstay of many traditional veterinary practices. Therapies similar to acupuncture may have arisen 7000 years ago in India, and have been used for at least 3000 years in China.

Life energy, or Qi, is said to flow along invisible pathways that communicate with specific organs or tissues throughout the body. TCM views all illness as an imbalance of the flow of Qi. Acupuncture seeks to cure disease by correcting the imbalance of Qi by pressure-stimulation of acupoints that fall along the pathways, or meridians, using needles.

To many people, talk of meridians sounds like magic, and science is still trying to explain how the acupoints and meridians really work. A Spanish study in humans that injected radioactive tracers at acupoints found that they traveled along similar pathways to the traditional meridians–the paths may be invisible, but they are there. Acupoints also appear to have lower electrical resistance than other areas of the body. Some studies indicate the meridians' energy flow may be a system of information transmission through neurochemicals. That's similar to the mechanism that carries thought processes from the brain throughout the body. Other theories propose a bioelectrical system independent of the nerves, which may be similar in concept to a computer software program that provides an internal operating system that's never seen.

Although the mechanism remains a mystery, even conventional medicine recognizes that stimulation of acupoints works. The National Institute of Health (NIH) has funded many studies in humans that point to relief of pain, nausea, addiction, and asthma, and the World Health Organization lists a variety of human health conditions that may benefit from these therapies. And in 1996, the American Veterinary Medical Association endorsed acupuncture, calling it an "integral part of veterinary medicine."

Fewer studies have been performed in animals, but the benefits appear to be similar. The stimulation of these points will actually release neurochemicals or endorphins in the brain that cause pain relief. Conditions in pets such as arthritis, reproductive disorders, back and musculoskeletal problems, skin conditions like allergies, pain relief, and neurological disorders such as epilepsy have been shown to benefit from this therapy.

Veterinarians follow a kind of body map developed by the Chinese thousands of years ago that locates the meridians and the point positions. Acupuncture points in the horse date back to around the same time as those for people because the horse was considered valuable property, and was so important to keep healthy. Many of the points in humans or horses also work in other animals, though, and over the years veterinarians have mapped dog and cat acupoints by transposing human and horse points to the dog and cat.

There are 14 meridians and 361 traditional acupoints; many of the points are duplicated in mirror images on either side of the body. Additional points may not be located directly on a meridian. The meridians and points have traditional Chinese names, but in the United States and Europe most commonly are designated by letters that correspond to the meridian's ruling organ (i.e., L=lung meridian, LI=large intestine meridian, ST=stomach meridian) along with a location number of the individual point. Therefore, ST25 refers to the 25th point on the stomach meridian.

Acupressure points are found in depressions between the muscles and the bones, and will feel like a slight dip in the tissue. They are almost never on a bone like the elbow, but will be immediately next to it. Some specialists say they can feel temperature changes at the acupoints which alert them to problems. A warm point indicates an area of an acute blockage, as compared to a cold point where it's more of a chronic state, and the energy has been depleted from that area. The acupoint is stimulated with the needle or sometimes gold balls inserted to either release an excess of energy, or to return energy to the point.

Pet owners of course cannot "needle" their own pets. But acupressure (pressing firmly in recommended body positions) may also offer therapeutic benefits.

Veterinarians study acupuncture and are certified to practice by the International Veterinary Acupuncture Society. Some also travel to China for specialized training. If your veterinarian is not able to provide acupuncture, he or she should be able to refer you to an experienced practitioner.

ADMINISTER MEDICATION

At some point, every cat owner will need to medicate their cat. The procedure is a daunting one, since most cats resist being forced to do anything. The sight of sharp teeth and claws gives even experienced veterinarians pause.

Yet topical treatments like lotions and creams, oral preparations such as pills or liquids, and even injectable medication can all be given at home, if the owner knows how. Handled correctly, medicating at home can be far less stressful to the cat than trips to the veterinarian's office.

It's helpful to have two people for any procedure, one to restrain the cat, and the other to apply the medicine. Using a cat sack or wrapping Kitty in a towel or blanket first may also be helpful. For some confident owners who have established a trusting relationship with their cats, restraints may not be necessary.

Topical Treatments: Cats generally tolerate skin medications well without restraints, unless the area is quite tender to the touch. But because cats are such unremitting self-groomers, care must be taken that the medication is not licked off. Follow your veterinarian's instructions regarding application. Some medication may be noxious enough to prevent Kitty from licking, but don't depend on that. Distract the cat by playing with him, or hold the cat for 15 minutes or so until the medication is dry or absorbed.

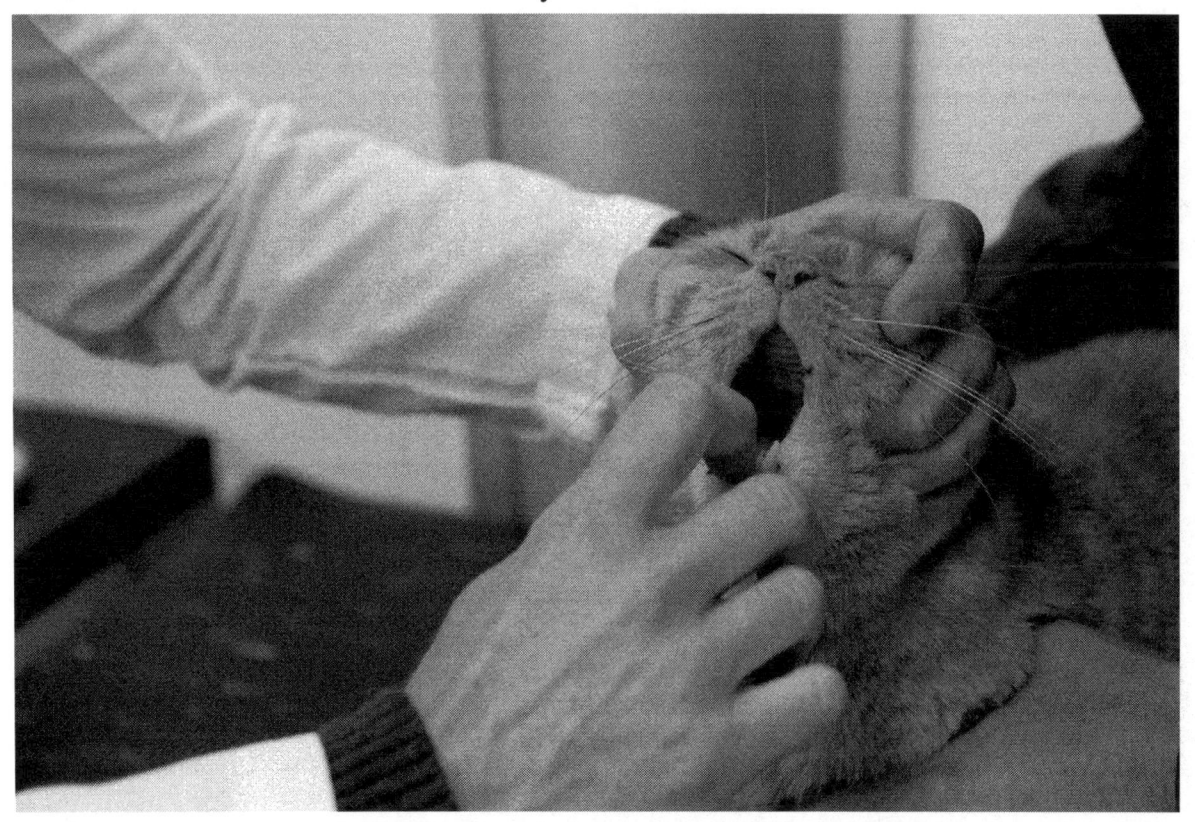

Medicating ears can usually be done with minimal restraint, unless the ears are extremely sore. Tip the cat's head so that the affected ear opening is directed at the ceiling, and simply drip in the medication. Let gravity move the treatment inside the ear, don't stick anything inside. Typically, liquids or ointments are applied, then the outside base of the ear is gently massaged to spread the medicine (see also EAR MITES).

Eye medication should be administered without actually touching the cat's eye. For liquids, tip Kitty's head toward the ceiling and drip the prescribed number of drops into the affected eye. For ointments, gently pull down the lower eyelid, and squeeze the medication in the

CAT FACTS

cupped tissue or simply apply the ointment into the corner of the eye. Then gently close the cat's eyelid to spread the medicine over its surface.

Oral Treatments: Oral medications come as liquids, pastes, or pills. Liquids and pastes are the easiest to use, and often employ squeeze bottles, eye droppers, or syringe applicators to squirt the medication into the cat's mouth. Insert the tip of the applicator between the cat's lips in the corner of his mouth, tip back his head and deposit the medicine into his cheek. Watch to make sure he swallows, and doesn't spit it out.

You may need to gently hold Kitty's mouth closed with one hand, and watch his throat until you see him swallow. When Kitty licks his nose, it's often a signal that he's swallowed. Most oral preparations are flavored to appeal to the cat, and are readily taken. Some paste medications, particularly those that are specifically for hairballs, can simply be spread on the cat's paw for him to lick off and swallow through grooming.

Pilling a cat involves opening the cat's mouth, placing the capsule or tablet on the back of Kitty's tongue, closing his mouth and inducing him to swallow. You may want to use the cat bag or other restraint for this maneuver, although sometimes it's easier without. Try kneeling on the floor with Kitty between your legs facing out, so he can't squirm away.

Place the palm of your left hand over the cat's head so that the thumb on one side and middle finger on the other fit behind the upper canine (long) tooth on each side. Tilt Kitty's head back so he's looking at the ceiling. Gently press the cat's lips against his teeth to encourage him to open his mouth.

Pressing one finger against the roof of your cat's mouth will also induce him to open wide, or use a finger of the other hand to gently press down on his lower teeth and prop the mouth open. Then quickly drop the pill as far back on his tongue as possible. Hold his mouth closed and stroke his throat until you see him swallow.

You may want to use a pill syringe available at most pet supply stores rather than risk your fingers when pilling your cat. Ask your veterinarian to demonstrate its use, though, so that you don't risk damaging the back of your cat's throat.

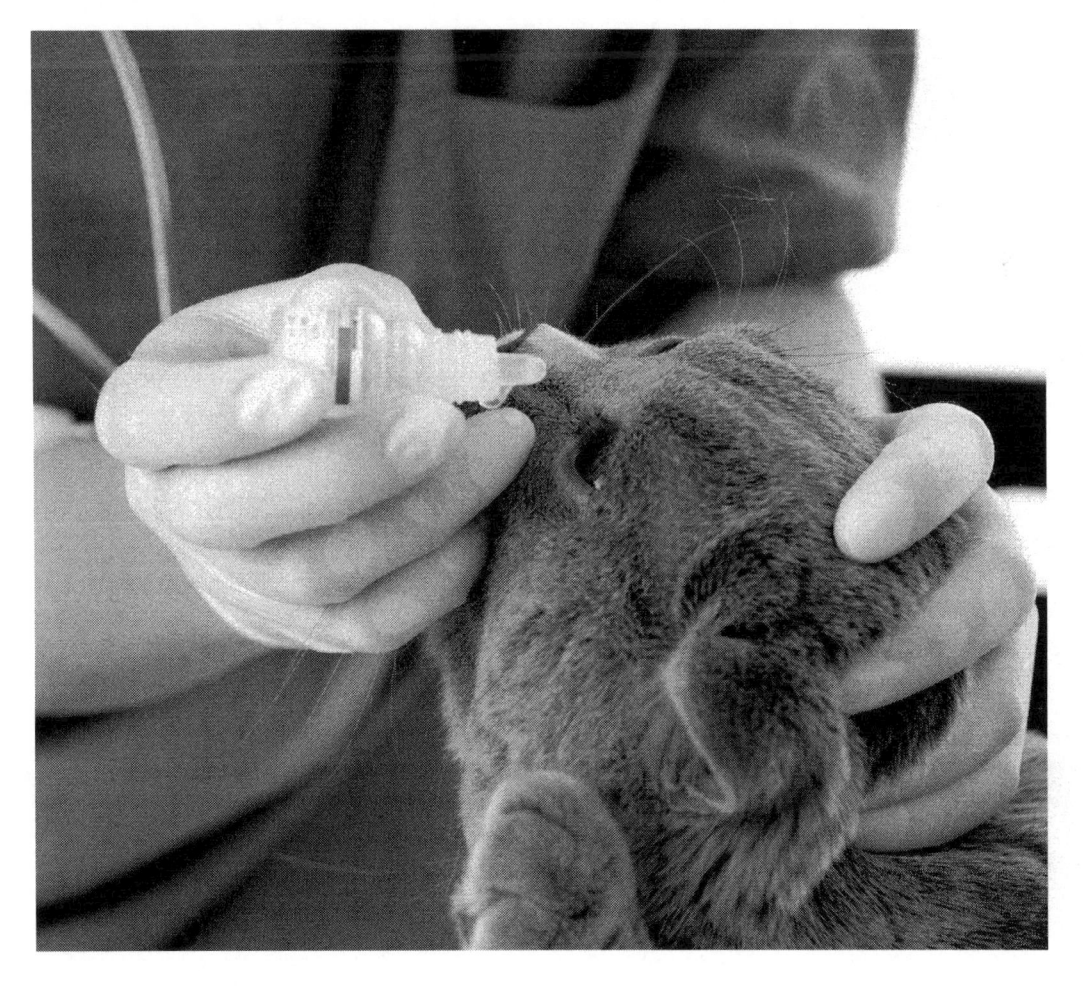

If pills are problematic, you may succeed by hiding the medication in a veterinarian-approved treat. Mixing medicine with food in the bowl isn't a good idea, because the cat won't get the full effect unless every bite is eaten. Hiding a pill in a hunk of cheese doesn't work well, either, since most cats eat the cheese away and leave the pill.

Unless the medication is a time-release treatment that's supposed to dissolve slowly, the pill can be crushed and mixed into a strong-tasting treat. Powder the pill with the bowl of a spoon, mix into one or two bites of a strong-smelling canned food, and feed to the cat. Offer it before meals to make sure every bit is eaten.

Always give your cat much positive attention following successful medication. Praise him, play with him, and if approved by your veterinarian, offer a tasty food reward so the next time will go even smoother.

ADOPTION, of CAT by HUMAN

Adoption describes the act of choosing to have a relationship with another being. A person who adopts a cat accepts responsibility for the life, health, and happiness of that cat.

Finding a cat to adopt is easy. "Free" animals are available through animal welfare organizations, friends, and newspaper advertisements. Often, a cat simply shows up on the back porch. For those seeking a particular feline look and personality, more than forty distinct cat breeds are available. Catteries breed cats to standards defined by various cat associations (see Appendix A, "Cat Associations and Cat Breeds"). These pedigreed and registered animals are more costly because of the expense involved in producing healthy animals of a particular type.

All cats require routine health care, nutritious food, and the basic comforts of litter box and scratching post. Successful adoptions match a cat that has the look, care demands, and personality to fulfill an owner's expectations. For instance, longhaired cats demand more grooming than shorthaired varieties; high-energy cats and kittens may require greater supervision; adult cats can have bad habits that make them hard to live with; unaltered male or female cats can display obnoxious behaviors (see NEUTERING and SPAYING); and the pets you already have need consideration (see INTRODUCTION).

A number of difficulties can be avoided by adopting a healthy cat. The sickly stray who appears on your doorstep may steal your heart, but it can also run up veterinary bills. It can also expose your other pets to illness (see QUARANTINE).

A healthy cat's coat is clean and shiny. Eyes, nose, and ears are free of discharge, and the cat's bottom is clean without any sign of diarrhea. A veterinary exam is always advisable to rule out hidden problems. Reputable shelters or catteries may provide preliminary health care prior to adoption, such h as basic first vaccinations or discount spaying or neutering. Some offer limited guarantees on the health of the animal. However, regardless of such guarantees, your cat should be taken to your veterinarian for a physical and checkup.

Adoption of a cat—or any pet—is for the life of the animal. We do not give back the human children we adopted when circumstances become difficult; neither should an adopted pet be forsaken when he becomes an inconven8ience, at its best, adoption is a joyful yet serious act, undertaken only after careful consideration.

ADOPTION, of KITTENS (OTHERS) by CAT

Cats have the capacity to show strong nurturing behavior towards others, in addition to their own kittens. Such cats appear to develop relationships and "adopt" other animals. This behavior has often been documented in female cats who are nursing. Such cats are hormonally ready to adopt, nurse, and care for another cat's young. This urge to mother may be so strong that predatory behavior is suppressed. Cats have been known to nurse and raise baby bunnies, puppies, and even rats.

Cats that have experienced motherhood may continue to exhibit such nurturing behavior, even after being spayed. These "aunties" cuddle, wash, and ride herd on their adopted charges, and take baby-sitting duties very seriously. Sometimes even male cats show strong protective behavior and seem to enjoy fostering kittens.

In most instances, cats that adopt other kittens or animals have enjoyed positive interspecies experiences during their impressionable weeks of life (see KITTEN SOCIALIZATION).

AFFECTION

Cats have an undeserved reputation as aloof, solitary creatures perhaps because people don't readily recognized feline signs of affection. Cats communicate their moods, emotions, and desires in a variety of signs that can be quite subtle. And affection is, after all, a two way street. The cat who is offered little interaction will return that indifference, while the beloved feline showered with attention blossoms into a loving pet. Cats are also individuals, with a wide range of personalities.

Cats show affection to other cats—and even dogs or other pets—by sleeping together and grooming each other. They indulge in subtle body contact, like bumping hips as they pass in the room. Affectionate cats share food, and enjoy playing together.

Cats show affection to humans in many of the same ways. They want to sleep on the pillow next to your face, they groom your hair. Often, cats will solicit owners to play. Affectionate cats twine around ankles, offer head bumps, purrs and trills, and knead with their paws to express contentment.

Some researchers are reluctant to say any animal experiences the same emotions as people. In fact, there is no way to know exactly what our cats are feeling. But from every indication, cats can and do become every bit as fond of us as we are of them.

CAT FACTS

AGGRESSION Aggression is the forceful reaction of a cat that feels threatened. Aggression can be a sign of illness, and cats in pain will often lash out when touched. A cat that suddenly bites for no apparent reason should be examined by a veterinarian.

Whether a shrinking violet shy cat, or boisterous in-your-face confident cat, any feline may become aggressive given the right circumstances. Growls, hisses, scratches, even bites are Kitty's way to take control of a situation.

Be aware that once aggression escalates, Kitty will remain upset for some time. Cats need to be left alone for up to two hours before they're ready to calm down.

There are several forms of feline aggression that experts categorize by the cause, or trigger, that instigates the behavior. Hostility can result from fear or anxiety, overly-enthusiastic play, predatory behavior, displaced aggression, or a combination of these or others. Physical punishment won't work, and will likely make the aggressive behavior even worse. Once aggression is a problem, the trigger must be identified and if possible prevented from recurring. An aggressive cat may pose a physical danger to the owner, so diagnosis and treatment of severe aggression in cats is best left to a professional animal behaviorist or therapist.

Status-Related Aggression Also known as "petting aggression," cats use the "leave me alone bite" usually when they want you to stop petting them. You have done nothing wrong, but these cats need to control when the attention ends and begins. Some cats do this by bite-and-leave behavior, while others simply hold the owner's hand in their mouth. Owners can learn to "read" the warning signs and stop the interaction by dumping the cat off a lap before she bites, and ignore her unless she behaves. Physical correction rarely works. The cat may view this as a challenge and intensify the aggression. Correction in the first second is ideal. These cats won't be cuddly but may learn to sit quietly on your lap for longer periods.

Redirected Aggression This behavior happens in response to a verbal or physical correction or thwarting of a desire, where the victim was not part of the trigger. For instance, a cat sitting in the window sees a dog outside invading the cat's territory. Unable to get through the window to protect her turf, the aggression has nowhere to go. So instead Kitty redirects the aggression to something within reach—like the owner, or another cat. Cats seem to stay hyped up for attack for a long period after an aggressive act is interrupted.

Fear Aggression Cats flatten their ears sideways, fluff their fur and turn sideways, or crouch, hiss and claw/bite, and run for cover. There is a genetic component in both shy and aggressive cats, and some cats become aggressive every time they become scared. Many behavior experts believe a fear component exists in all cat aggression situations.

Territorial Aggression In cats, territorial aggression is aimed at other cats or people. Cats mark their "property" with cheek rubs, patrol, and urine marking (spraying or otherwise). Cats may lure others into their territory and then "discipline" the other cat for trespassing. Feline territorial aggression is notoriously hard to correct, and marking behavior is a hallmark of potential aggression. Treatment includes modifying the environment, behavior modification, and sometimes drugs. One cat may need to be placed in a new home or one cat segregated from the other. Neutering before 12 months decreases or even prevents up to 90 percent of cat- on-cat aggression. Cats identify their environment and friends by scent, and cheek-rub/mark important feline property with pheromones. Commercial products that use pheromone therapy can help reduce aggression over territory.

Predatory Aggression is extremely dangerous. These cats silently stalk smaller animals or infants and/or stare at them silently and drool. High-pitched sounds, uncoordinated movements as an infant might make, or sudden silences (as happens with prey animals) may provoke an attack. Predatory aggression in cats includes components of stealth, silence, alert posture, hunting postures, and lunging or springing at "prey" that moves suddenly after being still. In cats, predatory aggression varies widely. Some pets target even inappropriate objects like an owner's hands and feet.

Play Aggression also includes components of stealth, silence, alert posture, hunting postures, and lunging or springing at "prey" that moves suddenly after being still. Nearly any type of movement, from walking to picking up an object, triggers the behavior. Over-the-top play is normal and hand raised kittens and those weaned early seem to have increased risk. They'll terrorize shy cats, bully smaller kittens, and pester geriatric felines as well as targeting owners. Confident adult cats usually put these obnoxious felines in their place, young kittens outgrow the behavior (see KITTEN).

To reduce the probability of aggression in your cat, be aware of situations likely to provoke Kitty to unbecoming behavior. Some cats will tolerate only limited petting, then suddenly reach their threshold and become aggressive if you continue. Know your cat's limits, and respect them.

Cats are creatures of habit that thrive on routine, which means any change at all could trigger fear or anxiety which can escalate into aggression in certain cats. A new baby in the house, change in work schedule, or even new drapes are potential problems. And new pets may prompt aggressive behavior in the cat who wants to assert his authority. Always ease Kitty into change slowly, and avoid surprises (see INTRODUCTIONS). Some pheromone products mimic the "friend" identification between cats and can help both with introductions and calming aggression between cats. Flower essences such as Bach Rescue Remedy can be very helpful as well.

Kitty may stalk and pounce upon moving feet, just as she'd attack a mouse. Rough handling of kittens encourages them to play rough, bite and wrestle human hands and feet. What's cute in a tiny kitten becomes painful or even dangerous in an adult cat. Hands and feet should never be available as cat toys; use a play mouse or fishing toy to satisfy the stalk-and-pounce urge.

Cats not properly socialized may strike out at strange people or animals. Kittens raised without human contact before age 12 weeks don't know how to react to people. If deprived of contact with other cats during this sensitive period, they never learn how to act toward other cats. Once they grow up, any forced contact with strange cats or with people may trigger extreme aggression. Each cat has her own "comfort zone," which is the distance strangers can approach without the cat feeling threatened. Invade the cat's space and, if there's not a way to escape, the cat may become aggressive.

However, behaviorists also recognize that a significant number of aggression cases stem from abnormal brain function. Those pets need extra help in the form of drug therapy.

Be aware of the signs of aggression (see COMMUNICATION) so that you can avoid escalating a borderline miffed cat into an attack animal. Give the cat some space and time to cool down, and if you're able to identify the triggers, avoid them when possible. Above all, do not hesitate to seek professional help. (see HUMAN-ANIMAL BOND, APPENDIX B)

ALLERGIES, CAT
Allergy refers to symptoms that result from the overreaction of the immune system. Special cells called antibodies protect the body by attacking viruses, bacteria and other foreign material. Sometimes these cells become overzealous, and

attack otherwise harmless substances like house dust, mold or pollen. The heightened reaction of the immune system to these substances, called allergens, causes the symptoms an allergy sufferer experience.

FLEA ALLERGY Like their human companions, cats can be allergic to virtually anything. But while allergic owners often suffer watery eyes, itchy noses, and explosive sneeze attacks, allergic cats most commonly itch and develop skin disorders.

Flea bite hypersensitivity is the most common allergy affecting cats. Sensitive cats react to a protein in flea saliva, and as a result develop skin disease. Just one bite can make the cat itch all over. Signs are usually seasonal, during flea season. A common sign are many tiny red bumps usually along the back and around the head and neck that become encrusted (see MILIARY DERMATITIS). Scabs may be hidden by the fur, but can be felt when you stroke the cat. Other insects like lice, ear mites, and mange may cause similar symptoms.

Effective treatment depends on eliminating the allergen. Flea control is essential for cats suffering from flea allergic dermatitis, and countless products are available to safely rid the cat and his environment of buggy intruders.

FLEA ALLERGY

SYMPTOMS: Seasonal itchiness; hair loss; scabby skin particularly along back and above tail
HOME CARE: Flea treatment
VET CARE: Steroids to reduce inflammation and itchiness
PREVENTION: Flea prevention

ATOPY or INHALANT ALLERGY Atopy, or inhalant/environmental allergy is the second most common allergy in cats. Also called atopy, the condition in people is often termed hay fever. Cats react to the same things people do. Pollen, mold, fungi and even the house dust mite make people cough, wheeze and have difficulty breathing, but atopic cats more typically break out in miliary dermatitis.

Eliminating the allergen means you must first identify it, which can be difficult. Blood tests are available but may not be reliable, but intradermal skin testing can help determine what causes the cat's reaction. Suspect allergens are injected into the shaved skin of the sedated cat. Positive reactions become swollen, red and elevated, while negative reactions fade away.

But even when the owner knows Kitty is allergic to grass pollen, it's difficult to eliminate exposure. A cat is a furry dust mop that collects and holds environmental allergens. Washing off dust, pollen and other debris is a good way to deal with feline atopy.

Controlling environmental allergens is critical for the atopic cat, and cleanliness is key. Rough surfaces like carpeting and upholstery act as reservoirs that collect and hold the particles. Smooth surfaces like linoleum and hard wood floors are easier to clean. Vacuums with water filters are more effective than sweeping, which tends to loft particles into the air. High Efficiency Particulate Air (HEPA) filter systems can be helpful, too.

ATOPY

SYMPTOMS: Itchiness all over
HOME CARE: Keeping cat's coat and environment clean
HOLISTIC HELP: Calendula ointment; Echinacea; vitamin C and E supplements; EFA supplements; flower essence remedies
VET CARE: Skin testing; allergy shots
PREVENTION: Avoiding dust, pollens, or whatever causes the problem

Eliminating all environmental allergens may be impossible, but other treatments can ease symptoms. Essential fatty acids (EFAs) may be helpful because they promote healthy skin and fur. In the proper balance, Omega 3 and Omega 6 fatty acids reduce the inflammatory response of the skin that results from some allergies. Your veterinarian can recommend appropriate products.

Holistic veterinarians recommend using calendula ointment two or three times a day to sooth the itchy areas. The herb Echinacea can help the immune system work more efficiently, particularly when given before allergies start in early spring. Vitamins C and E have both been shown to have anti-inflammatory effects. Holistic vets suggest cats under 15 pounds can take 250 milligrams of vitamin C daily during allergy season. Giving too much will cause diarrhea, so err on the side of caution. For vitamin E, you can give 50 international units (IU) once daily during allergy season to pets under 10 pounds, and no more than 200 IU daily for cats over 10 pounds.

Another option is immunotherapy, which consists of gradually increasing injections of the allergens to which the cat is sensitive. It's hoped these allergy shots will build up Kitty's resistance to the allergen and reduce sensitivity. Because improvement from immunotherapy is slow, injections are usually continued for at least a year. Maintenance injections may be continued for life.

FOOD ALLERGY

SYMPTOMS: Itchy face and/or vomiting and diarrhea
HOME CARE: Feed appropriate diet
VET CARE: Elimination diet to diagnose
PREVENTION: Avoid problem foods

FOOD ALLERGY Cats sometimes develop allergies to food ingredients. The incidence of food allergies in cats is suspected to be somewhere between five to 15 percent, but often is blamed when it's not really the culprit. A change in diet that coincides with the cat's symptom relief may be attributed to the food, when it's actually due to hay fever or flea season ending.

Signs of feline food allergies can be vomiting and diarrhea, and/or they may itch and scratch their face and ears. Like all allergies, food sensitivities develop from exposure. Animals typically become allergic to proteins like beef, milk, corn, wheat, and eggs which are the most common protein ingredients in commercial cat foods.

If the offending ingredients can be avoided, symptoms will disappear. But identifying the culprit is complicated because diagnosing food allergy can only be done by a weeks-long veterinarian supervised elimination diet.

Cats are fed a limited antigen diet containing only one unique meat source and one unique carbohydrate source Kitty has never before eaten, like rabbit and potato, or venison and rice. After symptoms disappear, ingredients from the cat's original diet are reintroduced one by one to see which provoke a reaction. Once identified, the owner feeds a food without the offending ingredient. There is no such thing as a hypoallergenic diet. What's hypoallergenic to your cat may be highly allergenic to another. The FDA says diets labeled to control allergies can only be prescribed and distributed by veterinarians, and there are several on the market.

But owners are often reluctant to go through tedious diagnosis which still may not pinpoint the problem, and may balk at feeding higher cost therapeutic diets. Some food allergic cats respond well to lamb and rice based commercial diets if the cat has never been exposed to these ingredients. But be aware that lamb and rice based diets may contain other ingredients to make them complete and balanced. And cats can develop allergic reactions to unique ingredients, too.

Diets using hydrolyzed proteins may offer help for some cats. Basically, the proteins are split into tiny pieces and concentrated. The immune system reacts to complete or large pieces of proteins. It doesn't recognize the protein fractions and so has no allergic response. There are several hydrolyzed protein diets for pets now available.

Like people, cats may be sensitive to more than one allergen. Allergies are cumulative. Whether or not a cat develops symptoms depends on each individual cat's allergy threshold, which is the amount of allergen necessary to produce a reaction.

Picture a measuring cup being filled with allergens. For some cats, the threshold is reached and they itch when the cup is one quarter full; others may not itch until the level reaches the halfway point. If the cat has a low allergy threshold, a single allergen—say a flea bite—may be enough to fill the cup beyond the line and cause itching. Other cats may start itching only if multiple allergens (i.e., both flea bites and grass pollen) fill the cup beyond

CAT FACTS

Kitty's level of tolerance. When enough allergens fill the cup beyond an individual cat's itch threshold, the cat will shows signs.

Conversely, a cat may stop itching once dropped below the itch threshold. Eliminate enough allergens—take fleas or a food ingredient out of the equation—and the cup level may drop to the point Kitty can handle exposure to other allergens without showing signs.

Allergies cannot be cured. Avoiding or eliminating the allergy source is the only way to control symptoms. That's not easy because multiple allergies make identification of the culprit(s) very difficult.

Only a veterinarian can diagnose allergy. Once the offending allergen has been identified, then you can try to eliminate or reduce exposure. Ultimately, identifying and dealing with feline allergies depends on an owner's dedication coupled with a veterinarian's expertise (see also EOSINOPHILIC GRANULOMA COMPLEX).

ALLERGIES, of HUMANS to CATS It's estimated that nearly 30 percent of cat owners are allergic to their cats. About 10 percent of the U.S. population suffers from allergies, and sensitivity to cats is quite common (and twice as common as dog allergies). Sensitive people don't react to the cat hair at all. Instead it's a specialized protein called Fel d1 found in the saliva and skin of all cats that causes the reaction. Any cat may provoke an allergic reaction.

Some cats produce more of this substance than others. The Siberian Cat breed produces far less than other cats and allergic people often can tolerate these kitties. Some commercial companies have sought to create "hypoallergenic" cats by selectively breeding, and then charging a high price for these cats. There are individual cats that also may be less allergenic, but there's no way to predict which cat is the least allergenic.

Microscopic particles of Fel d1, often referred to as dander, are so light they remain airborne, stick to rough surfaces and are hard to remove from the environment. Even after the cat has been removed from the home, the substance remaining in the environment can produce symptoms for up to six months.

Symptoms of cat allergy can be as simple as a stuffy nose and sneezing, or as complicated as a potentially fatal asthma attack. Itchy eyes, skin rash or hives, runny nose, or even tightness in the chest may develop. A specialist diagnoses the allergy, and may prescribe antihistamines, decongestants, or a class of drug called an allergy blocker to manage symptoms.

Immunotherapy (see ALLERGY, of cats) is another option. A new vaccine in development, called CAT-SPIRE that uses only a part of the Fel d1 protein, promising to reduce the desensitization process to only four injections with a two-year benefit. Phase 3 clinical trials are underway, spearheaded by Circassia Ltd., a British biotech firm along with the Canadian company Adiga Life Sciences.

Treating the cat is another option. Some experts advocate washing the cat weekly in plain water to dramatically reduce allergic reactions, and several products have been formulated to reduce or neutralize cat antigen. Researchers disagree on how effective these efforts may be, but if they work for you, use them.

Just as allergic cats have an itch threshold, allergic humans have a sneeze threshold. And, if a person is allergic to the cat, chances are they're allergic to other allergens as well. Therefore, cat allergy symptoms may be reduced by avoiding exposure to other allergens.

Avoid heavy odors like perfumes, cigarette smoke, insecticides or cleaning fluids that can trigger a reaction. Choose cat litter carefully; the dust or deodorant in litter may cause more reactions than the cat. Good ventilation helps lower the concentration of airborne particles, and opening the window a few minutes each day to circulate the air will help. Reduce dander reservoirs; carpet accumulates cat allergen at approximately 100 times the level of a polished floor. Vacuum daily with water filter machines that trap tiny particles, or use HEPA (High Efficiency Particulate Air) filters or air purifiers.

Cat allergic owners also benefit from a "cat free zone." designate an area in your house, like the bedroom, and keep it off limits to the cat. That provides you with at least eight hours of reduced exposure. Wash your hands after handling the cat, and especially avoid touching your face and eyes until after you've washed. Another family member should provide regular grooming of the cat to remove excess dander and hair. A quality diet lessens shedding and promotes healthy skin.

ALOOFNESS
Cats described as aloof act distant, keep to themselves, and seem to prefer their own company to that of humans. Aloofness may develop as a result of poor kitten socialization, neglect (see STRAY, and FERAL) or even outright abuse. But the attitude may be that cat's normal personality.

Remember that every cat is an individual. While some outgoing "people cats" thrive on attention and closeness, others want only limited cuddling or hands-on contact. Simply sharing a room with a human companion may be an intimate encounter for these cats.

To strangers, otherwise affectionate cats may appear aloof and distant. Many cats require time to develop trust before establishing close relationships.

CAT FACTS

ALTER see NEUTERING and SPAYING

AMPUTATION Amputation refers to the surgical removal of a limb. Nerve damage from frostbite or fracture may leave a leg or tail useless, infection can impair healing, and diseases like cancer may be beyond human skill to cure. When a leg or tail becomes so badly damaged that it impairs or endangers the cat's health, amputation removes the limb and preserves the integrity of the rest of the body.

Owners tend to notice the loss of the tail or leg more than the cat. Tailless cats rarely slow down at all. Most cats adjust quickly and do well on three legs, even flourish when longstanding pain has been removed. Cats with three legs navigate indoors nearly as well, and may even remain able to jump and climb.

ANAL GLAND PROBLEMS Two pea-size anal glands (also called anal sacs, or scent glands) are located beneath the skin on each side of the cat's rectum. They secret a liquid or sometimes creamy light gray to brown substance that scents the cat's stool. This signature odor identifies the cat as an individual, and is used in marking territory.

The glands are normally emptied by the pressure of defecation. Cats have few anal gland problems, but if odor is a problem due to overactive glands, they can be expressed manually. Impaction is uncommon in cats, but may occur if the sacs become plugged and can't empty normally. Manual emptying of the glands is the treatment.

Raise the cat's tail, and locate the openings at four o'clock and eight o'clock on each side of the anus. Place your thumb and forefinger on the skin at each side of the gland, and gently squeeze as you would to express a pimple. Use a damp cloth to wipe away the strong smelling material that appears as the sac empties. Wearing rubber gloves is recommended.

If the discharge contains blood or pus, if there is swelling on either or both sides of the anus, or if the cat shows pain or "scoots" on his bottom, Kitty may be suffering from an infection. Treatment requires weekly expression of the glands and application of an antibiotic directly into the sac itself; this should be done only by an experienced veterinarian. You can help the infection resolve by applying warm wet packs to the area in 15 minute periods several times a day.

ANAL GLAND PROBLEMS

SYMPTOMS: Excessive licking; scooting; strong odor
HOME CARE: Wet warm cloths applied for 15 minutes several times daily
HOLISTIC HELP: Add fiber to diet; treat with homeopathic Silica
VET CARE: Express contents of glands; apply antibiotic; sometimes surgical removal
PREVENTION: None; if this is a chronic problem, routine emptying of the glands by owner or groomer

Holistic vets recommend adding fiber to the diet, which absorbs larger amount of water and causes stools to get larger. The larger stools put more pressure on anal sacs during elimination, so they empty normally. Try offering your cat about one-eighth cup of minced veggies each day, mixed into the regular food. Run broccoli and carrots through the blender with no-salt chicken broth to make it more palatable for your cat.

The homeopathic remedy Silica is said to help anal sacs empty normally. You can give two or three drops, or three to five pellets of Silica 6C twice a day for three days to see if it helps.

Left untreated, anal gland infections can lead to abscesses. If infections continue to recur, surgical removal of the glands may be recommended.

ANAPHYLAXIS

An anaphylactic response refers to an extremely rare but potentially lethal allergic reaction. It can result from any substance, but most commonly is associated with reactions to medicine such as penicillin or a vaccination, or to insect bites and stings

CAT FACTS

The immune system over-reacts to the offending substances and responds by flooding the body with immune components like histamine that are supposed to neutralize the offender. Instead, the histamine causes intense inflammation both locally and throughout the body, with itchiness appearing on the head and face (sometimes in hives), and constriction of the respiratory system. Quite simply, the affected cat can't breathe. Severe anaphylactic reactions can kill a pet within minutes.

ANAPHYLAXIS

SYMPTOMS: Salivation; drooling; difficulty breathing; uncontrolled urination; incoordination; vomiting; collapse
HOME CARE: EMERGENCY, SEE VET IMMEDIATELY!
VET CARE: Intravenous administration of epinephrine (adrenaline) and oxygen therapy
PREVENTION: Avoid medicating cat without vet advice; prevent insect bites or stings

Signs of reaction include excessive salivation and drooling, difficulty-ty breathing, uncontrollable urination, incoordination, vomiting, and col-lapse. This is an emergency situation that needs immediate veterinary attention. The treatment of choice is administration of intravenous epinephrine (adrenaline), glucocorticoids, and fluid therapy along with oxygen therapy. (see also INSECT BITES/STINGS)

ANEMIA Anemia means a lower than normal volume of red blood cells. These cells are one of the major components of circulating blood, and they carry oxygen throughout the body. Anemia can affect any cat of any age or breed. Anemia can occur if not enough red cells are manufactured by the bone marrow, or if too many are lost out of the body (i.e., from bleeding). Signs include depression, increased sleep, weakness, weight loss, rapid pulse or breathing, and pale mucus membranes. Kittens have a lower blood volume to begin and are more seriously affected by anemia than adult animals.

The number of red cells is relatively fixed but cells of the body do not live forever. As they wear out, they are immediately replaced with new ones. In a cat, red cells live only about two and a half months. The constant turnover of red cells is like water flowing into a bucket from the top, while flowing out of a hole at the bottom. Anemia occurs when the incoming flow is shut off, or if too much flows out the bottom. If cells aren't replaced as quickly as they are lost, anemia results.

Anemia in pets has a variety of causes. The most typical causes are blood loss from traumatic injury; blood-sucking parasites like fleas; or a bone marrow disorder, often caused by chronic kidney disease that interferes with making new red blood cells.

A less common type, hemolytic anemia, develops from an abnormal immune system that mistakenly identifies the red blood cells as foreign and destroys them. In cats, kittens may be born in certain instances with a different blood type than the mother cat. When that happens, kittens develop neonatal isoerythrolysis, a kind of blood incompatibility reaction caused by the immune agents passed to them through the mother cat's milk, which attack the infants' red cells.

ANEMIA

SYMPTOMS: Depression; increased sleep; weakness; weight loss; rapid pulse or breathing; and pale gums or tongue.
HOME CARE: Nutritional support
VET CARE: Blood transfusion; treatment for underlying disease
PREVENTION: Flea treatment

CAT FACTS

Regenerative anemia occurs when bone marrow still functions and generates new red cells, but can't keep up with red cells being lost. There's too big a hole in the bucket. Blood losses due to trauma or from parasites like flea or hemotrophic mycoplasmas are the most common examples of regenerative anemia. Some breeds like Abyssinians and Somalis may inherit red cell defects that result in regenerative anemia.

Nonregenerative anemia occurs when the bone marrow stops making enough blood cells—the water is shut off from the top. These anemias are usually associated with diseases that affect the bone marrow (see FELINE LEUKEMIA VIRUS, FELINE IMMUNODEFICIENCY VIRUS, and FELINE INFECTIOUS PERITONITIS).

Chronic illness of any kind may affect the bone marrow's ability to make new red cells, resulting in anemia of chronic disease. Kidney disease can also cause anemia. That's because erythropoietin, a hormone that stimulates red cells to be produced, is made in the kidney. Cats can also have bleeding disorders that cause anemia when viral infections, cancers or other problems compromise the blood's clotting ability (see also BLOOD).

ANESTHETIC A drug used to block the sensation of touch, pressure, or pain with or without a loss of consciousness is called an anesthetic. Anesthetics are particularly important in feline medicine because cats typically refuse to hold still for necessary treatment. Anesthetics can be used to prevent pain, immobilize the cat for medical treatments, and prevent further emotional stress to the cat.

Anesthetic drug doses are determined by the weight of the cat. Because of Kitty's small size and sensitivity to such medications, often the drugs will be administered in repeated small doses until the desired effect is reached.

Local anesthetics like xylocaine are used to block sensation on the skin surface. They may be injected into the surrounding tissue, or applied topically as an ointment, spray or cream. A tranquilizer or sedative may also be given with a local to help make Kitty easier to handle. Local anesthetics may be used to treat problems like an abscess, but are not appropriate for major procedures like spay surgeries.

A general anesthetic leaves the cat unconscious, blocks the pain, and may have amnesiac properties so that Kitty does not remember anything traumatic. A variety of both injectable drugs like Telazol and inhalant anesthetics like halothane and isoflurane are available. Inhalant anesthetic is administered either by a tube that carries the gas into the cat's lungs, or by a mask that fits over Kitty's face. A veterinarian may use general anesthetic alone or in combination with other drugs depending on the health status of the cat, and on the procedure to be done.

The drugs are removed from the body by the lungs, kidneys and liver, and anesthetics also affect the way the heart works. Although care is taken with the administration of any anesthetic, complications can occur. Cats suffering from impaired kidneys, liver or heart function are at higher anesthetic risk. Screening tests prior to anesthesia may be recommended when the cat is very young, old, or ill to evaluate and reduce possible risks.

ANOREXIA

Anorexia is an ongoing loss of appetite that results in a refusal to eat. The cat may also show signs of weight loss, depression, and sometimes vomiting. Anorexia is common in cats, and may be triggered by a number of things.

Some cats develop strong food preferences. These finicky felines may starve themselves rather than eat anything but their favorite meal (see FOOD). But most often, cats stop eating because they feel bad either physically or emotionally. The stress of any change in routine such as moving to a new home, an absent owner, or a new pet may prompt an aversion to food.

Pain, fever, and metabolic disorders also can cause a loss of appetite. To cats, the smell of food is more important than taste, and nothing spoils Kitty's dinner faster than a stopped up nose. Virus and bacterial infections are common disorders that result in stuffy nasal passages (see UPPER RESPIRATORY INFECTION).

A refusal to eat can make well cats sick, and sick cats even sicker. There are few if any conditions when withholding food is necessary; chronic diarrhea or vomiting may be examples. But in most instances, appropriate nutrition is important to keep the cat from using his own body tissue for energy.

Kittens should go no more than 18 to 24 hours without eating, and adult cats probably shouldn't exceed 48 hours without a meal. Cats that stop eating for several days, especially overweight cats, are at high risk for developing a life-threatening condition commonly called Fatty Liver Disease (see FELINE HEPATIC LIPIDOSIS). See your veterinarian immediately.

Usually, the physical or psychological condition causing the anorexia must be addressed to solve the problem. Treatment is aimed at stimulating Kitty's appetite, and getting the cat to eat.

At home, an owner may prompt the cat to eat by moistening dry food with warm water, or warming canned food. Offering a bit of food to the cat with your fingers, then stroking his head and neck seems to stimulate some cats to eat. Placing the first bite in his mouth may be all that's needed to get Kitty to continue feeding on his own. Try smearing a bit on his nose or paw to induce him to lick it off.

CAT FACTS

Although adding treats to a balanced diet should never be done on a regular basis, all's fair when tempting a sick cat to eat. A drizzle of warm chicken broth, meat baby food or cottage cheese over the regular diet may do the trick.

Holistic vets suggest using aromatherapy to help jump-start the flagging appetite. Put one or two drops of the essential oils rose, or vetiver, on the cat's bedding. The homeopathic remedy Nux vomica as well as Lycopodium, also are helpful. Cats can take two pellets of either remedy (potency of 6C or 12x) twice a day for no more than 24 hours.

Your veterinarian may prescribe drugs to stimulate the cat's appetite. If Kitty still won't eat, force feeding may be necessary (see ADMINISTER MEDICATION). In these instances, a puree of the cat's normal diet and/or a high calorie special diet prescribed by the veterinarian, is fed to the cat. In severe cases, the veterinarian may resort to placing a feeding tube directly into the stomach to force feed the cat.

ANTIFREEZE Antifreeze is used in cars to protect them from freezing temperatures. Antifreeze is composed of ethylene glycol, an industrial solvent also used in the removal of rust. It is an odorless, colorless fluid with a sweet taste that appeals to many pets.

Drinking antifreeze is deadly. Less than one teaspoon can kill an average size cat, and there is an 88 percent mortality rate for antifreeze poisoning in pets.

All cats are at risk, but male cats younger than three years seem to be poisoned most often. Accidents occur in the fall, winter, and early spring during peak usage of antifreeze solutions.

Survival of the poisoned cat depends on prompt treatment, because antifreeze is rapidly absorbed into the body. The cat's system actually works against itself and turns the relatively harmless ethylene glycol into a more toxic form that poisons the cat.

When the liver breaks down antifreeze, ethylene glycol is changed into oxalic acid, a substance extremely toxic to the kidneys. Oxalic acid is used as a bleaching or cleaning agent, and is a substance that the cat's body cannot further metabolize. When passed in the urine, oxalic acid can literally eat away parts of the urinary tract. Often, it combines with calcium to form crystals which clog the kidneys and cause sudden kidney failure (see also KIDNEY DISEASE).

The first symptoms can appear as early as one hour after ingestion. The poison first enters the brain and spinal fluid and produces a narcotic effect. The affected cat acts drunk, and staggers about showing a severe loss of coordination. Vomiting, convulsions, diarrhea, loss of appetite, and rapid breathing or panting are also signs of antifreeze poisoning.

The substance stimulates the thirst, so a poisoned cat drinks lots of water, and an early sign may be a temporary increase in urine output. Significant amounts of the poison are passed unchanged in the urine, especially in the first 12 hours.

Animals often survive initial poisoning signs and may seem to return to near normal in 12 hours. But although Kitty may act fine, even more serious signs return at around 24 hours. Symptoms may progress over a week, during which time the cat stops urinating, and becomes severely depressed. Vomiting, diarrhea, loss of appetite, dehydration and weakness, and even seizures may be seen. Ultimately, the cat falls into a coma, and dies.

ANTIFREEZE

SYMPTOMS: Drunken behavior; thirst; diarrhea; vomiting; convulsions; loss of appetite; panting
FIRST AID: SEE VETERINARIAN IMMEDIATELY; if not available, induce vomiting, administer activated charcoal
VET CARE: Induce vomiting; pump stomach; treat with intravenous alcohol or antidote
PREVENTION: Use pet safe products; store out of cat's reach

Any time you know or suspect that your pet has been into the antifreeze, time is of the essence and you should see your veterinarian immediately. If help is far away, though, and you've actually seen cat drinking antifreeze, try to make the cat vomit if the cat is alert. Never attempt to make your pet vomit if he's acting depressed or is not fully conscious. DO NOT USE SYRUP OF IPECAC, WHICH CAN CAUSE TOXICITY IN CATS.

Fill a syringe, eye dropper or squirt bottle with hydrogen peroxide (three percent solution), and give one tablespoon for each ten pounds of pet. If Kitty doesn't vomit in the next ten minutes, repeat the dose once more. Cats are typically hard to make vomit, even for professionals (see ADMINISTERING MEDICATION).

Giving the cat activated charcoal also helps improve survival. It's available from the drugstore, and can be given as tablets or crushed and mixed with water. Charcoal binds the poison to prevent its absorption in the intestinal tract. Whether successful or not with home treatments, your cat should be seen immediately by a veterinarian.

Therapy is directed at preventing absorption, increasing excretion, and avoiding further metabolism of the poison. Typically, the veterinarian will flush Kitty's stomach with a saline/charcoal solution. Intravenous fluid therapy helps head off dehydration problems, and also encourages the cat to urinate as much antifreeze as possible before it's changed into its more lethal form.

Getting the cat drunk by using 100 proof ethanol alcohol has historically been the recommended treatment for cats. When the cat's blood/alcohol content is raised to a high enough level, the liver works overtime on the alcohol instead of changing the antifreeze to oxalic acid. It is hoped that the antifreeze will pass through the cat's system in its original, less-toxic form.

An antidote for antifreeze poisoning became commercially available in January 1997. It is expensive, but Fomepizole (4MP) given to the cat **within the first three hours** following ingestion can save the cat's life. It prevents the liver from metabolizing the poison so that the cat's body eliminates the antifreeze naturally through urination.

If treatment isn't in time, the kidneys will shut down from the poison. Humans with kidney failure have the option of dialysis machines, but this luxury is usually unavailable for our pets.

Instead, peritoneal dialysis may be used. Fluid is pumped into the abdominal cavity and absorbs waste the damaged kidneys can't process, and then is drawn back out. Ideally, this procedure gives the kidneys time to start healing, so that normal function can return.

Antifreeze induced kidney disease is sometimes reversible. Even if the kidneys are able to return to normal or near normal function, it may take three to four weeks for this to occur.

Today, antifreeze manufacturers throughout the United States may be required by law (or if not, may still voluntarily) add a bitter flavoring agent to their normally sweet-tasting products to make them less attractive to pets as well as kids. The nontoxic bittering agent, denatonium benzoate, commonly is used in dangerous liquids to deter tasting or drinking, as well as a prevention treatment for nail-biting in people. Pet owners will still need to remain vigilant, of course.

The best prevention is keeping antifreeze safely away from cats. Dispose of drained radiator fluid in a sealed container, and mop up spills immediately. Keep pets away from garages or other areas where antifreeze may be found. Some new antifreeze products contain safer chemicals such as propylene-glycol instead of ethylene glycol. As your veterinarian to recommend non-toxic products that address the safety of your pet (See also POISON).

AROMATHERAPY

Aromatherapy uses certain scents like medicines to affect the body on a biochemical level. The fragrant scents used in aromatherapy are absorbed by the mucus membranes in the nose, and go directly to the brain to cause the therapeutic effect. For instance, the scent of lavender oil causes temporary sedation and helps pets relax. Other types of aromatherapy can affect the blood pressure and heart rate, or impact the pet's emotional state by reducing fear or stress.

Essential oils used in aromatherapy are available from holistic veterinarians, health food stores, and online. These oils are derived from natural sources, although synthetic and less expensive products can be found. As with flower essences, you can purchase single or combination oil blends.

Not everything is known about effective doses or potential toxicities of essential oils, especially in cats, so it is best to work directly with a holistic veterinarian before using aromatherapy with your pet. Some oils, like peppermint and pennyroyal, can be dangerous or even fatal when used incorrectly on pets.

Once your veterinarian has recommended the appropriate essential oil for your pet's circumstances, they typically can be applied at home. The oils are very strong and can burn the skin at full strength, so typically are diluted half-and-half with vegetable oil. The diluted oil can be used either in a diffuser, or applied to the fur at the back of the pet's neck or inside tip of the ears, so the scent reaches him but he can't lick it off.

Aromatherapy usually works very quickly, so is a short-term therapy. The effect also wears off quickly within four to six hours, but often, a single treatment is enough. Holistic veterinarians say it's fine to use veterinary approved aromatherapy up to three times a day for one or two days if there's not an immediate improvement, but after that, you should call the veterinarian.

ARRHYTHMIA

An arrhythmia is defined as any abnormal heartbeat. Electrical impulses control the natural rhythm of the heart. Changes in the impulse may cause the heart to beat too fast (tachycardia), too slow (bradycardia), or irregularly. Turbulence in the blood flow through the heart results in a distinctive sound, referred to as a heart murmur.

Drugs, toxins, and electrolyte or a body acid-base imbalance resulting from severe vomiting or diarrhea, urinary blockage, hyperthyroidism, and cardiomyopathy are all potential causes of a4rrhytymias. Drugs are available that help control and regulate the beat of the heart. The underlying cause, however, must be addressed if the problem is to be resolved.

ARTHRITIS

Arthritis is a degenerative disease of the joints. It's caused by inflammation and degradation of the cartilage that results in increasing pain that interferes with mobility. Unlike dogs, cats with arthritis often show few if any symptoms until the condition has become severe. Recent surveys suggest up to 75 percent of senior cats suffer from some degree of arthritis. Rather than specific joints, feline arthritis typically is a systemic condition and affects the cat's entire body.

Cats, usually males, can suffer from Chronic Progressive Polyarthritis (CPP) in which the immune system attacks the joints and causes a condition similar to rheumatoid arthritis in people. CPP is considered rare. The cause isn't known, but the condition may be related to viral infection like Feline Leukemia Virus.

ARTHRITIS

SYMPTOMS: Stiff feverish joints; difficulty rising; lameness; reluctance to move particularly in cold weather; poor grooming
HOME CARE: Gentle massage of joints; applying heat to painful areas
HOLISTIC HELP: Nutraceuticals/supplements; chiropractic adjustment; acupuncture/acupressure; aromatherapy
VET CARE: Prescription pain medications
PREVENTION: Treat joint or bone problems promptly

The typical condition we think about in people, called osteoarthritis or degenerative arthritis, also affects cats. It is a chronic disease of aging that occurs when simple wear and tear slowly destroys the thin layer of cartilage protecting the joint surface.

Arthritis is seen most often in older cats, but can develop at any age from to injury to bone, cartilage or ligaments. The resulting inflammation of the joint can lead to even more cartilage damage, causing a vicious cycle of degeneration. Arthritis is a progressive disease that once started doesn't stop.

Cats mask arthritis quite effectively. Owners may not notice problems until the arthritis is quite advanced. Typically, arthritic cats have difficulty getting up after they've been resting. Cats may stop grooming because it hurts to move. Lameness is aggravated by cold, damp weather. Moderate exercise may loosen and warm up the joint and muscles, so that once the cat starts moving the lameness subsides.

Cats are understandably reluctant to move when their joints are painful, and restricting movement over time also causes the muscles and tendons to shorten. Sometimes called muscle tie-down, this limits the cat's movement even further. Rather than limping or holding up a leg the way arthritic dogs do, the arthritic cat typically stops moving around.

Feline arthritis often isn't diagnosed until the cat begins showing signs the owner notices. The veterinarian can palpate, or feel how the joint works by flexing the affected limb. Usually the joint is warm and painful. However, it's not always easy to locate the exact source of the pain, because cats are not always cooperative during examinations. Sometimes they don't want to be touched anywhere, and other times are so stoic they won't indicate if something bothers them.

When an area of soreness or unusual lump or bump indicates a problem, X-rays show what's going on. But arthritis is a disease of the cartilage, and changes in cartilage aren't easily seen in X-rays until damage is severe. In fact, painful arthritis may be present, yet won't be apparent on the X-ray at all.

Treatment of osteoarthritis is aimed at relieving the cat's pain. Medications like aspirin and Tylenol, or other over the counter pain medications that are often used for arthritis in people are highly toxic to cats, and should not be used (see POISON). Human arthritis ointments are not only messy when applied to fur, they can be poisonous. Menthol products are particularly dangerous for cats.

Carprofen, trade name Rimadyl, is approved for dogs and with care it can be used off-label in cats. Metacam (meloxicam), made by Janssen Animal Health, is another one licensed for dogs but there is a feline dose some veterinarians use. Ketoprofen is probably the most commonly used NSAID in cats, also currently used off-label.

Another group of drugs—steroids—can help ease feline arthritis pain, particularly since feline veterinarians say cats are very steroid-tolerant as a species. The smallest dose possible that keeps them comfortable is given.

Narcotics can help manage feline arthritis pain, particularly acute flare-ups or after failure of an NSAID. Buprenorphine has been demonstrated to be effective in cats, and oral liquid morphine also has been used, although many cats dislike the taste.

Special "joint diets" are also available, and typically contain high levels of omega-3 fatty acids, alpha linoleic acid, carnitine, various antioxidants and glucosamine/chondroitin sulfate.

Glucosamine/chondroitin sulfate is a group of compounds thought to help diseased cartilage work a little better, and may slow or stop the progression of arthritis. A glucosamine and chondroitin sulfate combination product, called Cosequin, is one of the few that's actually been tested in scientific trials, and it is most often recommended by veterinarians. It is, however, more expensive than many health food products.

Medical marijuana (or cannabis) today is also available for pets, but must be formulated so that pets receive the medical benefits of the cannabis (hemp) plant while reducing potential toxic concentrations of the herb. Hemp can be used to control pain and inflammation. Ask your veterinarian if this supplement may benefit your pet.

Injections of Adequan (polysulfated glycosaminoglycan) in combination with Cosequin also work well for cats. Cosequin comes as a tasty powder you sprinkle over the cat's food. It takes several weeks for the Cosequin to begin to work, but the Adequan results in measurable improvement within a few days.

Acupuncture can relieve the pain of arthritis and can be used with drugs, or nutraceuticals such as Cosequin. The insertion of needles in proscribed locations throughout the body prompts the release of natural painkillers called endorphins. Most cats tolerate these needles quite well. Acupuncture is particularly helpful for cats because it has no side effects (see ACUPUNCTURE).

The "aspirin" point (BL60) is located on the outside of the rear ankle. Use the eraser end of a pencil to press this spot gently for about 60 seconds, once or twice a day, to help relieve pain.

Your veterinarian may recommend PEMF therapy, which stimulate the electrical and chemical processes in the tissues to relieve inflammation and pain. Devices may be designed for whole body treatment or targeted areas of the body. Some of these devices have successfully completed efficacy studies and are FDA-approved. Therapeutic products may be available in mats, wraps or other devices from your veterinarian or over the counter (see PULSED ELECTROMAGNETIC FIELD).

Gentle massage may be helpful to loosen the joint, soothe tight muscles, and relieve the ache. Use circular rubbing motions down both sides of the cat's spine, from head to tail. Gently flex Kitty's joints to keep them limber. But don't force the cat to submit, that's counterproductive. Only massage as much as Kitty will allow.

Warmth applied to sore joints seems to help as much as anything. Use hot water bottles, recirculating water blankets or heating pads, but always buffer them with several layers of towels to prevent burning the skin. Be sure Kitty can move off the area if it gets too warm.

There's no way to prevent age-related arthritic changes in cats, and no way to predict which cats will have problems. But watching for early signs and treating them can help make cats more comfortable.

Extra weight puts stress and strain on bones and joints, so keeping Kitty slim may help slow down arthritis (see OBESITY). Fractures, sprains or ligament injuries should receive prompt treatment to minimize the chances of developing arthritis in the future (see FRACTURE).

ARTIFICIAL RESPIRATION

Artificial respiration is the means of getting air into a cat that has stopped breathing. Common causes include electrical shock, drowning, asthma, smoke inhalation and trauma. Penetrating chest wounds can damage the lungs, and a blow such as being hit by a car can tear the diaphragm, a muscle separating the abdomen from the chest cavity that normally works to expand the lungs.

Signs of respiratory distress in cats include gasping, panting, or slowed breathing. A pale or blue tinged color to the cat's gums or rims of the eyelids indicates oxygen starvation from poor circulation. Cats in respiratory distress may simply pass out (see ASTHMA and RESPIRATORY DISTRESS).

If you suspect your cat is choking on a swallowed object like a bone or part of a toy, try to remove it with your fingers or tweezers. However, never pull on swallowed string, which may be anchored at the other end by a needle or fish hook; leave that to your veterinarian (see SWALLOWED OBJECTS).

When respiratory distress isn't due to obstruction, you'll need to help your cat breathe until you can get her to a veterinarian. Remove the cat's collar, and place her on a flat surface on her right side. Open her mouth, and pull the tongue forward; a piece of gauze or washcloth makes the tongue easier to grasp. Gently close Kitty's mouth with her tongue extended outside. Raise her chin so the neck stretches forward and keeps the airway open. Place one hand flat on Kitty's ribs, and press sharply to express the old air from her system, then release. If the diaphragm is intact, when you release the pressure elastic recoil will fill the cat's lungs with air.

If this recoil mechanism doesn't work, you must breathe air into your cat's lungs. The mouth-to-nose method is the most effective. Keep his tongue forward, then place both hands about your cat's muzzle to seal his lips so the air will not escape. Then place your lips over your cat's nose.

Blow two quick breaths just hard enough to move his sides, and watch to see if his chest expands. Blowing into his nose directs air to the lungs when the lips are properly sealed. For small pets, think of blowing up a paper bag—gently does it!—or you could over-inflate and damage the lungs.

Between breaths, pull your mouth away to let the air naturally escape before giving another breath. Continue rescue breathing at a rate of 15 to 20 breaths per minute until he starts breathing on his own, or you reach the veterinary clinic (See also CARDIOPULMONARY RESUSCITATION).

ASPIRIN TOXICITY

Aspirin (acetylsalicylic acid) is a common pain reliever used by people. Although it is often used in home veterinary use for dogs, aspirin can kill your cat. The cat's body breaks down aspirin more slowly than people, so the drug stays in the cat's system for days rather than hours. Giving your five pound cat one adult aspirin tablet is roughly equivalent to you taking 30 pills. Aspirin dosage in cats may be prescribed by a veterinarian in certain instances, but must be carefully regulated to avoid a fatal overdose.

Signs of aspirin toxicity include dehydration, loss of appetite, salivation, hyperactivity or depression, incoordination, vomiting, and diarrhea. The vomit and/or diarrhea often contain blood from gastrointestinal bleeding. If you know or suspect your cat swallowed aspirin, prompt veterinary attention is necessary. Treatment is aimed at supporting the cat with fluids, and administering drugs that help the kidneys get rid of the aspirin.

ASTHMA

Feline asthma is breathing distress that results from a sudden narrowing of the airways. The condition is thought to be caused by an allergy. Asthmatic cats have the same symptoms as people with asthma.

Something triggers the body to have an asthmatic reaction, and if that trigger can be avoided, asthmatic attacks can be eliminated. But identifying the trigger is difficult because it can have single or even multiple components.

Potential triggers include substances that often cause other types of allergic reactions, like inhaled pollens, molds, perfume, smoke, even cat litter dust. Asthmatic cats often seem to suffer from other allergies, but they may also react to air pollution, stress, exercise, or simple changes in the temperature. Usually, the trigger remains a mystery.

ASPIRIN TOXICITY

SYMPTOMS: Loss of appetite; salivation; dehydration; hyperactivity or depression; blood in vomit and/or diarrhea; incoordination.
HOME CARE: Induce vomiting if within two hours of swallowing
VET CARE: Fluid therapy; drugs to stimulate elimination of drug
PREVENTION: DON'T GIVE CATS ASPIRIN

When the triggering event occurs, an asthmatic will have a reaction within minutes. Muscles and glandular structures surrounding the lower airways—the bronchials—seem more developed in asthmatics. That means the size of the airways is probably already smaller in these cats. The trigger prompts muscles to forcibly contract, which closes down the passageways like a fist.

At the same time, inflammatory cells flood the area to try and neutralize the mysterious trigger. But inflammation causes swelling which narrows passageways even further. On top of this, local glands in the lungs release great amounts of mucus to soothe the inflammation, but this acts to clog the little breathing space that remains. The cat is probably left feeling like he's breathing through a straw.

Early signs like breathing a little fast or increased effort during breathing are so subtle they can be easily missed. Some cats may cough or wheeze, but often the first sign is a full-blown asthma attack. Gasping, panting, and open mouth breathing are very dangerous signs in cats; get the cat to a veterinarian immediately.

CAT FACTS

The incidence of feline asthma isn't known, but experts agree it's fairly common. Siamese and Burmese cats seem to be affected more often than other cats, and although the condition affects cats of all ages, it's usually seen for the first time in a two to four year old cat. Asthmatics seem to have a more difficult time during the spring and fall when pollen and mold counts are high.

ASTHMA

SYMPTOMS: Gasping; panting; wheezing; loss of consciousness
HOME CARE: EMERGENCY: SEE VET IMMEDIATELY
HOLISTIC HELP: Flower essences; acupressure
VET CARE: Steroids, oxygen therapy; bronchodilating drugs
PREVENTION: Reduce dusts or other triggers; use humidifier

Diagnosis is based on signs, clinical tests, and response to treatment. X-rays of asthmatic lungs may show thickened bronchials, but sometimes the lungs appear normal. A tracheal wash may offer clues. This procedure takes a sample of the fluid in the airways to look for inflammatory cells. If treatment for asthma in these cats offers relief, it's presumed that cat is asthmatic.

Allergic cats frequently are sensitive to more than one allergen, and each individual has an allergy threshold; below the threshold, Kitty remains symptom free. If an asthmatic cat's condition is aggravated by a combination of things, eliminating some may help relieve the signs (see ALLERGIES, CATS).

Treatment is aimed at reducing inflammation and opening up the lungs with medication so Kitty can breathe. Anti-inflammatory drugs like corticosteroids are the mainstay of feline asthma treatment.

Historically, asthmatic cats have been given low doses of steroids only for a couple of days to control immediate problems. Recent studies have shown that these cats often suffer ongoing airway inflammation, even when they aren't showing clear signs of the disease. Some veterinarians now recommend long term high-dose steroid therapy to manage the disease. Once diagnosed with asthma, cats generally stay on medication for the rest of their lives. Even if it's well controlled, an acute asthma attack can happen at any time and can be fatal.

Inhalers that human asthma sufferers use aren't practical in cats, so pills or injectable bronchodilators that open the airways are used. In emergency situations, the cat may require oxygen therapy and other drugs that help relax the muscles so Kitty can exhale more easily. Owners may be taught by their veterinarian to give the cat an injectable bronchodilator should an emergency happen at home.

During an asthma attack, holistic veterinarians say acupressure can help quieting the distress. The area between the shoulder blades has "association points" for the lungs. Use the balls of your fingers and rub forward and backwards, in the head-to-tail direction. Also, since asthma can be linked to stress, routinely using a flower essence to reduce the angst, like Rescue Remedy, may reduce the number of attacks. Put three or four drops on the inside ear leather (pinna) and smooth quickly with your finger.

Asthma cannot be cured, but can usually be managed. It's helpful to eliminate or reduce anything that might bring on an attack, such as dust or stressful conditions. A humidifier may make breathing easier.

In most species including dogs and people, a compound called histamine plays an important role in allergy. Histamine triggers certain inflammatory reactions, and antihistamine drugs help relieve these symptoms. However, antihistamines don't seem to work in cats.

Many of the symptoms of asthma in cats are instead prompted by a compound called serotonin, which is released by specialized immune cells in response to the presence of the triggering substance. In the same way antihistamine drugs block the effect of allergy symptoms in people, drugs that block serotonin may reduce or even prevent asthma signs in certain cats. Some veterinarians are now using anti-serotonin drugs like cyproheptadine as a preventative in feline asthma.

Medical marijuana (or cannabis) today is also available for pets, but must be formulated so that pets receive the medical benefits of the cannabis (hemp) plant while reducing potential toxic concentrations of the herb. Hemp can be used to reduce bronchial spasms in asthma. Ask your veterinarian if this supplement may benefit your pet.

56
CAT FACTS

57

CAT FACTS

BAD BREATH Offensive mouth odor, also called halitosis, should not be considered normal for the cat. Strong smelling canned foods may tinge Kitty's breath for a short time after eating, but a persistent bad smell more commonly points to a health problem.

Cats aren't able to brush their own teeth, yet are subject to some of the same dental risks as people. One of the first signs of gum and tooth infections is bad breath (see PERIODONTAL DISEASE).

Offensive mouth odor can also indicate a sore mouth, like stomatitis. Certain types of breath odor can signal disease or poisoning. A strong garlic breath may indicate the cat has been poisoned with arsenic. One sign of late-stage diabetes is acetone breath that smells something like nail polish remover. And signs of kidney disease include mouth ulcers and ammonia-like mouth odor.

Halitosis is more than a nuisance, and cannot be fixed with a breath mint; diagnosis is necessary before treatment can cure the problem. Often, bad breath that results from periodontal disease can be prevented with routine dental care.

BAD BREATH

SYMPTOMS: Mouth odor
HOME CARE: Feed dry crunchy foods; clean teeth
VET CARE: Anesthesia and dentistry
PREVENTION: Routine brushing of cat's teeth

59

CAT FACTS

BALANCE The cat's finely tuned sense of balance is regulated by a specialized organ called the vestibular apparatus found deep inside the ear. Balance allows Kitty to travel great heights and effortlessly leap long distances.

It is the cat's uncanny flexibility and motion control, coupled with intricate balance sense that allows the falling cat to land on her feet. She uses a series of spine, shoulder and flank contractions to twist in midair during a fall, and right herself.

The cat is instantly able to distinguish between up and down, and can determine acceleration as she falls because of the specialized balance organs. Inside the cat's inner ear are tiny fluid filled tubes and structures called the semicircular canals, utricle and saccule. Each is lined with millions of microscopic hairs, and the utricle and saccule also contain tiny particles of chalk that float and move with every motion. Whenever the cat's head moves, the fluid moves against the hairs. When the hairs move, they relay information to the brain about body position, and speed of movement.

Ear infections can affect the cat's balance (see OTITIS and EAR MITES), and falls from short distances may not allow enough time for the righting mechanism to work. Landing on her feet does not prevent Kitty from sustaining serious injuries during falls (see HIGH RISE SYNDROME).

BATHING see GROOMING

BEHAVIOR see AFFECTION, AGGRESSION, ALOOFNESS,

COMMUNICATION, DOMINANCE, EATING, FEAR, HUNTING BHEAVIOR, KITTEN, KNEADING, MARKING, PLAY, REPRODUCTION, SCRATCHING, SLEEP, and SOILING.

BLEEDING Bleeding is the body's way of cleansing a wound. Injuries to soft

tissue that can cause bleeding include cuts, abrasions, and lacerations. Factors in the blood cause it to clot and seal minor wounds, and protect the area while healing takes place. Any deep or gaping wound requires veterinary attention, whether the cat is bleeding profusely or not.

Scratches and abrasions may result in oozing wounds. When an artery has been cut, bright red blood will flow in spurts in time with the cat's heartbeat. Blood from a vein flows evenly, and is a darker red.

In most instances, bleeding can be stopped by applying even, direct pressure. Use a sterile gauze pad or clean cloth to cover the wound, and press firmly for five to seven minutes. Gently lift the pad to see if bleeding has stopped; if not, continue the pressure. Don't pull the material away from the wound if it sticks, or you risk tearing away the new scab. Instead, place another clean cloth or pad over the first.

If direct pressure doesn't stop the bleeding, indirect pressure on the arteries may help. Apply pressure between the heart and the wound. Pressure points are inside the legs; that's the "arm pit" on front legs and the crotch where the hind legs connect. The underside at the tail base is another pressure point. With a cut vein, apply pressure below the injury to stop the bleeding. Elevate the wound above the level of the heart; that lets gravity reduce the blood pressure to the wound, which helps slow the bleeding.

If none of these procedures work and the wound is on the leg or tail, then a tourniquet may be used, but only as a last resort. Improper use of a tourniquet may so severely injure the tissue that amputation of the affected limb may be necessary.

Make the tourniquet using a wide strip of cloth, gauze, or other material; the leg from a pair of pantyhose works well. The material must be at least one inch wide to prevent cutting into the cat's skin. Wrap the material twice around the limb approximately two inches from the wound, and tie once. Then securely knot a pencil or stick on top of the first tie. Gently twist the pencil, stop immediately when the bleeding is a trickle, and fasten the pencil in place. Remember to release the tourniquet for a brief time every 15 minutes. In the meantime, get your cat to the veterinarian immediately.

Internal bleeding is harder to notice, and may indicate a number of critical conditions. Bruises or swollen areas may result from these injuries, but are often hidden beneath the fur (see HEMATOMA). Danger signals indicating possible internal injury include bleeding from the mouth or anus, blood in the stool or vomit, or loss of consciousness. Spontaneous bleeding from the nose or mouth and blood in the urine or stool can also indicate poisoning or advanced liver disease. Blood tinged urine is a sign of cystitis or lower urinary tract disease. With the exception of simple abrasions, any cat that is bleeding should see a veterinarian immediately.

BLOOD
In its simplest terms, blood is a mass transit system that shuttles the components of life throughout the cat's body. The yellow liquid portion, called plasma, transports waste products, various nutrients, antibodies, and certain clotting proteins. The solid portion is made up of red cells, white cells, and platelets.

Platelets and plasma clotting proteins make clotting possible, so that when Kitty tears a claw, the bleeding will stop. White cells are a part of the body's immune system. White cells and antibodies guard against and fight off attacks by foreign invaders, like viruses and bacteria.

The red cell's major function is to carry oxygen. The oxygen-carrying pigment (hemoglobin) gives blood its red color.

Not all feline blood is the same. Antigens, a kind of protein on the surface of blood cells, define a blood type. The immune system responds to a foreign antigen by producing antibodies against it. Like people, cats have very strong antibodies against the wrong blood type, and they attack and destroy the foreign blood the same way they would a virus or bacteria. Consequently, giving an incompatible blood transfusion can quickly kill a cat. Because blood type is inherited, certain cats are more likely to have one kind over another.

Researchers have identified one feline blood group system made up of three types: feline type A, type B, and type AB. More than 95 percent of domestic shorthair and domestic longhair cats are type A. Pedigreed Siamese, Burmese, Tonkinese, Russian Blue, American Shorthair, and Oriental Shorthair are all type A.

Up to 10 percent of Maine Coon and Norwegian Forest Cats are type B, and up to 20 percent of Abyssinian, Birman, Persian, Somali, Sphynx, and Scottish Fold are type B. Up to 45 percent of British Shorthair, Cornish Rex, Devon Rex, and exotic cats are type B.

Blood type AB is rare, but has been found in a number of breeds and domestic shorthair cats. Type AB has been observed in some domestic shorthairs and breeds with Type B.

Feline blood type matters because blood type B cats have very strong antibodies against blood type A. When a type B cat receives type A blood, antibodies in the type B blood attack the foreign type A red cells. Type A cats that receive Type B blood will likely also have a reaction, but it is often not as severe or fatal, and can usually be successfully treated. Type AB cats are very rare, and are considered "universal recipients", but should receive Type A blood if possible.

Knowing blood type not only is important in case of needed blood transfusions, but also when breeding. Newborn kittens receive antibodies from the colostrum (first milk) they nurse from their mother. If the kittens have type A blood, but the mother cat is type B, the newborns will swallow antibodies that don't like the kitten's red blood cells.

That results in a hemolytic reaction called Neonatal Isoerythrolysis (NI). The antibodies from the queen's colostrum attack and destroy the kitten's red blood cells. Called "fading kitten syndrome," such kittens start out healthy but grow weak and usually die within the first week of life.

It's crucial for breeders to identify each cat's blood type before planning any kitty matchmaking. NI can be prevented by breeding type B females only to type B males.

But for all cats, blood compatibility can be a matter of life and death. Transfusions of whole blood, plasma, or other blood products are used to treat a variety of blood disorders. If a cat is given a transfusion with the opposite blood type, he can have a deadly reaction on the very first transfusion.

When a type B cat receives type A blood, antibodies in the type B blood attack the foreign type A red cells. Call a hemolytic transfusion reaction, the breakage of the red cells causes almost immediate signs of distress in the cat, including reduced heart rate, low blood pressure, slowed breathing, vomiting, defecation, and urination. The affected cat can die within only a few minutes. To avoid such problems, only compatible blood should be given.

If your cat is a breed that has a high prevalence of type B blood, it's important that the cat's blood be typed. Specialized tests are necessary, and only a few places in the United States, such as veterinary schools and certain commercial labs and animal blood banks have the capability.

Cross-matching can be done in your veterinarian's office. The procedure doesn't determine the type, but will tell if the donor's blood is compatible with the recipient's—in other words, whether a transfusion reaction will occur or not.

To cross-match blood, a drop of serum or plasma from the recipient cat is mixed with a drop of blood from the prospective donor cat. Clumping indicates the blood is incompatible.

Many veterinarians keep a clinic cat that serves as a blood donor when necessary. Teaching hospitals at veterinary schools often operate their own animal blood banks, and commercial animal blood banks also make a variety of products available.

BLINDNESS

Cats can become blind at any time, but it occurs mainly when they are older (see GERIATRIC CAT). Vision loss often is gradual, but may be sudden, complete or partial. Injury or eye disease such as infections, cataracts or glaucoma can frequently cause blindness.

Hypertension can also develop as a consequence of kidney disease or heart disease. Reginal detachment can cause vision loss due to the high blood pressure symptomatic of one or more of these diseases.

Even if the cat loses vision, the owners typically aren't aware of it—at least not at first. Blind cats remember the layout of the house, and rely on sound and scent landmarks to get around. Vision loss typically causes problems when they're in unfamiliar surroundings. Owners may suddenly realize there's a problem if they rearrange the furniture, for example.

Catching vision loss in the earliest stages has the best chance of preserving the cat's sight. Specific drug treatments and sometimes surgery are available for glaucoma and cataracts, discussed further in the chapters on those topics. Eye infections and inflammation may also respond to prompt medication (see UVEITIS).

Similarly, cats suffering from kidney or heart disease often benefit from anti-hypertensive drugs. If you catch it early and treat it medically you may catch it before the retina completely detaches, or it may reattach so there's still some viable vision afterwards.

Cats that have lived their whole life in one place have memorized their home or yard, and show few if any signs of vision loss. Symptoms of vision loss are therefore noticed more in an unfamiliar environment.

Blind cats to tend to become a little more withdrawn as they lose their vision. The cat hides, and her activity level decreases. She'll become reluctant to navigate stairs or jumps, especially in unfamiliar places. Blind cats may become clingy, move slowly and cautiously and when touched or startled unexpectedly the cat may bite. Depending on the cause, the pupil of eye may stay dilated (see EYES).

When blindness due to disease or injury can't be reversed, you need to adjust your cat's environment to help her better cope in a sightless world. Blind cats compensate for the loss by relying more on other senses, and won't be nearly as concerned about the deficit as the owners.

CAT FACTS

Cats prefer the status quo anyway, and this becomes even more important when they can no longer see. Don't rearrange the furniture. Keep things in the same place so the cat can map the house, and doesn't become disoriented. Keep food, water and bed always in the same spot so the animal knows where things are at all times. Cats don't tend to run into objects, but they may decide to stop moving altogether in a strange landscape.

As long as the environment stays the same, blind felines become adept at compensating and may still be able to accurately judge well-known leaps simply by memory. But take care to block off danger zones, such as the basement stairway, to protect your blind cat from an accidental fall. If you must pick up and carry the cat, set her down in a place she recognizes—near her litter box, for example—or she may become disoriented. Setting her on high unfamiliar surfaces could cause her to fall off because she doesn't know where she is.

A blind cat is still a very happy cat. She can enjoy and remain engaged in life and the world around her.

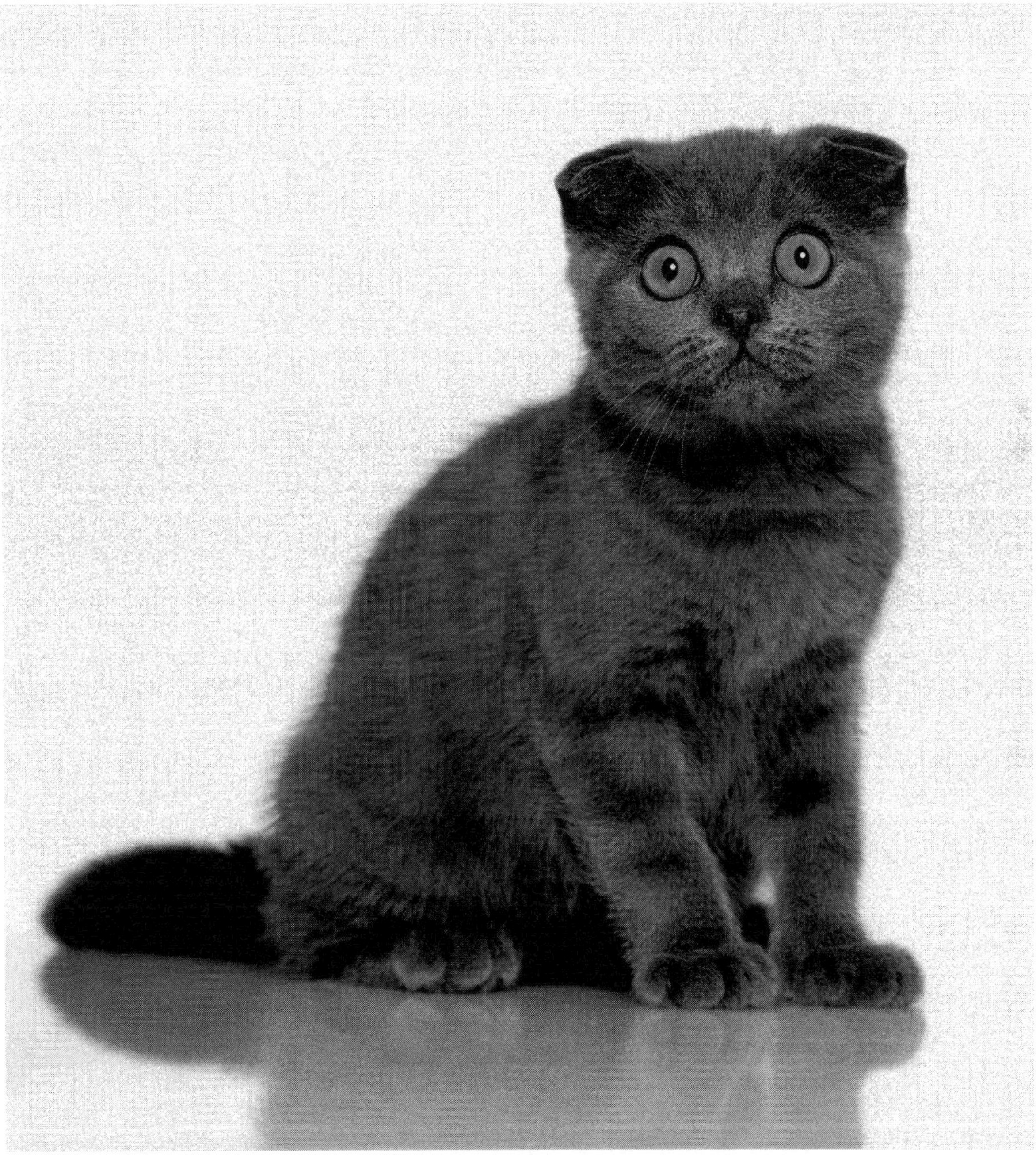

CAT FACTS

BREED Breed refers to a particular cat type that has distinct and predictable physical and/or temperament characteristics that are consistently reproduced in the offspring.

A cat of a particular breed has a known, traceable ancestry referred to as the pedigree. A "pedigreed" cat is one produced by the mating of a male and female cat of the same breed. To authenticate breed status, kittens must be registered with a cat association. There are over 100 distinct cat breeds recognized around the world; more than forty are described in this book (see APPENDIX A, CAT ASSOCIATIONS and CAT BREEDS).

"Natural" cat breeds like the longhaired cobby Persian appeared in nature, and selective breeding by cat fanciers refined the type. "Man-made" breeds like the Bombay are hybrids created by combining existing breeds to form a new one. "Spontaneous mutations" are the third breed type, and are inexplicable deviations of nature; examples are the taillessness of the Manx, the folded ears of the Scottish Fold, and the baldness of the Sphynx.

Every cat's basic shape is the same, but some are wirier and others more heavily muscled. Cat body types are described as the extremes of cobby and foreign, with degrees in between. The cobby type (i.e., Persian) is a heavy boned, short bodied cat with a round head and usually thick tail. Foreign body types (i.e. Siamese) have long slender bodies with fine bones, and wedge-shaped angular heads. Oriental type takes this foreign look to an extreme. Body types that fall somewhere between cobby and foreign, like the American Shorthair, may be referred to as domestic type.

The fur comes in a variety of lengths. Shorthair cats include the peach fuzz coat of the Sphynx, the fine single coat of the Bombay, to the plush double coat of the Chartreux. Most shorthair coats are straight, but the rex coat curls, waves or ripples (see American Wirehair, Cornish Rex, Devon Rex). Longhair coats vary from two to six inches in length depending on the breed.

Coat color and pattern are equally diverse. Cats in solid colors are referred to as self-colored. Tipped refers to the hair tip color contrasting with the rest of the hair. When the tip is lighter, it's called "Chinchilla," medium contrast is called "Shaded", and dark ends with light undercoat is "Smoke."

Tabby refers to a pattern of darker stripes, spots or swirls on a lighter background. The classic tabby pattern is a combination of circles and stripes, while the mackerel tabby is more clearly defined stripes. The spotted tabby has various sizes and shapes of spots.

Any solid-color coat with patches of white is referred to as parti-color. Bi-color is when the two colors are divided two-thirds to one. Van marking is a white coat with patches of color on the head and tail, as in the Turkish Van breed. Cats with a solid colored coat with patches of cream or orange are called tortoiseshell or tortie; when white is mixed in, it's called calico.

CAT FACTS

Mixed-breed cats come in a rainbow of colors and types that rival that of any registered kitty. A mixed-breed cat, also referred to as random-bred or "mutt" cat ("moggy" in Great Britain), is the result of unplanned breeding of various pedigreed or other mixed-breed cats. They have no pedigree, are not often registered, and rarely resemble any pedigreed standard. It is impossible to predict what the offspring will be like. They make wonderful pets, though, and make up the majority of household pet cats throughout the world.

Breeding see REPRODUCTION

Burns

Cats may suffer burns from walking over hot stoves or fresh tar; being exposed to accidental spills of hot water, cooking oil or chemicals (see POISON); and by chewing electric cords (see ELECTRICAL SHOCK). They also may be burned due to sun overexposure (see SUNBURN) and rarely, direct contact with fire. Frostbite resembles a burn injury (see FROSTBITE).

A minor burn will cause the skin to turn red and sometimes blister or swell, and the area will be tender. Deeper burns turn the tissue white or even char it, and the fur will loosen; severe burns are extremely painful. Severe burns are usually accompanied by excessive loss of fluid and shock, and when 15 percent or more of the body surface is burned, the outlook is grim.

BURNS

SYMPTOMS: Red skin; blistering; swelling; tender-to-painful area; severe burns are sometimes charred, with fur easily pulled out

FIRST AID: Flush with cool water; apply cool water compress; see vet as soon as possible

VET CARE: Depending on severity, cold compresses, salves, or ointments; surgical removal of dead tissue; sometimes fluid therapy or pain medication

PREVENTION: Confine cat in safe place when hazards are unavoidable; prevent sunburn with sunscreen; tape down electrical cords; keep caustic solutions out of reach

CAT FACTS

If your cat is burned, flush the area with cool water for five to ten minutes to stop the "cooking" process. If the burn covers more than 25 percent of the cat's body, soak a towel in cool water and apply to the injured area to alleviate the pain. When the burn is on the head or neck, be sure to remove the collar so swelling doesn't make the cat choke. Then see your veterinarian. Even minor-appearing injuries may be more serious than you think; the full extent of the damage may be hidden by the hair coat.

To avoid burns, make the stove off-limits to your cat; perhaps confine him in a safe place when you're cooking. When open flame is accessible, such as candles or a fireplace, either confine your cat to a safe place or increase your vigilance to prevent accidents.

73

CAT FACTS

CANCER Cancer is the abnormal out-of-control growth of cells that invade and replace normal tissues and interfere with body processes. Such growths are called neoplasms, or tumors. Those that are localized and relatively harmless are called benign; more often, feline tumors are malignant.

Malignant tumors may be localized, but more frequently they metastasize, which means tumor cells spread throughout the body. A malignant tumor, becomes deadly when it interferes with normal body processes. Approximately 80 percent of the tumors found in cats are malignant.

Feline cancers can strike at any age, and the kind that is often associated with feline leukemia virus (FeLV) and feline immunodeficiency virus (FIV) tends to strike young to middle-aged cats. But cancer mostly strikes older cats, and the Veterinary Cancer Society says cancer accounts for nearly half of the deaths in cats over the age of ten.

In the normal course of a cat's life, old cells throughout the body die and are replaced by new ones in a process called mitosis, where one cell splits into two new ones identical to the parent cell. Sometimes something goes wrong in this process, and the new cells aren't identical—they mutate to something different from the parent. Usually the immune system gets rid of mutated cells, and there's no problem. But for reasons that aren't clear, mutation sometimes creates abnormal, fast-growing cancer cells. Like parasites, they invade and replace healthy tissue with abnormal growth. In most cases, a healthy immune system recognizes and eliminates foreign cells. But when the system breaks down, the abnormal cells proliferate into tumors.

Localized, relatively harmless tumors are termed benign, while malignant refers to the most dangerous, life-threatening form that often tend to spread— metastasize—throughout the body and interfere with normal body processes. The degree of malignancy determines the seriousness of the disease. "Low- grade" cancers may grow to enormous proportions but tend not to spread until late in the disease. The most dangerous cancers spread very early, even when the point of the origin (the primary tumor) is tiny or nearly undetectable.

The exact mechanism that prompts cancer to form isn't known, but a variety of factors are probably involved. Some families or breeds of cats are genetically predisposed. Viruses like feline leukemia virus and feline immunodeficiency virus can cause cancer, and vaccines cause injection site tumors in some cats. Cats with white on their face around the nose, eyelids and ear tips, and cats with white thin-haired abdomens are at risk for tumors caused by sunlight.

Some cancer-causing agents, referred to as carcinogens, have been identified. Cumulative exposure over a cat's lifetime may be why older cats develop cancer more often.

Cats can develop many of the same types of cancers that affect people, but some are more common. The most common sites for feline tumors are 1) lymph glands, 2) skin and subcutaneous and 3) mammary tissue. The most common of the skin and subcutaneous tumors, in descending order of frequency, are basal cell tumors, mast cell tumors, squamous cell carcinoma, fibrosarcoma, and sebaceous hyperplasia and adenomas.

Nearly 90 percent of lymph gland cancers are caused by FeLV, and affect the lymphatic system and blood cell-forming organs such as bone marrow and spleen. Skin cancer, the second most common types, usually affects the face and head, often due to overexposure to sunlight. Fibrosarcoma is a malignancy of the connective tissue of the body, with a wide range of subtypes—collectively referred to as soft tissue sarcomas. Vaccine-associated fibrosarcomas are included in this category. Breast cancer is also very common in cats, and Siamese are reported to have twice as much risk as other breeds. Other common old-cat cancers include digestive tract tumors, oral tumors, and bone cancer.

One in five cats that are sick with FeLV suffer from FeLV-related cancer. FeLV causes several kinds of cancers, including cancer of lymphoid tissue (lymphosarcoma) and bone marrow cancers. A mutant form of FeLV called feline sarcoma virus (FeSV) causes cancers of connective tissue called fibrosarcoma. Preventing these diseases reduces the chance of a cat developing virus-associated cancers.

CANCER

SYMPTOMS: see **VETERINARY CANCER SOCIETY'S TOP 10 CANCER SIGNS**
HOME CARE: Maintain good nutrition; nursing care
VET CARE: Surgery; chemotherapy; radiation
HOLISTIC HELP: Vitamin supplements; nutraceuticals; herbal therapy; homeopathy
PREVENTION: Spay females before first heat cycle, neuter mails before puberty; avoid sun exposure in light-colored cats; remain alert to lumps and bumps

Over-exposure to sunlight is associated with a skin cancer called squamous cell carcinoma that affects the ears and face, particularly of white-faced or sparsely furred cats. Older outdoor cats that have been exposed over their lifetime are especially susceptible, but even indoor sun-bathers can be victims. These tumors are seen more often in the Sunbelt areas of the United States, with the highest incidence in Arizona, New Mexico, California, and in Colorado where elevation makes ultraviolet exposure more intense. Siamese are less likely to develop this cancer, possibly because of their dark faces and ears.

A cat's risk of developing breast cancer can be greatly reduced by spaying before the first heat cycle. Using a medication called Megestrol acetate (Ovaban) can lead to breast cancer in both male and female cats, whether neutered or intact. Ovaban is a progesterone-type compound sometimes used as a behavior-modification medication.

Vaccinations can also be a culprit. In 1992, researchers first noticed fibrosarcoma tumors developing in some cats in the place where they'd been vaccinated, between the shoulder blades or in the upper thigh. Rabies and FeLV vaccines containing adjuvants (immune-stimulating compounds) were most commonly implicated. Today, effective vaccines are available that do not contain adjuvants, so ask your veterinarian for the best options for your cats.

It's still a mystery why some cats develop vaccine-induced tumors while most do not and the best frequency guess is one to two cats per 10,000. Current recommendations are to vaccinate as far down the leg or tail as possible, to be able to save an affected cat's life through amputation of the affected limb. Cat owners should continue vaccinating their cats, because the risk of contracting infectious diseases like rabies is much greater than the possibility of developing these tumors. After your cat is vaccinated, monitor the vaccination site for small bumps. These are common, but if they fail to disappear in four to six weeks, consult your veterinarian.

Many cancer-related symptoms are confusingly similar to other illnesses or conditions. Most feline cancers are internal, so until they make the cat sick you may not notice anything's wrong. Even external lumps or sores may be hidden by fur. Since early detection significantly improves treatment success and chance of survival, cat owners should immediately alert their veterinarians to any physical or behavioral change in their cat.

Diagnosis can only be made by microscopic examination and identification of specific tumor cells. The veterinarian may collect a sample by inserting a needle directly into the tumor and withdrawing cells into the syringe (see CYTOLOGY). Other times, cancer cells may be identified in the blood, or even in a urine specimen. Most often, diagnosis requires a biopsy, the removal of a piece of tissue for specialized laboratory analysis. The tumor type and its state of progression must be evaluated before a prognosis and treatment can be determined.

The prognosis is defined by how far the cancer has spread; cancer treatment is designed to kill the cancer cells, and stop the progression. Cures are possible if tumors are detected and treated during the very early stages. The three major cancer treatments used in cats are the same as those used in people; often, a combination treatment that attacks the cancer from multiple angles works best.

Surgical removal of tumors is the primary method of treating cancer in veterinary medicine, and cost varies widely depending on the cancer involved. Surgery may gain the cat an additional six to 12 months, but rarely cures the disease because it's often difficult to remove the entire tumor. Leaving behind even a single cancer cell can allow the tumor to return. Surgery may be followed by other treatments that address any cells left behind.

Some cancers are impossible to treat with conventional surgery because of the location or invasiveness of the tumor, and the danger of damaging vital tissues and organs. Tumors that can't be surgically removed in their entirety are commonly treated with chemotherapy.

Chemotherapy is a systemic treatment that attacks cancer that's spread throughout the body. Cytotoxic or cell-poisoning drugs, referred to as chemotherapy, often are used in various combinations, along with surgery or radiation. Nearly all chemotherapy drugs used in pets are taken from human medicine and adapted for animals. Examples include gemcitabine and temazolamide. Chemotherapeutic drugs may be injected into the bloodstream, given as pills, or both.

Chemotherapy is used to destroy as many cancer cells as possible, and/or to slow the growth rate of the tumor. Specific treatment and drug choice depends on the type of tumor, but normally a variety of drugs are given in sequence; initial therapy is quite intense, then becomes less so as therapy progresses.

These drugs can't specifically be targeted to the cancer, so they also affect healthy tissue. This is what often causes side effects in people. But although prolonged treatment may occasionally cause a loss of whiskers, generally cats don't lose their hair, or suffer nausea and vomiting. Cats don't tend to get sick at all.

Because dosage is based on body weight, the cost of the drugs is relatively low. But such cats are also commonly affected by other medical problems and expense can quickly mount.

About 50 to 80 percent of lymph gland cancers treated with chemotherapy shrink in size, or even go away. Every case is different, and success depends on the type of lymphoma and how advanced it is when treatment is begun, but generally about 75 percent of treated cats will go into remission for nine months to a year. Although cures are very rare, they do sometimes happen.

Cancers of the face and head, or those that surround nerves and vital organs may be impossible to remove with surgery. Conventional beam radiation that shoots intense X-rays directly into the cancer works well as an alternative, particularly against cancers of rapidly dividing cells like skin or bone marrow. Radiation doesn't discriminate between cancerous and healthy tissue, though. It can damage normal areas of the body, and so it is best used on cancers confined to one area.

Cats tend not to have the same severe side effects with radiation, either. At most, they may lose their whiskers or appetite temporarily. Radiation cures up to 80 percent of some kinds of cancer cats. The pet must be anesthetized to target the cancer, which raises the cost, as well as risk for older animals that may not tolerate anesthesia well.

Radiation therapy machines can be found in nearly all veterinary universities and in many specialty hospitals across the country. Some of the newest linear accelerators, like the one at Washington State University, feature a computerized 40-leaf collimator similar to the iris on a camera. That allows the radiologist to shape the X-ray beam to fit the tumor, and target with pinpoint radiation. The head of the machine rotates around the pet's body, adjusting the beam as it travels. That spares the surrounding normal tissue from being irradiated. The laser-sighting system built into the linear accelerator means patients can be positioned in the exact same position for every treatment.

VETERINARY CANCER SOCIETY'S TOP 10 CANCER SIGNS

1. Abnormal swelling that persists or continues to grow
2. Sores that do not heal
3. Weight loss
4. Loss of appetite
5. Bleeding or discharge from any body opening
6. Offensive odor
7. Difficulty eating or swallowing
8. Hesitation to exercise or loss of stamina
9. Persistent lameness or stiffness
10. Difficulty in breathing, urinating, or defecating

Although surgery, chemotherapy and radiation therapy alone or in combination represent the most common and successful cancer therapies currently available, veterinary medicine is constantly researching new treatments. Immunotherapy enhances immune responses to help the body itself destroy tumor tissue. Immune-boosting drugs like acemannan are being studied, and seem promising when used against fibrosarcoma.

Cryosurgery has successfully been used on localized, shallow tumors to freeze and destroy cancerous tissue. A substance that produces intense cold—usually liquid nitrogen—is applied directly to the tumor itself, leaving surrounding healthy tissue intact. Hyperthermia, or heat therapy, is the opposite of cryosurgery; it heats the cancer cells to kill them. The proper temperature destroys the tumor without damaging normal tissue.

An innovation is photodynamic therapy (PDT), a kind of light-activated chemotherapy using lasers. Photosensitizing agents, similar to chlorophyll, are used. For unknown reasons, the tumor tends to absorb these agents, and they respond to different wavelengths of light. Once the agent has been absorbed, then the laser light is either shined on the area or laser fibers are implanted in the tumor. The agent releases the laser light energy inside the tissue and kills the tumor cells. It's used for some skin cancers, oral tumors, and bladder tumors.

Holistic veterinarians recommend a variety of therapies to help support pets with cancer, and these may be used alongside (not instead of) conventional treatments. Be sure to consult with your vet before adding a holistic treatment, though. An herb or vitamin may affect the impact of chemo, for example, so that less of a conventional drug is needed.

Medical marijuana (or cannabis) today is also available for cats, but must be formulated so that pets receive the medical benefits of the cannabis (hemp) plant while reducing potential toxic concentrations of the herb. Hemp can be used to control pain, inflammation, nausea and anorexia and may be helpful to mitigate side effects of cancer treatments. Ask your veterinarian if this supplement may benefit your pet.

Your veterinarian may recommend PEMF therapy, which stimulate the electrical and chemical processes in the tissues to relieve inflammation and pain. Devices may be designed for whole body treatment or targeted areas of the body. Some of these devices have successfully completed efficacy studies and are FDA-approved. Therapeutic products may be available in mats, wraps or other devices from your veterinarian or over the counter (see PULSED ELECTROMAGNETIC FIELD).

Extra antioxidant vitamins C and E have been shown to slow the growth and spread of some kinds of cancer. The mineral selenium also helps slow cancer growth, as do the omega-3 fatty acids in fish oil.

The herbs maitake and green tea help support the immune system, and have an antioxidant effect. Turmeric is thought to inhibit the growth of cancer cells. Noni juice, available in health food stores, is made from the morinda plant from the South Sea Islands. Noni juice can relieve pain often associated with cancer.

The best preventative measure is for owners to pet the cat everywhere. The smaller the lump or bump is when found, the more likely you are to cure it.

Available cancer therapies may help prolong the cat's quality of life even if a cure isn't possible. Your veterinarian can help you make difficult decisions for your cat when a longer life is no longer necessarily the best choice (see EUTHANASIA).

CARBON MONOXIDE POISONING

Carbon monoxide is an odorless, colorless, tasteless gas that is deadly to people and their pets. This natural by-product of fuel combustion is present in car exhaust and improperly vented gas furnaces or space heaters.

The gas affects pets the same as people. However, carbon monoxide is lighter than air, so cats that lounge on higher perches may show signs earlier than people. If you notice any change in your cat's behavior or your own symptoms that coincides with cold weather or the furnace coming on, consult your veterinarian and doctor.

CARBON MONOXIDE POISONING

SYMPTOMS: Confusion; disorientation; difficulty walking; vomiting; lethargy; extreme sleepiness; cherry-red color to gums
FIRST AID: Provide fresh air. EMERGENCY! SEE VET IMMEDIATELY!
VET CARE: Oxygen therapy
PREVENTION: Have heating units safety-checked each fall before using them

Carbon monoxide passes into the lungs, and then binds with hemoglobin, the oxygen-transporting component of blood. This effectively prevents the hemoglobin from utilizing or transporting oxygen to the body. The gas creates a kind of chemical suffocation (see BLOOD).

The most common symptom of human carbon monoxide poisoning is headache, confusion and disorientation, and flu-like symptoms with vomiting. Ultimately, the poison victim falls into a coma, and dies. We don't know if poisoned cats suffer headaches, but they do act confused, lethargic, and drunk like human victims. A distinctive sign common to both people and pets are bright cherry-red gums in the mouth. When the victim is asleep during exposure to the poison, the cat, or the person, may never wake up.

The body can only get rid of the poison bound to the hemoglobin by breathing it out, or by replacing the poisoned hemoglobin with new. The liver and spleen replace hemoglobin about every ten to fifteen days. When only a small amount of the blood is affected, the victim recovers without treatment as long as no more poison is inhaled.

But high levels of blood saturation will kill the person or pet unless emergency treatment is given. Twenty-five percent saturation level is considered dangerous for people. Usually, though, both people and pets should be treated when the carbon monoxide saturation level is ten percent or higher.

Administering high concentrations of oxygen is the treatment of choice, because it increases the amount of gas that is breathed out. Many hours of oxygen therapy may be required. In some cases, ventilation may be necessary. To protect yourself and your pets from carbon monoxide poisoning, have heating units inspected each fall before you start using them.

CARDIOMYOPATHY

Cardiomyopathy simply means "heart-muscle disease," and can refer to any disease that affects the heart muscle. Based on distinct features of the disease, cardiomyopathies affecting cats are categorized as hypertrophic, dilated or congested, and restrictive forms. Cardiomyopathies that don't fit into these categories may be classified as intermediate or intergrade.

Dilated cardiomyopathy is a disease of systolic dysfunction, which means the muscle isn't able to adequately contract, and has trouble pumping blood out of the heart. The heart becomes enlarged and globular like a balloon, and the muscle walls become quite thin.

Between 1987 and 1994, researchers discovered dilated cardiomyopathy in cats was associated with a dietary deficiency of taurine in genetically susceptible cats. Taurine is an essential amino acid (see NUTRITION). Since cat food manufacturers started adding more taurine into their diets, at least 90 percent of the disease has disappeared in the United States. In fact, if a cat's dilated cardiomyopathy results from taurine deficiency, giving the cat taurine cures the disease.

However, dilated cardiomyopathy in a cat that isn't due to taurine deficiency does still occur. When the cause isn't known, the disease is called idiopathic. Today, dilated cardiomyopathy constitutes at least 50 percent of the heart failure cases diagnosed, and its cause is primarily still unknown.

Hypertrophic cardiomyopathy is a disease of diastolic function, of filling rather than contracting. The muscle wall of the heart thickens and reduces the size of the heart chambers until they cannot fill adequately with blood.

Restrictive cardiomyopathy is a more recently recognize form, with only a few documented cases in the veterinary literature. The heart muscle or the lining of the heart chambers become so stiff that the heart cannot fill properly. Affected cats may have a condition where portions of the heart wall don't function well, but other portions appear normal or may just be thicker than normal.

Cardiomyopathy represents the majority of feline cardiovascular disease. But it's hard to know how many cats are truly affected, since no one's ever looked at incidence across the general cat population. It's been seen cats of every breed or mixture.

However, research indicates hypertrophic cardiomyopathy has a genetic component, and has been identified in some Maine Coon cats. If a cat does inherit the condition, then their kittens and related cats will probably also be affected. Any cat diagnosed with cardiomyopathy should not be bred anyway, because the stress of breeding may kill such cats.

CARDIOMYOPATHY

SYMPTOMS: Labored breathing; lethargy; weakness; loss of appetite; hind limb pain or paralysis
HOME CARE: Nutritional support
HOLISTIC HELP: Nutraceuticals; herbal treatments; homeopathy; flower essence
VET CARE: Drug therapy to get rid of excess fluid and control heart action; possibly taurine supplements
PREVENTION: Heartworm preventive medication; feed appropriate complete and balanced nutrition

Cats can be affected at any age, but hypertrophic cardiomyopathy is most common in young and middle-aged male cats. With dilated cardiomyopathy, all breeds can be affected, but Siamese, Abyssinian and Burmese seem to be predisposed. The disease has been reported in cats anywhere from five months to 16 years of age.

Severity of symptoms varies from cats that appear totally unaffected, to those who suffer sudden death. Very mildly affected cats may live a totally normal life with the disease, and only be diagnosed when symptoms suddenly develop due to a stressful event that makes the heart work too hard, such as a flea bath or a teeth cleaning at the vets. Stress causes an increase in the cat's heart rate, which means there's less time for the heart to fill. If the heart is already difficult to fill, and the time it's allowed to fill is shortened, that may push the cat over the edge.

Affected cats may exhibit labored breathing from fluid-filled lungs, called pulmonary edema, or from fluid in the chest cavity called plural effusion which may be present due to congestive heart failure. Poor cardiac output may result in lethargy, weakness, and/or mental depression. Heart failure that results in poor circulation to the intestines and liver may cause reduced appetite or anorexia.

Another dramatic symptom is hind limb pain or paralysis, which results from blood clots secondary to the cardiomyopathy. The formation of a blood clot, called thrombosis, is common within the cardiac chamber or a vessel in cases of cardiomyopathy. Embolization occurs when the clot breaks off and gets "stuck" in another location, and blocks normal blood flow. Clots usually lodge in the hind legs where the aorta splits. The result is a "saddle thrombus" that causes pain and/or paralysis in one or both rear limbs.

Diagnosis is based on symptoms, and diagnostic tests. An electrocardiogram may pick up abnormal heart rhythms. X-rays can reveal the presence of fluid in the lungs and chest cavity, as well as the silhouette of the heart itself. The hypertrophic heart is typically shaped like a valentine. Echocardiograms show how thick the wall of the heart is, and how well the blood is being pumped.

Obvious clinical signs generally indicate the presence of severe disease. In these cases, treatment probably won't prolong the cat's life, but may improve the quality of the time the cat has left. Cats without symptoms may not require any therapy, but once heart failure is apparent, drug therapy is usually recommended.

Congestion and fluid in the lungs or chest are commonly controlled with a diuretic drug like Lasix (furosemide) that forces the kidneys to get rid of excess salt and water. Vasodilator drugs open up the constricted blood vessels, and help control congestion which makes it easier for the cat to breathe. Calcium channel blockers and beta blockers may be used to slow the heart rate in hypertrophic cardiomyopathy to give the heart more time to fill. Digoxin may help strengthen heart muscles and regulate blood pressure.

CAT FACTS

Holistic veterinarians may recommend giving cats hawthorn berries, said to make the heart muscle stronger. The homeopathic remedy Apis is a mild diuretic that can help get rid of excess fluids of plural effusion. Pets with heart problems also may benefit from supplements with coenzyme Q10.

About 40 percent of cats with blood clots regain rear limb use within a week without treatment. Surgery is rarely an option because affected cats are high anesthetic risks. Clot-reducing drugs help reduce the "stickiness" of blood platelets and so decrease the chances of clots from forming, but their use is controversial. Up to 50 percent of cats that undergo corrective surgery or anticlotting drugs will suffer another clot.

Cats with dilated cardiomyopathy due to taurine deficiency have a good prognosis, if they survive the initial two weeks while taurine is being given. But cats with idiopathic dilated cardiomyopathy have a very poor survival rate, and so do those suffering from restrictive cardiomyopathy. About 50 percent of cats showing signs of hypertrophic cardiomyopathy die within three months of diagnosis, while most cats without clinical signs can be expected to survive more than five years.

CARDIOPULMONARY RESUSCITATION (CPR)

CPR is the means of providing mechanical heart action and artificial respiration for cats whose breathing and heartbeat have stopped. Heartbeat and respiration may stop due to poisoning, electric shock or injury like being hit by a car. CPR is a short-term method of keeping your pet alive, while stimulating her heart and breathing to resume working on their own.

Use CPR only when both the heart and breathing have stopped, and the cat is unconscious; you risk injury to the cat if CPR is administered when the heartbeat or respiration are normal. Monitor the motion of the cat's chest to check for breathing. To find the heartbeat, place your flat palm on the cat's left side just above and behind the elbow of the front leg. When the heart is beating, but the cat isn't breathing (see ARTIFICIAL RESPIRATION).

CPR requires two people to apply artificial heart contractions and artificial breathing, one after the other, in an ongoing rhythm. A third person can drive you to the veterinary clinic while CPR is administered. Experts agree that it is difficult and nearly impossible to restart a heartbeat without specialized veterinary equipment. Although rare, an arrested heart may resume beating when stimulated by external compressions.

To find the heartbeat, place your flat palm on the cat's left side just above and behind the elbow of the front leg. If you still can't tell for sure, use the blink test. Tap her closed eyelid.

Even unconscious cats will blink unless the heart has stopped. If there's no movement, start CPR immediately.

Cats Under 20 Pounds: Perform the *cardiac pump technique* with compressions over the heart. That squeezes the motionless heart so that it pumps blood. Veterinarians recommend 100 to 120 compressions each minute, of 1/3rd to 1/2 of the chest width, according to the latest veterinary guidelines. It's also highly recommended to perform CPR in 2-minute cycles, and switch who does the compressor in each cycle, so you don't wear yourself out.

Find the heart by flexing your cat's front left foreleg backwards. The center of the heart falls directly beneath where the point of the elbow crosses her chest.

Situate your cat on her right side on a flat, firm surface. Cup your hand over the heart, and squeeze firmly. Press in about ½ inch with your thumb on one side and fingers on the other.

For very small kittens that fit in the palm of your hand, perform compressions between your fingers. Cradle her in the palm of your hand, with your thumb over the heart and fingers on the other side, and squeeze rhythmically.

Cats Over 20 Pounds: When a cat weighs more than 20 pounds, the space between the strong ribs and heart interfere with successful compressions. Cats this size best benefit from the *thoracic pump method*. When she's on her side, place your hands over the highest part of the chest and compress. That changes the chest cavity interior pressure which can move blood forward. Place one hand flat on her chest, and the other over top of the first hand, and press down 30 to 50 percent.

Acupuncture Resuscitation: When the pet's breathing and heart has stopped and resuscitation methods have failed, veterinarians suggest stimulating an acupuncture "alarm point." That prompts the body to release natural adrenaline (epinephrine), a drug commonly used in human and veterinary medicine in cardiac arrests to stimulate the heart and breathing.

The alarm point is in the center (midway point) of the slit found between your cat's nose and upper lip. Stick a needle, safety pin, paperclip, or even your clean fingernail into this point. Jab deeply to the bone, and repeatedly wiggle back and forth.

Don't be squeamish—this is your cat's life you hold in your hands! Continue administering the emergency acupuncture treatment for at least twenty minutes, until the pet revives or you reach the hospital.

Puppies and kittens dead at birth treated with this method have been revived more than an hour later, and survived to live long, healthy lives. A needle jab, with rescue breathing, can ensure your cat survives.

CAT FACTS

CARNIVORE A carnivore is an animal that eats other animals. The name comes from specialized teeth. Molars in the side of the jaw called carnassial teeth evolved with early meat eating mammals. These teeth provide a scissor-like action that slices flesh and makes it easier to eat.

Cats are obligate carnivores. That means they have a nutritional requirement for specific amino acids and other nutrients found only in animal products. A cat cannot survive on an exclusively vegetarian diet (see FOOD and NUTRITION).

CAR SICKNESS

SYMPTOMS: Agitation; crying; creaming, throwing fit
HOME CARE: Situate carrier so cat has a view, or drape carrier to block view
HOLISTIC HELP: Acupressure; homeopathy
VET CARE: Prescription sedative or Dramamine-type car sickness medication
PREVENTION: Withhold food for 12 hours prior to trip; acclimate cat to car in short trips; use favorite toys/games to make experience more pleasant

CAR SICKNESS Fortunately, cats don't often get sick during car rides. They more frequently become agitated and fearful, and meow a great deal; some actually throw a fit.

Introduce your cat to car rides slowly, and always be sure he's contained in a secure carrier to protect him. While he's still a kitten, take him on short trips around the block, and end the ride with a special treat or favorite game so he associates the car with good things. If the only experience in the car your cat ever has ends with unpleasantness at the vet, you can only expect him to protest.

Offering a favorite toy may help calm his nerves. Depending on the cat, seeing where he's going may help calm him down; other cats, though, do better with a towel draped over the carrier.

Holistic veterinarians suggest using acupressure on the PC6 point to relieve nausea. This spot is located in the small depression on the underside of the front legs, just above the pad on the wrists. Press this point for one minute before you get into the car, and as often as needed during the trip, to help calm the tummy. A homeopathic remedy, Tabacum 30C also calms nausea. Put a couple of pellets on the cat's tongue two hours before traveling.

Your veterinarian may prescribe a mild sedative to calm your cat's nerves or a drug like Dramamine to soothe possible upset stomachs. Never give your cat anything for car sickness without first consulting your veterinarian.

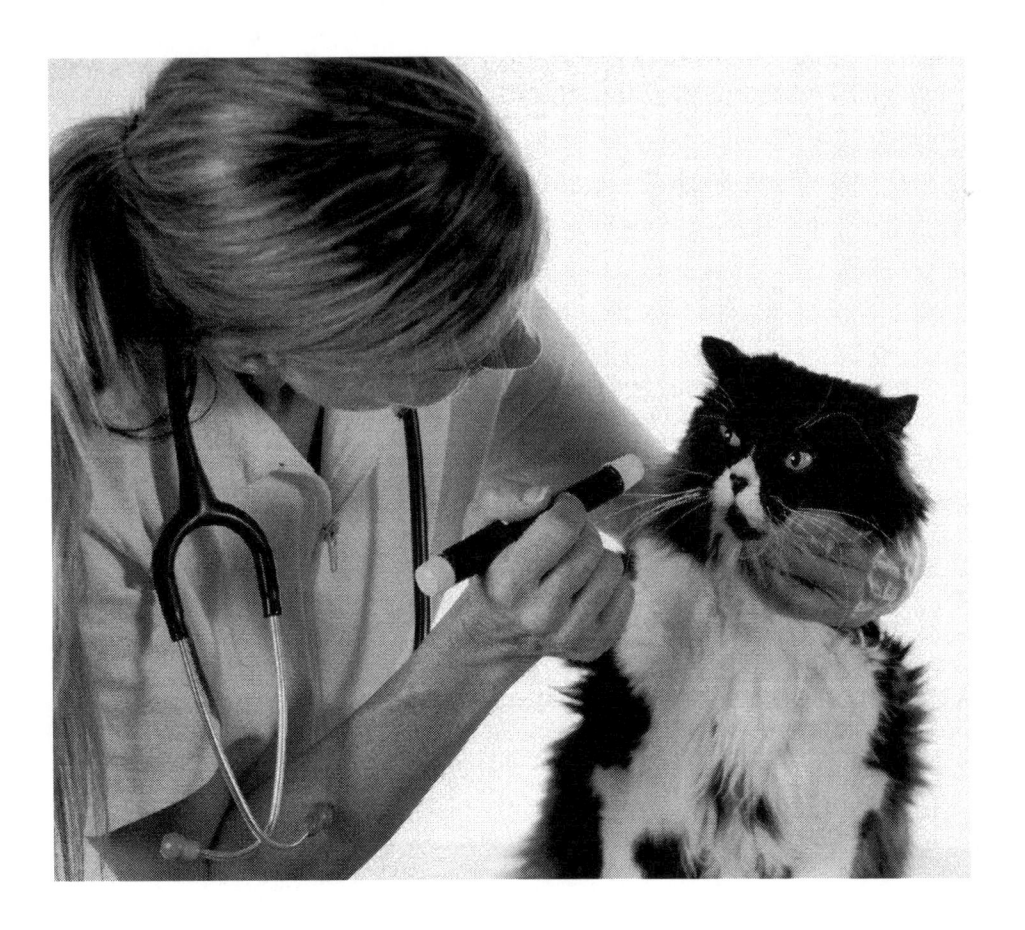

CAT FACTS

CATARACT A cataract is cloudiness within the lens of the eye. The lens is inside the eye directly behind the pupil (see EYE). In a normal eye, the lens is clear. A cataract interferes with sight by partially or completely blocking the clarity of the lens. The cloudiness can vary from a little spot of white to a totally opaque structure that affects the entire lens. If the lens becomes completely masked, the result is blindness.

Fortunately, cataracts in cats are not terribly common. Still, they can affect any age and every breed; no cat is exempt. Cataracts are extremely common in dogs, but cats do not suffer from diabetes-related, or "old age" cataracts that are often found in dogs. But just like dogs, cataracts are reported to be inherited in some breeds of cats. Birman, British Shorthair, and the Himalayan are reported to be affected most often.

With a cataract, the lens turns from a clear protein to one that precipitates, just the way the clear raw portion of an egg turns white as it cooks. Any number of things can cause such changes in the lens. Injury to the eye or the resulting inflammation may cause a cataract, usually to only one eye. Some kittens are simply born with the cataracts. These are probably due to an infection that happens while they're in the uterus.

Cataracts may also result from poor nutrition, but because of modern advances in feline diets, such causes are rare. And in some cases, the cataract is idiopathic, which means the cause cannot be identified.

Most feline cataracts are associated with inflammation inside the eye due to systemic disease. Many cats will have chronic inflammation inside the eye as part of feline infectious peritonitis, feline immunodeficiency virus, or feline leukemia virus and develop this type of cataract.

Because a cataract can affect only a tiny part of the lens of one eye, some cats may show no signs at all. A cat can have a significant cataract, and not have any meaningful vision loss. Other times, the cataract may cover the entire lens of one or both eyes, causing blindness. And although a vision-impaired cat may do well in familiar surroundings, he may bump into walls when faced with rearranged furniture or a new environment.

Don't make the mistake of confusing a cloudy eye surface with a cataract. A cloudy skin on the eye is more likely a treatable injury to the cornea, the clear surface of the eyeball. With a cataract you may notice cloudiness within the pupil space. It looks like there is a little white marble inside the eye.

Treatment depends on how severe the cataract is. When trauma or inflammation is the culprit, the underlying cause is treated. Many times when small cataracts cause little vision problems, no treatment is necessary. As long as only one eye is affected, cats tend to do quite well with one working eye.

CATARACT

SYMPTOMS: Cloudiness to lens of eye; loss of sight
HOME CARE: None
VET CARE: Address underlying cause; sometimes surgery is done
PREVENTION: Prevent infectious diseases

Kittens born with congenital cataracts can have a lot of trouble seeing when they're young, but their vision usually improves with age. The lens grows as the cat matures, while the area of cloudiness on the lens remains the same size and, at maturity, is relatively small. By adulthood, most cats born with cataracts are able to compensate and see "around" the cloudiness.

In certain instances, surgery is helpful, although it is not indicated when the cataract is caused by inflammation. But when the cat is blind or going to go blind in both eyes, surgery may be recommended. The same surgical techniques used on people for cataracts are applied to dogs and cats. Most veterinary ophthalmologists in private practice or at a university can do the surgery. It is a long procedure done under general anesthetic that removes most but not the entire affected lens. The lens itself is contained in a kind of capsule like an egg shell. Most commonly, surgery removes the front part of the shell and the contents inside, while leaving the back half of the capsule/shell intact. In some cases, the whole lens is removed and a new lens is transplanted to replace the damaged lens.

A device called a phako unit is used in the surgery. The unit produces high frequency sound waves—ultrasound—to break up the lens, which is then removed by suction, or aspiration. Cats that have the surgery do quite well. (See also EYE)

CAT ASSOCIATIONS see APPENDIX A

CATNIP

Nepeta cataria, or catnip, is a strong-scented mint that cats find extremely attractive. The plant contains a volatile oil that's major component is a chemical somewhat like sedatives found in the valerian plant. The chemical may also be similar to one of the substances in tomcat urine, which often triggers the same kind of reaction.

Cats are affected by the scent, and will bite and roll on the plant to release the oil into the air. The smell is interpreted by the cat's highly specialized Jacobson's organ. Cats can detect catnip oil in the air at saturations as low as one part per billion.

Catnip in cats affects the same biochemical pathways that are affected by marijuana and LSD in people. Catnip is a feline hallucinogen; the "high" lasts from five to 15 minutes, and basically causes a loss of inhibition. Catnip-intoxicated cats act like furry fools who roll and flop about on the floor, drool, and have a wonderful relaxing time. Catnip builds the confidence of some shy cats.

Not all cats are affected by catnip. Cats rarely respond until they are about six months old, and some cats never do. The trait is an inherited one, with only two out of three domestic cats being affected; male cats seem to respond more strongly than females. Most scientists agree that catnip provides a harmless recreation for cats, but it can be overused. Overindulgence causes cats to lose their response to the plant. An occasional treat, perhaps once every two or three weeks, is plenty.

CAT SCRATCH DISEASE (CSD)

Formerly called Cat Scratch Fever, CSD is a bacterial infection caused by the tiny bacteria *Bartonella henselae*. The syndrome was first described in 1950, but until recently, researchers couldn't agree on what caused the disease. Much still remains unknown. We do know the bacteria infects the cat's bloodstream without making the cat sick. Cats infected with CSD remain perfectly healthy. Research shows that approximately 40 percent of cats are exposed to the bacteria sometime in their life. About 41 percent of pet cats are actually infected with the disease.

Problems arise when the organism is transmitted to people, who do become sick. Historically CSD has been diagnosed most often in children, but recent surveys indicate 43 percent of affected patients were older than 20 years old, and more than half were women. The disease is estimated to affect about 22,000 people each year in the United States.

92
CAT FACTS

No one really knows just how the bacteria gets into the cat, or into people. The cat connection, though, is a strong one. About 90 percent of those diagnosed with CSD have had contact with a cat, and 80 percent report having been scratched by a cat. The risk of infection is highest for people owning kittens.

It's not been established but is considered highly likely that the bacteria is spread from the blood stream of one cat to another by biting fleas. Therefore, risk of the disease goes up if the kitten has fleas. Just how the bug gets on Kitty claws where scratches spread the disease to people isn't known. It's theorized that the bacteria may be in an infected cat's saliva, and transferred to his claws when he grooms himself; or, that infected blood contaminates the claws when Kitty scratches himself.

However, that doesn't explain the 20 percent of people ill with CSD who never have contact with a cat. Researchers believe, but haven't yet proven, that the fleas may be able to spread the disease directly without the cat's help. That may be why the highest incidence of disease is during the summer months of flea season.

Signs in otherwise healthy people are often mild and go away without treatment. A healed cat scratch may again turn red, swollen and sore, and the lymph node closest to the injury swells. Scratches on a hand or arm tend to affect lymph nodes in the armpit, while those on the ankles and legs affect lymph nodes in the groin region. Vague feelings of fatigue or even flu-like symptoms may develop and last up to three months before going away. Ten percent of cases develop conditions affecting the eyes, liver, kidneys or central nervous system, and require hospitalization; with treatment, even these rare conditions usually resolve within two weeks.

Diagnosis is based on the signs of the disease, a history of cat exposure, and blood tests. A variety of antibiotics are used to treat the condition. CSD represents a much greater risk for people with compromised immune systems, such as transplant recipients, people with HIV or AIDS, patients undergoing anticancer treatments, and others. A suppressed immune system may allow the bacteria to infiltrate the walls of the blood vessels, resulting in a condition called Bacillary Angiomatosis (BA). The most common sign is raised, red skin lesions, but BA also compromises liver and kidney function, and can cause death. A microscopic examination of affected tissue diagnoses the condition. BA looks quite similar to Kaposi's Sarcoma which commonly affects AIDS patients; but unlike Kaposi's Sarcoma, BA responds extremely well to treatment, and typically infections are cured within a month or so using antibiotic therapy.

CAT SCRATCH DISEASE

(HUMAN) SYMPTOMS: Swollen cat scratches; flu-like signs; swollen lymph nodes
(HUMAN) HOME CARE: Nutritional support
(HUMAN) DOCTOR CARE: Antibiotics
(HUMAN) PREVENTION:
- Get rid of the fleas (see FLEAS);
- Avoid rough play that prompts bites or scratches (see PLAY);
- Wash bites or scratches immediately with soap and water, and disinfect; and
- Prohibit the cat from licking open wounds on your body.

CAT FACTS

Preventing the disease is desirable, particularly for those people in high risk groups. However, until we know how the disease is transmitted, testing and treating cats isn't effective or practical. And doing without a beloved cat is rarely something owners are willing or even need to consider.

The emotional and physical benefits of owning pets have been well documented in the medical literature, and most experts agree that high risk groups should not be denied the joy of cat ownership. The risk for transmission from contact with cats is considered quite low, and can be reduced even further by using simple precautions. Sensible interaction with adult cats rarely leads to scratches, and declawing isn't generally recommended. Nail covers might help prevent claws from breaking the skin.

If you are in a high-risk group, your physician should know you have a cat. Be aware that adopting an adult cat poses less risk for you than a kitten. Ask a friend to medicate or groom your cat for you to lower the risk for scratches or bites, and always wash your hands after handling Kitty.

Getting scratched doesn't automatically result in infection, though. There are more than 86 million pet cats in the United States, and most owners will never be affected by CSD (see also ZOONOSIS).

CESAREAN A cesarean procedure is a surgical delivery performed by the veterinarian when a natural birth is not possible. Healthy queens rarely have problems with delivery, but those in poor health may need assistance. Trauma or a nutritional deficiency may cause pelvic deformity that makes natural birth difficult. Medications may be administered to stimulate uterine contraction, which means surgical intervention is rarely necessary.

When it is necessary, the surgery is performed under general anesthesia by the veterinarian. Generally, the risk to the queen is not great. Prolonged labor, dead kittens, uterine rupture, or toxicity increase the risks for the queen. Usually, within a few hours the mother is awake and able to nurse her kittens. She may or may not require a cesarean with future pregnancies, depending on the circumstances for the first (see also REPRODUCTION).

CHERRY EYE

SYMPTOMS: Red, swollen tissue at inside corner of the cat's eye, sometimes with a discharge
HOME CARE: None
VET CARE: Anti-inflammatory ointments; more often, surgery
PREVENTION: None

CHERRY EYE This condition occurs when the pinkish-red tear gland at the inner corner of the eye protrudes, or prolapses. The smooth mass of this third eyelid swells to the size of a small cherry. There may be a purulent discharge if infection is present.

It is most commonly associated with a congenital weakness in the anchoring tissue of the gland in the cat's eye. The cause of the prolapse could be due to scrolled or everted cartilage in the third eyelid, abnormal cells in the third eye, or a prolapse of fat in the cat's eye. It's not known if this is inherited, but it does appear to be more common in younger animals and certain breeds.

Cherry eye can occur in one or both eyes of any cat. However, it is most common in Burmese and Persians. Prolonged exposure of the gland can cause irritation to the eye. Sometimes, anti-inflammatory topical medications may resolve the problem. More commonly, surgery is necessary to correct the condition or to remove the entire gland if the condition is severe.

CHIROPRACTIC Chiropractic care is a holistic manipulative therapy that carefully flexes the affected joints to return them to proper alignment. Treatment plans are customized to the individual pet. Advocates say that appropriate adjustments can affect your pet's emotions, as well as how the organs work, due to the viscera-somatic, or "organ-to-muscle" reflex.

Manipulative therapies also include physical therapy and massage. While massage focuses on the tissues surrounding the bones, chiropractic care and physical therapy focus on the proper functioning of the joints and related muscles, including the spine.

Both science and holistic methods work hand-in-paw with these hands-on modalities both in people and in pets. Veterinary chiropractors often require X-rays before attempting any adjustments. While a human chiropractor can't prescribe drugs (unless also an M.D.), a veterinary chiropractor with a veterinary degree can incorporate medications to help.

It may take only one "adjustment" or instead require several. The longer the problem has existed, the more treatments will be necessary, and chiropractic manipulations (especially of the spine) require a trained veterinary chiropractor because it can be very easy to injure your pet unless you know what you're doing.

Physical therapy techniques, though, can often be performed by you at home to help loosen up your pet's stiff legs, shoulders and necks. This increases joint mobility, and also stimulates production of synovial fluid, a fluid manufactured by the body that nourishes and lubricates the joints to keep them healthy.

Be careful not to over-extend a muscle or joint, though, and pay attention to the cat if he tells you to stop. Flinching or crying out during physical therapy means it's painful and you should stop and have a vet check out the pet or any problems.

A chiropractic technique called motion palpation can be safely done at home. Motion palpation helps flex and extend the joints of the back. It can have an additive effect, so that even tiny amounts done daily help pets feel better over the long term. It's particularly helpful for creaky older pets, but athletic animals will enjoy and benefit from this gentle treatment that keeps them flexible and may help prevent injury.

Ask your pet to stand or lie down in a comfy position. Feel for the individual vertebrae, the bumpy bones in the back. Pay particular attention to the dents or "valleys" between each bone.

Start at the neck, right where his skull meets the spine. Position your thumb and index finger on each side of the first dent between the first vertebrae and his skull.

Press down very gently with your fingers, and release. Then move to the next dip, and repeat the quick gentle pressure—each press shouldn't take more than one second, so you can count, "One-one-thousand" and then move on. Continue to move downward from his head toward his tail, pressing each "valley" in turn and then releasing.

CHLAMYDIA (PNEUMONITIS) see UPPER RESPIRATORY INFECTIONS

CHOCOLATE TOXICITY

Chocolate may appeal to a pet's sweet tooth, but it's toxic to both dogs and cats. Poisonings usually happen around the holidays when pet owners have more candy available.

Chocolate contains a substance called theobromine that's toxic to pets. Milk chocolate found in candy kisses contains about 1.5 milligrams of theobromine per gram. A toxic dose of milk chocolate is five ounces per pound of body weight; that's nearly two pounds of milk chocolate for a seven pound cat. But unsweetened baking chocolate contains nearly ten times as much theobromine as milk chocolate. A seven pound cat can become sick by eating as little as 2.5 ounces of baking chocolate, about the amount if your cat licked the frosting off a large cake.

Theobromine is related to caffeine, and acts as a stimulant to the cat's nervous system. Essentially, theobromine shifts the cat's nervous system into overdrive.

Affected cats show a wide variety of signs. Some cats drool and most eventually suffer vomiting and/or diarrhea. Occasionally, poisoned cats pass so much urine, they appear to be incontinent. Affected cats typically become hyperactive, and run around with great energy. The drug not only stimulates the nervous system, but can also speed up the heart or cause irregular heartbeat. If Kitty eats enough of the poison, the signs of toxicity can progress to muscle tremors, seizures, coma, and ultimately death.

There is no specific antidote for theobromine toxicity. Treatment consists of maintaining life support, preventing further absorption of the poison, hastening elimination, and symptomatic treatment of the signs of poisoning.

If Kitty ate the chocolate within the last two hours, it's generally recommended that the owner make the cat throw up. DO NOT GIVE SYRUP OF IPECAC, WHICH CAN BE TOXIC IN CATS. Administer one tablespoon of a three percent solution of household hydrogen peroxide for every ten pounds of pet (see ADMINISTERING MEDICATION). Repeat the dose in ten minutes if the first dose doesn't do the trick. If you have difficulty making the cat throw up, bring the cat to the veterinary hospital so it can be done there.

CHOCOLATE TOXICITY

SYMPTOMS: Drooling; vomiting and/or diarrhea; excessive urination; hyperactive behavior; muscle tremors; seizures; coma
FIRST AID: SEE VET IMMEDIATION: if ingested in last two hours, induce vomiting
VET CARE: Induce vomiting; flush stomach; supportive care
PREVENTION: Keep chocolate out of Kitty's reach

The veterinarian may administer activated charcoal to help prevent additional absorption of the theobromine into the cat's system. Fluid therapy may be needed to counteract signs of shock. Seizures, heart irregularities, vomiting and diarrhea are each specifically treated with appropriate medications. The treatment is often prolonged, because the half-life of theobromine—the time it takes the body to eliminate it—is 72 hours in dogs, and is thought to be the same or longer in cats.

The best way to deal with chocolate toxicity is to prevent the problem from ever happening. If your cat has a sweet tooth, keep chocolate out of reach (see also POISON)

CHOKING see SWALLOWED OBJECTS

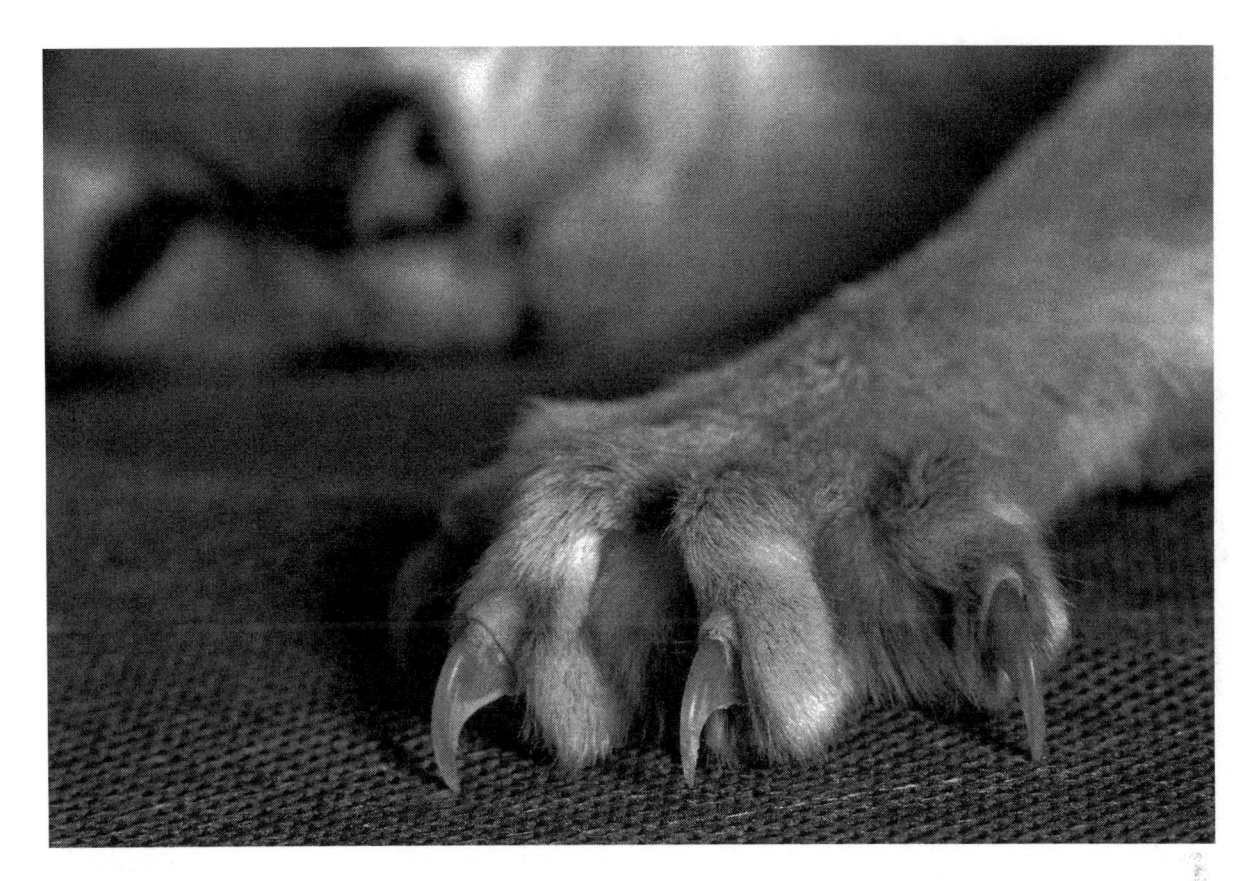

CLAWS Cats have a toenail, or claw, on the end of each toe. Sharply pointed and curved, claws function as grooming tools for combing fur, grappling hooks for climbing and holding prey, and daggers for protection. While most animals, including humans, have hard protective nail tips, cat claws are unique because they are retractable.

Cats normally have five toes on the front feet and four on the hind feet. The fifth claw on the inside of the front paws that does not reach the ground is called the dewclaw, and is a left over toe inherited from ancient cats that is no longer truly functional.

About ten percent of cats have extra toes. Extra toes are referred to as polydactylism. Front paws are most often polydactyl, but rear paws can have extra toes, too. Polydactyl cats, often called "mitten" cats for the way the paw looks, may have up to seven toes on each foot.

Claws are an extension of two small bones found at the end of each toe. The bones rest nearly on top of each other, and are "hinged" by tendons. When relaxed, the claws are sheathed inside a skin fold at the end of each toe, and paws look softly furred, smooth, and almost dainty.

100 CAT FACTS

To extend his claws, a cat flexes the tendon and straightens the folded bones; that pushes the claws down and forward. The action also spreads the paw to nearly twice its former width.

The exterior claw is composed of a hard, non-living protein or cuticle that is white to clear in most cats. Inside this rigid structure is the living tissue of the nail bed, called the quick, which contains the blood supply and nerve endings. Claws grow out of the quick, and the outer horny layer of claw is periodically shed to expose new growth that is razor sharp.

Cat claws do not wear down during normal activity the way a dog's do, but new claw tips lose their edge. Cats sharpen their front claws by scratching hard surfaces. Nibbles and bites remove outer claw layers on their rear paws, while sinking front claws deep into softer surfaces and pulling downward strips away the dead outer layers on their front claws. Unless this necessary maintenance is attended, claws can overgrow, split or break off, and result in painful infections (see GROOMING and DECLAWING).

CLIMBING

Cats seem to prefer high locations that offer them the best view of their surroundings. Some breeds tend to climb more than others. Indoor cats may leap to refrigerator and door tops, or lounge in lofty book cases. High ledges, fences and even trees are favorite outdoor cat lookouts.

The cat was designed with climbing in mind. Strong rear leg muscles enable the cat to jump up to seven times her height. The cat's shoulder blades located on her sides, rather than on the back like human shoulder blades, give her greater flexibility. Cats have no collarbone; front legs are instead attached to the chest only by muscle. Because they are not connected to a fixed point, the cat's front legs have a superior range of motion. This allows Kitty to walk, run and jump with her front legs close together, which is invaluable when traversing narrow high areas. Cats also have the ability to "hug" a tree by spreading their front legs wide as they climb up or down.

Claws curved outward and back help the cat to grasp vertical objects to pull herself up. Even cats missing front claws may be able to climb when rear claws remain intact (see DECLAWING). Because of the curve of their claws, cats that willingly climb upwards may be reluctant to descend. Often, they simply yowl for an owner's assistance to avoid the embarrassing necessity of backing down tail first.

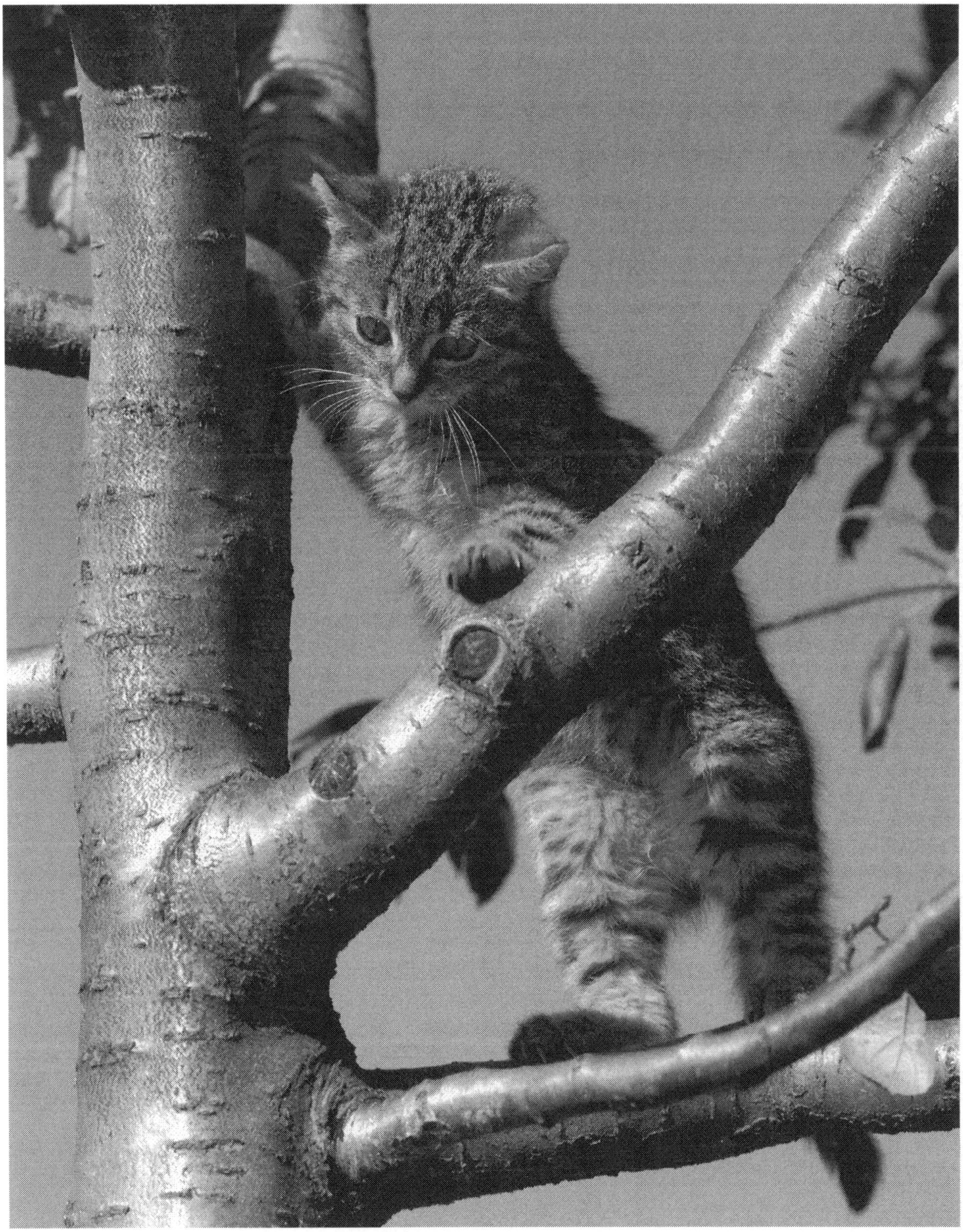

COCCIDIOSIS

SYMPTOMS: Loose stool with mucus and blood that comes and goes
HOME CARE: None
VET CARE: Sulfa type drug; sometimes fluid therapy or blood transfusion in severe cases
PREVENTION: Prompt cleaning of litter box

COCCIDIOSIS

Coccidiosis is caused by coccidia, a common protozoal parasite seen in cats that colonizes and attacks the lining of the intestine. Adult cats commonly have a few coccidia in their system that cause no problem. However, kittens that are infected may develop a fatal diarrhea that's mixed with blood-tinged mucus.

Cats are infected by swallowing the immature parasite. The developing eggs, called oocysts, are passed in an infected animal's stool. These microscopic oocysts require several days in the soil to become infective. Cats contract coccidia by swallowing this infective stage. Kitty can become infected by washing himself after walking through contaminated soil, or by eating other animals like rodents that are infected.

Signs of infection in adult cats tend to come and go. Affected cats may pass blood and loose stool with a lot of mucus for two to three days, get better, then a week later have the signs return. Diagnosis is made by finding the oocysts during microscopic examination of a stool sample.

Generally, cats are treated with a sulfa-type drug, and it typically takes a week before improvement is seen. In severe cases, hospitalization may be required to treat dehydration with fluid therapy or a blood transfusion (see BLOOD).

Routine and prompt cleaning of the litter box helps prevent infection or reinfection. Environmental control includes daily washing of the cat's quarters with boiling water to destroy infective organisms

COGNITIVE DYSFUNCTION SYNDROME

As they age, cats can develop signs of senility, or cognitive dysfunction syndrome (CDS). CDS represents a loss of memory and learning, or a reduction in learning memory. The syndrome has long been recognized in elderly dogs, and cats age 15 and older also are affected. Some of the brain changes in these cats are similar to those seen in the early stages of human Alzheimer's. Affected cats also have deposits of amyloid material in the brain.

COGNITIVE DYSFUNCTION

SYMPTOMS: <u>Disorientation</u>: wanders aimlessly; acts lost and confused; may not recognize family members or other familiar people or places; gets "stuck" in corners or lost in the house
<u>Interaction changes</u>: no longer greets family members; dislikes or avoids petting; not as interested in getting attention, interaction changes with other pets
<u>Sleep changes</u>: is awake and active at night; sleep cycles are disrupted or reversed
<u>Housetraining is forgotten</u>
<u>Anxiety or compulsive behaviors</u>: tremors, yowling and crying, repetitive pacing, floor or object licking
HOME CARE: None
HOLISTIC HELP: Nutraceuticals
VET CARE: Sometimes drug therapy
PREVENTION: Keep cats active and their minds engaged

CAT FACTS

In the past, these symptoms would have been brushed off as a normal part of feline aging. Affected cats typically seem to forget how to do normal cat activities. For example, they are unable to find the litter box, or simply sit in the middle of the room and cry.

The acronym D.I.S.H. (disorientation, interaction, sleep changes, housebreaking) was created to help identify cognitive disorders in dogs, and because the drug Anipryl was licensed for use in those specific categories. However, the acronym doesn't account for anxiety or compulsive behaviors such as howling and repetitive pacing that tend to be quite common in both older dogs and aged cats.

A cat study indicated that 20 percent of eleven-to-twelve-year-old cats were positive for one or more categories. Only 3 percent were positive for two or more categories—a very small amount. As the cat's age increased, so did the prevalence. The percentage of thirteen-to-fourteen-year-olds positive for one or more categories was 33 percent, but only 8 percent were positive for more than two categories. 42 percent of the fifteen-to-sixteen-year-olds were positive for one or more categories; 16 percent of this group was positive for two or more categories. Finally, 61 percent of seventeen-to-nineteen-year-old cats were positive for one or more categories with 43 percent were positive for two or more.

Once properly diagnosed, the human medicine selegiline hydrochloride (Anipryl) has been FDA-approved in the United States to treat canine cognitive disorder and has been successfully used off-label in cats. It acts on one of the neurotransmitters in the brain responsible for nerve-to-nerve communication, and slows the natural destruction of the chemical compound dopamine in the brain.

Cognitive dysfunction is a progressive disease, and medication can slow or reverse these behavior changes but not on a permanent basis. Time will catch up with the cat, and there will be an eventual decline. But selegiline can buy time and improve the cat's quality of life for perhaps a year or more. And when your cat is 17 or 18 years old, another year or two is golden. Generally the cat will need to be on the drug for about four weeks before any results can be expected.

A natural component of some foods, called phospholipids, can help reverse some signs of cognitive disorders by helping brain cells send and receive nerve impulses more effectively. Choline and phosphatidylcholine, two common message-sending compounds, are found in a dietary supplement called Cholodin FEL, which is a less expensive alternative to Anipryl. The product is available through veterinarians, and comes in a pill form or powder flavored to appeal to cats, to be mixed into the food.

Medical marijuana (or cannabis) today is also available for pets, but must be formulated so that pets receive the medical benefits of the cannabis (hemp) plant while reducing potential toxic concentrations of the herb. Hemp can be used to help mitigate signs of dementia. Ask your veterinarian if this supplement may benefit your pet.

Although many therapies may hold promise for the future, cat owners today can't afford to wait years for them to become available. Environmental enrichment is easy, costs nothing and your cat can benefit today. If the cat works the brain on a regular basis, the memory ability is preserved longer.

Offer your cat lots of play sessions to keep her mind as healthy and well-toned as her body. This can also help wear her out in a nice way, especially prior to bedtime, to help curb unwanted nighttime activity and vocalizations

COLITIS

Colitis is an inflammation of the colon, the large bowel which is at the very end of the gastrointestinal tract. The colon removes water from the solid waste that's passed. When the intestinal lining becomes inflamed, it interferes with water removal and compromises the way the organ contracts and moves fecal matter along.

COLITIS

SYMPTOMS: Frequent liquid stools containing mucus and blood
HOME CARE: None
VET CARE: Addresses the specific cause; oral medications and high fiber diets
PREVENTION: Prevent intestinal parasites; keep litter box clean; avoid abrupt diet changes; don't feed milk to cat

Colitis accounts for 15 to 20 percent of diarrhea complaints in cats. Lots of straining is often involved. Cats with colitis produce a very frequent (several in an hour) liquid stool that has a great deal of mucus and bright red blood.

In some parts of the country, particularly in outdoor cats in the south, colitis is associated with intestinal parasites like hookworms or giardia. When the causative parasites are eliminated through proper treatment, the colitis usually goes away. Other times, the inflammation may be due to a food allergy, and avoiding the food ingredient will relieve the situation. Your veterinarian may prescribe oral medications or high fiber diets to help control the problem (see DIARRHEA, ALLERGY, GIARDIA, HOOKWORMS, TRICHOMONIASIS and INFLAMMATORY BOWEL DISEASE).

Communication

Cats have often been regarded as mysterious, solitary, unpredictable creatures. This is largely because humans have been unable to understand what Kitty is saying. Current research indicates cats are social creatures; they rely on a distinct feline language to communicate with other cats, other pets, and the humans who make up their world.

But while people rely primarily on speech to communicate, "felinese" is predominantly a silent language. Cats speak by using complex combinations of sign language, vocalization, and scent cues (see MARKING).

Cats have the ability to learn a large human vocabulary, though, especially when words are used with consistency (see TRAINING). But since cats are more highly attuned to body language, they tend to give silent communication more weight. That means when the words reprimand but the face smiles, Kitty reacts to the amusement rather than the aggravation, and acts accordingly.

Cats may have built their mystical reputations by reacting to subtle non-verbal cues people don't realize they're broadcasting. Kitty seems psychic when in fact she's simply reading a facial expression, posture or action she knows indicates a particular emotion or intent. The cat's ability to figure things out makes her look psychic, but actually she's just an excellent observer. Cats pay exquisite attention to the details of our behavior.

Our own limited hearing and scenting ability renders us deaf to many of the nuances of feline language. But an attentive owner can learn to read and translate the more obvious feline signals, and pave the way for smoother interspecies communication.

Verbal expression is a relatively small part of cat communication, although some breeds like the Siamese are more vocal than others. There are as many as 16 distinct feline vocal patterns, which fall into four generally recognized categories.

CAT FACTS

Murmur patterns include purrs and trills, which seem to express contentment. Meows are classified as vowel patterns, and are almost exclusively directed at humans. Cats have a variety of meows, which are invariably used when the cat wants something from her human (i.e., petting, being fed, going outdoors, coming inside). Usually, the more agitated Kitty becomes, the lower the pitch of the meow drops. Articulated patterns a sign of solicitation or frustration. Cats produce chirping, chattering sounds when they can't reach the squirrel teasing them from the other side of the window. Finally, strained intensity patterns are used as warnings to increase the distance between the cat and a perceived threat. These sounds include spits and hisses, growls and screams, and are the feline equivalent to "back off, buster!" Strained intensity sounds are used in defense, attack, and in mating.

AGGRESSIVE, THREATENING ATTACK

ALERT AND INQUISITIVE

FRIGHTENED

MEOW-DEMAND

NORMAL RELAXED

Feline faces

Nonverbal signals offer a number of advantages over verbal ones in the animal kingdom. Vocalizations give away a cat's location to adversaries, while posturing can't be overheard. Non-verbal communication also lasts longer. Sign language can be sustained nearly indefinitely with no need to stop and take a breath. The silent semaphore language of cats is accomplished through facial expression and body position, and even the elevation of the cat's fur speaks volumes.

CAT FACTS

A cat's mood is indicated by the position of the eyelids, and the dilation of the pupil (see EYE). Any strong emotional arousal such as fear, anger, pleasure, or excitement can result in the sudden contraction of the cat's pupils. Cats open their eyes wide when they are alert. A wide-eyed cat that bumps your face with his cheeks is showing his trust, by leaving those eyes open and unprotected. But a direct unblinking stare from a distance is a sign of dominance and aggression or defensiveness, as are slit-eyed looks. Avoid locking eyes with a cat you don't know. A relaxed, trusting cat has droopy, sleepy-looking eyelids.

Ear position indicates the cat's mood. Forward facing ears express interest. The ears turn to the sides as the cat feels threatened or uneasy, and flatten tight to the head when fearful or angry.

The curious cat's whiskers fan forward, as though to embrace the object of interest. The whiskers of happy relaxed cats are extended out. Whiskers slick back and down against the cheeks when Kitty is frightened or agitated.

CAT FACTS

The cat's tail speaks volumes. Kittens greet their mothers, and confident, happy adult cats greet owners with tails held straight up, with just the end tipped over like a finger waving, "hi, there." The end of the cat's tail may twitch or flick as an expression of the cat's frustration or irritation, and is a warning to cease and desist. If polite tail flicks are ignored, the tail movement may escalate to lashing or even thumping the ground, which is a final warning to lay off or be smacked. The relaxed, content cat's tail curves down and up in a gentle U, and goes higher to show interest. A straight tail with bristled fur indicates aggression, but a bristled tail held in an inverted U indicates fear or defensiveness.

Cats use communication to smooth relationships. A cat who blunders into another's territory must be able to apologize, and the offended cat must understand, or constant fights would erupt. Cats avoid fights by bluffing with universally understood feline postures. Confident cats face the unknown head on, their body ready to strike if necessary.

113

114
CAT FACTS

Fearful cats turn sideways and arch their backs to bluff their way out of the situation. Fur normally lies close and smooth against the cat's skin, but cats that are uncertain or afraid puff up their fur to make themselves look larger and more impressive to warn off possible threats.

Cats cry uncle in surrender by flattening themselves on the ground, all four feet beneath them, with ears and tail tucked tight. Cats may posture 15 minutes or longer without fur ever flying, until finally one backs down. The cat who chases off the less dominant cat wins the confrontation.

Finally, cats place themselves in vulnerable positions to communicate affection and trust. They groom one another or their owner, solicit play by rolling and presenting their tummies, and may sleep, cuddle, or play together. The cat sleeping with his back to you is showing ultimate trust. Other types of body contact, like touching noses or bumping hips when they pass each other can be signs of affection. And just as human speech is colored by regional dialects, accents, and a variety of languages, cat communication varies somewhat from cat to cat.

CONSTIPATION

Constipation is the infrequent elimination of small amounts of dry, hard, dark-colored stool. When feces are not passed for two or three days, the colon removes too much moisture which makes passing the waste painful.

Cats afflicted with constipation may squat and strain for long periods of time with little result. Constipated cats may stop eating, and begin to lose weight. Sometimes chronic constipation can cause inflammation of the bowel lining, which stimulates a release of fluid. In these instances, the fecal matter remains hard and dry, but may be accompanied by dark watery liquid.

A number of conditions (see HAIRBALLS and SWALLOWED OBJECTS) can cause the cat to become constipated. Diets low in fiber with a high meat protein concentration may result in stools that are difficult to pass, particularly if the cat drinks little water. The stress of new surroundings, or a dirty litter pan may induce the cat to delay defecation. Constipation is a common problem of elderly cats due to weakness of abdominal muscles, lack of exercise, and improper diet (see GERIATRIC CATS).

Veterinary assistance is often necessary to initially clear the colon. Some cats need to be sedated to have hard feces mechanically removed. Veterinary-approved suppositories and enemas may be helpful, but should only be administered by your veterinarian. Over-the-counter products may contain ingredients like phosphates which can be lethal for your cat.

CONSTIPATION

SYMPTOMS: Straining without passing stool; hard dry stools accompanied by dark brown liquid
HOME CARE: Hairball medication
HOLISTIC HELP: Homeopathy
VET CARE: Suppositories; enemas or laxatives
PREVENTION: High fiber diets; grooming to remove excess fur

The treatment depends on the actual cause, but in most instances constipated cats are treated the same as people. High fiber diets and laxatives prove beneficial. Veterinary approved stimulant laxatives are available, but can interfere with normal colon function if overused. Many cats like the flavor of plain canned pumpkin, which can be used as a high fiber treat.

The homeopathic remedy Nux vomica 6C liquid may help. Holistic veterinarians recommend diluting 20 drops of the remedy in an ounce of spring water, and giving your pet half a dropperful three times a day to relieve the constipation.

Bulk-forming laxatives that contain cellulose ingredients attract water and add bulk to the stool. One to three tablespoons of Metamucil a day mixed into the cat's diet will help. Wheat bran works as well, is less expensive, and is a natural product without known side effects. Mix about two tablespoons for each fourteen ounces of the cat's canned diet (canned provides more water) as a maintenance program to help keep Kitty regular (see MEGACOLON).

CRYPTORCHID

Male kittens are born with their testicles already descended into the scrotal sack. The tiny organs are easily felt by about six weeks of age.

Testicles that fail to descend and are retained in the abdomen are referred to as cryptorchid; when only one descends, it's called monorchid.

When both testicles are undescended, the cat is rendered sterile. Hormonal therapy administered prior to sexual maturity to affected kittens may sometimes cause the testicles to descend. Cats with one descended testicle may be able to father kittens, but because the condition is thought to be inherited, cryptorchid cats should not be bred.

Retained testicles continue to generate male hormones, so these cats will exhibit the same behavior as any intact male (see REPRODUCTION). Cryptorchid cats are also at higher risk for testicular cancer. It is recommended that cryptorchid cats be neutered. The veterinarian must surgically go into the abdomen to find and remove the organs.

When a cat appears to have been neutered but behaves otherwise, the veterinarian should be able to tell if Kitty has a retained testicle. The penis of a mature intact male cat has prominent spines; once neutered, the spines disappear.

CUTEREBRA

Cuterebra is the larva of the bot fly, a parasite that usually afflicts rodents. Cats and dogs come in contact with cuterebra from exploring rabbit or mouse habitat. Outdoor cats, particularly hunting felines, seem to be at highest risk, with kittens and younger cats affected most often. Cuterebra infection is seen most often during the summer months.

The eggs of the bot fly are deposited five to 15 at a time in the soil or vegetation surrounding the animal burrow. The body heat of a nearby host triggers the egg to hatch, and emerging larvae attach themselves to the animal's skin. The larva enters the animal's nose or mouth during grooming, and migrates through the host's body to a location just beneath the skin. This area swells as the parasite matures.

At first, the swelling feels firm, then become fluid-filled and soft with a central breathing hole for the parasite that leaks blood-tinged fluid. The cuterebra continues to grow and molt, until the cyst beneath the skin that contains the worm is quite noticeable.

Spine-covered brownish larva may reach over an inch in length and a half inch in diameter before breaking free of the host's skin, dropping to the ground and spending the winter in a pupal stage. Pupae hatch into adult bot flies in the spring, which can lay more than 2000 eggs, completing the cycle.

In cats, cuterebra usually follow the normal route of migration. Typically cats are affected only by one parasite, but they may have more than one. The swelling often looks like an abscess on the neck or in the chest region (see ABSCESS). Other than the swelling and draining, cats rarely show distress from the encounter, but the cysts may become infected. The parasite remains in the cat's skin for about a month before they emerge.

CUTEREBRA

SYMPTOMS: Soft swelling beneath skin of usually the neck or chest
HOME CARE: None
VET CARE: Surgical removal
PREVENTION: Keep cats indoors; prevent hunting

Never try to remove the parasite at home, and do not try to squeeze or express the cuterebra from the skin. Crushing the parasite can cause a life-threatening anaphylactic reaction in the cat (see INSECT BITES AND STINGS). The veterinarian carefully removes the parasite through the vent hole, enlarging the opening surgically if necessary, then cleans and treats the wound.

In rare instances, cuterebra infestation results in an aberrant migration into the nostrils, spinal column or scrotum, or even into the brain, which can have life-threatening consequences (see FELINE ISCHEMIC ENCEPHALOPATHY and STROKE). Prevent cats from cuterebra exposure by keeping them inside.

CYST A cyst is a thick capsule of tissue containing foreign matter that develops abnormally within the body. Cutaneous cysts (those found in the skin) are uncommon in cats, but can appear anywhere on the body.

Cutaneous cysts are firm to soft, well defined round areas often bluish in color that move freely beneath the skin. They may reach an inch or more in diameter, and are filled with a greasy, yellow-to-brown cheese-like substance that may drain from a central opening. Cutaneous cysts tend to progress to ulceration and infection, and most should be surgically removed.

Ovarian cysts may develop in females allowed to repeatedly experience heat without being mated (see REPRODUCTION). Called cystadenomas, these tumors are quite common in intact female cats. Affected queens develop many thin-walled cysts on the ovaries that contain watery fluid, and in time these cysts can completely replace normal ovarian tissue.

Ovarian cysts result in an abnormally high production of the hormone estrogen. This can cause the queen to experience a prolonged or even continuous heat cycle. Affected cats tend to fight with other cats, and either refuse to mate, or will mate frequently but be unable to become pregnant. Surgical removal of the cysts may correct the problem and allow conception to occur. More often, spaying the cat surgically removes the ovaries and uterus. Spaying the cat before her first heat cycle prevents the problem from ever occurring.

CYSTITIS
Cystitis in cats is a condition most commonly associated with Lower Urinary Tract Disease (LUTD). The warning signs for cystitis and LUTD are identical.

Bacteria, virus or fungus that irritate the lining of the urinary bladder causes cystitis. Pets that feel discomfort or even painful urination from cystitis typically lose housetraining. They probably will feel the need to urinate more frequently. Cats may cry or appear to strain during urination, and may also pass blood.

More than two-thirds of cystitis cases in cats are idiopathic, which means the cause is a mystery. Estimates indicate that this disorder affects nearly half a million cats every year. Researchers believe some cases are the same as interstitial (or idiopathic) cystitis that some women tend to suffer. In feline idiopathic cystitis (FIC), stress appears to be the major trigger of inflammation. Something as simple as a change in diet may bring on an episode.

Treatments for FIC seeks to address the stress, inflammation and discomfort and/or environmental influences. Narcotics such as oral buprenorphine or a fentanyl patch may address the cat's pain. Prazosin or phenoxybenzamine are sometimes prescribed in male cats with obstructive FIC. Antibiotics are not recommended unless the cat urine culture is positive. In most cases, litter box management and owner interaction are also influences on recovery. The vast majority of these cats will resolve within five to seven days, and up to one-third of cats will have a recurrence of signs after that initial episode.

CYSTITIS

SYMPTOMS:
- A housebroken cat dribbling urine or urinating in unusual locations;
- Frequent voiding of small quantities of urine;
- Bloody urine;
- Urine with a strong ammonia odor;
- Squatting or straining at the end of urination; and
- Listlessness and poor appetite and/or excessive thirst.

HOME CARE: Therapeutic diets
HOLISTIC HELP: Herbal treatment; homeopathy
VET CARE: Antibiotics
PREVENTION: Reduce stress

Amitriptyline (brand name Elavil) works in people to counter anxiety and depression, and this stress relief helps calm the urinary condition as well. Amitriptyline also inhibits the release of mast cells in the bladder wall, which is thought to be the root cause of bladder inflammation. By stabilizing these cells, inflammation in the bladder wall is reduced. The drug's antipsychotic activity also seems to reduce how much the cat cares about whether their bladder hurts.

However, clinical trials with amitriptyline haven't shown consistent effectiveness, and the drug has in some cases made the signs worse. Behavior drugs like amitriptyline may take several weeks to make a difference, although some cats show improvement more quickly, even within days. That may be due to the anti-inflammatory properties, or might even create a kind of placebo effect. In other words, giving the drug builds confident expectations in the cat owner, and this human confidence reduces the cat's stress caused by owner displeasure, and that helps relieve the symptoms.

Amitriptyline doesn't help in all instances, and some veterinarians consider other experimental treatments promising. Pentosan polysulfate, derived from beechwood cellulose and approved for use in humans for treatment of interstitial cystitis, may also help the condition in cats. Researchers have also noted the similarity between the chemical structures of amitriptyline, and hydroxizine (a common antihistamine).

Medical marijuana (or cannabis) today is also available for pets, but must be formulated so that pets receive the medical benefits of the cannabis (hemp) plant while reducing potential toxic concentrations of the herb. Hemp can be used to control pain and inflammation. Ask your veterinarian if this supplement may benefit your pet.

A pilot open label clinical trial using L-theanine (Anxitane®) in cats with anxiety related behaviors relieved some signs of anxiety, suggesting this product may be helpful in cats with FIC. L-theanine is an amino acid found naturally in green tea leaves.

Using synthetic feline facial pheromone products to reduce stress, such as Feliway, may also be beneficial. Several of these products are now available commercially.

Holistic veterinarians may recommend using an herbal tincture called Goldenrod Horsetail Compound to reduce the bladder's irritation. You can also look for a combination of goldenrod, horsetail, parsley, marshmallow root and elderberry, sometimes called Urinary Tea Blend. Cats can have one teaspoon of the cooled tea three times daily until symptoms go away.

The homeopathic remedy Cantharsis 30C helps to reduce the pain of urination, particularly when there is blood in the urine. Cranberry, often recommended for the same condition in people, also works well in cats, but most pets hate the taste. You can use the supplement called CranActin from health food stores. Ask your vet for the proper dose.

In some instances, the cat's urinary tract may become lethally blocked by crystallization of minerals in the urine (urolithiasis) and/or by sticky urethral plugs. COMA AND DEATH HAPPENS WITHIN 72 HOURS FOLLOWING COMPLETE OBSTRUCTION. Cats exhibiting any one or combination of these signs should be seen by a veterinarian immediately (see LOWER URINARY TRACT DISEASE).

CYTAUXZOON

A protozoal parasite *Cytauxzoon felis* transmitted by the American Dog Tick causes the disease. Don't let the tick's name fool you. In its different life stages it feeds variously on rodents, livestock or deer, and skunk, raccoon, dogs, and cats. While this tick also may transmit other diseases to dogs and people, Cytauxzoon affects only felines.

Cytauxzoon was first recognized in 1973 in Missouri and for many years was largely confined to this area and its neighboring states, Cytauxzoon has also been identified in Arkansas, Oklahoma and Kansas, and as far east as the Carolinas. The American bobcat serves as the primary reservoir in nature, and only becomes sick from the parasite for a short time. Bobcats can live for years walking around perfectly healthy but infective. Wooded areas that host bobcats and ticks offer a good situation for the disease to be present. In order to transmit the disease the tick must attach and feed for a period of time, and it's likely that any lifestage of the tick can transmit the infection.

CYTAUXZOON

SYMPTOMS: Lethargy; anorexia; sudden spiking fever; jaundice; respiratory distress
HOME CARE: None
VET CARE: Supportive care; drug therapy
PREVENTION: Keep cats indoors; prevent hunting; tick prevention

Once the organism enters the cat's body, it multiplies and infects a wide range of tissues. This schizont stage infects and fills up cells like blowing up a balloon until the cells block off the vessels, blocking blood supply to multiple organs at the same time: liver, spleen, lungs, brain. It causes anemia (see ANEMIA), but cats essentially die of multiple organ failure. Bobcats survive the tissue phase, recover, and when the next stage of the parasite infects red blood cells, ticks become infected when they feed.

The course of the disease lasts about two weeks, but the early signs, lethargy followed by refusal to eat, are so vague many cat owners won't notice. Late signs typically include sudden fever as high as 107 degrees, and jaundice, which is yellow tinge to the eyes and mouth. Sick cats feel uncomfortable, have trouble breathing, often vocalize and howl, and temperature drops to sub-normal just before they die.

"The whole course of the disease is generally less than five days from the first time the owner sees a sign to the death of the cat. Once the temperature becomes low almost no cats recover at that point (see TEMPERATURE).

There is no blood test available at this time. A definitive diagnosis relies on signs of disease along with careful microscopic examination of cells from lymph nodes, bone marrow, liver or spleen. Molecular diagnosis of *C. felis* via polymerase chain reaction (PCR) of whole blood has become available.

More than 50 percent of cats diagnosed with the disease will die, even with treatment. The outcome depends on the strain of the disease, as some appear to be more virulent than others. Prompt diagnosis followed by supportive care with intravenous fluid therapy and nutritional support is vital. Severe cases may require a blood transfusion (see BLOOD).

Current research supports using a combination of the drugs atovaquone and azithromycin. Imidocarb diproprionate following premedication with atropine or glycopyrrolate, can also be used for treatment.

Any cat allowed outside should also be protected with a commercial tick product. Some of the flea or heartworm medications also protect against the American dog tick that carries Cytauxzoon. Even indoor cats treated with a good parasite control product can get sick. Owners living in a rural setting bring ticks in, and while the infected tick won't give Cytauxzoon to your dog, he could carry the tick to your exclusively indoor cat. Check your cats routinely for ticks, especially if you live in a Cytauxzoon-endemic region.

Ticks are most active in the morning because they're very sensitive to moisture. When morning dew is on the ground, ticks climb up on the grass leaves waiting to jump on anything that passes nearby, and as the moisture evaporates ticks retreat lower into the grass. Carbon dioxide (the exhalation of your breath) attracts them. So wait until dew has dissipated to let pets outside, and keep grass cut as low as you can around the house. Also keep pets away from leaf litter and mulch where ticks like to hide.

CYTOLOGY
A lump or sore you find on your cat raises concern, and nobody wants to worry for days to find out if it's a serious health problem. Diagnostic tools like CT-scans and MRIs provide important information, but it can be pricy and take time to reveal results. One of the simplest in-office tests provides quick, inexpensive answers.

Cytology looks at cells under a microscope. It's a noninvasive, pain-free way to screen for many health conditions, including inflammation, infection, fungi, parasites, bacteria and cancer. Cytology often can determine within minutes if your cat's bump or that fluid in the tummy is a cause for concern.

A trained pathologist can look at cells and tell what kind of cells they are. The veterinarian can make informed decisions about best treatment options once cells are identified.

Cytology is most commonly used to diagnosing a lump or bump (see CANCER). Cells are collected in a technique called a "fine needle aspirate." A syringe similar to what's used to give your cat vaccinations is used. The needle is inserted into the mass and the plunger drawn back on the syringe to draw material from the mass into the needle. A fine needle aspirate can be used to collect cells from masses on the skin surface, from deeper in the tissue, or even from a mass or fluid inside the chest or abdomen. For targets deep within the cat's body, a longer needle would be required, as well as sedation to keep the cat from wiggling and an ultrasound probe to so the needled doesn't hit the wrong target.

Cells that are collected aren't very visible until they're stained. The cells are squirted onto a slide to be examined under the microscope and then dunked into a series of jars of fluid that contain different stains, leaving the cells purple.

Pathologists are specialists able to diagnose conditions by examining the cells under a microscope. Often they can distinguish benign from malignant processes by how the cells look, and sometimes even identify the type of cancer.

But some tumors are more easily diagnosed with cytology than others. That depends on how readily the tumor exfoliates—sheds cells. Some tumors don't exfoliate very well and very few cells are collected during the fine needle aspirate.

Round cell tumors such as lymphomas exfoliate best and are very easy to diagnose with cytology. Carcinomas—basal cell and squamous cell carcinomas are two examples—arise from epithelial tissue found in the lining of the mouth, eyes, intestinal tract and can also be readily diagnosed with cytology.

Tumors that don't exfoliate well or are difficult to sample with a needle may not be candidates for cytology. For instance, sarcomas—tumors of connective tissue such as muscle, ligament and tendon—are often the most difficult to diagnose cytologically. A biopsy may be needed in conjunction with a fine needle aspirate to get a definitive diagnosis of a cat's fibrosarcoma tumor, for example.

Biopsy is the gold standard for making a diagnosis because it preserves the tissue architecture. While cytology examines only a few individual cells, biopsy looks at a slice of tissue. The veterinarian collects a sample with a larger bore needle or an incision that removes a piece of tissue with a blade. After preserving the sample in formalin, it's embedded in paraffin wax, stained, and then fine slices are made. The cells look the same under the microscope as with cytology, but biopsy preserves the relationship of cells to each other.

A pathologist can "grade" the seriousness of a cancer by evaluating the biopsy—an assessment of how bad it's likely to behave. Grading can be done with biopsy but not with an aspirate. A biopsy typically costs two or three times more than cytology because it requires general anesthesia, a pathologist's report, and hospital stay. It also takes two or three days to get the results. But it offers a more complete and accurate diagnosis than cytology.

However, cytology almost always is your cat's first step to getting a diagnosis. It doesn't require a specialist, or sedation, so the cost stays low. The sooner you have answers, the more quickly your cat can receive the proper treatment. Cytology is a fast, economical way for your veterinarian to diagnose many feline conditions. It also can deliver the best news of all—that you have nothing to worry about.

126
CAT FACTS

127

DEAFNESS Hearing loss may develop due to inner ear infection (see EAR MITES and OTITIS). Sometimes white cats, especially those with blue eyes, are born with a condition that causes the cochlea to degenerate, which results in deafness. Deafness also can develop due to age, because the bones of the middle ear lose their mobility and the nerves of the cochlea degenerate with time.

Chemical or noise-induced damage can also cause irreversible or progressive hearing loss. Nearly 200 drugs and chemicals can prove toxic to hearing. The most common including certain antibiotics, diuretics, the anticancer drug cisplatin and some antiseptic preparations.

Age-related hearing loss (presbycusis) is not associated with a specific cause, but is a gradual degeneration of one or more areas of the ear. It is believed to be the most common form of hearing loss in cats.

Cats often overcome deficits in one of their senses by compensating with another. That's why it's hard to detect hearing loss in pets, even if present from birth. Cats normally have a range of hearing of sound frequency that's close to three times that of humans, so pets can often suffer hearing loss but the owner never notices.

Diagnosis can be tricky. Impedance audiometry measures changes in the eardrum mobility as pressure in the external ear changes. In a healthy ear, the air pressure in the external ear canal will be the same as the air pressure in the middle ear. By comparing the two, a hearing impairment can be diagnosed.

Acoustic reflex, another test using impedance audiometry, is the involuntary action of the middle ear in response to a sound. When a loud noise is heard, the muscles of the middle ear in normal pets contract to decrease the movement of the eardrum, protecting the inner ear from damage. The reaction can be measured, and an acoustic reflex less than normal indicates inflammation of the middle ear, or disease of the cochlear nerve, which transmits the sound impulses to the brain.

Holistic veterinarians don't know why it sometimes works, but some hearing problems can be improved with acupressure. There are two points near the base of the ear that you can stimulate. TH17 is located just below the ear, and SI19 and GB2 are both located just in front of the ear. Press each point with your finger once a day for 30 seconds to a minute, then release.

Most cats with a hearing loss compensate and do well as long as they remain in familiar, safe surroundings. Routine ear cleaning is important to stay ahead of possible health problems (see EARS and GROOMING).

DECLAWING

Declawing is an irreversible surgical procedure that removes a cat's claws. This elective surgery is not necessary or beneficial for feline health, but rather is a means of eliminating normal feline scratching behavior that an owner may find objectionable.

Declaw operations remain controversial, with some cat experts declaring the procedure unnatural and psychologically and physically damaging to the cat. The procedure is illegal in some parts of the world, and certain cat breed associations will not allow a cat to be shown if declaw surgery has been done. Some kitties will experience a personality change after the surgery. Detractors argue that loss of the claws changes the cat's gait and stance, and can contribute to arthritis as he matures (see ARTHRITIS). Another common complaint is hit-or-miss litter box issues, stemming from painful paws and possibly the association of the box with the discomfort. The cat remembers the pain, and so avoids the litter box.

The American Association of Feline Practitioners 2015 position statement on declawing urges veterinarians to council clients on alternatives to declaw, and states in part, "There are inherent risks and complications with declawing that increase with age such as acute pain, infection, nerve trauma, as well as long term complications like lameness, behavioral problems, and chronic neuropathic pain."

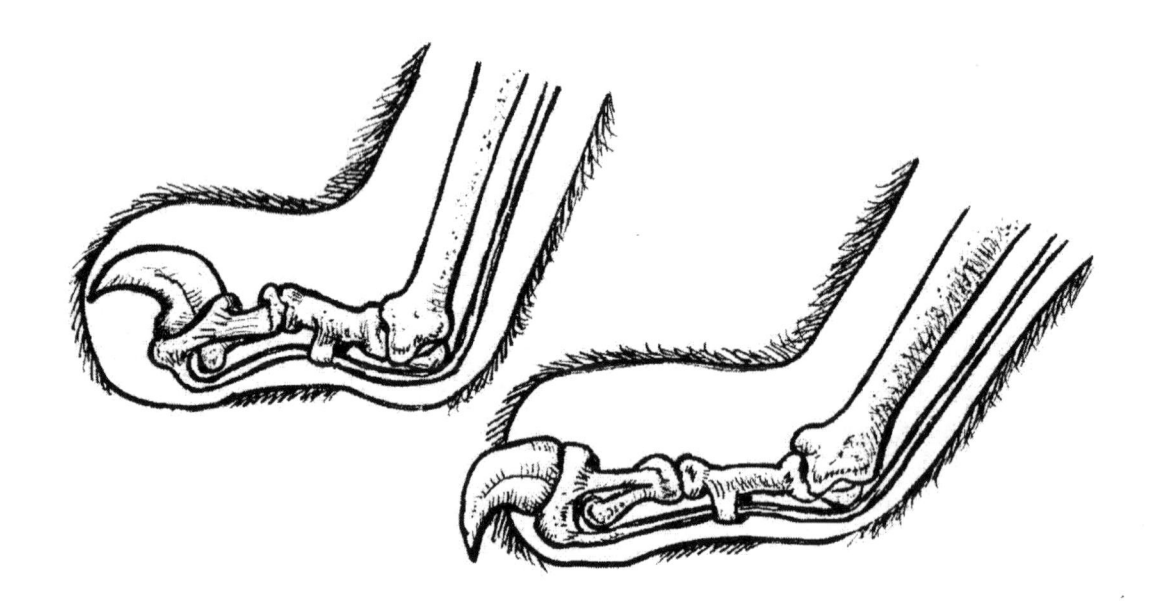

Proponents argue that when properly performed, a cat suffers no ill effects, and is more likely to enjoy a permanent home when destructive scratching is eliminated. Many kittens and cats show absolutely no negative effects to losing their nails. Do not let the presence—or absence—of claws interfere with your choice of adopting a lovely shelter cat, since some may have already had the procedure done.

Claws are the outdoor cats' first line of defense, and impact their climbing ability, stride and balance, which means outdoor cats should not be declawed. When behavior modification techniques have proved unsuccessful for an indoor cat, surgery may be an option.

The procedure is performed under a general anesthesia so that the cat feels no discomfort. Because youngsters tend to cope with the loss of claws more quickly than adult cats, veterinarians often recommend kittens be declawed at three to five months old. Usually, only the claws from the front paws are removed, since rear claws are not used to scratch furniture. Cats with rear claws are likely to still be able to climb small trees.

There are three bones in each toe, with the claw growing from the end of the last bone. Declawing surgically amputates the end section of this last bone along with the nail to remove the claw and prevent regrowth.

The cat's feet are prepared for surgery by scrubbing and soaking them in an antiseptic surgical solution, such as betadine and alcohol. The fur is not shaved, but may be clipped if extremely long. A tourniquet is placed to stop the bleeding, then each claw is expressed in turn, and surgically removed at the joint leaving smooth white bone. Each toe is sewn closed with absorbable suture material that will not need to be removed. Once all the claws on a paw are removed, the foot is bandaged snugly to control post-operative bleeding, and the tourniquet is removed.

A day or more of hospitalization is required. Bandages come off in a day or two, but the feet will remain tender for up to a week. Until the toes completely heal, gritty or abrasive litter box fillers should be avoided to prevent introducing dirt into the cat's healing incisions. Shredded newspaper is often recommended (see LITTER BOX).

Most cats are up and walking quite well within 48 to 72 hours. But if limping or favoring of paws persists, or the incisions begin to bleed or appear swollen, return to the veterinarian for further evaluation. If not all of the claw bed is properly removed, the claw may regrow or produce a misshapen claw, and a repeat of the surgery will be necessary.

Cats without front claws may still go through the motions of scratching furniture. Even without toenails, Kitty feels impelled to scratch, which leaves invisible scent marks on the upholstery (see MARKING). A percentage of cats appear to be impacted by loss of claws that disrupts normal stride and balance, or may increase biting when unable to use claw-defense. Cats that associate paw-discomfort with the litter box may develop litter box aversions.

A newer, supposedly less stressful procedure called a flexor tendonectomy is another option. This procedure leaves the cat his claws, but prevents him from extending them.

A tendon connects the second and third bones of the cat's toes, and controls the extension of the claws. The cat is anesthetized, then each tendon is cut and a tiny portion removed, so the cat cannot flex and extend the claws. Incisions are closed with skin glue, the cat spends the night at the veterinary hospital for observation, and usually goes home the next morning. Following this procedure, the claw base tends to thicken and nails may become blunter, probably because of a limited ability of the cat to shed and sharpen the claws. Owners need to monitor the cat's toenails, and clip them as necessary.

Advances in surgical techniques have reduced post-operative pain, and current declaw surgeries are more humane than in the past. The surgical laser has allowed veterinarians to remove claws, and seal the blood vessels and nerve endings so the animal is much more comfortable after the surgery. However, laser surgery, which uses heat energy (burns!), takes longer to heal than cuts from a scalpel. So although the cat feels better, he may bounce around on his feet too soon and develop complications if the incisions open. Bottom line, declaw surgery is designed to benefit the human's objection to a normal feline behavior, rather than pose any health benefit to the cat. (see GROOMING).

DEHYDRATION

Dehydration is the excessive loss of body water. Normal water loss occurs in the cat's litter box deposits, through moisture exhaled with the breath, and through sweat. These fluids are replaced when the cat eats and drinks.

Any illness may prompt the cat to stop eating and drinking, and prolonged fever increases the loss of body fluid. Specific disease conditions or injuries may result in excessive urination (see DIABETES MELLITIS and KIDNEY DISEASE), and vomiting, diarrhea, and bleeding are all common causes of dehydration.

DEHYDRATION

SYMPTOMS: Loss of skin elasticity; dry mouth; stringy saliva; delayed capillary refill time; sunken eyeballs; muscle twitches; cold paw pads
HOME CARE: Give lots of water, and/or solutions like Pedialyte as directed by vet
VET CARE: Possible fluid therapy
PREVENTION: Provide lots of fresh water at all times; offer shelter from the heat

A normal adult cat's total body water is approximately 60 percent of his body weight. Signs of dehydration become apparent when the cat loses as little as five percent of normal body water. A 12 to 15 percent loss of total body water results in imminent death (see SHOCK).

The earliest noticeable sign of dehydration is the loss of skin elasticity. When the loose skin at the cat's shoulder blades is gently grasped and lifted, it should quickly spring back into place upon release. When slightly dehydrated, the cat's skin retracts slowly; more serious dehydration causes retracted skin to remain in a ridge, and spring back little if any.

Dry mucus membranes are another sign of dehydration. The cat's mouth is dry, the gums are tacky instead of wet, and saliva may be stringy and thick.

Also, capillary refill time, the time it takes for blood to return to tissue after pressure is applied, is delayed. Gently press one finger to the side of your cat's gums; this will briefly block blood flow, and turn normally pink tissue white when the pressure is quickly released. Normally it takes less than two seconds for the white to return to pink. At seven to eight percent dehydration, capillary refill time is delayed by another two to three seconds. Longer than four or five seconds indicates severe dehydration. Such cats may also have sunken eyeballs, involuntary muscle twitches, and their paw pads feel cold.

A cat with noticeable dehydration needs immediate veterinary attention. Fluid and electrolyte (mineral) loss will be replaced, and steps taken to prevent further loss. Intravenous fluid therapy may be necessary.

In mild cases in which the cat is not vomiting, oral hydration with plain water may be sufficient (see ADMINISTER MEDICATION). Your veterinarian may prescribe a balanced electrolyte solution such as Ringer's lactate with five percent Dextrose in water. Fluids for treating dehydration in children, such as Pedialyte, are also suitable for cats. They should be given as directed by your veterinarian (see DIARRHEA and VOMITING).

DERMATITIS

Dermatitis is inflammation of the skin. It can be generalized and involve the entire body, or confined in isolated areas. Dermatitis in cats is most often associated with allergy, but may be induced by sunburn, and very rarely is a psychological disorder related to stress. Signs and treatment vary depending on the cause (see ALLERGY and HAIR LOSS).

CAT FACTS

DESTRUCTIVE BEHAVIOR see AGGRESSION, SCRATCHING, and SOILING.

DIABETES MELLITUS Diabetes mellitus is a common disorder of the endocrine system in cats. The pancreas, a gland located near the stomach and liver, produces the hormone insulin, which stimulates the movement of glucose (sugar) from the blood into the cells of the body where it is used. Diabetes mellitus is a disorder that results from conditions that either suppress the action of existing insulin (Type II, non-insulin dependent), or interfere with the production of insulin (Type I, insulin dependent). In other words, although food eaten by the pet may be turned into glucose by digestion, without insulin the cat's body can't use it.

The onset of disease is so slow that the condition often goes undiagnosed until it becomes quite advanced. In the past several years, the incidence of the disease appears to be increasing. This is associated with a variety of known risk factors such as obesity, increased longevity (older than seven years old), sedentary cats, and high carbohydrate diets. More male neutered cats are diagnosed than female. Studies from Australia, New Zealand and the United Kingdom have found a larger percentage of Burmese cats diagnosed. Long term use of certain medications (corticosteroids), and any concurrent health conditions may also contribute to the increase.

Excessive drinking, increased urination, and/or increase of the appetite along with weight loss occur because the cat's body can't use food; he becomes very hungry and weak, and eats more and more trying to compensate. The level of glucose in the cat's blood continues to increase because it's not being used, and instead the glucose is excreted in large volumes in the urine. The sugar in the urine actual pulls more water out of the cat's system in a process called osmotic diuresis.

As the cat's need to urinate greater quantities more frequently continues to increase, cats may have "accidents." This excessive loss of water through urination tends to make the cat thirsty, so he drinks more water to compensate. The result is a vicious cycle; drinking more water increases the need to urinate, which causes more thirst and drinking, and on and on. Pet owners may notice sticky urine.

DIABETES

SYMPTOMS: Increased eating, drinking, and urination with weight loss; possibly "accidents" when cat can get to litterbox to urinate in time; "plantigrade" posture; walking on heels
HOME CARE: Administer insulin injections as instructed by veterinarian
HOLISTIC HELP: High protein diet
VET CARE: Stabilize cat with fluids and other medication; regulate diet and monitor urine and blood to determine proper insulin dosage
PREVENTION: Prevent obesity; trim down tubby tabbies

Diagnosis is based on the signs of disease, along with an evaluation of the blood and urine. This can be tricky because a cat may "spill" excess glucose into his system when he becomes stressed from visiting the veterinarian. A test that measures the serum fructosamine level may be run to determine the average blood glucose level over the past week. The cat's "stress-response" typically does not affect this measurement. Sugar and sometimes acetone in the urine along with a high blood sugar indicate diabetes mellitus.

Today, Type I diabetes is considered very uncommon in cats. Cats most frequently suffer from non-insulin dependent diabetes, designated Type II. Insulin is present in the body but other factors suppress its function. When the cat's cells become resistant, this ultimately leads to a lack of insulin as this disease process progresses. Obesity is thought to be a major player in Type II diabetes mellitus because fat cells may become resistant to insulin when exposed to it. Diet and weight loss may help control certain cases of non-insulin dependent diabetes mellitus.

About 20 percent of cats have an in-and-out phase of diabetes, and this transient diabetes is most commonly associated with pancreatitis (see PANCREATITIS). Those cats are ones that are amenable to just diet sometimes, or diet and oral medicine. Also, cats that are fed a high protein/low carbohydrate diet are ten times more likely to lose their dependency on insulin injections.

Without treatment, the diabetic cat develops life-threatening ketoacidosis. When the body isn't able to metabolize glucose for energy, eventually it switches to catabolism, which means the body burns its own fat and muscle tissue. This condition results in an excess of ketone bodies in the blood and urine. Ketone bodies are a normal part of fat metabolism, but too many results in a diabetic coma and death. Treatment for ketoacidosis may include fluid and electrolyte replacement, along with bicarbonate to correct acid-base balance.

Many cats with diabetes develop a nervous system disorder called peripheral neuropathy. This nerve disease leads to weakness and wasting away of muscle, especially of the hind limbs, which causes a rear-leg plantigrade stance. Instead of walking normally on her toes, her stance drops until she's on her "heels." This neurologic disorder can be reversed once the diabetes is under good control.

Neuropathy in diabetic cats is reported as 8 percent, but many veterinarians believe the percentage is much higher. What causes the condition and how it works isn't known.

Diabetes mellitus cannot be cured, but in many cases it can be managed. Treatment is aimed at supportive therapy for any complications of the disease, and replacing insulin that the body is no longer able to produce.

Oral medications such as Glipizide promote the secretion of insulin from the pancreas and may be helpful for owners unable to give insulin injections. The stress of "pilling" often makes injections the better choice.

Most cats require insulin injections, usually twice a day. Various types of insulin are available, and different ones may work better for individual cats.

The amount and frequency of insulin injections varies from cat to cat and depends on activity level and metabolism. Usually it takes time and experimentation to find the right dose, best insulin, and ideal schedule. Most owners become quite adept at giving insulin injections. Diet and exercise influence insulin requirements, and should be kept constant. Unauthorized snacks or an exuberant chase around the room can be devastating to the diabetic cat.

Usually, blood tests are monitored for blood sugar levels, and the amount and frequency of insulin shots are adjusted accordingly. An instrument called a glucometer tests the blood, and a sample is obtained by performing an ear prick. Put a damp washcloth in a plastic baggy, warm it in the microwave for about 5 to 10 seconds, and then massage the damp warm cloth against the ear for about 30 seconds. That brings the circulation to the ear, and then you use the lancet to prick a drop of blood just as a human diabetic does on their fingertip. Home monitoring can be a big advantage because stress can affect the reading, and bringing the cat to the hospital may mean the tests aren't as accurate as when done by the owner. Just be sure your glucometer is calibrated to match your veterinarian's testing parameters.

Too much insulin can cause insulin reaction, referred to as hypoglycemia. Symptoms include disorientation, weakness and hunger, lethargy, shaking, or head tilt. Without treatment, the cat's symptoms progress to convulsions, coma, and then death. Giving the cat a glucose source, such as Karo syrup or honey, should reverse signs within five to 15 minutes. Then get your cat to the veterinarian immediately.

Insulin coma occurs when not enough insulin is given, and may result from a variance in diet or exercise, or if the insulin has expired and isn't effective. This is an emergency that your veterinarian must address.

DIARRHEA

Diarrhea refers to more frequent than normal bowel movements that are abnormally soft or fluid. Diarrhea is not a disease, but rather is a symptom of ill health. Any prolonged change of bowel habits should be addressed by the veterinarian.

Gastrointestinal upsets occur fairly frequently in cats, and diarrhea is one of the most common signs. The condition is generally classified as either acute, which happens suddenly, or chronic, which is an ongoing condition.

Diarrhea can result from a number of things. Common causes include intestinal parasites or viruses (see FELINE PANLEUKOPENIA VIRUS, GIARDIA, HOOKWORMS). Eating too much, or an abrupt change in diet may bring on diarrhea. Unhealthy food supplements like table scraps can upset Kitty tummies. Milk causes problems for many cats, because they may lack the dietary enzyme that allows them to digest it properly (see MILK AS FOOD). Outdoor cats are more likely to suffer diarrhea when they capture and eat rodents or birds, or ingest toxic substances (see POISON). Some cats develop allergies to their food. And swallowing foreign material may also result in diarrhea (see HAIRBALLS and SWALLOWED OBJECTS).

Diarrhea is treated in three ways. Symptomatic therapy treats the signs. For example, an antidiarrheal medication would be given to control diarrhea. Supportive treatment is given when the cat has become debilitated by the disease; a dehydrated cat would be given fluid therapy (see DEHYDRATION). Specific therapy treats the underlying disease when a specific diagnosis has been made. If signs are caused by parasites, worm medicine would be given.

With acute disease, treating the symptoms often works. Start by withholding food for at least 24 hours to rest the gastrointestinal tract. Offer only small amounts of water, or ice cubes for licking during this period. When you again offer food, make the first meal bland, and divide it into several small servings rather than offering it all at once. Try a mixture of one part skinless white chicken meat, or chicken baby food. The second day, mix the chicken half and half with Kitty's normal diet. Reduce the mixture until by the fourth day, Kitty's back to eating a normal ration. Sometimes mixing in a tablespoon of a fiber supplement helps firm the stool; try natural wheat bran or non-flavored Metamucil.

DIARRHEA

SYMPTOMS: More-frequent-than-normal bowel movements that are soft or fluid
HOME CARE: Withhold food for 24 hours; offer minimal water or ice cubes to lick; feed bland first meal (one part white chicken and two parts rice) in several small servings
HOLISTIC HELP: Homeopathy; acupressure; add natural fiber
VET CARE: Treat parasites; antidiarrheal medication; sometimes fluid therapy, or other medications depending on diagnosis
PREVENTION: Vaccinate; keep cat indoors to prevent him from eating vermin; avoid sudden diet changes

In addition, your veterinarian may suggest you treat the cat with antidiarrheal medication. Ask for an expert's recommendation; it could be dangerous to give your cat over-the-counter medication without your veterinarian's direction.

The homeopathic remedy Nux vomica may help stop the diarrhea. Mix six drops of a 6X potency in an ounce of spring water. Give your pet half a dropperful three times a day. Holistic vets also use acupuncture to relieve diarrhea, and you can try using acupressure (firm pressure) on three points that may help relieve the problem. The LI4 point is located in the web of skin between the dewclaw and the first long toe on the front feet. LI11 is located on the outside of the front legs at the elbow creases. And ST25 is located just below the last rib. For cats, you can use the eraser end of a pencil to give firm pressure in these locations. Stimulating each of these points for about 30 seconds a day until your cat feels better (see ACUPUNCTURE).

In cats with chronic disease, simply treating the diarrhea usually doesn't work. If you suspect your cat has ingested something dangerous that's causing the problem, or if the stool contains blood, see a veterinarian immediately. Your cat should see a doctor when diarrhea doesn't resolve with the above steps, and persists for more than 24 hours. A further diagnosis is necessary to understand what's causing the problem before it can be appropriately treated (see also COLITIS, ENTERITIS, TRICHOMONIASIS and INFLAMMATORY BOWEL DISEASE).

DISTEMPER see FELINE PANLEUKOPENIA VIRUS

DOMINANCE

Dominance is behavior used to achieve a desired result. Most cats aren't satisfied with anything less than being King Cat and getting their way. That's because the feline social system is not a hierarchy with one ruler and lesser ranking individuals in a stair step order below. Rather, feline ranking is described as despotic, which basically means each cat considers himself the cat that counts, with other cats/people below and having no particular ranking whatsoever.

A confident cat may exhibit dominant behavior toward family members, using anything from aggression to trickery to get his way. Cats that meow constantly for more food, attention, to go inside or out are asserting their dominance. To turn off this behavior and establish yourself as King Cat, don't let Kitty push your buttons. If he meows for you to pet him, then only pet him when he's quiet and ignore him when he's noisy. If he meows to be fed, feed him before he turns up the noise, and don't give in to pleas at any other time. Consistency is key; owners reinforce the cat's identity as despot by giving in just one time. Cats know that if it worked once, it will likely work in the future.

A cat's sense of self has a great deal to do with the territory each "owns." Dominant cats defend their territory against interlopers. Your cat may identify the entire house, a portion of the house, or even individual furniture as his territory. His sense of possession may extend to the front yard visible from the window even if he's never allowed outdoors. And his territory most certainly extends to you.

If he feels his territory is threatened—a strange cat crosses the yard, a new boyfriend is taking your time, the other cat sits in his chair—the dominant cat may react with aggressive behavior or some other action to reestablish who is King Cat.

For instance, some cats need only stare intently at a subordinate cat to induce them to move. Others make their point by hissing or posturing. And some devious cats even use subtle aggravation—grooming the other cat until he can't stand it and moves away, or simply leaning against him to make him leave. Kitty may simply get between you and the new boyfriend when you sit on the sofa.

Most cats sort out their own social order with compromises that avoid face-offs. As long as each cat has enough "territory" to satisfy his or her sense of ownership, the chance for feuds is lessened. Cat One may rule the first floor, and makes way for Cat Two on the second floor, and vice-versa; Cat Two "owns" the sofa, while Cat One claims the top of the television.

Dominance becomes most problematic in multicat households because dominance struggles increase in direct proportion as the amount of available territory decreases. An apartment that was adequate for one or two cats to share may be insufferable for five. And when there's not enough territory to go around, dominant cats will constantly jockey for position and ownership, and be in constant turmoil. They may resort to marking behavior and/or fighting each other. A good rule of thumb is to have no more cats than there are bedrooms in your house; that gives everybody a room of his own, and is handy if separation becomes necessary (see AGGRESSION, FEAR and MARKING.

Dreaming

Cats, like other animals with highly developed brains, dream. Feline fantasies are born during the deep sleep phase, and cats spend up to three hours each day enjoying kitty dreams. People only dream one and a half to two hours each day.

The exact purpose of dreams, for either people or animals, isn't known, but cats seem to relive the activities of everyday life in their dreams just like humans do. The dreaming cat's muscles relax, and his eyes move rapidly beneath his eyelids (REM, or rapid eye movement phase). During dream sleep, Kitty is hard to awaken. A trusted owner whose scent and touch are familiar may even be able to move the cat without awakening him. During dreams, the cat's paws may twitch and tail switch, he may purr or growl, and whiskers bristle with excitement as he pounces on dream mice.

Drinking see EATING

CAT FACTS

DROWNING Drowning is suffocation caused by submersion in water. Being natural swimmers, drowning is an infrequent occurrence in cats. Although some breeds like the Turkish Van relish swimming, many cats dislike getting wet and avoid water hazards. Cats that drown are typically youngsters that fall into water and are unable to climb out. With very small kittens, even a water bowl may be dangerous, but outdoor hazards like swimming pools, ponds, rivers and streams are more often involved.

Treatment consists of removing water from the lungs and getting air back into the cat. Position the cat head down, holding her with both hands around the lower abdomen, and swing her back and forth for 20 to 30 seconds. This should remove most of the water.

Then begin resuscitation to get the cat breathing again. If the water was cold, the cat's body will need to be warmed as quickly as possible. Seek veterinary attention immediately. Such cats are frequently at higher risk for pneumonia (See ARTIFICIAL RESPIRATION, CARDIOPULMONARY RESUSCITATION and HYPOTHERMIA).

DROWNING

SYMPTOMS: Loss of consciousness; no breathing apparent; cat found in or near water
FIRST AID: Hold cat upside down and swing; artificial resuscitation; keep warm and get to veterinarian
VET CARE: Oxygen therapy; rewarming therapy, precautions against pneumonia
PREVENTION: Bar the cat from exploring dangerous waterways

143

EAR MITES

These tiny parasites are common in cats, and causes otodectic mange, more commonly known as ear mite infestation. Ear mites (*Otodectes cynotis*) are a kind of arthropod that are actually related to and look something like spiders. The first four legs of all stages bear unjointed short stalks and suckers, and adult males also have suckers on the rear legs.

The mites live on the surface of the skin of the ear and ear canal. Adult females lay eggs with cement that sticks them in place. After incubating four days, eggs hatch into six-legged larvae. Larvae feed for three to ten days, consuming the debris of the ear canal, and piercing the skin to suck lymph. Each larva hatches into an eight-legged protonymph, which then molts into a deutonymph. The deutonymph becomes attached to an adult male end to end by the suckers on their rear legs. If a female adult emerges from the deutonymph, fertilization occurs and the female becomes egg bearing. The life cycle lasts three weeks.

EAR MITES

SYMPTOMS: Black to brown tarry or crumbly substance inside ears; itchy ears; scratching or rubbing ears
HOME CARE: Clean ears with prescribed medication
HOLISTIC HELP: Herbal treatment; oil the ears
VET CARE: Initial treatment to flush out debris; sometimes medication to reduce inflammation or itching
PREVENTION: None—monitor ears, prevent contact with other animals

Ear mites are the most common cause of ear inflammation (see OTITIS). Symptoms of ear mite infestation include brown, waxy debris in the ear canal, and/or crust formation. The crawling mites inside the ear canal produce intense itching and discomfort. Infested cats will shake their heads, dig at their ears, and show a variety of restless behavior.

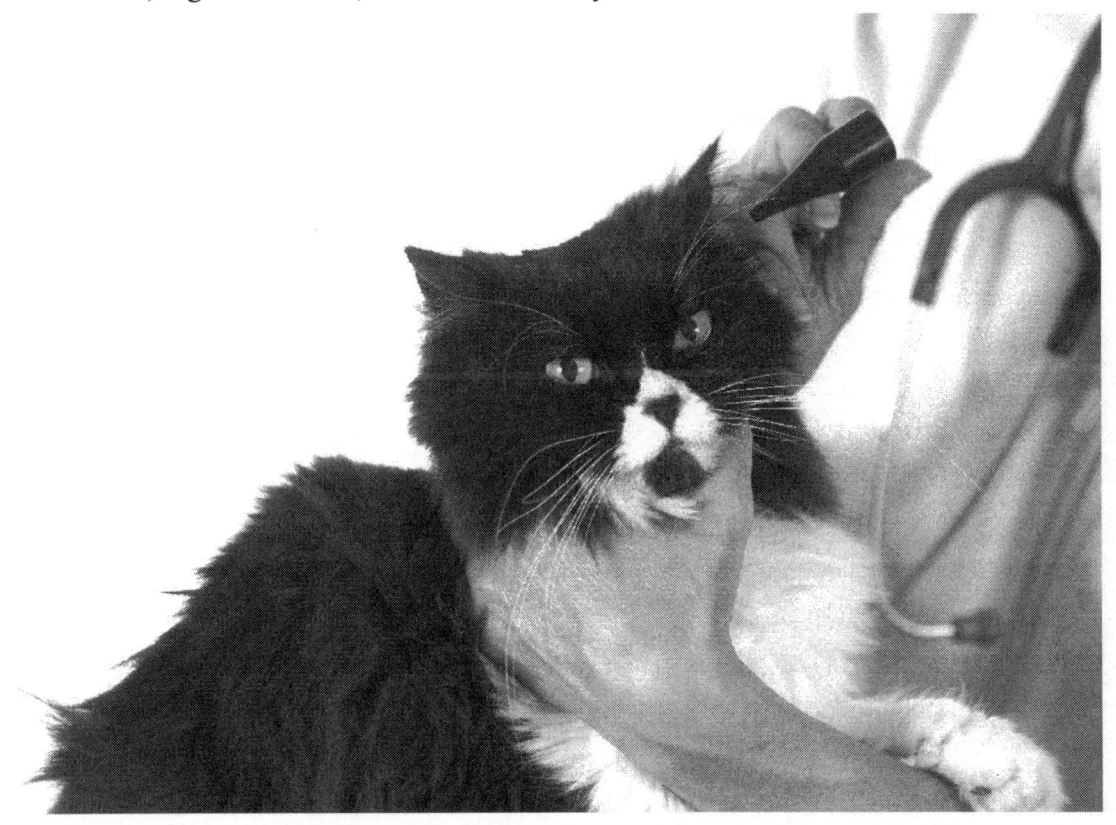

Excessive head shaking or scratching at the ears caused by ear mites can result in secondary trauma to the pinna, the external portion of your cat's ear. This can cause a kind of blood blister (see HEMATOMA).

Ear mites are extremely contagious, and outdoor cats are most commonly affected. These parasites aren't selective; they infest many species, including cats, dogs, rabbits, ferrets and other pets. Kittens often acquire ear mites from their mother.

If one pet is diagnosed with ear mites, all the animals in a multi-pet household must be treated to prevent reinfestation. When left untreated, ear mites can cause severe problems of the middle and inner ear, which may affect the cat's hearing and balance (see EARS and BALANCE).

CAT FACTS

Diagnosis is made by actually seeing the mite. The parasite is tiny, white, and nearly impossible to see with the naked eye. Generally, the veterinarian will make a slide of a sample of the ear debris, and examine it under the microscope to identify the parasite.

Treatment consists of flushing out the debris, and applying insecticide to kill the mites. Bland oil, like mineral oil squirted into the ear canal followed by gentle massage helps flush out the crumbly material. Because of the three week lifespan of the mites, more than one treatment may be necessary to kill the mites as they hatch.

A number of over the counter ear drop medications are available for treating ear mites in cats. Many of them contain insecticides such as carbaryl or pyrethrins in a mineral oil solution. Sometimes, steroids are necessary to help the inflammation subside, and antibiotic ointment may be indicated to treat bacterial infections.

Holistic veterinarians may recommend using a green tea rinse, since it's a natural antiseptic and can gently remove the ear debris caused by the mites. Steep a tablespoon of green tea leaves in a cup of hot water for three or four minutes, strain it, and allow to cool to room temperature. Flush your pet's ear canal with the tea, using a small dropper.

A natural traditional way to treat ear mites is to suffocate the bugs with oil. Place two or three drops of vegetable oil in the pet's ears, and massage. The oil also soothes the itch, but you'll need to treat the ears daily for at least a month to catch all the maturing bugs, and your cat's oily head may not be to his (or your) liking.

Not all of the mites are in the ear at any one time, so whole body treatments are ideal. Sores may be limited to the external ear canal, but are commonly found on other parts of the body, especially the cat's neck, rump and tail. This condition is called otodectic mange, and some of these cases look very much like flea bite allergy. In severe cases, the body of the animal may need to be treated weekly for four weeks to kill the mites not in the ear canal. Products that kill fleas will also eliminate ear mites (see ALLERGY).

Just as fleas infest the environment, ear mites may live in the premises for months. Control is especially difficult in homes with many pets. The same procedures for premise control of fleas works for eliminating ear mites in the environment. Repeat premise treatments weekly for four weeks at a minimum; experts suggest treating the environment two weeks beyond the pet's apparent cure.

When the cat's ears are very sore, sedation may be necessary to properly clean his ears. Even when ear drops are effective, some cats object to having their ears cleaned and treated, and unless the entire course of treatment is completed, the problem will recur. In addition, some cats are resistant to certain medications, or are hard for owners to handle and medicate at home.

For these stubborn cases, an injectable medication may be the answer. One or two beneath-the-skin injections of an insecticide called Ivermectin is effective, but not FDA approved for this use. Veterinarians may use the drug "off label" with the informed consent of their clients.

EARS

The ear is a sensory organ that provides cats with both the ability to hear and their sense of equilibrium, or balance. Ears can be divided into three parts; the sound-collecting outer ear, a sound-transmitting/amplifying middle ear, and the inner ear that translates vibration into meaning. The cat's sound sense is extraordinarily sensitive; she relies on hearing for protection from danger, for enhanced hunting skills, and for everyday living.

There are 19 separate muscles that allow the large external ear that you see, called the pinna, to swivel 180 degrees. The pinna is triangular cartilage covered by skin on both sides. The pinna normally functions as a furry funnel to collect and direct sound waves to the tympanic membrane, or eardrum, situated inside the ear canal.

Unlike human ears that have straight canals, the cat's auditory canal runs straight down from where the pinna joins the head, and then turns inward until it ends at the eardrum. Sound waves cause the sensitive membrane of the eardrum to vibrate.

The middle ear begins on the other side of the cat's eardrum. It's here that sound is amplified by a chain of three tiny bones, called ossicles. The first bone, the hammer, is attached to the ear drum. The middle bone called the anvil and the third called the stirrup lie against the hammer.

The greater the ratio between the length of the hammer compared to the length of the anvil, the better the cat will hear low-intensity sounds. This measure is nearly tripled in the cat's ears compared to that of humans, explaining why we are deaf to many of the interesting sounds cats detect. Together the bones augment and transmit sound deep into the inner ear.

The middle ear also contains the eustachian tube, a short canal that connects from the middle ear to where the nose empties into the throat. This tube equalizes pressure on the inside of the ear with the atmospheric pressure on the outside. Mostly, the changes are so subtle they aren't noticed, but when sudden extremes occur people notice this phenomenon when their ears "pop" during a yawn or plane flights.

Vibrations intensified by the bones of the middle ear are transmitted by the stirrup to the chamber of the inner ear. This bony opening contains fluid filled structures called the semicircular canals, the utricle and the saccule. These organs dictate equilibrium, and define what is up and down for the cat (see BALANCE).

CAT FACTS

The utricle and saccule carry the vibration on to the tiny organ responsible for hearing. Called the cochlea, this fluid filled tube is coiled like a snail shell, and lined inside with a membrane called the cochlear duct that spirals its length. The "organ of Corti," a specialized area of this lining, is where hearing actually takes place.

The organ of Corti is covered with minute hair cells sensitive to sound vibrations. These vibrations are transmitted as signals to the brain via the auditory nerve, and there the sound is interpreted.

This complex system enables cats to hear high frequencies beyond the detection of human hearing. Young cats hear better than old cats, and in her prime Kitty can detect the high frequency squeaks of mice that are 50 to 60 kilohertz, while people can only hear as high as 20. However, cats can't hear sounds as low as people can. Cats are able to pinpoint sounds that are only three inches apart at a distance of three feet away (see also DEAFNESS).

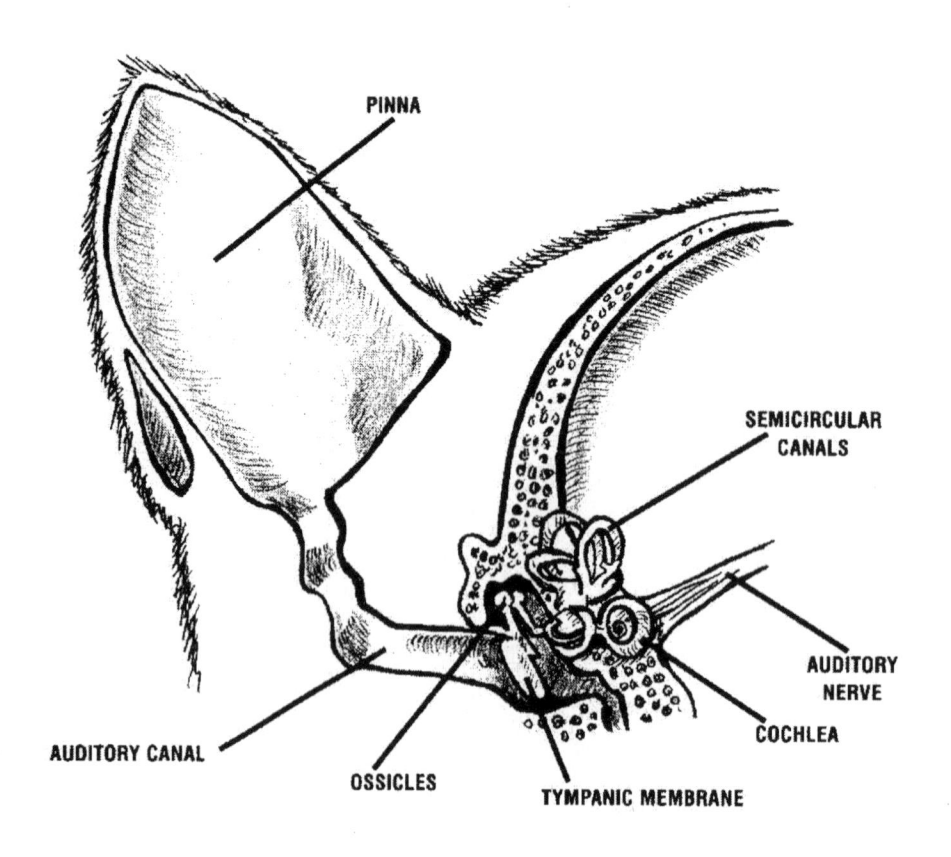

EATING

There is no doubt that eating is one of the cat's dearest pleasures. Every cat has individual eating styles and food preferences, but owners must cater to the cat's taste buds only after ensuring the diet is appropriate.

The cat that must hunt for his food typically catches small game like mice, rats, birds or rabbits, crouches over the kill, and swallows small prey headfirst, fur, feathers and all. Larger birds like blackbirds may be plucked first to remove obnoxious tail feathers. Rabbit-size prey are eaten more slowly.

The cat's teeth are designed for a carnivorous lifestyle. The dagger-shaped canine teeth are used to kill, while the tiny incisors across the front of the jaw pluck feathers or skin from the prey. Rather than chewing, cats shear off manageable portions of food with their molars, then swallow these chunks. The specialized teeth are located in the side of the cat's mouth, so Kitty typically tilts his head to the side while eating. Nibbling with incisors and licking with his rough tongue rasps off smaller pieces (see TEETH and TONGUE).

Because cats evolved in the desert, their bodies are designed to conserve water. Cats waste very little water, which means his urine becomes quite concentrated before he uses the litter box, and he may not "go" nearly so often as dogs do. Of course, this urine concentration can also predispose some cats to urinary problems.

In the wild, cats get a large percentage of liquid from the animals they eat. Indoor cats rely on water from a bowl or fountain. To drink, the cat uses his water-absorbent tongue curled into a spoon shape. But rather than scooping up a tongue-spoon-full of liquid, your cat defies gravity and "levitates" the liquid up into his mouth. Lapping liquid creates an efficient bio-mechanical process that forms a column of liquid the cat swallows before gravity sucks it back into the bowl. Larger cats lap more slowly than smaller cats to adjust for the size/process. They swallow about every four to five laps.

Cats appreciate routine, so establish a dinner habit early. Feed the cat in the same place and at the same time every day. A low-traffic area is best so the cat isn't disturbed during meals. A corner of the kitchen or the laundry room is often appropriate. Be sure the feeding station is some distance away from the litter box, or the cat may refuse to eat in that location.

Cats relish food that is body or room temperature. Food cooler than this may be refused, or even vomited when eaten cold, so always allow refrigerated foods to warm before serving. A few seconds in the microwave often helps, but don't overheat.

A bowl of clean water should be available at all times. Cats often take advantage of any water left out, and an owner's glass is fair game. Fountains are even better, with recirculating water that always tastes fresh. Some cats share food bowls with no problem, but dinner time is less stressful when everyone has his own place. When you have more than one cat, feed them in separate bowls some distance apart to help avoid confrontations.

Several bowl choices are available, from trendy designer crockery to paper plates. Consider what the cat likes before making your choice.

Cats dislike chasing a lightweight bowl over the floor. They are turned off by a dirty or smelly dish. Longhaired and flat-faced cats prefer shallow bowls that allow them to eat to the bottom without bending their whiskers or getting their face dirty.

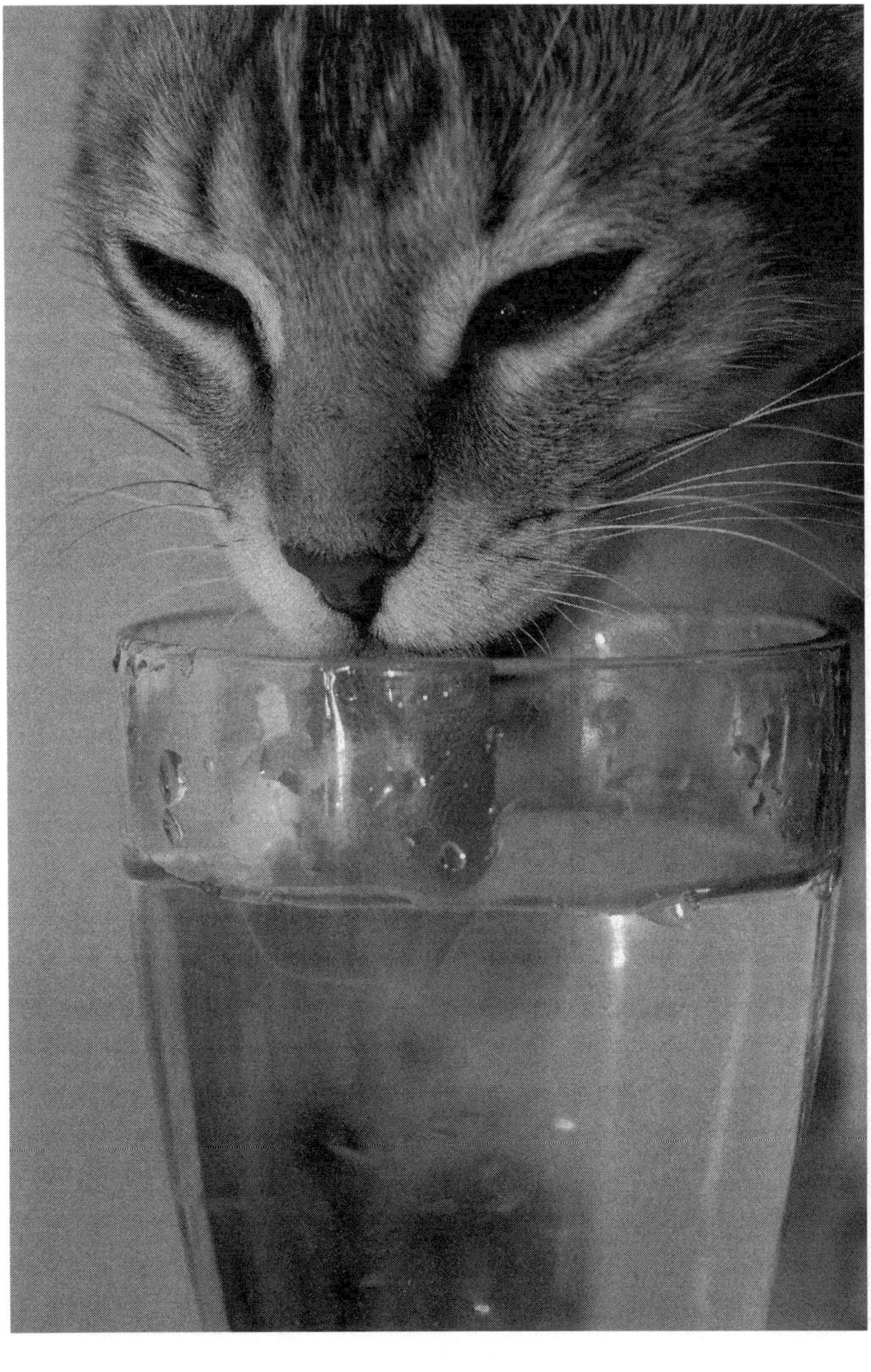

CAT FACTS

Plastic bowls tend to hold odors, are hardest to keep clean, and their light weight allows them to slide around the floor. Some cats may suffer skin problems like acne resulting from plastic food bowls (see ACNE).

United States-made ceramic bowls are better choices because of their solid weight and ease in cleaning. The glazes in ceramic bowls manufactured in some foreign countries, though, may contain lead.

Heavy non-breakable glass bowls are also good choices, and cats may drink more water from glass containers because they like the taste. But care must be taken if the glass is breakable. Stainless steel bowls are the choice of veterinary clinics because they are easily sterilized and are non-breakable. Some cats object to the taste of water or food offered in such containers, though. You may need to experiment before finding a safe, practical alternative for your cat.

By the age of six to seven weeks, kittens should be completely weaned and eating an appropriate commercial kitten ration. Offer the food three times a day. Moisten dry foods to soften the kibble and make it easier for a youngster to eat. Use three parts dry food to one part water (not milk) to soften the food.

The kitten's tummy is too small to allow him to eat the amount needed for proper nutrition all at one time. Instead, kittens tend to eat many small meals, perhaps only three or four bites at time, leave and then return later to nibble again. Give the kitten about an hour to eat his fill, then throw out the uneaten portion. Wet food spoils if left out longer, but dry diets may be fed free choice throughout the day without risk of spoilage.

Soft diets may be fed for the cat's lifetime. Kittens are able to eat plain dry food by about three months of age. Once the kitten is six months old, his meals can be reduced to twice a day. He should continue to eat kitten ration, though, as long as he continues to grow, until at least a year old.

After one year of age, the cat should be fed an adult maintenance ration. Never change the diet abruptly, because this can cause upset stomachs and result in diarrhea. Instead, introduce the new food over a week's period by mixing it with the familiar food. Gradually increase the proportion of new food while reducing the amount of old ration until the cat is eating only the new diet.

The amount of food the cat needs depends on the cat and the individual food. Outdoor cats and those that are more active require more food than indoor couch potato felines. Cats need to eat less of nutrient dense super premium foods than other category diets. But an average cat that weighs seven to nine pounds and has normal activity will require about six to eight ounces of canned food, or about two to three ounces (one half to one eight-ounce measuring cup) of dry food each day.

Kitty's appetite may vary some from day to day, but a loss of appetite over several days may indicate illness so see your veterinarian. Commercial cat food products offer feeding suggestions on the packaging as a guideline only; you may wish to consult with your veterinarian as well. Holistic veterinarians recommend home prepared foods and sometimes raw diets, and can recommend appropriate formulations for your specific cat's needs.

Adult cats tend to be "occasional" feeders. They like to come and go from the food bowl, and nibble rather than eat an entire meal all at one time. For this reason, cats should have access to their food for several hours at a time. Canned food, however, tends to spoil if left out for long periods, and should be meal fed two to three times a day (see also FOOD and NUTRITION).

ECLAMPSIA

SYMPTOMS: Restlessness; pacing; ignoring kittens; stiff-legged movements; incoordination; rapid breathing; elevated fever; grimacing expression; pale lips and gums; drooling; collapse with muscle spasms.
HOME CARE: EMERGENCY! SEE VETERINARIAN IMMEDIATELY!
VET CARE: Intravenous calcium treatment; therapy to counteract heatstroke
PREVENTION: Don't breed the cat

ECLAMPSIA (MILK FEVER)

Also called milk fever, this condition is caused by a low calcium level. Much more common in dogs than in cats, eclampsia is associated with the birth of a large litter of kittens that deplete the queen's calcium stores from nursing.

The mother cat will at first simply appear restless and anxious. She leaves her kittens and paces, breathing rapidly, with a stiff-legged uncoordinated gait. Her temperature may sore as high as 106 degrees (see TEMPERATURE). The condition causes facial muscles to tighten which may expose her teeth, and her gums and lips will appear pale. Finally she collapses, exhibits muscle spasms and drools. Left untreated, eclampsia can be fatal within a few hours. This is an emergency that must be immediately addressed by a veterinarian.

The antidote is an intravenous organic calcium solution, such as calcium gluconate. Given in time, treatment results in a rapid, dramatic improvement within 15 minutes of administration. When the cat's temperature exceeds 104 degrees, Kitty should also be treated for heatstroke (see HYPERTHERMIA).

Kittens should be bottle-fed and not allowed to nurse from the stricken queen for at least 24 hours. Your veterinarian can best advise you whether it's safe for Mom to return to nursing at all. Cats afflicted once with eclampsia are at higher risk for a recurrence, and such cats may benefit from calcium supplements during subsequent pregnancies.

ELECTRICAL SHOCK

SYMPTOMS: Mouth burns; difficulty breathing; convulsions; loss of consciousness; shock

FIRST AID: Shut off current; artificial resuscitation; get veterinary help immediately; nutritional support during convalescence

VET CARE: Oxygen therapy; drugs to rid fluid from lungs; surgical removal of burned tissue; antibiotics; possible placement of feeding tube.

PREVENTION: Supervise cats and kittens around electrical cords

ELECTRICAL SHOCK Injury and death from high voltage electricity may be caused by lightning, contact with fallen electrical cables, or faulty circuits. Most often, electrical shock affects kittens when they chew through an electric cord. The current may cause muscle contractions that make Kitty involuntarily bite down even harder and prevent the cat from releasing it.

Should you find your cat in contact with an electrical wire, shut off the current and disconnect the plug before attempting to touch the cat or you may be shocked as well. If the cat has stopped breathing, begin rescue breathing (see ARTIFICIAL RESPIRATION).

Injury varies depending on the degree of the voltage and the pathway taken by the current. Death is usually instantaneous if lightening is involved, but this more typically affects farm animals than cats. The exception might be a tree hit by lightning in which a cat is perched.

The most common sign of electrocution is burns in the mouth area (see BURNS), and water in the lungs often develops within 12 hours after the incident. This pulmonary edema is caused by the current damaging the tiny capillaries in the lungs, which then leak fluid and make it difficult to breathe.

The current passing through the heart can also cause an irregular beat and circulatory collapse, and the involvement of the central nervous system may affect breathing and other bodily functions. Without treatment, the pet may fall into a coma, suffer convulsions, and finally death; those who survive may have permanent nerve damage. Cats may go into shock from the trauma, and should be treated accordingly (see SHOCK).

Treating the burns may require surgical removal of damaged tissue, antibiotics, and possibly use of a feeding tube passed through the nose to bypass the damaged oral cavity. Heartbeat irregularities are usually addressed with drugs to stabilize the rhythm, and with fluid therapy to prevent circulation problems. The edema may be treated with diuretic drugs like furosemide that help the body get rid of the excess water, along with bronchodilating drugs and oxygen therapy that help the cat breathe. Some cats may need mechanical help breathing until their lungs can compensate. Any cat suffering electrical shock should be seen by a veterinarian as soon as possible.

Electrical shock is better prevented than treated after the fact. Kitty-proof your home particularly when young cats are present. Unplug appliance that aren't in use, tape down cords to keep them from being tempting playthings, and watch your cats at all times when they have access to electrical cords.

ELIZABETHAN COLLAR

The Elizabethan collar is a practical tool used to prevent the cat from further injuring herself by licking or biting healing wounds, suture lines, itchy skin, or other problem areas. Some cats refuse to eat or drink while wearing the collar; if that's the case, remove it for dining. Cats aren't able to navigate as well wearing the collar, and should not be allowed outdoors wearing one.

The collar is named for the elaborate wide stand-up dress collars (usually ruffled) used during the Elizabethan period. The stiff material, which typically is plastic or cardboard, fits snugly around the cat's neck and extends outward approximately one foot in a cone shape. Pet supply stores and veterinarians offer the collars in various sizes. A soft collar restraint more similar to a human cervical collar may be more acceptable and work equally well for your cat.

Owners can also make the collars themselves using stiff cardboard. Cut out a 12 inch circle of cardboard, and at the center cut an opening the size of your cat's neck (plus one inch or so). Measure the cat's collar to get the right length. Remove a pie-shaped slice from one side of the circle about 1/4th of the diameter. Use tape around the inside opening to buffer the edges that will fit about the cat's neck, and punch a small hole in this inside border in three places to accept a string. Place the collar around Kitty's neck, and tape the cut sides together to form the cone. Use the three strings to secure the Elizabethan collar to Kitty's existing collar.

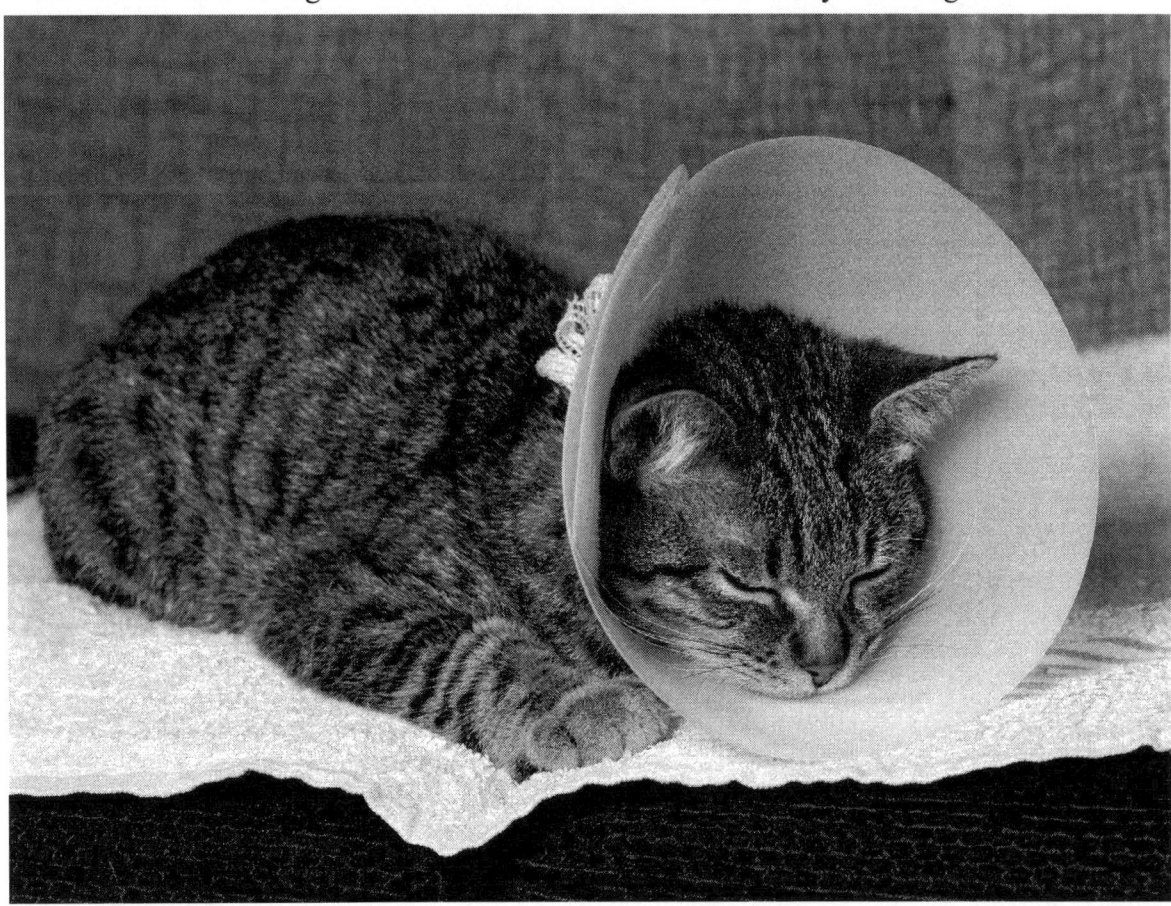

ENDOSCOPE The term endoscopy means "looking within," and the technique is another noninvasive way to examine the internal structures of a pet's body. The respiratory, digestive, and urinary tracts, as well as some areas of the abdomen or chest, can be viewed with an endoscope. Before the method became available, the stomach and intestines were most commonly examined by having the pet swallow a contrast medium, like barium, and then taking pictures with radiographs (see X-RAY). Exploratory surgery was often the only way to gain a true diagnosis.

Today, the fiberoptic endoscope and the video chip endoscope produce images of the internal body structures on a viewing screen, via a tiny incision. The fiberoptic endoscope is the older of the two, and can transmit light (including lasers) through optical fibers. The newer video chip cameras are less fragile, produce better images, and tend to be more versatile. In either case the veterinarian inserts the long tube of the endoscope into the appropriate part of the body and literally "sees" what's going on. This tool also can be used to take tissue samples and perform biopsies from deep inside the body.

In addition, the endoscope can be used to find and retrieve foreign objects such as inhaled grass seeds or swallowed objects that have lodged in the respiratory or digestive tract (see SWALLOWED OBJECTS).

ENTERITIS Enteritis refers to an inflammation of the stomach and small intestine, and can be a sign of several diseases. The cat with enteritis may suffer a simple loss of appetite, to intermittent vomiting and/or watery diarrhea (see DIARRHEA and VOMITING).

Inflammation of the gastrointestinal tract can result from a variety of things. Most often, tummy upset occurs when Kitty eats something he shouldn't. Cats that gorge themselves and overeat commonly suffer from vomiting; this can be controlled by offering feline gluttons smaller portions.

ENTERITIS

SYMPTOMS: Loss of appetite; vomiting; watery diarrhea
HOME CARE: Withhold food and only offer ice cubes to lick for 12 to 24 hours to rest the system
VET CARE: Fluid therapy; diagnostic tests to determine cause; treatment specific to that cause.
PREVENTION: Feed smaller portions; cut out table food; change diets gradually

Although cats are considered fastidious creatures, some are not above swiping a slice of bacon from their owner's plate or raiding the garbage. Any food item unfamiliar to the cat, even a change in commercial diet, may cause enteritis. Cats that hunt and eat their prey are also prone to digestive upset. Acute signs usually resolve simply by resting the gastrointestinal tract and treating the symptoms. When the problem is dietary in origin, in most instances withholding food for 12 to 24 hours may be all that's required. An antidiarrheal medication prescribed by the veterinarian may be given to control diarrhea.

Cats with chronic disease won't respond to symptomatic therapy, and the veterinarian must play detective to discover what's causing the problem so that specific treatment can begin. Eating non-edible objects can be life-threatening, and viruses may also result in enteritis. Parasites are a common cause of tummy upset. Supportive treatment, such as fluid therapy for a cat dehydrated by diarrhea, may also be required.

Should you see your cat swallow something he shouldn't, call your veterinarian immediately. Depending on the object, you may be asked to simply monitor the litter box for a day or two to see that the object passes without further incident. Other times, your cat may need to be seen immediately. And anytime you see signs of distress following ingestion of foreign material, get your cat veterinary help.

Most cases of enteritis are preventable. Protect your cat with vaccinations against viral illnesses, and prevent exposure to intestinal parasites. Keep him from hunting and eating vermin and from swiping unauthorized snacks from your plate or the trash. Feed feline gluttons in smaller portions several times a day to slow down their gulping (see also FELINE PANLEUKOPENIA, GIARDIA, HOOKWORMS and SWALLOWED OBJECTS).

EOSINOPHILIC GRANULOMA COMPLEX

Sometimes called "lick granulomas," eosinophilic granulomas are skin diseases that result in three kinds of skin sores. Eosinophilic plaque affects young to middle aged cats most often, and is thought to be associated with allergy. It's an extremely itchy area of elevated skin that's bright red and oozing. It can appear anywhere on the body, but usually is located on the inside of the cat's thighs or on the abdomen. Diagnosis is made by skin biopsy, and allergy treatment often cures the problem (see ALLERGY).

Eosinophilic granulomas are also believed to be allergy related, and most commonly affect kittens and cats less than a year old. They are yellow to yellow-pink raised sores that form straight lines, and usually are found on the back of both hind legs. Like the plaques, eosinophilic granulomas are diagnosed by biopsy, and usually go away when the allergy is treated.

The rodent ulcer (also called indolent ulcer) is a non-itchy, non-painful red-to-brown thickened, glistening area usually found on the cat's upper lip. Female cats are affected three times more often than male cats. Because rodent ulcers may evolve into cancer, aggressive therapy is indicated. Cortisone given either orally or by injection is administered until the ulcer disappears. Ulcers that have become cancerous should be addressed with appropriate therapies (see CANCER).

EPILEPSY

Epilepsy is a generic term used to describe a condition characterized by recurrent seizures. Also called convulsions or "fits," seizures result from the misfiring of electrical impulses inside the brain.

The neurons of the brain normally discharge electrical impulses as "messengers" that travel the highways of the nervous system to direct bodily functions. When neurons misfire, they generate a kind of power-surge that literally blows out the breakers of normal processes, so the brain temporarily shuts down; the result is seizures.

EPILEPSY

SYMPTOMS: Seizures; falling; involuntary jerky or padding motions; grinding teeth; loss of bladder and bowel control
FIRST AID: Keep cat cool; reduce stimulation; see veterinarian for diagnosis
HOLISTIC HELP: Acupuncture
VET CARE: Sometimes medication to control episodes
PREVENTION: None

Seizures are caused by injury to the brain, toxicity, or metabolic disease. In cats, most seizures result from poisoning. Head trauma from being hit by a car may also cause seizures, with the onset often delayed until several weeks after the injury. Severe kidney or liver disease, tumors, or organic or infectious disease like feline leukemia or feline infectious peritonitis may cause seizures. There is evidence that some food allergies may be the culprit in certain instances. When they happen for the first time in a pet older than six years old, tumors often are the cause. If the cause can be identified and successfully treated, seizures are usually eliminated.

Unfortunately, often the condition is considered idiopathic, which means the cause cannot be determined. Such cats may have been born with a brain disorder that causes convulsions. Idiopathic epilepsy tends to appear at age six months to three years old, while cats with acquired disease are more likely to be affected for the first time later in life.

The most common seizure activity seen in cats is the major motor seizure, also called the grand mal. This type of convulsion affects the entire body. A partial motor seizure affects only specific groups of muscles; for instance, a leg may twitch or one side of the cat's face may spasm. Psychomotor seizures affect behavior; the cat may suddenly become aggressive or fearful, or perhaps attack invisible objects or even himself (see HYPERESTHESIA SYNDROME).

Typically, there is an altered period of behavior that occurs immediately prior to the seizure, called the aura. Cat owners may be alerted by the cat acting disoriented or staring into space. During the first ten to 30 seconds of the convulsion itself, the cat loses consciousness and falls over, the legs extend rigidly, and breathing stops. This rigid phase is followed by the agitated phase in which Kitty exhibits jerky running or paddling leg movements, chews and grinds his teeth, and drools. Cats often lose control of their bowels or urinate, their eyes dilate, and the fur stands on end.

Do not interfere with your cat during a seizure. The muscle contractions are involuntary, and you may be severely bitten while the cat remains unaware you are even there. Move the cat only when he is in danger of falling or injuring himself further, then stand back. Turn on the air conditioner or a fan to help keep the area cool. A seizure burns so many calories, it can overheat your cat. Outside noises or sights can prolong the seizure or prompt a new one, so avoid talking or touching your cat. Turn off the lights and any music, and cover with a sheet to help shut out external stimulations. Most episodes last ten seconds to three minutes. Very young kittens may suffer seizures as a result of low blood sugar if they don't eat enough, so giving your kitten a dribble of honey or Karo syrup may be helpful, after the seizure ends. When the seizure stops, take Kitty to the veterinarian.

Recovery varies. Some cats act normal within a few seconds or minutes. Others suffer from restlessness or lethargy following seizures, and may act confused or even blind for hours.

Seizures lasting longer than five minutes are dangerous. Wrap the cat in a towel or blanket and get Kitty to your vet's emergency room immediately. Status epilepticus is the name given to rapidly recurring convulsions without recovery in between, or of prolonged, ongoing seizure activity. Convulsions burn many calories, which can cause body temperature to rise and blood sugar levels to drop. Either of these conditions can stimulate seizures to continue. Uncontrolled ongoing seizures may cause severe metabolic abnormalities, irreversible brain injury, and even death. Typically, a drug is administered intravenously to bring the cat out of ongoing convulsions.

A single seizure does not usually warrant anticonvulsant medication, and cats that suffer infrequent seizures may not require medication at all. Epilepsy cannot be cured; treatment is aimed at reducing the frequency, shortening the duration, and/or reducing the severity of seizures, with a minimum of side effects. Realistically, limiting episodes to one or two seizures per month is considered a success.

Some of the same human medications for controlling seizures are also used in veterinary medicine. Primidone doesn't seem to help cats, but they benefit from Phenobarbital or oral Valium. Dilantin, which works well in people, is metabolized too rapidly in dogs to be particularly helpful, and it is toxic to cats.

Pets that suffer from psychomotor seizures have been helped with medications that control obsessive/compulsive disorders. Several universities, including Ohio State and Texas A & M, have researched potassium bromide (an easily metabolized salt) alone or in combination with other anticonvulsants like Tranxene or Phenobarbital.

Acupuncture has offered benefits to some epileptic cats. Ask your holistic veterinarian if acupuncture might be an option for your cat.

Regulation of the medication requires veterinary supervision and strict owner compliance to be successful. Missing a dose can actually cause a seizure. Most patients improve with therapy, but about 20 to 30 percent don't respond well to drugs. Generally, cats with idiopathic epilepsy can, with treatment, enjoy a quality life.

EUTHANASIA

As it applies to veterinary medicine, euthanasia is the act of causing merciful death when the cat is ill, injured, and/or suffering with no reasonable hope of recovery. Choosing euthanasia—putting your cat "to sleep"—is not an easy decision, and should be made with the understanding and guidance of a compassionate veterinarian.

When we take a cat into our hearts, we must inevitably face the loss of that pet. That's the deal we make when we love and care for these unique creatures. Elderly cats can continue to enjoy a quality life with special care, and even chronically ill or injured felines benefit from modern veterinary medicine, but eventually age takes its toll.

As your cat's best friend, you often will know when a longer life isn't necessarily a better life. If you aren't sure, that's normal, too, and you should ask your veterinarian to help you decide when awakening is no longer a feline delight; when pain outstrips pleasure; and when Kitty yearns for the next life, beyond your lap. When that time comes, you have it in your power to grant your cat the greatest gift of all, a merciful death.

Before the time comes, ask your veterinarian to explain the usual procedure so you're prepared. Private rooms are generally provided so that you have time alone with your cat before, during, and after the euthanasia. Usually a catheter is placed in the vein as a first step, to make it easier to administer the euthanasia solution when the time comes.

Chronically ill cats may already have an IV catheter in place. Sometimes the cat will be sedated first, and that makes her very sleepy. You may prefer to forgo the sedation so that she remains alert up to the end, and you are better able to interact with the friend you know and love during your goodbyes.

The veterinarian will return after you've had time to visit. As the drug takes effect, it relaxes the cat and she'll sometimes involuntarily urinate, so if you want to hold her on your lap, cuddle her in a towel. If she's not been sedated before, she may receive that injection now so she's relaxed and has a smoother transition.

Then a slow IV injection of the euthanasia solution, an overdose of a barbiturate anesthetic-type drug, is administered. It can be very quick-acting. Usually the cat will die within only a minute or two, and the veterinarian will listen for a heartbeat to confirm that she's gone. There may be a few involuntary muscle spasms, or last-minute breaths, but the cat is already gone at that point.

Most people wish to spend some time alone with their pet afterward. Don't hesitate to ask for this consideration if it's not offered. Her final moments are difficult for your veterinarian and staff as well as you; many practitioners offer counseling and emotional support (see GERIACTRIC CAT and GRIEF).

EYES Two eyes grace the front of the cat's face and provide Kitty not only with her sense of sight, but play an important role in silent feline communication. These highly specialized organs are quite similar to human eyes, but are designed with the night-hunter in mind. Their shape and function have evolved to make the most use of light, along with the ability to detect the slightest movement. Vision brings the cat a finely tuned understanding of spatial relationships, and that coupled with superb motor skills—as well as hearing and scent sense—make Kitty an exceptional hunter (see HUNTING BEHAVIOR).

The eye is nothing so much as a camera that records images carried by light to the brain, which translates the images into meaning. The eyeball is cushioned in fat and situated deep inside a bony socket in the skull. The eyelids support the front of the eye, and ride over the surface of the eyeball on a thin layer of tears. Cats also have a third eyelid, called the nictitating membrane or haw, that normally is invisible and originates at the inside corner of the eye. This membrane lubricates and protects the eye by sliding across and wiping the surface clean.

The clear front surface of the cat's eye is called the cornea. The outer edge is the sclera, the "white of the eye" that's more apparent in people than cats. A thin layer of tissue called the conjunctiva covers the sclera, the inner eyelid, and the sides of the nictitating membrane. Tears produced in glands found in these structures not only lubricate and clean the eye, they contain immune substances that help fight bacterial infection. Directly behind the cornea is the anterior chamber filled with aqueous fluid.

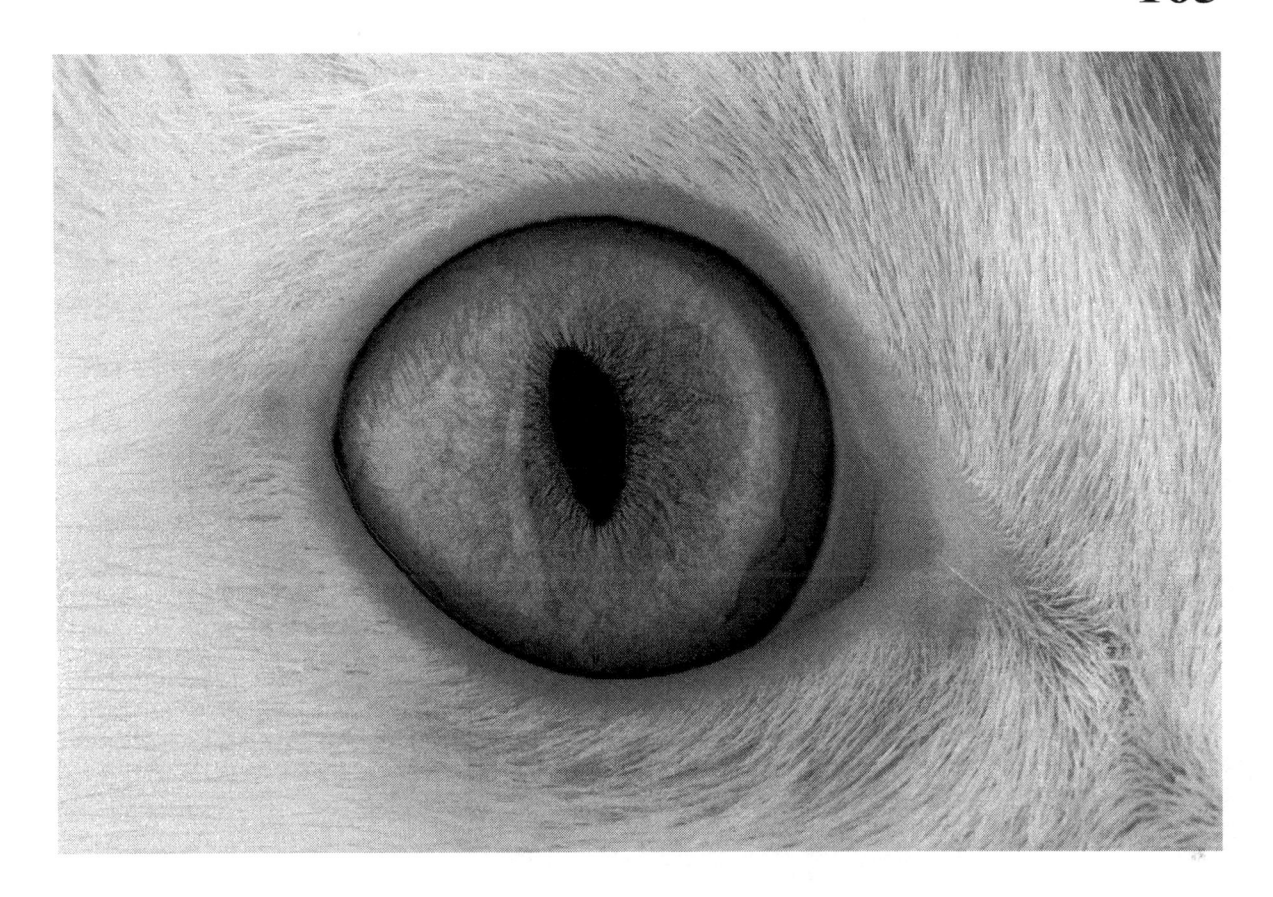

At the center of the eye is a dark opening, called the pupil, through which light passes. The pupil is surrounded by the beautiful colored portion of the cat's eye, called the iris. The iris is a figure-eight muscle that opens and closes the pupil in response to light to regulate the amount that passes into the eye. In very low light, the pupil is opened wide in a circle to capture as much light as possible, while in very high light the iris closes the pupil to a vertical slit. The cat's eyelids may further reduce the amount of light by squinting; this also helps to focus images for the cat.

166
CAT FACTS

PUPIL DILATING

IRIS CONTRACTING

RETINA

CONJUNCTIVA

UPPER EYELID

TAPETUM LUCIDUM

CORNEA

ANTERIOR CHAMBER

LENS

OPTIC NERVE

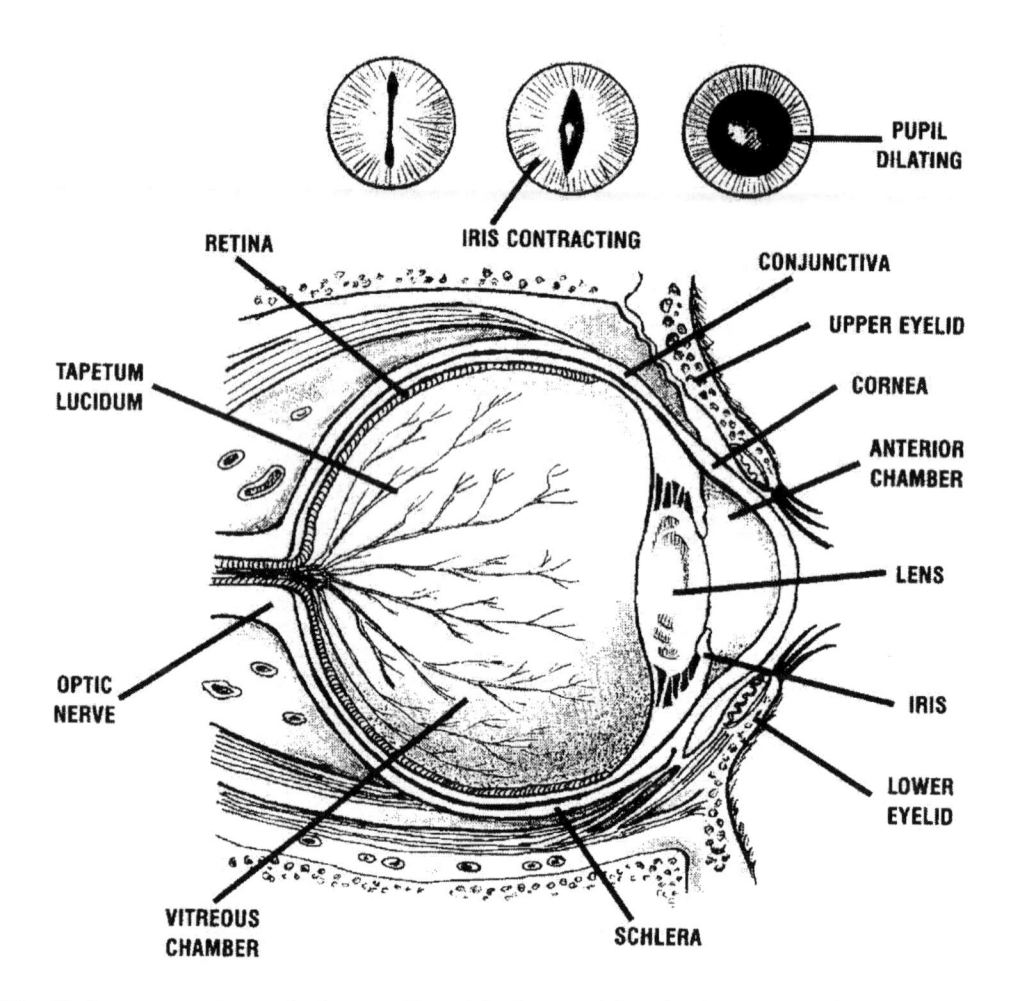

IRIS

LOWER EYELID

VITREOUS CHAMBER

SCHLERA

    The light passes through the pupil and is focused by the lens onto the retina at the back of the eye, like a movie projector shining an image onto a screen. The area between the lens and retina contains gel-like substance called vitreous which helps hold the retina in place. Millions of light-receptor cells on the retina called rods and cones gather the information. Other cells send signals through the optic nerve to the brain's visual center, where the impulses are translated into meaningful images.

Rods allow Kitty to see shades of white, black and gray, while cones provide color sense. Although the cat does have the ability to detect differences between certain reds, greens, blues and yellows, it's uncertain how important colors are to cats. Perhaps Kitty sees color, but does he care? We don't know.

Cats require only 1/6th the illumination level and use twice as much available light as people because their rod-to-cone ratio is much higher than ours. They also benefit from a layer of highly reflective cells, called the tapetum lucidum located behind the retina. The tapetum lucidum captures and reflects back any light the eye captures, in effecting making the light do double duty. It's this eerie reflection you see at night when light shines in your cat's eyes.

Proportionally, the cat has the largest eyes of any carnivore; a similar eye-to-face ratio in people would make our eyes eight inches across. By facing forward, the cat's field of vision

CAT FACTS

overlaps and gives her three-dimensional sight, which is critical when judging distance. This provides Kitty with 130 degrees of binocular vision, compared to our own 120 degrees. In addition, cats have 155 degrees of peripheral vision (compared to humans' 90 degrees), and are experts at detecting motion from the corners of their eyes.

Near vision isn't as sharp as ours, because the muscles that focus the lens are rather weak. Kitty must focus long and hard on stationary objects, near or far. Cats typically rely on movement to locate and identify objects.

The eye is prone to conditions which can be extremely painful to the cat and require immediate veterinary attention. Signs of a painful eye include squinting, tearing, avoiding light, and tenderness to touch. A visible nictitating membrane is often a sign of pain. Flat faced breeds of cat that have more prominent eyes like the Persian may require routine cleaning of their eyes (see GROOMING). Signs of injury and/or disease may include any kind of eye discharge, redness, crusting, cloudiness to the eye, or a hard or soft eye. (See also BLINDNESS, CATARACT, GLAUCOMA and UVEITIS)

169

CAT FACTS

FALLING see BALANCE and HIGH-RISE SYNDROME.

FALSE PREGNANCY This is exactly what it sounds like; the cat shows some of the signs of pregnancy when in fact there are no kittens.

False pregnancy occurs when ovulation takes place but the eggs that are released are not fertilized. Following ovulation, hormones like progesterone prepare the cat's body for nurturing kittens. This may result in Kitty eating more and gaining weight, or even prompt nesting behavior. Rarely, cats suffering a false pregnancy produce milk.

Treatment is not necessary for this condition, which will resolve by itself within about forty days following the heat cycle. However, cats are prone to repeated false pregnancies. When kittens are not desired, the cat should be spayed to prevent future occurrences. (See also SPAY and REPRODUCTION)

FATTY LIVER DISEASE see FELINE HEPATIC LIPIDOSIS

FEAR Our feline friends come by the term "scaredy cat" honestly. Cats are creatures of habit that dislike change, and the unknown can be frightening to them. A new house, new pet, or new person in your life may seem threatening, and such cats typically run away and hide if they can. But when escape isn't possible and the cat feels cornered, a fearful cat can become hostile when he feels he must defend himself (see AGGRESSION). Your cat communicates his fear using hisses, fluffed fur and/or flattened ears (see COMMUNICATION).

Fear is a strong emotional response associated with the close proximity of another object, individual or social situation that threatens the animal. This common emotion becomes abnormal or inappropriate only within certain contexts. For example, it's perfectly reasonable to fear water if you can't swim and fall out of the boat—but it's unreasonable to fear a glass of water.

Anxiety is the fearful anticipation of a future event, and this tends to be an ongoing but less severe response that can turn into full-blown fear. Phobias result, on the other hand, in an immediate, extreme and severely abnormal response, like a panic attack or catatonia. Some experts believe that one phobic experience "primes" the individual to fear future events. Just the memory of the first event is enough to trigger subsequent attacks.

Properly socialized cats tend to be more confident when faced with new experiences, and they are less likely to suffer abnormal anxiety or fearful behavior later in life. Pets frightened by something during this impressionable period, though, may forever after react with anxiety when faced with a similar situation. For instance, a kitten traumatized by a small child is likely to be fearful as an adult when exposed to any other toddler or male. Pets either try to escape the scary situation and run away, or when that's not possible, they may become defensively aggressive to drive off the perceived threat.

Punishing pets for fearful behavior doesn't help. More likely, punishment makes the fearful behavior worse or escalates the fear into aggression toward the owner.

Little is known about the mechanics of how fear works, but researchers have determined that a functioning amygdala is required to learn fear, and a functioning forebrain is required to unlearn fear. The amygdala is a tiny portion of the brain considered the "primitive brain." It deals with emotions and the fight-or-flight response. The forebrain is the seat of personality, and it also deals with logic. Many human fear disorders seem to result from the inability to inhibit a fear response. It's theorized that fear arises in part from the overreaction of the amygdala, or the failure of the amygdala to switch off once the threat is gone.

The best way to prevent fear in cats is to build confidence at an early age by exposing them to novel experiences (see KITTEN SOCIALIZATION). Mature cats need to be introduced slowly to new experiences, so plan ahead before throwing something new in the cat's face. For older cats, try to identify the cause of the fear before addressing the problem.

Soothing music seems to calm frightened cats, particularly classical pieces and harp music. Harp music has been used in human medicine particularly in hospice situations, to alleviate pain and distress. Music, especially from the harp, lowers heart rate and blood pressure, slows respiration, increases endorphin levels (natural pain control factors produced in the brain), and possibly increases longevity.

CAT FACTS

Special chemicals called pheromones are secreted by the cats' cheek glands and can soothe feline fear and anxiety. Cats rub objects to make themselves feel comfortable by spreading this calming scent. Certain parts of these pheromones (an analogue of the F-3 fraction) are used in a spray product called Comfort Zone with Feliway, and help to prevent urine spraying and claw marking behavior by signaling the environment is safe. The F-4 fraction, though, has proven to be even better for calming aggression or fractious behavior between cats and unknown individuals. It is commercially available in a spray product called Felifriend (see MARKING).

Environmental enrichment also helps. Offer Kitty some escape routes, like elevated perches or a cat bag on a dresser. Cats feel more secure when they have an unobstructed view. And playing with the cat is a great confidence-builder. Some of the best toys are fishing-pole styles. Nothing makes Kitty forget her fears like attacking—and capturing!—that fierce toy mouse on the end of the string.

An extremely fearful cat, particularly one that becomes aggressive, may need more help that you can offer. Clomicalm (clomipramine, Novartis Animal Health) prevents the metabolism of serotonin, a natural hormone produced by the brain that affects behavior. It has not yet been approved for use in cats but has been safely used off-label to treat feline anxiety. The pet version of Prozac ™ has been released by Eli Lilly under the brand name Reconcile™. The drug fluoxetine has been used in many animal behavior issues (see SOILING, SEPARATION ANXIETY, AGGRESSION and HYPERESTHESIA SYNDROME). Consult a professional animal behaviorist for advice (see APPENDIX B, VETERINARY RESOURCES).

FEEDING see **EATING and NUTRITION**.

FELINE AIDS see **FELINE IMMUNODEFICIENCY VIRUS**.

FELINE CALICIVIRUS (FCV) see **UPPER RESPIRATORY INFECTIONS**.

FELINE ENTERIC CORONAVIRUS see **FELINE INFECTIOUS PERITONITIS**.

FELINE HEPATIC LIPIDOSIS (FHL) Feline Hepatic Lipidosis (FHL), commonly called Fatty Liver Disease, is the most common liver ailment affecting cats. The condition refers to the accumulation of fat cells within the liver which interferes with normal function.

Although cats of all breeds and any age are at risk, those most often afflicted with FHL are middle aged obese felines. The major trigger of the condition is when the cat stops eating (see ANOREXIA).

An adult cat should not go without eating for more than 48 hours without consulting a veterinarian. Monitor the amount your cat eats as well; cats that drastically reduce their caloric intact over several weeks also run the risk of developing FHL.

The reason why cats develop FHL is not known, but researchers speculate it may have something to do with the cat's unique metabolism as a meat eater. Fasting trigger's the cat's body to find new energy sources normally supplied by food; fat stores are moved into the liver, and become trapped. A microscopic examination of tissue from the liver reveals cells throughout the liver packed with fat globules. Once fat invades these cells, the liver can't work properly. That makes Kitty feel sicker and sicker, so she continues to refuse food, creating a vicious cycle which if left untreated will result in death.

The treatment of choice for FHL is simply getting the cat to eat. In such cases, tempting the cat with special treats rarely works. An extremely aggressive feeding program that forces the cat to eat offers the best hope of success, and veterinarians report up to a 90 percent recovery rate when a feeding tube is used.

A gastrostomy tube is surgically placed in the stomach through the body wall. The tube extends about eight inches outside the cat's side, and is kept clean with a bandage covering. Another option is the smaller nasogastric tube that runs through the nose into the stomach, or an esophagostomy tube may be placed down the cat's throat through the esophagus and into the stomach. The look of the apparatus typically bothers owners more than their pets; cats tolerate feeding tubes quite well.

FELINE HEPATIC LIPIDOSIS

SYMPTOMS: Anorexia in obese cat
HOME CARE: EMERGENCY! SEE VETERINARIAN IMMEDIATELY! Nutritional support once diagnosed and stabilized by veterinarian.
VET CARE: Supportive care; placement of feeding tube; force feeding
PREVENTION: Keep cats trim; don't allow obesity to develop

A high calorie soft food is given to the cat through the tube three to four times a day. Calorie dense prescription formulas are available, but even good quality kitten rations are appropriate; canned food forms are easier to use. Mix the food in the blender with water to the proper consistency, and warm in the microwave to about 100 degrees to prevent upsetting tummies.

Liver disease typically requires other supportive care as well. Fluid therapy helps replace lost nutrients and liquids, and antibiotics may be administered to help fight infection. Special medication may be necessary to help reduce toxins the liver is unable to handle. Cats with liver disease typically have trouble moving food from their stomach into the intestinal tract where it can be processed, and often suffer from vomiting; medication addresses these problems.

Once stabilized, the cat can go home with the owner continuing to feed Kitty through the tube as instructed by the veterinarian. The recovery time depends on how far the disease had progressed. A majority of cats feel better soon after tube feeding begins, but it can take anywhere from two to 18 weeks before the cat begins eating again on her own; most begin eating within the first month. Aside from the tube, these cats live an otherwise normal life during their convalescence.

The best way to prevent this devastating condition is to keep your cats trim to reduce the risk of FHL. To slim down tubby tabbies, always consult with your veterinarian before implementing a safe, gradual weight loss program (see OBESITY and LIVER DISEASE).

FELINE IMMUNODEFICIENCY VIRUS (FIV)

Sometimes referred to as feline Aidsis a lentivirus similar to simian and human HIV, and was first identified in 1986. Just like in monkeys and people, the virus suppresses the immune system and makes the cat susceptible to other kinds of illnesses. However, people cannot be infected with the cat virus, and cats cannot be infected with the human virus; although similar, they are species specific.

FIV is found in both domestic and wild feline populations throughout the world. Unlike some other feline viruses, FIV is relatively difficult to catch. Mutual grooming, shared food bowls and litter boxes, or sexual contact are considered unlikely methods of infection, and the virus is not transmitted from the mother cat to kittens through close contact.

The Banfield Pet Hospital annual 2014 State of Pet Health showed a 48 percent increase in the prevalence of FIV. Approximately one in every 300 cats seen in Banfield hospitals in 2013 was infected with FIV. With the possibility of this virus continuing to rise, it's important to know as much as possible about FIV and how to protect and care for your cats.

The virus is found in the blood, saliva, and cerebrospinal fluid of infected cats. It is a fragile virus outside of the cat's body that does not survive in the environment, and only rarely is transmitted through close contact. Unborn kittens may be become infected if the mother is infected during pregnancy.

To become infected, a cat must be nearly "injected" with the virus, and this is primarily accomplished through cat bites that transmit infective saliva. For that reason, intact male cats allowed to roam and fight tend to be at highest risk for the disease.

Shortly after infection, the cat's white blood cell count begins to decline and the immune system becomes progressively impaired over time. However, many FIV-infected cats remain asymptomatic for many years. Most cats are diagnosed at age five years or older.

Cats positive for feline leukemia virus (FeLV) are up to twice as likely to also suffer from FIV. The reported incidence of FIV varies, but is thought to be one to three percent of the pet cat population.

Cats infected with FIV may take up to 60 days before they test positive, so to be sure, even if the first test is negative, a second test should be run 60 days later to confirm the cat's negative status.

Cats are diagnosed using an ELISA (enzyme-linked immunosorbent assay) test, which evaluates a blood sample to detect the presence of antibodies to the virus (not the virus itself). When the test is positive, a follow up test (PCR test) can help tell the difference between a truly infected cat, and one that has been vaccinated against FIV.

FIV

SYMPTOMS: Nonspecific signs including fever that comes and goes; swollen lymph nodes; weight loss; dehydration; trouble breathing; loss of appetite; vomiting; claw or mouth sores; chronic skin infections
HOME CARE: Supportive care; good nutrition
VET CARE: Supportive care; good nutrition; treatment to relieve individual symptoms
PREVENTION: Vaccination; reduce exposure to strange cats

The earliest signs appear four to six weeks after infection, and include a transient fever, swollen lymph nodes, and low white blood cell count. Cats may act lethargic, suffer diarrhea, or simply have a poor coat condition. These signs often go unnoticed by the owner, and most cats recover from the first stage of disease.

FIV-infected cats may stay healthy for five to ten years, yet all the while be potential carriers of the disease. FIV actually turns the cat's body against itself by changing healthy cells into factories that manufacture more virus.

Once true immunodeficiency develops, cats suffer chronic infections throughout their body. Inflammation and chronic gingivitis are commonly seen (see PERIODONTAL DISEASE). Signs include any one or combination of weight loss, dehydration, trouble breathing, loss of appetite, vomiting, claw or mouth sores, or chronic infections of the skin, intestines, bladder or respiratory tract. Many of these signs are similar to those exhibited by FeLV-infected cats. Some cats also suffer from neurological signs which vary from strange behavioral changes to convulsions (see EPILEPSY).

Cats remain infected for life; there is no cure. Treatment is aimed at soothing specific symptoms and making the cat as comfortable as possible. Infected cats may lead happy lives for many years when owners are attentive and promptly and aggressively treat each illness.

FIV-positive cats should be kept indoors. This protects them from exposure to diseases, and prevents them spreading FIV to healthy cats. High quality nutrition is particularly important in immune-compromised cats, and regular veterinary exams are essential.

Ultimately, FIV-positive cats no longer rally with treatment, and usually die of secondary illnesses. Euthanasia is the humane choice for cats that can no longer be made comfortable.

Vaccination is available to protect certain populations of cats that may be at risk for the disease. The FIV vaccination is considered "non-core" and not currently recommended for all cats. Consult with your veterinarian to see if this is a good option for your individual cat.

Remember that giving your cat the FIV vaccination will cause your cat to test positive for FIV. Be sure to identify your cat's FIV-vaccination status in some permanent manner. The information can be included on a collar tag or microchip information, for example.

The best protection against FIV is prevention of exposure. Cats that are kept indoors and not allowed contact with free-roaming cats are at low risk for becoming infected.

FELINE INFECTIOUS ANEMIA (FIA) see HEMOTROPHIC MYCOPLASMAS.

CAT FACTS

FELINE INFECTIOUS ENTERITIS see FELINE PANLEUKOPENIA VIRUS.

FELINE INFECTIOUS PERITONITIS (FIP) FIP is a deadly viral disease of cats first described in the late 1950s that continues to challenge our understanding today. It has been identified in all species of *Felidae*.

The virus acts on the tiny blood vessels throughout the cat's body, particularly those in the abdomen, lymph nodes and internal organs. The disease arises from the mutation of a relatively benign virus (Feline Enteric Coronavirus/FECV) within the infected cat's body. At least three specific mutations have now been associated with the FECV-to-FIP virus biotype conversion. It is estimated that FIP affects as many as one in 300 cats, and virtually all that contract the disease will die.

FECV is highly contagious, but rarely produces signs of disease, or only mild digestive tract disturbances in young cats and kittens. It's estimated that FECV incidence is 30 to 40 percent in pet cat homes, cats, and as high as 80 to 100 percent in shelters and breeding colonies. Pretty much all cats will be exposed to FECV during their lifetime.

But cats suffering from FIP are not believed to be directly contagious to other cats. That's because once the virus mutates into FIP virus, it lives inside a type of white blood cell and is no longer shed in feces.

Nobody knows exactly why the virus mutates in some cats but not others. This mutation could happen years after the initial infection, but in most cases, if FIP virus is to develop, it will happen within six months to a year of the initial infection. Most cats with FIP are between six months to two years old.

Researchers believe cats have a genetic predisposition that either promotes natural resistance to the FIP virus, or susceptibility that allows mutation to occur.

One study of Birman cats identified five regions on four different chromosomes that could harbor genes involved in susceptibility, but this may be specific to Birman cats. Today there are tests that purport to identify genetic markers for resistance, but these may have limited benefit if the genetic influence arises from a combination of gene expression and pathways, rather than a single marker.

In fact, research indicates that breeding "resistant" cats together may actually make their offspring even more susceptible. Heritability can only explains 50 percent of FIP virus susceptibility, and the remaining factors are due to genetic changes that take place after birth in combination with environmental factors. Researchers do recommend not breeding cats that have produced FIP-afflicted kittens in the past.

Outdoor cats, cats raised in multi-cat environments (shelters, catteries), cats stressed from infection, malnutrition or overcrowding, and cats treated with high doses of immune-suppressing drugs like steroids are at the highest risk for FIP. Most cases occur in pedigreed cats less than four years old, and those infected with feline leukemia virus and/or feline immunodeficiency virus are at increased risk.

FIP is an immune-mediated disease which means the cat's own body actually speeds the progress of disease. Virus first infects lymph glands, then within a week after exposure infects blood cells which transmit virus throughout the body, particularly to the liver, spleen and lymph nodes. Virus infects the walls of the blood vessels and produces an intense, destructive inflammation that allows fluid to escape, which eventually accumulates in body cavities.

FIP

SYMPTOMS: Nonspecific signs; anorexia; weight loss; depression; persistent fever; progressive painless swelling of the abdomen
HOME CARE: Supportive care; good nutrition
VET CARE: Supportive care; good nutrition
PREVENTION: Prevent overcrowding; vaccinate for FeLV and FIV; reduce exposure to other cats by keeping them inside

Clinical signs may occur suddenly, or progress slowly over time. Periodic loss of appetite, weight loss, and depression are general signs, along with a persistent fever. In addition, there are two major forms of FIP distinguished by the accumulation of fluid, or its absence, within the body.

The effusive, or "wet" form of the disease has the most dramatic symptom, consisting of a progressive, painless swelling of the abdomen with yellowish fluid. Fluid may also accumulate in the chest cavity, and make breathing difficult. Yellowing of the pale areas of the skin, called jaundice, and a mild anemia may develop. Cats typically survive only two to three months after onset of clinical signs. This form is most typical of random bred and most pedigreed cats.

The noneffusive or "dry" form is more typical of Birman and Burmese cats and is the more prolonged form of FIP. Inflammatory lesions called pyogranulomas are found throughout the body, including the eyes, kidneys, liver and nervous system, and symptoms vary depending on which organ is affected the most. Anemia, fever, weight loss and depression are typical. Cats also may show signs of specific organ failures, such as kidney or liver disease. The most common signs of the dry form include incoordination and partial or complete paralysis of the hind legs, convulsions, personality changes, and eye disease. Some of these cats may survive a year or more after clinical signs first appear.

Diagnosis is based on the cat's age, where acquired, clinical signs and veterinary exam. Cats four to thirty-six months of age from high-density environments that have a persistent fever unresponsive to antibiotics are highly suspicious, since FIP is one of the few infectious diseases with these signs. When partnered with the signs of either "wet" or "dry" forms, the diagnosis for FIP is considered reasonably certain. Indirect tests of the cat's blood, analysis of the effusions, and ultrasound may further confirm the suspicion.

Controversy remains over using feline coronavirus antibody titer tests because both FECVs and FIP viruses, being identical, cause the same test result. Since virtually all cats are exposed to FECV, even healthy cats may test "positive" with one of these tests. A number of other indirect tests are available today, but none are definitive and their results must be weighed alongside other factors.

A definitive diagnosis requires either a biopsy or post mortem examination of tissue and/or fluid to find viral RNA using PCR-based tests, or identifying viral proteins in samples. Immunohistochemistry and real time RT-PCR are very useful for identifying FIPV antigens in tissues with lesions or effusions and, if done properly, can provide a definitive diagnosis.

There is a vaccine currently available but it is not widely recommended due to questions about effectiveness. There is no effective treatment for FIP, and treatment most typically aims to keep the cat comfortable as long as possible.

Experimental treatments include one or more combination of drugs designed to inhibit viral replication, control the inflammatory response (perhaps with interferon type treatments), or attempts to stimulate the immune system non-specifically so that it might overcome the infection. Providing good nursing care and feeding a balanced, high nutrition diet makes the cat more comfortable in the terminal stages of disease.

FELINE ISCHEMIC ENCEPHALOPATHY

This mysterious condition is caused by a disruption of blood supply to part of the brain and results in sudden signs of nerve damage. The syndrome has been around for years, but was only first described in the veterinary literature in the late 1960s. Feline ischemic encephalopathy is like a stroke in in humans.

The problem rarely affects kittens, and is seen most often in outdoor cats. It usually occurs during the hot summer months. No studies have been done to determine the frequency of the condition, but experts believe the syndrome is common in cats.

FELINE ISCHEMIC ENCEPHALOPATHY

SYMPTOMS: Sudden behavior changes; mild depression with fever; pacing; circling; seizures; blindness
HOME CARE: Keep cat quiet; administer prescribed seizure medication when seizures are ongoing
VET CARE: Little can be done; sometimes, parasite medication; seizure-controlling drugs, and/or behavior modification medications; often, euthanasia is the final option
PREVENTION: Prevent cat's exposure to cuterebra infestation by keeping cat indoors and curtailing hunting

The onset of symptoms is typically abrupt—cats are normal one moment and stricken the next. However, signs vary greatly depending on the severity of the brain damage. Some cats suffer only a mildly depressed state, sometimes with fever. More dramatic symptoms include obsessive pacing and circling, blindness, and/or seizures (see EPILEPSY). Following the initial onset, cats tend to recover significantly over the first several days, but oftentimes, weakness on one side of the body or seizure episodes may continue. In many cases, the attack leaves the cat with a permanent personality change for the worse; typically, the cat becomes hostile and is no longer a suitable pet, in which case owners may choose to euthanize the cat.

The exact cause of feline ischemic encephalopathy remains a mystery. Atherosclerosis, a narrowing and hardening of the arteries from deposits of fatty substances, like cholesterol, is commonly associated with stroke in people. However, cats don't suffer the problems with cholesterol. Certain features of the feline disease suggest the syndrome may be due to a parasite (see CUTEREBRA), because the time frame during which cats are most commonly affected parallels the parasite's life cycle. Also, the syndrome has never been reported in New Zealand or Australia—where cuterebra is not found—but is common in the continental United States, where the parasite is native. Some researchers speculate that aberrant migration of the parasite into the cat's brain causes this vascular disease, possibly due to a toxicity released by the cuterebra that may cause a spasm or stricture of the vessel that blocks the blood supply.

Once the cat suffers brain damage, there's little treatment available. Some veterinarians may prescribe a medication called Ivermectin that is used to kill other parasites, but it is not clear whether this experimental therapy helps or not. Some seizures can be controlled with anticonvulsant medications, but behavior changes due to brain disorder rarely can be modified.

Because a definitive cause of the syndrome has not been determined, it's difficult to suggest how best to prevent the condition in your cat. Preventing exposure to cuterebra by keeping your cat indoors and curtailing hunting activity is probably the best way to reduce the risk (see STROKE).

FELINE LEUKEMIA VIRUS (FELV)

Feline Leukemia Virus (FeLV) is a retrovirus and was first identified in 1964. It is considered one of the leading causes of pet cat deaths. The disease gives rise to a complex of diseases that are either directly or indirectly caused by the virus.

FeLV causes lymphosarcoma, a variety of bone marrow cancers, anemia, and certain reproductive disorders (see CANCER). The virus also results in suppression of the cat's immune system, which makes the cat susceptible to a wide array of illnesses (see IMMUNE SYSTEM).

A great many cats suffering from severe bacterial infections, haemobartonella, or toxoplasmosis also are infected with FeLV. Often cats suffering from feline infectious peritonitis or feline immunodeficiency virus also are positive for FeLV.

Symptoms of the many associated diseases are extremely varied, but the affected cat frequently undergoes a chronic wasting disease marked by anemia, sluggishness, and poor appetite. Any time a cat loses weight, has recurring colds, bloody stool, diarrhea, swollen glands, trouble breathing, excessive urination, periodontal disease or sores around the claws, FeLV should be suspected.

The virus is fragile in the environment but extremely contagious, and is shed in the cat's milk, feces, and urine. FeLV can also be passed from the queen to her kittens either through the placenta before they are born, or through her milk when they nurse. The primary transmission is through saliva during grooming, licking, biting and sharing dishes and litter pans. Blood transfusion can also spread the virus, so any blood donor cats must be tested prior to giving blood.

FeLV

SYMPTOMS: Wasting away; sluggishness; loss of appetite; weight loss; chronic respiratory infections; dental disease; sores around the claws
HOME CARE: Supportive care; good nutrition; prevent/reduce stress
VET CARE: Supportive care; good nutrition
PREVENTION: Vaccinations; reduce exposure to other cats by keeping them inside

CAT FACTS

All cats are susceptible, but outdoor cats and those in multiple cat households are at highest risk for the disease. Those cats who are very young, very old, and cats already ill are more vulnerable to infection. Kittens four to six months old are at highest risk, since their immune system is not yet fully mature.

Virus enters the membranes of the eyes, nose, or respiratory tract, and infects nearby lymph nodes. From there the virus infects the bloodstream, and is distributed throughout the body within two weeks of initial infection. About 30 percent of cats are able to fight off the infection and develop immunity to the virus. Another 30 percent or so develop latent infections, which means they harbor the virus in their body but do not become sick; they are not infective to other cats, but nursing kittens may become infected through their milk. These cats are permanently infected and will enter an asymptomatic state that can last months to years.

The remaining 40 percent of exposed cats become sick. It appears that repeated or continuous exposure is necessary for successful disease transmission. The retrovirus has the ability to insert its genetic code into healthy cells, which turns these cells into virus factories; in effect, FeLV programs the cat at the cellular level to self-destruct. About 50 percent of persistently viremic cats die within six months of infection, and more than 80 percent die within three years.

The virus is diagnosed using the ELISA (enzyme-linked immunosorbent assay) or IFA (immunofluorescence assay) test, which identifies components of the virus in the infected cat's blood. Because virus is present only during certain stages of the disease, and because a cat may not test positive until 30 days after exposure, more than one test may be needed for accurate diagnosis.

There is no cure for FeLV. For the most part, treatment is aimed at preventing the spread of the disease to healthy cats while keeping the infected cat comfortable as long as humanely possible. Survival rates vary, and may be enhanced by supportive care and/or aggressive treatment. Indoor confinement and isolation from other cats help reduce exposure to bacterial, viral, and fungal infections. Stressful situations should be avoided.

Preventing exposure to infected cats is the best way to safeguard your cat. Quarantine and test any new cat you plan to bring into your home. Should one of your cats be diagnosed with FeLV, consult with your veterinarian how best to safeguard your other cats. Isolation of the infected cat coupled with daily disinfection of all feline items (food bowl, litter pan, bedding) will help but not ensure safety.

Several vaccinations are currently available to help prevent the disease. The FeLV is considered a non-core vaccination recommended for all cats at risk for exposure, and especially kittens. Cats must test negative for FeLV before being vaccinated. Vaccinations do not affect test results. Consult with your veterinarian for the best way to protect your cat.

FELINE PANLEUKOPENIA VIRUS (FPV) Previously referred to as "cat distemper," FPV is also called feline infectious enteritis or feline parvovirus and is a highly contagious viral disease that affects all members of the cat family, both wild and domestic. Any age cat is at risk, but kittens are at highest risk. Outbreaks of the disease appear to be seasonal, and coincide with the births of kittens.

This parvovirus causes, among other things, an overall drop in the numbers of circulating white blood cells, which is what "panleukopenia" actually means. FPV is closely related to canine parvovirus type 2.

PANLEUKOPENIA

SYMPTOMS: Sudden high fever; refusing to eat; depression; vomiting; diarrhea; painful abdomen (hunching posture).
HOME CARE: EMERGENCY! SEE VETERINARIAN IMMEDIATELY!
VET CARE: Supportive care; fluid therapy; blood transfusions; drugs to control vomiting and diarrhea
PREVENTION: Vaccinate your cat

Infected cats shed virus in all their body secretions, such as saliva, urine, vomit and feces, and infection usually results from direct cat-to-cat contact. However, during some stages of the disease, fleas may carry the virus from an infected cat to susceptible cats. Virus may survive for years in the environment, and can be spread from contact with contaminated litter pans, food bowls, bedding, or on the hands and clothing of owners. Most cats allowed to roam outside are exposed to the virus during their first year of life. Feline Panleukopenia Virus is highly resistant to most disinfectants, but can be killed by using a mixture of one part bleach to 32 parts water.

Cats are typically infected by swallowing the virus during self-grooming or other oral contact. Incubation is two to ten days after exposure. The virus multiplies in the most quickly-reproducing cells of the cat's body; in very young kittens, that's the brain. If kittens survive, the brain damage results in cerebellar hypoplasia. Signs include permanent incoordination that includes tumbling or rolling when walking, shaking, or swaying and twitching of the head or body. In older cats infected with FPV, the lymphoid tissue, bone marrow and intestinal lining are most seriously affected.

Signs vary from cat to cat, with some showing none to few signs at all. But generally, the condition is characterized by a sudden onset of 104+ degree fever, refusal to eat, and depression, followed by vomiting and diarrhea that leads to severe dehydration. Sick cats may crouch with their head between their front paws, crying with pain, and vomit immediately upon swallowing water or food. Late in the disease, a profoundly low body temperature often develops, generally followed by coma and death within a few hours.

The illness rarely lasts more than five to seven days; mortality rate is high. In acute cases, kittens die within 12 hours of onset of signs. Diagnosis is generally based on clinical signs. Laboratory tests to measure the white blood cell count may be required to confirm diagnosis.

There is no specific treatment once the cat is infected. The disease must run its course until the cat's system mounts a defense and circulating white blood cells are replaced. Antibodies generally appear three to four days after first signs of illness (see IMMUNE SYSTEM). Therapy is aimed at supportive nursing care which includes rehydration using fluid therapy, possibly blood transfusions, and medications to help control vomiting and diarrhea. Sick cats are at higher risk for contracting concurrent upper respiratory infections.

Food and water are withheld until vomiting subsides, and then frequent small amounts of water and bland easily digestible foods are offered. Cats that survive for five to seven days probably will recover; however, cats may continue to shed virus for up to six weeks following recovery, and should be isolated from other cats during convalescence.

Vaccinations to prevent this disease are available. They are highly effective and provide long-term immunity. FPV is a devastating disease that is highly preventable (see VACCINATIONS).

FELINE PNEUMONITIS (CHLAMYDIOSIS) see UPPER RESPIRATORY INFECTIONS.

FELINE RHINOTRACHEITIS, see **UPPER RESPIRATORY INFECTIONS.**

FELINE UROLOGIC SYNDROME (FUS) see **LOWER URINARY TRACT DISEASE.**

FERAL The term feral as it applies to cats refers to a domesticated feline that has reverted to the wild state. In contrast to abandoned or lost cats which may relish human contact but are forced to live on their own (see STRAY), the feral feline usually has been reared without benefit of human contact.

Feral cats are extremely shy of people, and are often unapproachable. They behave as any wild animal would. Feral cats can and do live anywhere in the country, but colonies are often found living in cities near food sources like restaurant dumpsters where scraps and vermin for hunting are available.

The typical feral cat's lifespan is short—three to five years—due to injury, disease, and malnutrition. Well-meaning individuals who feed feral populations without addressing the other issues may perpetuate the problem. Unmanaged feral colonies are not only a nuisance, but also pose a health risk to pets and people because they may spread diseases like FeLV, FIV, and rabies; and uncontrolled breeding creates more and more feral kittens destined for short, sad lives. Local health departments may resort to ineffective and/or inhumane trap-and-kill programs to control the problem.

As a rule, feral cats do not make good pets. With great effort, some can learn to tolerate or even appreciate attention from one or two individuals. Most, however, lead a tortured existence if forced to live indoors when "rescued" by concerned cat lovers. TNR programs, however, can be an effective and humane alternative.

TNR stands for "trap-neuter-return," a program designed to control and decrease the numbers of roaming felines. Trapped cats receive a health exam to identify very sick cats, which are euthanized. Healthy kitties are sterilized and vaccinated, to prevent reproduction or illnesses such as rabies.

CAT FACTS

Friendly adult cats and tame-able kittens are adopted while the feral (wild) adults live out their lives–sometimes a decade or longer–in the managed colony. The removal of one ear tip identifies these cats as managed. The caregiver(s) monitor the colony and provides food and shelter. Well managed colonies improve the life and well being of these cats, and not unusual for them to live six to ten years or longer.

TNR first appeared in Europe, and became better known once animal welfare societies in Great Britain began advocating the approach. It took longer for the idea to reach America. One of the best known advocacy organization of TNR, Alley Cat Allies, was founded in 1990 and began to get national attention in 1995-96 when Joan Miller of the Cat Fanciers Association presented a talk on cat lifestyle diversity at the AVMA Animal Welfare Forum. The next year she and Dr. Patricia Olson (then affiliated with the American Humane Association) co-coordinated the first National Conference On Feral Cats in Denver.

Not everyone supports TNR. The most common objections focus on protection of the cats themselves. People argue that as a domestic species, it's our responsibility to keep cats safely confined. But feral cats can rarely be tamed or easily contained. Relocating them becomes difficult when sanctuaries fill up. When cats are removed from an area that offers shelter and food, others quickly move into that niche–a "vacuum effect" that argues for maintaining the colony in its original location. Even if trap and kill programs weren't expensive and ineffective, most Americans dislike the notion of treating cats as vermin.

As an introduced or "exotic" species, critics argue cats should be removed from the environment to protect native wildlife, particularly endangered species. Cats cause the most problems where ecosystems are already in the most trouble such as on island ecosystems where *any* predator is a problem. TNR is not a good choice in these fragile environments.

But proponents argue that for the most part, cats hunt more rodents than birds, and usually only catch sick, old, or very young birds. For instance, rats also are an introduced species, and quite good predators of many birds. Even critics of TNR often support the programs in situations such as barn or city cat colonies since no endangered species are at risk.

Alley Cat Allies and other educational resources have made great strides in educating the public about feral cat solutions. How much TNR has grown isn't easy to determine, though, because most programs involve volunteers and little tracking information is available.

There is common ground. People on both sides of the TNR fence agree that owned cats should be sterilized and identified, and safely confined in some way. Feral cat programs have impacted our world in an intangible but perhaps even more important way. TNR demonstrates that *all* cats have a value, even those that can't be touched. We as human beings now recognized our ethical responsibility toward these *community cats* and that they should be cared for and treated humanely (see APPENDIX B).

FEVER see TEMPERATURE.

FIGHTING see AGGRESSION.

CAT FACTS

FLATULENCE Flatulence, or passing gas, can be highly offensive and even embarrassing to the cat owner. Intestinal gas is a natural part of digestion, and in most cases is more a nasty nuisance than a danger. Some cats simply produce more gas than others; however, flatulence can be the sign of a health problem.

Eating highly fermentable substances, drinking milk or gulping air when eating or drinking is usually the cause. High fiber or carbohydrate diets may make the condition worse, and so can inappropriate food supplements. Any sudden diet change, from treats to raiding the garbage, may result in a tummy upset with predictable results. Eliminating these culprits from Kitty's diet often solves the problem.

Providing a more highly digestible diet also helps. Check the ingredient list on the package (see READING FOOD LABELS) or ask your veterinarian to recommend an appropriate choice. Make food changes gradually over a week's period. Start by mixing two-thirds of the old diet with one-third of the new, progress to half and half, then one-third to two-thirds, and finally the new diet entirely.

FLATULANCE

SYMPTOMS: Passing gas; bad odor
HOME CARE: Provide more digestible diet; avoid soy-based diets; cut out table scraps; feed activated charcoal; add yogurt to the diet.
HOLISTIC HELP: Flower essences; digestive enzymes
VET CARE: Prescription for gas control
PREVENTION: Slow down gulping of food (and air) by feeding free choice; offer smaller meals several times a day; feed away from other pet competition

A too-full tummy gives food extra time to ferment. Slow down the gluttons by feeding your cats at different times, or in separate bowls at opposite ends of the room to reduce food competition. Free feeding—leaving dry food available at all times—may allow your cat to eat more leisurely, rather than gulping everything down at once. Try offering meals in a puzzle toy cats must play with and manipulate to shake out the food, so they eat more slowly.

Plain yogurt contains bacteria that helps digestion and reduces flatulence, and many cats relish the flavor. Try adding a teaspoonful as a food topping.

The flower essence crab apple can help bring the body back into balance. Add two or three drops onto your pet's tongue or in his drinking water each day. Adding digestive enzymes to your cat's food may also help. Ask your holistic veterinarian for a recommendation.

As a last resort, your veterinarian may prescribe a human medication like Flatulex that contains simethicone and activated charcoal to control the gas. There is also an anti-gas veterinary product called CurTail that contains an enzyme that aids food digestion and reduces flatulence.

FLEAS This is an insect parasite that feeds on blood. Fleas are the most common complaint of cat owners. All cats are at risk for flea infestation, except for those living in mountainous areas above 5000 feet, or extremely dry environments that are inhospitable to fleas. Although fleas tend to be more prominent during warmer summer months, indoor cats can harbor fleas all year long.

Flea bites cause everything from mild skin irritation and itchiness, to severe allergic reactions. But more than mere itchy aggravations, fleas are potential carriers of other parasites and diseases such as plague and tapeworms. In large enough numbers, fleas cause severe blood loss and even death (see ANEMIA).

Piercing-sucking mouthparts allow fleas to actually cut into skin and insert a sucking tube to feed. Fleas belong to the insect order *Siphonaptera*, which means "wingless siphon." Fleas have six legs equipped with hooks used to snag a host as the animal walks by. An elastic-like protein called resilin is compressed in the flea's abdomen by leg and thorax muscles which, when released, catapults the flea upward. That's why fleas are tiny athletes able to jump eight inches vertically and 16 inches horizontally.

The flea body is flat from side to side, and covered in protective cuticle plates that make it nearly impossible to crush. Its narrow profile allows rapid movement through the thickest forest of cat hair. Fleas remain on the cat unless physically removed; individuals typically live

194 CAT FACTS

about 30 days. But the adult flea only represents about five percent of the total bug count; 95 percent of the flea population is found in the "invisible" life stages of egg, larva and cocoon.

After mating, the female flea stores sperm for use as needed. A blood meal stimulates egg laying. A mamma flea can lay 50 eggs a day, and over 2,000 eggs in her lifetime. Most eggs fall off the cat into the environment, where they may remain dormant for six months or longer. More typically, eggs hatch into tiny, maggot-like larvae within two to three weeks. They feed on the undigested blood passed by adult fleas (sometimes referred to as "flea dirt), and other organic material.

In another three weeks, the larvae spin cocoons, where they undergo further development. Once mature, the flea uses antennae and bristles sensitive to body heat and odor, changes in light, touch and moisture, and even traces of carbon dioxide exhalation, to detect when a host is nearby, and only then leaves the cocoon and mounts a furry host. The cycle from egg to adult takes about 30 days.

Cats are diagnosed by finding the fleas themselves, or evidence of flea presence such as the dark brown specks of digested blood excreted by the flea. The adult flea is visible, but so fast it's hard to detect in thick cat hair. Cats also tend to groom away many of the nasty nuisances, so they may not be seen.

Fleas seem to prefer your cat's hindquarters, and flea dirt can be found on the skin near the base of the tail. Simply part the fur and look, or comb Kitty after standing the cat on a light-colored towel; flea dirt will pepper the towel below as you groom the cat. When the specks are placed on a damp cloth, they dissolve and turn red. Evidence of tapeworms, which are usually contracted from swallowing fleas, also points to flea infestation. Look for dried rice-like grains in the litter box, or in the fur below the cat's tail (see TAPEWORMS).

There is a wide array of flea products available for controlling the problem. However, flea control is complicated by both flea biology and feline sensitivity. There is no quick fix for controlling fleas.

To stay ahead of fleas, it's essential to treat both the cat and the environment. When the cat is an inside pet, "environment" means the house. Outside cats pose a dilemma, since it's nearly impossible to control reinfestation if Kitty's allowed to roam the great outdoors. All pets in contact with the affected cats must also be treated.

Traditional flea control relied on various classes of chemical insecticides used in various forms, such as sprays, powders, shampoos and dips. However, cats are very sensitive to a number of chemicals, and what kills a flea may also make Kitty sick, or even dead. Flea products for dogs are often toxic to cats, and even products that are safe for cats may prove deadly if applied inappropriately or in the wrong combinations. The first rule when treating your cat for fleas is to read, understand, and follow product directions for use.

Products that use a class of chemicals called cholinesterase inhibitors should be used only with extreme caution on cats. Their effects can be cumulative; using an environmental spray that contains these chemicals when the cat has been dipped with a similar product can result in toxic levels for the cat. This group includes organophosphates such as chlorpyrifos (Dursban), malathion, diazinon, cythioate and fenthion, and carbamates like carbaryl and propoxur. Also beware of products containing chlorinated hydrocarbons, which include DDT, lindane, and methoxychlor; they are poisonous to cats.

CAT FACTS

FLEAS

SYMPTOMS: Presence of fleas; black pepper-like residue on skin; itchiness; scabby skin; tapeworms; sometimes lethargy and pale lips or gums from anemia
HOME CARE: Treat cat and environment with appropriate cat-safe insecticides
HOLISTIC HELP: Use flea comb; diatomaceous earth; homeopathy; borax salts; nematodes
VET CARE: For anemia cases, fluid therapy and/or blood transfusion, then appropriate flea treatment
PREVENTION: Routine flea control

Pyrethrins, made from a relative of the chrysanthemum flower, are one of the safest insecticides for cats available. Synthetic pyrethrins called pyrethroids include permethrin and provide a broader and longer flea-killing action than natural pyrethrins. Products may be combined with compounds like piperonyl butoxide (PBO) that are synergist which increase the effectiveness of insecticides and allow lower, safer concentrations of the chemical to be used. However, PBO makes some cats drool. Some products use microencapsulation; this reduces toxicity to the pet while enhancing the product's long-term effect by delivering small amounts of insecticide inside permeable microcapsules that release the product over a longer period of time.

Insect Growth Regulators (IGRs) are extremely safe for cats because they're formulated specifically to affect insects, not mammals. Methoprene and phenoxycarb are two of these hormone-like compounds that work by turning an insect's own natural metabolic process against itself. Adult fleas aren't killed, but immature fleas are prevented from maturing, which breaks the life cycle. One example is lufenuron (Program) which is mixed in Kitty's food once a month; fleas that bite a cat treated with lufenuron won't produce eggs that hatch. However, fleas that bite can still cause itchy skin disease, so this product isn't appropriate for flea-allergic cats. Lufenuron is available only through veterinarians.

New insecticides affect only the insect's nervous system, not the cat's. Examples include imadacloprid (Advantage) which kills adult fleas, and fipronil (Frontline Top Spot) which kills both adult fleas and ticks. Both products are waterproof and applied once a month as drops to the skin of the cat's shoulder blades. Fipronil actually spreads to the hair follicles, where it coats each hair as it grows. Check with your veterinarian for the safest, most effective products for your cat.

Flea products are usually applied topically, but some forms are more effective and/or easier to use than others. Traditional delivery systems include collars, shampoos, dips, powders and sprays. Flea collars seem easiest to use, but in the past have been the least effective; recent products are better able to spread their "cargo" over the entire pet, but unless they are equipped with safety break-away catches, collars can be dangerous if they catch on something and strangle the cat. Shampoos only kill fleas as long as they're on the cat. Powders and dust last longer, but are messy to apply and can be drying to the skin. Sprays offer a good initial flea kill, and offer residual protection as well; but cats may object to sprays, and alcohol-based sprays can be drying. Dips are applied wet and allowed to dry; they penetrate the hair coat and have some lasting effect, but extra care must be taken with these stronger products that toxicity doesn't occur. Monthly "spot-on" products today offer convenience and effective protection.

Concerned cat owners may seek out "natural" means to control parasites, and some do work. Rotenone and d-limonene are considered botanicals, insecticides made from roots and citrus fruit extracts. Desiccants are drying agents that cause fleas to dehydrate and die; derivatives of borax used by some commercial pest control companies on carpet do kill flea larvae which helps break the life cycle. Desiccant diatomaceous earth (DE or Diatom Dust) also has a drying effect against a certain percentage of fleas and larvae, but is messy to apply. Certain kinds of nematodes (worms) that eat immature fleas are sold in pet stores and garden shops to be mixed with water and sprayed in the yard.

A host of "natural" products flood the market each year; please be aware that compounds claiming to have activity against parasites must pass EPA guidelines for safety and effectiveness claims, and will have an EPA registration number on the label. Avoiding insecticidal claims and calling themselves "natural" allows some products to avoid expensive safety and efficacy tests. Just because a product is natural doesn't necessarily mean it's safe-- or that it works.

A flea comb with tines very close together is the safest "natural" way to rid a cat of fleas. Comb the cat from head to tail, and after each stroke, drown the fleas captured in the comb in a bowl of soapy water. A flea comb, though, won't do the job if Kitty has a substantial problem.

If your cat spends any time outdoors, you must treat the yard for fleas. Fleas prefer moist, cool habitat and shun the sun, so treatment is only necessary in shaded areas. Keep grass clipped close and brush cleaned up; letting the sun shine in will go far toward chasing the bugs away. Check with your local County Extension Agent to learn what environmental insecticides are approved for use in your area. Some products containing IGRs can control fleas for up to 12 months, but be aware that some IGRs may also affect beneficial insects, like bees or butterflies, so choose your weapons wisely.

For inside premises, vacuum carpets several times to lift the flea eggs and larvae to the surface of the pile so flea products can reach them. Change the vacuum bag frequently to keep surviving bugs from reinfecting the house. Follow product directions to treat the house and yard, and don't allow pets or people access until these areas are completely dry.

FLOWER ESSENCES

Flower essences are a type of "vibrational therapy" made from the essential oils of wild plants, trees, and bushes said to offer benefits to the emotional state of pets. Several brands are available. One of the best known, Bach Flower Remedies, consists of 38 individual essences made by infusing spring water with wild flowers either by steeping in the sun or by boiling.

Bach Flower Remedies were created by British physician Dr. Edward Bach in the early 1900s. He believed disease to be a physical sign and end product of unhappiness, fear and worry, and identified twelve "pathological emotional states" in people that the essences are designed to treat: fear, terror, mental torture or worry, indecision, indifference or boredom, doubt or discouragement, over-concern, weakness, self-distrust, impatience, overenthusiasm, pride or aloofness. We can't know with certainty that pets feel the same emotions as people do, but holistic veterinarians have used the remedies with success, by attempting to identify the emotional state.

The great thing about Bach Flowers is they can be used safely by anyone. Even if you use the wrong remedy, although it may not help it won't cause problems. The essences are easy to use. They don't work in all cases, but when they do, they tend to work very quickly. You can combine them, but will get the best results by limiting to no more than three at a time.

Each individual flower essence treats a specific type of anxiety. The essence Mimulus, for example, is good for soothing fears while Rock Rose deals with terror. Vervain calms nervous energy and Vine helps stop aggression. Holistic veterinarians also attribute some physical healing properties to various flower remedies. They won't cure behavior or health problems by themselves, but can help when used alongside other techniques.

Occasionally more than one flower essences is combined into one remedy. The premixed Rescue Remedy, for example, contains the essences of Impatiens, Star of Bethlehem, Cherry

Plum, Rock Rose, and Clematis. Rescue Remedy is considered an "emergency remedy" good for any kind of sudden stress or shock.

You can find Bach Flower Remedies at most human health food stores. A number of veterinarians and pet product stores also carry them, and they're available over the Internet. They come in individual glass bottles, and need to remain in glass and be kept away from direct sun, microwaves or heat.

While you can take the remedies undiluted, it's best to prepare a treatment bottle from the full-strength "stock bottle" you purchase. Obtain a glass 30 ml (1 oz.) dropper bottle and fill with spring water (not tap water).

Add two drops of your chosen Remedy to the new bottle of spring water. It's best to limit this to three Remedies in the same bottle. Shake well, at least ten times (practitioners call this "succussing").

(Optional) Add one teaspoon of EITHER brandy, apple cider vinegar or vegetable glycerin to the treatment bottle as a preservative. Be aware that this changes the flavor so choose wisely based on how you plan to administer the remedy to your pet. Most pets do best with no preservative or the vegetable glycerin.

Store the stock bottle and treatment bottle in a dark, cool place. The stock bottle should last for a very long time in this way.

To treat your cat, use the treatment bottle and shake it each time before putting three drops in the water bowl for Kitty to sip all day. It won't hurt if the other pets also drink. Alternatively, you can mix the drops into a teaspoonful of plain yogurt for the cat to take as a treat.

Since it's a vibrational energy medicine, practitioners say that simply dripping the two drops on the cat's forehead or a paw also works. But when giving the drops directly don't let the dropper touch the skin, fur or mouth or you'll contaminate the bottle.

Holistic veterinarians usually advise giving three drops, one to four times a day as needed, until your pet acts like she feels better. More is NOT better—Bach Flower Remedies work best over a longer period of time.

FOOD Food is organic material used by the body to sustain growth, repair tissue, maintain vital bodily processes, and provide energy. Historically, cats viewed small mammals and insects as food and, given their choice, modern felines may still relish the occasional grasshopper or mousey morsel. But pet cats can't be depended on to choose proper foods, and owners must take responsibility for providing a balanced and complete diet.

An appropriate food must address the individual cat. The age, the lifestyle, even health status influences the optimal formulation. Growing kittens have higher energy needs than adult cats, and geriatric cats or those with special health problems may require specific diets. Designing cat foods is extremely difficult, even for professional feline nutritionists. Homemade diets are a good choice for your cat, when you have the proper expertise and/or veterinary guidance to provide a consistent balanced formulation.

Good nutritional choices for your cat can be found in a variety of commercial products that provide an appropriate food for every cat and condition imaginable. Reputable pet food companies invest years in ongoing research to ensure the diets they produce fulfill the various needs of pet cats.

Pet food companies design cat food to please owners, as well. The product must be appealing to you because unless the food is purchased, the cat will never eat it. Some components, like the color of the food, are aimed specifically at getting owners to open their pocketbooks. Your cat could care less what a food looks like. To make the best choices, consider the cat's requirements ahead of anything else.

Commercial cat food products can be divided into three broad categories: super premium products, premium products, and low-cost products. The category that is best depends on the age, the body condition, and activity level of the individual cat.

The super-premium foods are typically higher in nutrient density and digestibility than the other categories of cat foods. They are more expensive because higher quality ingredients that cost more are used. Higher fat content makes this category extremely palatable; in other words, the food tastes very good to cats. Nutrient density means the cat doesn't need to eat as much volume as in other categories. And high digestibility means the cat's body is able to use a high percentage of nutrients, which results in less waste; consequently, the amount that ends up in the litter box is reduced. Super premium foods typically are available at specialty pet stores or veterinary clinics. Some super premium cat foods can be purchased at the grocery store.

Premium name brand products are usually sold through grocery stores, large pet stores and some department stores. The nationally distributed brands are considered a more economical choice than super premium cat foods. The average cat tends to do quite well eating these diets, but because they are not as nutrient dense, the cat must eat more of these foods to obtain the same calories. In this category, look for products made by reputable manufacturers that have been tested through feeding trials; this provides a consistent quality diet that offers complete and balanced nutrition.

Low cost products are typically the cheapest category of food, and may be sold in the grocery store, sometimes as the "store brand." This category uses the least expensive ingredients, and products may not be as tasty or digestible as more expensive products. Low digestibility can increase the stool volume in the litter box. A cat may need to eat much more of these foods to obtain adequate nutrition. House-brand products claim nutritional value equal to national name brand products, but at a lower cost, and to be sure, some cats may do well on these foods. However, the quality of such low cost products is extremely difficult to predict and can be inconsistent from batch to batch. Avoid generic cat foods. Choose quality over cost to ensure your cat receives the best possible nutrition.

Your veterinarian can advise you whether a super-premium, premium, or other product is most appropriate for your cat. Also consider the form of the food.

There are three basic forms of cat food; semi-moist, canned, and dry. High quality semi-moist foods are quite palatable, easy to serve, and can be stored without refrigeration. Ingredients like corn syrup are added to keep the food moist and prevent it from drying out, but these ingredients may also make the cat thirsty. Semi-moist forms are convenient for using on trips when traveling with your cat, because they're packaged in individual servings. Usually they're more expensive than dry forms. Semi-moist foods on average contain 16 to 25 percent protein, 5 to 10 percent fat, 25 to 35 percent carbohydrate and 25 to 34 percent water.

Canned cat food is processed in the same way as human canned products. After the formulation, or recipe, is determined, the ingredients are ground together and the mixture is delivered into the cans at high-speed filling lines run by computers. The food inside the cans is then cooked and sterilized in giant pressure cookers, sealed, then labeled and shipped. Canning preserves food without adding chemicals. As long as it's not opened, a canned product stays fresh nearly indefinitely. Canned foods contain about 10 to 20 percent protein, between 2 and 10 percent fat, and 72 to 78 percent water.

Dry food ingredients are mixed into dough or batter, cooked under extreme pressure for a short time, then pushed through a die plate to give the food its characteristic shape. Called extrusion, this process dries the kibble and gelatinizes the starches in the grain ingredients to make them more digestible. Dry cat foods generally contain 28 to 36 percent protein, 8 to 22 percent fat, and less than 12 percent water.

Quality of the food—whether name-brand, premium or super premium—depends much more on the ingredients and proper processing than on the form of the food. All three forms are capable of providing complete and balanced nutrition, but there are certain misconceptions as well as advantages associated with each.

Canned cat foods tend to consist of more protein and fat than dry forms. Carbohydrates aren't as useable in the canning process, and are incorporated in smaller quantities than in dry food forms. Some canned cat foods are entirely composed of meat and fat, with necessary vitamins and minerals added to balance the diet. And while meat meal is used in dry foods, canned products often contain fresh meats cited on the label as beef, fish, chicken, and meat byproducts.

But some canned products don't contain any fresh meat at all. These products may incorporate an extruded soy product that is less expensive but looks like meat. It is typically identified on the label as textured vegetable protein, soy protein, or soy protein isolate. When formulated correctly, these products are perfectly fine for the cat.

Some cats have a softer stool when fed canned products as compared to dry forms. That may be because canned food rarely includes a fiber source, which helps form fecal material. Because of the difficulty using carbohydrates in canned diets, it's more difficult to create lower calorie foods in canned than dry forms. Carbohydrates help food retain its form. Since lower quantities of carbohydrates are found in canned products, canned foods may include gum Arabic, xanthan gums and vegetable gums as viscosity enhancers to help the food set up. This is what makes the "gravy" that owners (not necessarily cats!) are so fond of in canned products. Color enhancers like iron oxide and caramel may be added to make cat food look more like something the owner would want to eat. Some cat foods are designed to look like human luncheon meat.

Canned cat foods do tend to rate more highly on palatability because water releases odor, and odor stimulates the cat's appetite. Liquid is required for the canning process, and raw meat is approximately 83 percent water. That's why canned foods typically are so high in moisture.

Added moisture is a benefit for those cats that won't drink enough water, and soft foods are easier for some cats to eat. However, canned and semi-moist foods may impact the cat's dental status (see PERIODONTAL DISEASE).

Canned foods are also attractive to cat owners who don't want Kitty to become bored with one food. Dry foods typically are sold in larger quantities, while canned products can be purchased in single servings. This makes offering a kitty smorgasbord easier for the owner.

Also, canned diets spoil quickly once opened, cannot be fed free choice, and leftovers must be refrigerated. The biggest drawback to canned cat foods compared to dry forms is the cost. Ounce for ounce, both forms may cost the same, but cats need to eat three times as much canned food as dry to compensate for the bulk added by water.

The greatest advantage to dry cat foods is convenience for the owner. Dry diets are easier to store, and do not require refrigeration. They can be fed free choice. The cat's bowl can be filled to allow Kitty to nibble at her convenience, which is more consistent with the cat's preferred style of eating. Some nutritionists believe multiple small feedings are better and more efficient for the cat than one or two meal feedings a day.

Dry diets typically are only eight to ten percent moisture, which means the food is more energy dense. The cat can eat less of the food, while getting the same amount of energy. Because of the packaging, dry diets are more economical to purchase in bulk than canned products. However, dry formulations typically contain higher carbohydrate content, which experts believe may impact the cat's health (see OBESITY and DIABETES MELLITIS).

Some cats prefer crunchy foods over soft ones. Palatability is influenced not only by flavor and smell, but also by the way the food feels in the cat's mouth. Mouth appeal preferences probably have a great deal to do with what the cat experienced as a kitten, and what she saw her mother accept as food.

Fat makes foods taste good, but if unprotected, it begins to break down and deteriorate within hours of dry food manufacture. To prevent the fat from turning rancid, preservatives keep dry food fresh for up to a year after manufacture so that optimum nutrition is delivered when the food is eaten. Antioxidants like vitamin E and vitamin C are often used to help maintain freshness. (See also FOOD ADDITIVES, NUTRITION and READING FOOD LABELS).

FOOD ADDITIVES

A food additive refers to an ingredient incorporated in the diet formulation that provides desirable characteristics to the food. Additives can be further divided into those that are nutritional, and those that are non-nutritional.

Vitamins, minerals, fats and amino acids like taurine are nutritional additives which may be incorporated in the diet formulation to assure it is nutritionally complete and balanced. Flavorings, texture enhancers, colors and preservatives are non-nutritional supplements.

Pet food regulations require that additives in pet foods be proven harmless to pets. Many currently in use are also approved for use in human foods.

Additives are used to enhance the taste and appearance of food. Natural colors like caramel or carotene, and artificial dyes like iron oxide provide a consistent appearance, or distinguish between various particles in multi-particle foods. Texturizers like guar gum, gum Arabic, xanthan gum, carrageenan and cellulose flower are sugar-type substances. The jelly in canned foods, its aspic appearance, or pseudo-gravy is created using these additives, and are designed to "feel good" to the cat's mouth when eaten. They also make cat food look more like human food, which appeals to owners who must choose to buy a particular product.

Flavor enhancers are often added to increase palatability. Enzymatically degraded (pre-digested) fish or animal organs are called animal digest, and this flavor enhancer is sprayed on dry foods to make them taste good to the cat. Palatability is extremely important, because even the best food provides no benefit unless the cat actually likes and eats it.

Preservatives protect food from degrading, and guard the nutritional quality of the product. Canned diets are preserved by the canning process, but dry and semi-moist forms of food require preservatives to prevent the break down (oxidation) of the nutrients. Oxidation is kind of biological rust, and is the reaction between oxygen and other compounds, especially fats.

Antioxidants prevent fat from turning rancid, preserves the flavor of foods, and keeps essential fatty acids and fat soluble vitamins at optimal nutrient value (see YELLOW FAT DISEASE).

A variety of synthetic and natural antioxidants are used by commercial pet food companies. Chemical preservatives such as sorbic acid or potassium sorbate are humectants that hold water and help keep semi moist products moist, and also protect these foods from mold and bacterial growth. WARNING: In the past, propylene glycol was used for these purposes in semi-moist foods, but recent studies show high levels of propylene glycol can damage a cat's red blood cells. Most reputable pet food companies have suspended the use of this chemical; avoid any cat food that lists propylene glycol on the label (see READING FOOD LABELS).

Synthetic antioxidants used most widely in dry pet foods include ethoxyquin, BHT (Butylated Hydroxytoluene) and BHA (Butylated Hydroxyamisole). Ethoxyquin has been used in pet foods since the mid-1950s when five year efficacy and safety studies were done. Many pet food nutritionists consider ethoxyquin to be the most effective preservative on the market, with BHA and BHT rating fairly close behind. Although the FDA has endorsed safe levels for use in pet foods, many pet food companies have suspended the use of ethoxyquin due to pet owner concerns over safety.

Natural antioxidants are preservatives found in nature. They include ascorbic acid (vitamin C), and tocopherols which are chemical compounds collectively referred to as vitamin E. Natural antioxidants used in combinations with each other usually provide good preservation, but typically do not last as long as synthetic forms. Foods preserved with mixed tocopherols should usually be used within three to six months of manufacture, or by the product's expiration date (see FOOD SUPPLEMENTS, NUTRITION and READING FOOD LABELS).

FOOD SUPPLEMENTS

Food supplements are defined as anything fed in addition to an otherwise complete and balanced diet. Cats eating homemade diets, cats that refuse to eat, and cats with specific medical problems may benefit from dietary supplementation. Your veterinarian's recommendation is important in these instances.

Food supplements can be anything from vitamin and mineral mixes, to treats and table scraps. Unauthorized supplementation of an otherwise nutritionally adequate diet risks throwing the nutrition out of balance. To find a complete and balanced commercial diet for your cat, learn to read pet food labels.

Cats require nutrients in the proper amounts and combinations, and too much can sometimes be as bad as too little. Supplements are not only unnecessary when feeding a balanced and complete diet, giving your cat a vitamin or mineral supplement or other food item when it's not needed can be downright dangerous.

For instance, adding raw eggs to the diet can cause a vitamin deficiency. A protein called avidin is found in raw egg whites; avidin destroys biotin, one of the B vitamins, and can result in poor growth and hair loss in the biotin-deficient cat.

Vitamins D and E are found in wheat germ and cod liver oils, and cats may relish these treats. But too much can cause toxicities that can result in skeletal deformity, reproductive problems, and even calcification of soft tissues.

Raw foods may be the natural choice in the wild, but it's not smart for house cats unless you get expert advice from your holistic veterinarian. Raw meat carries parasites and bacteria (see SALMONELLA and TOXOPLASMOSIS). Habitual eating of raw liver causes vitamin A toxicity that results in deformed bones, weight loss, anorexia, even death.

Table scraps place your cat at risk for obesity, gastrointestinal problems that result in upset tummies with signs like vomiting or diarrhea, or even metabolic problems (see PANCREATITIS). The quality of table scraps of course depends on what you feed yourself. Small amounts of lean meats are usually fine, for example, while fat alone isn't healthy for you or your cat. Table scraps should make up no more than five percent of the total amount of food your cat eats.

Highly palatable food treats like tuna or meat baby foods may create food addictions which can result in many problems. Unlike humans who need variety in their diet to achieve nutrient balance, many cats are perfectly content to eat the same food day in and day out. It's fine to find a complete and balanced diet your cat accepts, and stick to it.

There are few regulations that apply to products marketed as "natural" supplements, so pet owner beware. Approach such products cautiously; just because something is natural does not necessarily mean it's harmless. After all, poisonous mushrooms are natural, too. Ask questions of the manufacturer, and if you don't like the answers—or can't get any answers—avoid the product to protect your cat. Rely on the reputation of well-known companies that have been around for a while, and have the nutritional research to back up their claims.

An occasional treat probably won't hurt your cat. There are many commercial cat treats on the market, some that claim to be complete and balanced. That way, you don't risk unbalancing the nutrition, but both you and the cat will feel special.

If you feel Kitty would benefit from eating more, adding a teaspoon of warm chicken broth to the food usually increases calorie intake of dry food by about ten percent. An even better choice would be finding a more nutrient dense ration that provides the cat with more calories even if he doesn't eat a great deal (see NUTRITION, NUTRACEUTICALS and FOOD).

FRACTURE

SYMPTOMS: Floppy limbs; limping; swelling; exposed bones
FIRST AID: Immobilize with temporary splint, then get cat to the vet
VET CARE: Application of casts; surgical plating; wiring or pinning; sometimes antibiotic therapy; occasionally amputation
PREVENTION: Keep cats indoors away from car accidents; lock windows to prevent falls

FRACTURE Fracture refers to the breaking of a bone. Bones are the solid support of the body that gives the cat his shape. The feline skeleton is composed of approximately 244 separate bones, which is about 40 more than people have. Extras are located mostly in the spine and tail. Individual bones can withstand only small amounts of stress without fracturing.

Fractures are categorized into three broad classifications: fatigue fractures, pathologic fractures, and traumatic fractures. Repeated stress to a bone results in fatigue fractures, which are rare in cats. Pathologic fractures are caused by systemic conditions like malnutrition or cancer that weaken individual bones or the entire skeleton and make them more susceptible to being broken. In these cases, the underlying problem as well as the fracture must be treated. In cats, most fractures are the result of trauma, with injuries due to falls or car accidents leading the way.

208
CAT FACTS

Cats suffering broken bones due to trauma may also suffer other injuries. Conditions such as bleeding and shock take precedence over fractures, and should be addressed before anything else. A veterinarian should be seen as soon as possible (see BLOOD and SHOCK).

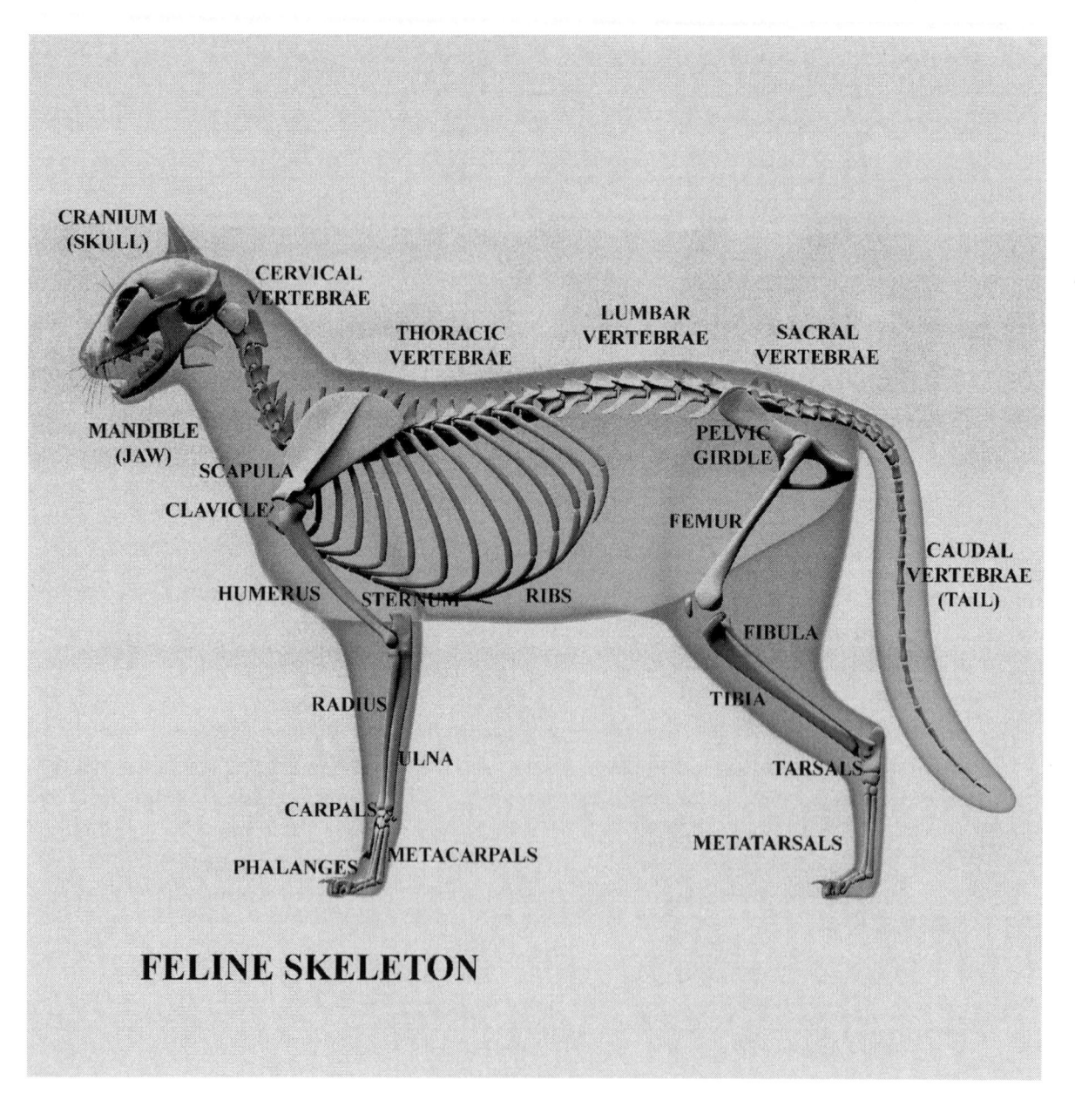

FELINE SKELETON

In young kittens, bones tend to crack or split rather than break; these fractures are called greenstick fractures. Complete breaks are classified according to whether or not the skin is broken. They are called closed fractures when the skin is not broken, and when bone protrudes from the skin, the fracture is called an open or compound fracture. Open fractures put cats at higher risk for tissue or bone infections, which are painful and can be fatal.

Although every bone can be broken, the cat's femur (thigh bone) is fractured most often and accounts for nearly 30 percent of all feline fractures seen. Pelvic fractures are also very common, and make up about 22 percent of feline fractures.

Head injuries result in skull fractures, and a broken palate or jaw often happens during a fall. Although the cat may try to land on his feet, the speed of the fall usually causes Kitty's chin to smack the ground (see BALANCE). Other common fracture sites include the rear leg (tibia/fibula), lower foreleg (radius/ulna), and upper foreleg (humerus). Fractures of the cat's tail often occur.

Signs of fracture include the affected limb moving or flopping loosely, or the cat holding the leg at an odd angle. Injured tails may hang limp, and cats with pelvic fractures aren't able to stand and support their weight. Bleeding and the white bone itself is visible in compound fractures. With greenstick or other closed fractures, the cat may exhibit pain by refusing to move, limping, or holding up the affected limb, which may be swollen.

Cats suffering fractures should be moved as little as possible. Do not try to feel or manipulate the injury; broken bone is sharp, and can damage the tissue and nerves. Movement may turn a closed fracture into an open one, or damage internal organs. Handle your cat with care so that you don't further injure him, and aren't injured yourself (see RESTRAINT).

If you are more than thirty minutes away from the vet, fractures of the leg below the elbow or knee are best immobilized using a temporary splint. The splint must extend both above and below the injury to be effective. Cover open wounds with sterile gauze or a clean cloth before splinting to help prevent infection. If the fracture is above the elbow, wrap a towel about Kitty to hold the limb snug against the body.

Nearly any long, stiff material will work as a temporary splint. A rolled newspaper, or a cylinder of cardboard from the core of a roll of paper towels may work. Split cardboard tubes up the center so that the injured limb can be laid inside without any attempt to straighten or reposition the fracture. A simple hand towel or bubble wrap about the limb may be sufficient, just enough to stabilize the injury. Place the stricken cat on a towel in a box or carrier, and get your pet veterinary attention as soon as possible.

Veterinarians palpate (feel) the injury and use X-rays to learn the extent of the injury and determine the best treatment. Setting fractures is called reduction, and various techniques are used to hold bone in the proper position for healing to take place.

Splints and casts are generally used with fractures in the mid-portion of legs below the elbow. They work best when the bone fragments fit back together easily. But the closer the fracture is to a joint, and the more pieces there are, the more difficult it is to fix. Internal surgical fixation with wire, metal plates or pins may be necessary.

Broken jaws are often wired to help them heal, metal plates replace missing section of bones and hold multiple breaks in correct alignment, and metal pins thread the breaks in long bones together like beads on a string. The hardware may become a permanent part of the cat, or may be removed after the fracture heals.

Feline bones heal relatively quickly and easily, especially those of growing kittens. Some types of feline fractures, particularly minor breaks in the pelvis, heal by themselves even when multiple fractures are present. If the cat is kept from moving, new bone called callus forms across the fracture site and helps stabilize it. Hard bone formation follows shortly, with an eventual return to normal function.

Cats suffering fractures in the ball and socket formation of the hip often regain most limb function within three to five weeks simply by resting the affected leg. Other times, the damaged femoral head and/or neck are surgically removed, and the body creates a new false joint out of tissue that functions like the original.

When the fracture won't heal properly, typical of broken tails or toes, amputation may be necessary. Cats typically adjust quite well to missing toes, tails, or even legs, should that happen.

Your veterinarian may recommend PEMF therapy, which stimulate the electrical and chemical processes in the tissues to relieve inflammation and pain. PEMF therapy may aid in bone healing, too. Devices may be designed for whole body treatment or targeted areas of the body. Some of these devices have successfully completed efficacy studies and are FDA-approved. Therapeutic products may be available in mats, wraps or other devices from your veterinarian or over the counter (see PULSED ELECTROMAGNETIC FIELD).

Outdoor cats are at highest risk for broken bones when they encounter vehicles, but indoor cats suffer more often from falls. Prevent injury by staying alert to rocking chairs that can crush legs or tails, slippery perches that a cat may misjudge, and open windows (see HIGH RISE SYNDROME).

FROSTBITE Frostbite is the partial or complete freezing of specific parts of the body, usually the extremities. In cats, frostbite most often affects the ears, toes, scrotum and tail.

Because our bodies contain more than ninety percent water, freezing can cause great damage. Just like an overfilled ice cube tray expands over the top as it freezes, living cells also expand when frozen. But the frozen matter has nowhere to go, and when the integrity of the cell ruptures, tissue is destroyed. Severe cases of frostbite can lead to infection and a loss of affected body parts.

Initially, a mildly affected area looks white and pale; as blood circulation returns, the area turns red and may swell. Severe cases result in blisters that actually look like burns. In these cases, tissue may peel, and dead skin eventually sloughs off.

CAT FACTS

Treating frostbite involves rewarming the frozen area, and first aid at home is extremely important. To thaw the area, soak in lukewarm 104 to 108 degree water for 15 to 20 minutes until the skin becomes flushed. Don't apply snow or ice, and don't rub or massage the injury; that will further damage the tissues and compromise recovery. Apply an antiseptic ointment like Neosporin to the affected area.

Your cat's injury should be evaluated by a veterinarian. It may require several days to determine the extent of the injury. Antibiotics, pain medication, or even surgery to removed damaged or dead tissue may be necessary in severe cases. Healing may take several weeks. Cats that have suffered frostbite in the past are prone to recurrence.

Frostbite can be prevented by confining cats indoors during cold weather. Outdoor cats should have access to warm, dry shelter away from the wind (see HYPOTHERMIA and OUTDOOR SHELTER).

FROSTBITE

SYMPTOMS: Pale, swollen or blistering ear tips, nose, testicles, tail or toes
FIRST AID: Thaw areas with warm water; apply antiseptic ointment
VET CARE: Antibiotics; pain medication; possible amputation of dead tissue
PREVENTION: Confine cats indoors during cold weather; provide shelter from wind and wet

FUNGUS see RINGWORM.

213

214
CAT FACTS

GERIATRIC CAT

GERIATRIC CAT The term geriatric refers to the aged. A cat may be considered geriatric when she reaches eight to ten years old. However, just like people, the signs of aging are extremely individual and vary from cat to cat.

The feral cat that lives on her own has a relatively short lifespan, and can expect to live only about six years before succumbing to disease or accident. But pet cats live much longer than in the past, because of better nutrition, medical care, and a more protected lifestyle (see OUTDOOR SHELTER). Today the average housecat typically lives to age 15 or more. It's not unusual for well cared for felines to enjoy healthy lives into their late teens, or even twenties. Longevity means caretakers must deal with more age-related issues of their pet cat. Many do not impact the cat's quality of life, and parallel

the infirmities people can expect as they age. Older cats become more sedentary, and they sleep more. Athletic cats may lose muscle tone, and start to appear wobbly on their feet. Joint pain from arthritis can make cats reluctant to move, and may cause irritability (see ARTHRITIS).

As they age, the senses become less sharp, and this can be distressing for the cat. Many older cats suffer from painful dental problems, including periodontal disease. Weight loss may be due to pain when eating or other problems, and is an indication something is wrong. Elderly cats often have problems grooming themselves, and an owner's help in this area is particularly important to keep Kitty feeling like herself. Irregularity may plague geriatric felines (see CONSTIPATION). Very old cats (17 and older) can suffer from senility, and may wander and cry with bewilderment and need comforting. Senile cats may lose litter box training, but medications are available that may help (see GOGNITIVE DYSFUNCTION SYNDROME).

An elderly cat's health is more fragile than a robust youngster's, because the effectiveness of the immune system also tends to fade with age. Geriatric felines get sicker quicker, and take longer to recover than healthy young cats. Prompt veterinary attention is vital to keep older pets healthy (see IMMUNE SYSTEM).

Remember, your cat ages much more quickly than people; each year added to an adult cat's life is roughly equivalent to four human years. Health checks should be performed more frequently, annually at a minimum, as the cat ages. Care is aimed at reducing physical discomfort and emotional stress, while slowing the signs of aging as much as possible.

A number of diseases and conditions typically affect geriatric felines. Renal failure is probably the most common cause of death in aged cats (see KIDNEY DISEASE). Kidneys just seem to wear out more quickly than other organs. Although it also affects cats of other ages, hyperthyroidism is also quite common in geriatric felines and if left untreated, hyperthyroidism can lead to heart failure (see CARDIOMYOPATHY). The risk of diabetes is greater in older cats, and the chances for cancer increase as the cat ages. And because of a compromised immune system, geriatric cats may suffer a wide range of opportunistic infections. Old cats do not tolerate hospitalizations well, though, and prescribed treatments are often most successful when done by owners at home.

AGE COMPARISON

Each cat ages differently. The rate at which a cat ages depends on his lifestyle, health status, the care he receives early on and throughout his life, and even his genetics. Certain breeds of cat mature more slowly, while some may be longer lived. The 2010 AAFP/AAHA Feline Life Stage Guidelines suggests six broad age categories of cats:
- **KITTEN** is said to be from birth until six months; at six months old, the kitten is the equivalent of a ten-year-old human child.
- **JUNIOR** is seven months until two years; at one year, your cat is about equal to a fifteen year old human, and at two years is equivalent to a 24-year-old human.
- **PRIME** is three to six years, the equivalent of 28 to 40 year old human.
- **MATURE** is seven to ten years, or a 44 to 56 year old human.
- **SENIOR** is eleven to fourteen years, or 60 to 72 years old. **GERIATRIC** is fifteen years and beyond.

Good nutrition is important to maintain the geriatric cat's health. Commercial diets are now available that are formulated for the special needs of older cats. Older cats benefit most from food that's easily digested and/or chewed.

Modify the cat's living quarters to make her more comfortable. If she can no longer leap to a favorite window perch, a ramp that allows her access will do wonders for her self-esteem. Grooming her daily not only makes her feel good, but provides an opportunity for you to check for problems. Make the litter box more accessible, and provide her with cozy warm spots to sleep near her favorite thing—you.

GIARDIA Giardia is a protozoa, a single cell organism that inhabits the small intestine. The parasite interferes with the cat's ability to properly process food. Consequently, cats infected with giardia may have soft to normal-appearing stools, poor hair coats, a swollen tummy from gas, and tend to have trouble gaining or maintaining weight.

The infective cyst stage of the organism lives in the environment. Cats catch the parasite from contact with infected soil or water. A mud puddle is a perfect giardia environment. Cats can transmit giardia to each other through contact with feces.

GIARDIA

SYMPTOMS: Soft stools; poor hair coats; swollen abdomen; trouble gaining or maintaining weight
HOME CARE: None
VET CARE: Treatment with drug to kill parasite
PREVENTION: Keep litterbox clean; restrict access to outdoors

Diagnosis is difficult, because the organism is so small it's hard to find in stool samples even using a microscope. Complicating matters, giardia may not be present in the stool all the time, and repeated microscopic examination of fresh stool may be necessary to detect the parasite. Giardia can be treated with a drug called Flagyl (metronidazole) to kill the parasite. Keeping the litter box clean and restricting the cat's access to the outdoors helps prevent the chance of infection.

CAT FACTS

GINGIVITIS Gingivitis is the inflammation of the gums that surround the teeth. The tissue will appear red, and may be tender or bleed when the cat chews hard food. Gingivitis is an early sign of dental disease (see PERIODONTAL DISEASE).

GLAUCOMA Glaucoma is a disease characterized by increased pressure inside the eyeball which damages the retina and optic nerve (see EYES). Glaucoma is considered uncommon in cats.

The sphere of the eye is filled with a specialized fluid that holds the structures of vision in place. But the liquid is not static like the air in a balloon. It's constantly replaced while at the same time it drains out.

The front portion of the eye directly behind the cornea contains watery fluid called aqueous humor, while the rear chamber of the eye holds a clear, gel-like material called vitreous humor. A membrane called the ciliary epithelium constantly replaces the aqueous fluid, which normally drains through the iridocorneal angle where the cornea and iris meet. If the normal input/output balance is disrupted, glaucoma results from the increased pressure from this liquid inside the globe of the eye.

It's like filling your bathtub with water when the stopper is out; if the faucet puts in the same amount being drained, the water level stays constant. In glaucoma, the drain is plugged, and the eyeball keeps filling and swells when the fluid has nowhere to go. The increased pressure is extremely painful for the cat. The pressure also pushes the internal structure of the eye into abnormal positions until the cat's vision is destroyed.

The condition is categorized as either primary or secondary glaucoma. The primary form, in which the condition occurs without any preceding disease, is rare in cats and may result from defects in the eye that the cat is born with. This form of the disease is thought to be genetic, and is seen most often in Siamese and Persian cats.

Cats suffer more commonly from secondary glaucoma which results from underlying injury or disease. Inflammation of the eye (see UVEITIS) is a common finding, and most often results due to infectious diseases like feline leukemia virus, feline infectious peritonitis, feline immunodeficiency virus, or toxoplasmosis. Tumors or injuries can also cause glaucoma.

GLAUCOMA

SYMPTOMS: Painful eye with squinting; pawing at the eye or tearing; bloodshot or cloudy-looking eye; swelling of the eyeball; non-responsive pupil
HOME CARE: None
VET CARE: Medications to control pressure, pain, and possibly surgery; sometimes removal of affected eye
PREVENTION: Prevent exposure to predisposing viral diseases

Signs of pain may be hard to detect, and often involve behavior changes (see PAIN). The cat with a painful eye may squint or paw at the eye, or the eye may tear. The cat's eye may become bloodshot or appear cloudy. By the time signs are more obvious, it may be too late to save the cat's vision. Late signs include swelling of the eyeball, and a dilated pupil that doesn't respond to light.

Diagnosis is made using a Schiotz tonometer, an instrument that measures pressure inside the eye. The veterinarian administers eye drops so Kitty will feel no discomfort, then the instrument is gently balanced on the cornea. A mercury level on the tonometer measures the pressure within the eye. Sometimes a special examination of the interior of the eye is done using a special contact lens placed on the cat's eye.

Glaucoma may be reversible when inflammation is caught early and is not too severe. Many times, only one eye is affected, but usually both are treated to prevent involvement of the second eye. Drugs help transfer water and decrease the production of fluid. Other medications help contract the pupil and control the pressure by inhibiting nerve impulses, while steroids may reduce the inflammation. Surgery may be used to remove the membrane that produces the fluid.

220
CAT FACTS

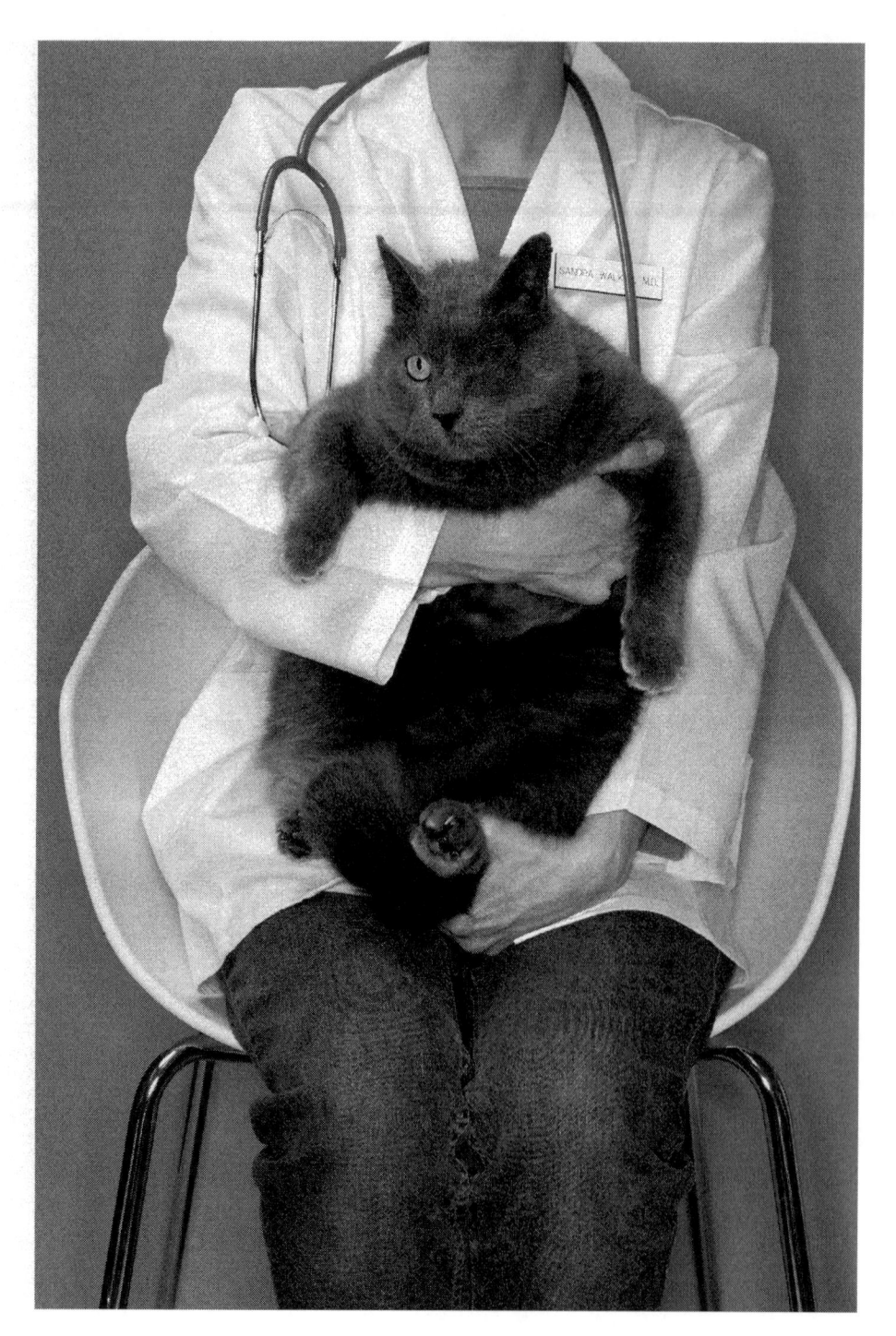

Laser ciliary body ablation selectively destroys the fluid-producing tissue in the eye and decreases the production of the fluid. The laser surgery takes place from the outside of the eye by placing the laser three to five millimeters behind the edge of the cornea, and zapping the structure. That can save the pet's vision.

When inflammation is severe, or the cause cannot be successfully treated, glaucoma may not get better even with treatment. When blindness is inevitable and medication doesn't relieve the cat's pain, removing the eye (enucleation) is necessary. Usually, the eyelid is sewn closed over the empty socket. Sometimes, a prosthesis is placed for cosmetic reasons.

Cats do quite well with only one eye. Once the pain is gone, they start to feel and act better almost immediately. Cats that become blind also do very well in familiar surroundings by relying on scent and sound (see BLINDNESS).

GRASS, EATING

Cats are obligate carnivores, which means they do not rely on vegetables or fruits in their diet, but require meat to survive. In the wild, the only vegetable matter a cat eats is found in the stomach and intestines of his prey.

Yet for unknown reasons, most cats occasionally eat grass. Usually, they carefully choose and eat the tips of only a few blades at a time. The grass may be used as a natural emetic to stimulate vomiting of hairballs. Or, cats may simply like the flavor and enjoy grazing from time to time. There is some speculation that eating grass may provide trace elements of vitamins in the cat's diet.

Whatever the reason, cats seem to enjoy chewing grass. Indoor cats may nibble houseplants when they feel the urge to graze, and depending on the plant, that can be dangerous (see POISON). Pet supply stores offer planting kits that contain wheat grass or other appropriate greens for grass-craving felines.

GRIEF

Grief over pet loss can be difficult and heartbreaking for people, but it can be an even greater challenge to help the surviving pets deal with pet loss. Cats do, indeed, grieve.

They cannot tell us how they feel. And the owners in the family may overlook behavior changes while dealing with their own sense of loss. Not every pet will react at all, while a percentage seems to suffer greatly. When pets grieve, they usually show their sense of loss with behavior changes. Separation anxiety is one form of grief—your cat only understands someone she loves is gone.

The surviving pets often begin to act differently when the cat or dog first becomes sick or starts to decline. For people, this can be a time of preparation, and some of our grieving may be done well in advance of the pet's actual death. Grief counseling often is part of what caring veterinarians naturally do.

We can't know if surviving pets realize their companion animal friends will soon die, but they certainly do act as though aware a change has—or will—occur. In fact, many sensitive cats (and dogs) react to their owners' emotional upset and grieve in response to our own changes of behavior over the heartache.

The surviving pet may seem withdrawn and depressed. Often the personality changes and a shy cat could become more demanding of attention, while a demanding cat instead hides. One of the most heartbreaking situations occurs when the surviving pet cries and looks everywhere for the missing loved one for days or even weeks.

Although it sounds macabre, sometimes it can be helpful to allow the surviving pet to say "goodbye" to the body after a furry friend has died. They may sniff and examine the body, cry or ignore it all together. aAy reaction should be considered normal.

That's the only way we can explain to them what has happened to their friend, and why a beloved cat- or dog-friend has disappeared from their life. Viewing the friend's body allows them to understand he's not coming back. They still grieve, but aren't driven to look for their missing buddy.

People go through several stages of grief—denial, anger, bargaining, depression, acceptance—but not necessarily in this order. While anthropomorphic to think pets might "bargain" *(I'll let you have my catnip toy if only you come back!)* it's certainly within the realm of possibility that they might feel anger or depression over the loss. Pets do in fact seem to finally work through the situation to acceptance. It takes some pets much longer than others just as people get over a loss in different time frames.

Many of the same things we do for each other can help our pets. Allow the grieving and even validate it with each other by simply offering compassion and support. Help your pets manage grief with these simple tips.

Talk to them. Try to be positive around your grieving pets. They may not understand the words but will pick up on your emotions. Simply say, *I'm sad, and I feel awful, but it's not your fault—and I know you feel awful, too.* You'll want to avoid babying, though, because that can reward the pet for acting depressed.

GRIEF

SYMPTOMS: Change in behavior; acting withdrawn or depressed; hiding; searching for missing pet friend; crying; refusing to eat
HOME CARE: Emotional support; spend time and talk with pet
HOLISTIC HELP: Flower essences; herbal therapy; music therapy; TTouch
VET CARE: Possibly medications
PREVENTION: None

Play music, particularly uplifting, faster tempos to lift depression. Harp music can have a soothing effect. But any music that your pet associates with positive times could be helpful.

Use TTouch, drawing clockwise concentric inch-diameter circles all over your cat's body. Pay particular attention to the ears, face and neck (see MASSAGE).

Flower essences also helps a percentage of pets. The Bach Flower remedy called Star of Bethlehem is said to be particularly helpful for relieving sorrow and grief. You can find Bach flower remedies or other brands at many health food stores, holistic veterinary clinics or online.

Pets depressed due to grief may be helped with the homeopathic Ignatia amara 30C. Give one or two drops of liquid or one or two pills, up to two days in a row. Only go to a higher dose if recommended by the holistic veterinarian.

Also, the herb Saint-John's-Wort acts as a natural antidepressant but must be dosed according to a veterinarian's advice. If the depression doesn't lift and lasts too long, your veterinarian may be able to prescribe an antidepressant drug.

Give your cat the gift of time to grieve. It hurts terribly, for you as well as your surviving pet. Still, the capacity to grieve honors the memory of the departed, and is a measure of the depth of our love. And that truly is a legacy to celebrate.

CAT FACTS

GROOMING Grooming is the act of cleaning and conditioning the body, and in cats refers specifically to the proper maintenance of the haircoat. Good grooming extends to proper attention to ears, eyes, claws and teeth.

Grooming is directly responsible for maintaining healthy skin. Sebaceous glands in the skin at the base of each hair release an oily secretion, called sebum, when the cat's grooming tugs at the fur. Sebum is spread by the cat's tongue during grooming, and lubricates and waterproofs the hair coat. Grooming also combs out loose hair, which if left in place can cause painful tangles, or mats. As they clean themselves, cats also search their skin and fur for parasites (see FLEAS, LICE, and TICKS).

A healthy coat does more than look good, it's furry insurance against injury. Hair normally falls in loose layers that help protect the cat's body from injury, and insulates her from temperature extremes. Cats do not have the same cooling system of sweat glands that people do, and instead rely on grooming to maintain their temperature. A well-groomed coat free of mats can be fluffed and allows air to pass between the hairs and cool the skin. Cats also pant to cool themselves when they are very hot, but licking the skin and hair is even more effective. Evaporation of saliva spread by grooming provides an extremely effective method of keeping Kitty cool.

Self-grooming is learned early, and a fastidious nature is a trait cherished by cat owners. Kittens learn to lick themselves by two weeks of age, and are washing themselves by the time they are weaned. As adults, they'll spend up to 50 percent of their awake time in some form of grooming.

Teeth and tongue are used for much of a cat's self-grooming, and cats often assumes odd positions to wash hard-to-reach areas. The specialized structure of the tongue makes it a perfect kitty comb, while teeth nibble and gnaw at tangles, dirt, and burrs caught in the fur (see TONGUE).

Typically the mouth, chin and whiskers are the first licked clean, followed by each shoulder and foreleg in turn. Kitty proceeds to wash both flanks and hind legs, the genitals, and then the tail from end to end. Dampened forepaws are used like furry washrags for scrubbing the face, head and ears. The paw is re-dampened by licking after every few swipes, and Kitty switches paws to do the other side. Rear claws groom the neck and ears by scratching. Rear claws are kept in shape by nibbling, while front claws are groomed by scratching objects.

Some cats are neatness freaks and seem to be constantly washing themselves, while others allow themselves to become quite shabby before cleaning up. Cats learn grooming technique from their mothers; consequently, if Mom-cat was less than meticulous about grooming, her kittens won't be as particular about their appearance, either.

Grooming of Others: Cats groom each other as a way to express their friendly relationship. Mutual grooming also helps cats take care of hard to reach areas, and usually focusses on the head and neck areas.

But the activity is usually more of a social gesture rather than a hygienic one. It can be a form of communication, an expression of comfort, of companionship, even of love. A cat that grooms an owner's hair or accepts the owner's petting is expressing affection by indulging in mutual grooming with that owner.

Displacement Behavior: It's thought that cats use grooming to make themselves feel better emotionally. Behavior that appears to be inappropriate to the situation is called displacement behavior, and cats employ grooming for this purpose more often than any other. Cats may groom themselves when fearful, to relieve tension, or when uncertain how to react to situations.

A cat confronted with an aggressive animal may, instead of running or attacking, suddenly begin to furiously groom. The same behavior is seen when the cat does something stupid, perhaps misjudges a leap and falls on his furry fanny. Such behavior usually prompts an intense session of self-grooming. Other times, cats use displacement grooming when other behaviors aren't allowed; perhaps you've put the cat on a diet, or are trying to convince an outdoor cat he should stay inside.

Animal behaviorists speculate self-grooming is a way for Kitty to deal with conflict. It's unknown whether grooming has a direct effect on the neurologic impulses in the brain, or simply is a way for the cat to distract himself. Some animal behaviorists suggest that strong emotion (fear? embarrassment?) results in a rise of body temperature which the cat cools by grooming. But with the benefits of massage and touch well documented, it appears that the mere physical action of massage could help calm feline anxiety.

227

228 *CAT FACTS*

Some displacement grooming is normal for the cat. If Kitty becomes obsessive about grooming, begins to lose fur or damage the skin, seek veterinary assistance. A number of medical conditions can result in the cat grooming excessively (see STRESS).

Besides meeting the cat's physical and social needs, grooming just plain feels good to the cat (see TOUCH). Grooming is a barometer of feline health; an unthrifty appearance often signals illness in the cat. Emotional and/or physical conditions may trigger grooming behavior that is inappropriate, or may cause the cat to stop self-grooming altogether (see HAIR LOSS).

Grooming Your Cat: Even the most fastidious cat benefits from grooming by the owner. A thorough once weekly brushing may be all that's required for shorthaired coats, but longhaired felines aren't able to do the whole job themselves and require more help.

Grooming your cat helps tones Kitty's muscles, and removes loose dirt, dander and fur that can contribute to allergies. Removing dead hair also helps prevents hairballs. A grooming routine doubles as an at-home exam for detecting problems with Kitty's eyes, ears, claws, or skin.

Cats groomed daily as kittens learn to relish and expect the attention. Cats also appreciate an established routine, so try to always groom at the same time and place. Keep grooming sessions brief so the cat won't lose interest, or patience. It's no fun to groom a reluctant cat, and forcing the issue just makes Kitty dread future grooming sessions.

Make the event as pleasurable for you both as possible. Plan ahead by having equipment handy, stop before your cat demands it, and finish with a favorite game or toy. You can always finish where you left off later.

The proper tools include a small table or counter top without a lot of distractions. This should be a place identified with grooming in which you can confine the cat's activity, like the top of the drier in the laundry room. Some cats do better with one person lightly holding them while a second person uses the comb or brush. Other cats go into ecstasy when groomed, and will be delighted with the attention anytime, anyplace.

Grooming brushes and combs are available at pet product stores, veterinary offices and mail order supplies. These come in a variety of styles, and your cat's haircoat defines the type you need. Longhaired cats may require an assortment, while shorthaired coats can often get by with one.

A rubber curry brush works well on shorthair cats. The slicker brush, with fine wire bristles in a rubber pad, also works well and tends to reach through thicker, longer hair. The pin-and-bristle brush has metal pins on one side for removing shed hair, and natural bristles on the other for smoothing the coat.

230
CAT FACTS

Combs come in fine, medium, and coarse teeth, which defines the amount of space between the tines. The ends of the teeth should be smooth and rounded. Teflon coated combs reduce the amount of static electricity, and reduce tearing or breakage of the hair. As a rule of thumb, cats with thick long fur should be combed with coarse combs where the tines are far apart, while shorthair cats benefit from medium to fine combs. Cats also enjoy being groomed with "cat gloves," special gloves with inset rubber nubs on the palm that smooth the hair coat and collect loose fur as you pet the cat.

Allow cats that have never been groomed before to sniff and investigate the equipment well ahead of time to familiarize themselves with the tools. Always begin a session with petting. This helps you learn the contours of the cat's body and alerts you to any mats or other problems ahead of time.

Cats with long heavy double coats like Persians and Himalayans develop painful mats very quickly when shed fur tangles with intact hair. These knots of fur tend to develop in the armpits of all four legs, behind the ears, and beneath the tail, places Kitty just can't reach. A badly matted coat is probably best left to the attention of a reputable feline groomer or veterinarian.

Minor problems may be teased out by using a coarse toothed comb. Rub cornstarch into the mat to help separate the hairs, then thread the comb through the mat to protect Kitty from painful pulling, and brush over the comb with a slicker brush. Begin at the tips of the hairs, and gradually work deeper into the mat. Don't use scissors; cat skin is quite thin and very tender, and you're liable to cut a wiggling Kitty as well as the fur. If gentle combing or brushing doesn't work, you may need to use an electric razor to break up the mat or shave out the area.

For routine grooming, run your fingers over the cat's body and through his fur until he is relaxed, then begin with light, short strokes with a brush in the direction the fur grows. Longhaired cats benefit from using the slicker brush first, followed by the comb. Begin and end at Kitty's "sweet spots," the area beneath his chin, his cheeks or throat that make him close his eyes and purr with delight. Talk soothingly to your cat throughout the session to help calm him, and keep him connected to you.

Progress from the face area to each side, taking care not to be too rough against the spine or nipples. Don't forget the flanks both inside and out, the area beneath the tail, and the tail itself. Cats tend to resist attention to their underside, so be alert to Kitty's mood and back off before he becomes too aggravated. Try lifting one hind food off the table while you attend to the other rear leg; that gives Kitty less balance and something else to think about, while allowing you access to the area.

CAT FACTS

Think of scratching the cat's skin rather than brushing. The cat will tell you by arching his back into the brush when he wants a heavier stroke. For longhaired cats, follow the brushing with a comb. Again, begin with a light touch and short strokes until you've reached through the haircoat to the skin. Finish with the cat gloves to polish the coat. A pair of pantyhose slipped over your hand also works well.

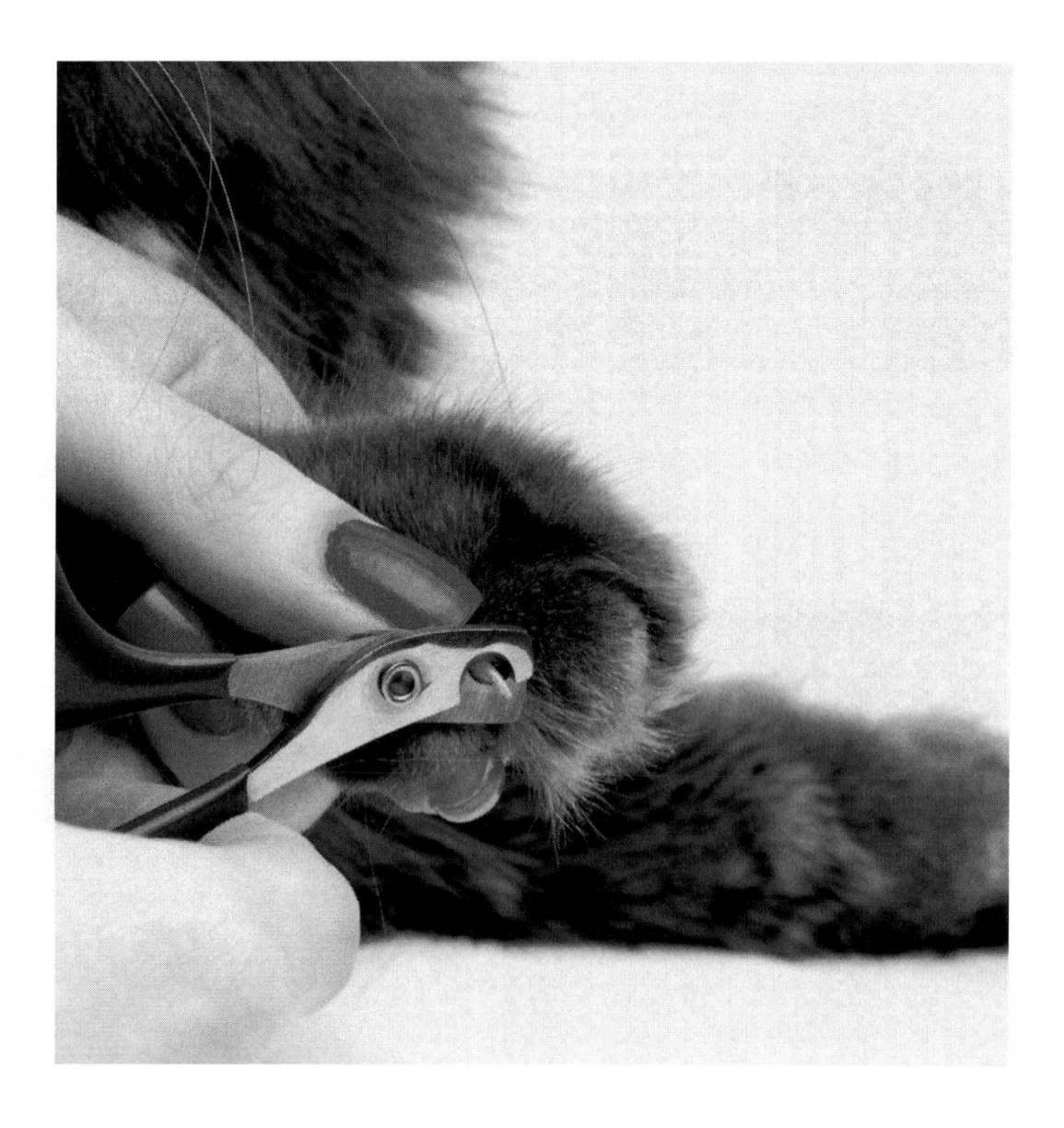

Clipping Your Cat's Nails: Most cats attend to their nails themselves, thank you very much. But claws can overgrow, tear and split causing painful infections. Trimming your cat's nails regularly reduces the chances of these problems, as well as tempering his urge to claw furniture. On average, a once-monthly trim should be adequate. Older cats may need trims more often.

Human nail clippers work well on some cats, particularly kittens with tiny claws. Commercial cat toenail clippers are available from your veterinarian, pet supply or online stores. These are designed to cut kitty claws at the proper angle without the risk of splitting or crushing the nail. There are trimmers designed like scissors, and also guillotine type clippers. The best clipper has very sharp blades, and is one you're comfortable handling.

Get Kitty used to having his paws handled while still a kitten. A good time to clip nails is when your cat is relaxed, perhaps after a nap. Often, it's easiest to have two sets of hands during nail clipping, one pair to hold and calm Kitty and the other to trim (see RESTRAINT). Trimming nails single handedly works well with trusting cats that have confident owners.

Grasp the paw and gently press it between your fingers and thumb to express the claws, using your other hand to clip the nails. Don't forget the dew claw. Trim only the end of the nail, which is usually white, and avoid the pink quick which will bleed. If you cut too closely, use a styptic pencil or corn starch on the nail, or rake the claw through a bar of soap to stop the bleeding.

Work quickly, and if Kitty begins to fret too much, let him go even if only one or two paws are done. You can finish later. Reward the cat with a play session or special treat, so he'll associated nail trimming with good things. Always trim your cat's nails before bathing (see CLAWS).

Bathing Your Cat: Although they are intrinsically clean creatures, all cats benefit from an occasional bath. Illness, poor grooming habits, parasite infestation, or simply getting themselves dingy may require more help than a brush can handle.

A bath stimulates the skin and removes excess oil, dander, and shed hair. But bathing too often can dry the skin. A good rule of thumb is to bathe shorthaired cats no oftener than every six weeks; two to three times a year during shedding season should suffice unless Kitty gets really grubby, or is a show cat. Longhaired cats benefit from more frequent baths.

Kittens should not be bathed until they are at least four weeks old. Elderly cats or extremely ill cats may be stressed by bathing. Babies and ill oldsters have difficulty regulating their body temperature, and can become chilled and develop pneumonia very easily. Follow your veterinarian's recommendation in these instances.

234
CAT FACTS

Just like with brushing, assemble your equipment beforehand. The cat should be thoroughly brushed and/or combed ahead of time. All mats must be removed before bathing, because water will just cement mats in place.

The bath area should be warm and draft free. The bathtub will do, but a waist-high sink is easier on your knees. Move all breakables out of reach, and push drapes or shower curtains that can spook your cat out of the way.

If you're de-bugging the cat, be sure your shampoo contains a cat-safe insecticide that will only affect the fleas. For routine cleaning, a simple grooming shampoo labeled specifically for cats is sufficient. Never use human products, or laundry detergent on your cat. At best, they can be harsh and dry out the skin; at worst, they can be toxic and kill your cat.

Assemble your shampoo, several towels, and washcloth near the sink or tub, and run warm water (about 102 degrees, or cat body temperature) before you bring in the cat. Some cats like the Turkish Van actually enjoy water, but no cat wants to be forced to do something. Don't create undo stress by making Kitty watch your preparations. Instead, make bath time a (hopefully) pleasant surprise.

One reason cats dislike bathing is they feel insecure on slippery surfaces. Placing a towel or rubber mat in the bottom of your tub or sink to give Kitty a foothold will do wonders for his confidence. Or, try standing the cat on a plastic milk crate which gives him something to clutch with his paws, while allowing you to rinse him top to bottom without turning him upside down.

Before you begin soaking the cat, place half a cotton ball inside each ear to prevent them filling with water. Some veterinarians recommend putting a drop of mineral oil in each eye before bathing, to protect them from soap.

For small cats or kittens, the bucket method of bathing often works best. Use the double sink in the kitchen, two or more large roasting pans, or a couple of buckets or wastebaskets set in the bathtub. Fill each with warm water, then gently lower your cat (one hand supporting his bottom, the other beneath the chest) into the first container to get him wet.

Don't dunk his face or splash water on him; that's what gets cats upset. Let him stand on his hind legs and clutch the edge of the container as you thoroughly wet him. Then lift him out onto one of your towels, and apply the shampoo, using the washcloth to clean his face. Once thoroughly soapy, dip the cat back into the first container to be rinsed. Get as much soap off as possible before removing him, and sluice off excess water before rinsing him in subsequent containers of clean water. Rinse his face with the washcloth.

Adult cats may object to being dunked, and running water can be scary. Another bathing method works better with large cats. Again fill a couple of buckets or wastebaskets with water ahead of time, but use a ladle to dip water over him. If you have a spray nozzle from the sink, use a low force, starting at his feet to get him used to the idea. Keep the nozzle close to the fur so he doesn't see the spray. Never spray in the face; use the washrag to wet that area. Keep one hand on the cat at all times to prevent escapes; it's doubly hard to catch a wet, soapy cat.

Professional groomers often use a figure-eight cat harness to tether the cat in place, which leaves the bather's hands free.

If flea shampoo is used, suds the neck area first to create a barrier the fleas won't cross. Lather from the neck down the body, to legs, feet and tail; use the washcloth on his face. For flea treatment, the shampoo must soak for up to ten minutes. Wrapping the soapy cat in a towel and holding him for the duration may be easier than keeping an unfettered foamy feline in the tub. Rinse Kitty's face with the washrag, taking care to avoid getting soap or water in his eyes or ears. Then rinse beginning at the neck and down his back; don't neglect beneath his tail or under his tummy.

When the water finally runs clear and you know he's clean, rinse him once more just to be sure. Don't forget to remove the cotton from his ears.

Wrap the squeaky-clean cat in a dry towel. Shorthaired cats dry quickly, but longhaired felines may need two or more towels to blot away most of the water. Some cats enjoy the blow dryer, but use only the lowest setting to avoid burning the cat. Combing long fur as you blow dry will give "oomph" to the longhaired coat.

Caring for Your Cat's Eyes: Flat faced cats like Persians have large prominent eyes that tend to water. Tears may stain the fur beneath the eyes, particularly of light colored cats. Normal eye secretions are clear and liquid, just like human tears; see your veterinarian if the discharge is cloudy or dark.

But even normal tears may turn crusty on the fur and irritate the skin, which can lead to infection. Daily maintenance prevents these problems. Use saline-soaked cotton balls to soften the secretions at the corners of Kitty's eyes and clean them away. There are also commercial preparations available from pet product stores that help remove the stain from fur (see EYES).

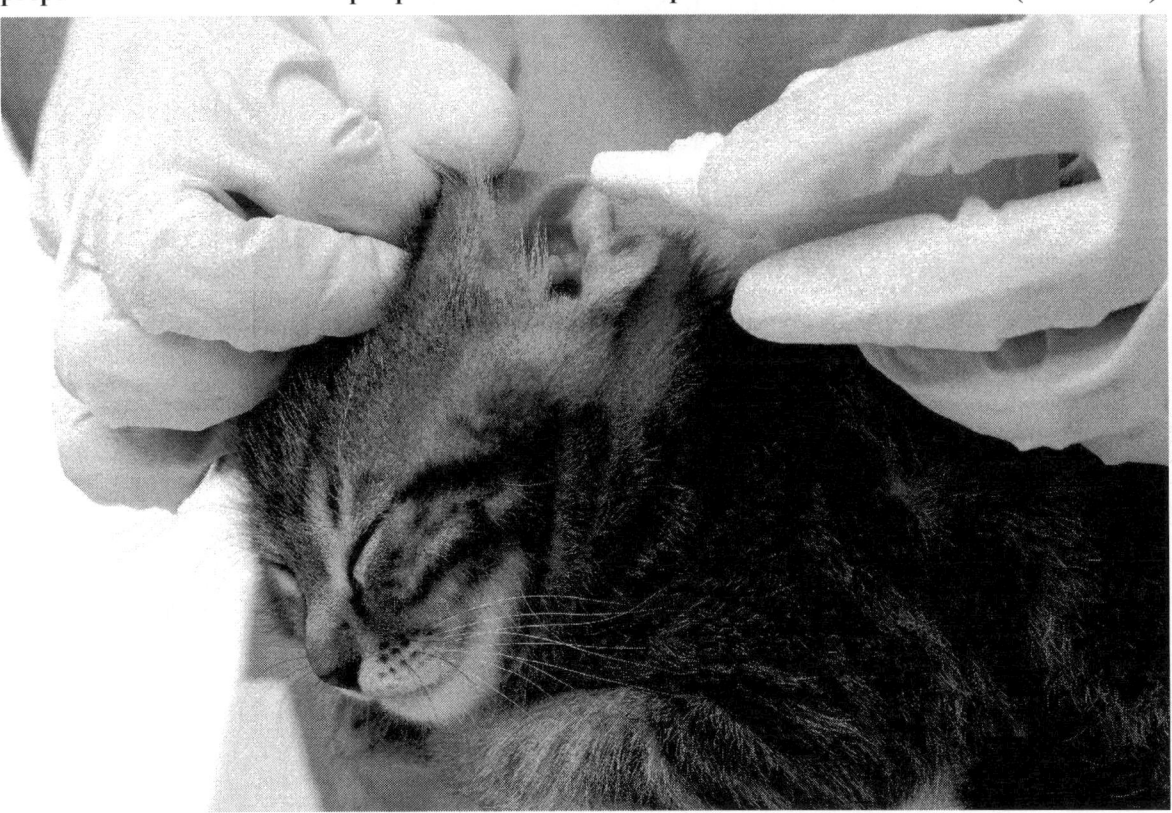

Caring for Your Cat's Ears: The inside of the healthy cat's ear is pink and free of discharge. Small amounts of light yellow wax is normal, but dark or crumbly material is not and may indicate the presence of ear mites. Check your cat's ears at least once a week during routine grooming sessions (see EAR MITES and OTITIS).

A cleaning solution suitable for cats is available from your veterinarian or pet store for routine maintenance, or use mineral oil or baby oil. Place a few drops on a cotton ball or swab, and gently wipe out the easily visible areas. Don't place drops of anything into the ear unless your veterinarian tells you to. When using a cotton swab to clean the tiny indentations, never go down into the ear further than you can see, or you may damage the cat's hearing (see EARS).

Caring for Your Cat's Teeth: (see PERIODONTAL DISEASE).

H

HAIR

Hair is the outgrowth from the skin of multiple thread-like colored filaments composed of keratin. These in combination make up the haircoat that covers the cat's skin.

Fur serves as a protective barrier between the cat's skin and the elements. All cats have fur, although the amount and type of haircoat varies from cat to cat and from breed to breed. Even "hairless" cats like the Sphynx breed typically sport a peach fuzz dusting of velvety fur.

Each hair is made up of the root seated within the skin itself, and the shaft which is the visible portion of the hair. Most cats have three types of hairs. Guard hairs are the coarse, long straight hairs found in the outer coat, awn hairs are medium length and make up the intermediate coat, and the undercoat is composed of soft, short downy fur that's curly or crimped. Sinus hairs, also called whiskers, are found on the face and legs and offer specialized sensory input.

Hair production is cyclic, growing from the root outward in a pattern of rapid growth, slower growth, and a resting period. Each cat hair grows about a third of an inch each month. That means Kitty generates about 60 feet worth of hair each day. Old hairs are pushed out by new (see SHEDDING).

Proper nutrition is essential for a healthy coat. Hair is 95 percent protein, and gains its sheen and healthy "glow" from the proper balance of fats and other nutrients. Poor nutrition often is reflected in the skin and haircoat first. Grooming is beneficial for all cats, and especially important for longhaired cats to keep their haircoat healthy.

HAIRBALLS

Hairballs are hotdog or cigar-shaped masses of compressed fur that are vomited by the cat. Cats spend a great deal of their time licking and cleaning themselves during self-grooming, and swallow fur as a part of this process.

Most swallowed hair passes through Kitty's digestive system, is expelled during bowel movements, and causes the cat no problems. Hair that doesn't pass collects in the stomach in a dense ball, and is expelled by throwing up. It is normal for cats to occasionally experience hairballs. Owner grooming reduces the amount of fur that cats swallow and helps prevent hairballs, which in some instances can become dangerous (see GROOMING).

Large amounts of swallowed fur may block the digestive tract, and become impossible for the cat to vomit or excrete. Impaction is the most common cause of feline constipation, with 50 percent of cases due to hairballs. Cats have been known to suffer hairballs as big as baseballs that require surgery to be removed. Frequent vomiting is the most common sign of intestinal blockage (see also SWALLOWED OBJECTS). A problem hairball may also result in diarrhea, loss of appetite, wheezing cough or dry retching, or a swollen abdomen. See your veterinarian immediately if your cat exhibits any one or more of these signs.

Commercial "hairball" high fiber diets and fiber supplements may be a better choice for chronic problems. The extra bulk helps carry the hairs naturally through the system so they're eliminated in the litter box. Commercial veterinary products are available. Plain bran, flavor-free varieties of Metamucil, or a teaspoon of canned nonflavored pumpkin (a favorite with some cats) added to the diet also provides the necessarily bulk.

Commercial products are available to help the hairball pass more readily, and usually are composed of a non-digestible fat-type ingredient. Take care to follow label instructions or your veterinarian's advice, because such products can interfere with the cat's use of fat soluble vitamins if overused.

HAIRBALLS

SYMPTOMS: Throwing up wads of fur; diarrhea; constipation; straining in litter box; loss of appetite; cough; dry retching; swollen abdomen.
HOME CARE: Hairball medication; non-medicated petroleum jelly; canned pumpkin; natural fiber supplements
VET CARE: Occasionally surgery to remove blockage
PREVENTION: Routine grooming, add fiber like Metamucil or pumpkin to diets or switch to higher fiber rations.

Occasional use of home products may also work well. Avoid digestible fats like butter, which tend to cause diarrhea or are absorbed before they can move the problem out. One of the most effective home treatments is non-medicated petroleum jelly, which many cats consider a treat. Spread the jelly on Kitty's forepaw for him to lick off.

Hair Loss
It is normal for cats to lose hair as new growth replaces old dead fur (see SHEDDING). Longhaired cats normally shed heavy undercoat in clumps, leaving a moth-eaten appearance that can look alarming to the owner. Most cats, particularly shorthaired cats, have areas of thinning hair at the temples.

Hair loss in isolated areas may be a sign of parasite infestation or skin disease (see ALLERGIES and RINGWORM). In these instances, the skin is often inflamed with scabs or sores. A veterinary diagnosis is necessary before the proper treatment can begin.

Occasionally, cats suffering stress react with over-grooming, which can result in hair loss. Displacement grooming can become a habit if the stressful conditions are not addressed (see STRESS).

While grooming is a normal response that seems to help cats calm themselves down, a few cats take the behavior to an extreme. They may worry an isolated area, and cause an ongoing sore usually on one leg, the belly or flank. More often, cats simply lick, nibble and scratch themselves until the hair begins to break off in single or multiple areas of hair loss. Called psychogenic alopecia, this condition generally results in a line or stripe down the back of very short stubbled hair; the skin beneath appears perfectly normal.

Removing the cause of the stress is a good first step in these cases, but psychogenic skin conditions usually result from behaviors that have become habit. Veterinary diagnosis followed by drug therapy and/or a feline behaviorist's intervention is probably necessary to break the cycle.

Heartbeat see PULSE.

Heart Disease Heart disease takes many forms and affects as many as 11 percent of the feline population. The most common condition, cardiomyopathy, affects the heart muscles in various ways. Today, hypertrophic cardiomyopathy is the most common cardiac condition seen in cats. It is also a genetic disease in humans and in some breeds of cats, such as the Maine Coon. Signs of the disease vary, from cats that appear totally unaffected to those who suffer sudden death. About 50 percent of cats that show signs die within three months of diagnosis, while cats with minor to no outward signs usually survive more than five years with medical help. Treatment won't cure heart disease, but it may prolong or at least improve the quality of the cat's life (see CARDIOMYOPATHY).

Heartworm Disease Feline heartworm disease (FHD) is caused by a type of roundworm that belongs to a group of parasites called *filarids*. Although FHD was first reported in 1922, dogs are the natural host and are much more commonly affected.

FHD has been diagnosed in all fifty states, and cats are at risk for heartworms wherever dogs are at risk. But because the resulting disease, FHD symptoms, diagnosis and treatment are quite different than that of dogs.

To become infected, a cat must live in an area that has infected dogs, and with mosquitos that have a taste for both dog blood and cat blood. The mosquito ingests baby heartworms, called microfilariae, when it bites an already infected dog. The heartworm spends about three weeks developing inside the mosquito, molting and growing until the larvae migrate to the mouthparts of the insect. It is this stage that is infective to the cat or dog. When the mosquito again takes a blood meal, larvae are deposited upon the skin and gain entrance to the host's body through the bite wound left by the mosquito.

During the next several months, the immature parasites undergo a number of further molts and development stages inside the animal's body, ultimately migrating to the heart and pulmonary arteries where they mature. In dogs, adult worms mate and shed microfilariae into the animal's bloodstream, completing the cycle. Cats are known as "dead-end hosts" because their small bodies are rarely able to sustain enough mature worms of both sexes for the parasite to be able to reproduce; consequently, cats almost never show the presence of microfilaria. Also, some cats appear to mount an immune defense against the parasite which kills the baby worms and effectively cures the cat. But an unknown number of cats die of the disease without ever being diagnosed.

HEARTWORM DISEASE

SYMPTOMS: Difficulty breathing; weight loss; sudden collapse; coughing; asthma-like signs; chronic vomiting not associated with hairballs or food
HOME CARE: Supportive care; reduce stress
VET CARE: Supportive care; reduce stress
PREVENTION: Heartworm preventative

All cats exposed to mosquitos are at risk, but indoor cats may be at highest risk because their natural resistance may not have been primed by past unsuccessful exposure (see IMMUNE SYSTEM). The incidence of FHD appears to parallel that of dogs, and current studies estimate the incidence of FHD to be about five to fifteen percent that of the disease in dogs in any given geographic location.

The majority of infected cats probably don't develop symptoms, and may recover without anyone knowing they were infected. However, the acute form of the disease occurs in cats more frequently than in dogs; such cats appear normal one moment, then suffer sudden respiratory failure and die within minutes.

Chronic FHD has vague signs different than the canine version of the disease. Dogs often develop signs of heart failure, which is rare in cats. Instead, cats suffer from diseases of the arteries of the lungs, have difficulty breathing, lose weight, become weak, and may suddenly collapse. FHD can cause breathing problems that may be misdiagnosed as asthma (see ASTHMA) or allergic bronchitis with coughing, which is actually part of the syndrome called heartworm-associated respiratory disease (HARD). Many cats suffer vomiting that isn't associated with eating.

Once infection in the lungs becomes established, the live heartworms appear able to suppress the cat's immunity, which may allow some cats to tolerate infections without problems for a short time. But once mature worms start to die, they create inflammation and thromboembolism (blockages) that often kill the cat with no warning.

Diagnosis is based on signs of disease, blood screening techniques, X-rays, and echocardiography. Traditional tests for dogs look for microfilariae in the blood, but this isn't helpful in cats that rarely have immature worms.

A better test for cats detects antigen that worms release into the bloodstream. A positive test is considered diagnostic, but the worms must be female, at least five months old, and in sufficient numbers to be detected. Cats usually host only two to three worms which typically die before becoming old enough to be identified by this test. False-negative test can results when infections are light, female worms are still immature, or only male worms are present.

Antibody tests can detect infection by both male and female worms as early as two months after infection. But antibody tests don't diagnose infection, but only indicate the cat was infected at one time. A positive test means exposure has taken place, but a negative test is inconclusive. Using the antibody and antigen tests together, though, can be helpful.

The canine drug treatment melarsomine dihydrochloride is toxic to cats in even small doses, and not recommended for treatment. Treatment in dogs consists of killing the worms in the heart, and allowing the body to slowly absorb the debris. But in cats, worms more typically are in the pulmonary arteries of the lungs. Worm debris can block the blood flow in the lungs, and this embolization can kill the cat. For that reason, heartworm disease in cats is usually treated only with supportive care aimed at relieving the cat's symptoms of distress.

Cats diagnosed with heartworm disease but not yet showing signs of illness may be monitored in the hopes the cat's own body will self-cure. Follow up antibody and antigen tests, along with X-rays, will show improvement if this approach is successful.

Prednisone in gradually reducing doses is the recommended supportive treatment of choice for any cat that shows signs on X-rays of heartworms. This helps control the inflammation. Heartworm preventative is available for cats.

The American Heartworm Society (www.heartwormsociety.org) recommends that all cats living in heartworm-endemic regions be protected with readily available preventative during the transmission season (mosquito season). Preventives should be started in kittens at eight weeks of age and continued thereafter.

HEAT STROKE see HYPERTHERMIA.

HEMATOMA

SYMPTOMS: Soft swelling on the ear flap
HOME CARE: None
VET CARE: Surgical drainage
PREVENTION: Routine ear cleaning to prevent self-trauma from scratching at parasites

248
CAT FACTS

HEMATOMA Hematoma refers to a swelling beneath the skin that contains blood. Hematomas are generally caused by a blow or bruise, and usually resolve by themselves. Large hematomas may require surgical drainage.

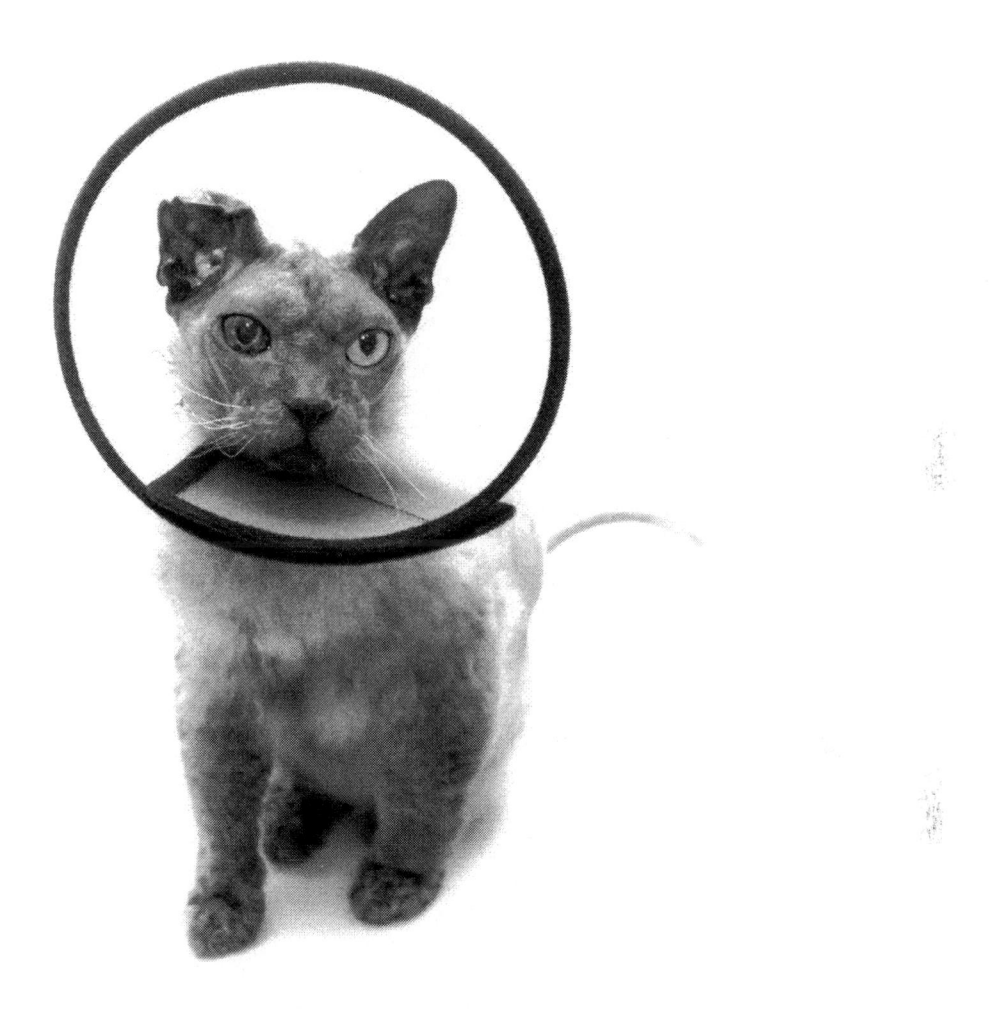

Aural hematomas, those occurring in the skin of the ear flap, often appear as a result of parasites or ear infection. The pinna swells suddenly when bruising separates the ear cartilage from the skin as the pocket between fills with blood and fluid. The soft swelling is usually on the inside but can be on the outside surface of the ear flap. The condition is much more common in dogs, particularly breeds with floppy ears. The underlying cause for the injury must be treated as well as the hematoma (see OTITIS and EAR MITES).

Unless the trapped blood is removed, the ear cartilage may scar and shrivel. Small hematomas may be treated by drawing out the blood with a syringe, followed by firm bandaging for seven to ten days. But often, the ear simply again inflates in a day or two with new blood and serum.

CAT FACTS

Surgery provides the best results. The cat is anesthetized, and a small incision is made to the inside surface of the cat's ear. Collected blood and other debris is removed, and the separated flaps of tissue stitched together, leaving a narrow opening at the incision line. This allows fluid to drain as the incision heals, and prevents the wound from re-ballooning with fluid.

In severe cases, a soft padding of bandage may be used to minimize deformity and help the ear retain normal shape as it heals. Typically, cats that undergo this surgery are fitted with a collar restraint to prevent them scratching at the wound (see ELIZABETHAN COLLAR).

HEMOTROPHIC MYCOPLASMAS

Hemotrophic mycoplasmas (previously called haemobartonellosis) is a disease caused by a specialized bacteria that lives on the surface of red blood cells. The parasite, called *Haemobartonella felis*, affects domestic cats around the world and was first recognized in the United States in 1953. Formerly the condition was called Feline Infectious Anemia, or FIA, because the most obvious sign of disease is anemia. *Mycoplasma haemofelis* (previously classified as the large form of *Haemobartonella felis*) and *M. haemominutum* (previously classified as the small form of *H. felis*) are the two types that cause this condition.

Half of cats with acute disease suffer a sudden high fever of 103 to 106 degrees, act depressed or weak, lose their appetite and have pale to purple gums. Some cats also become jaundiced from the rapid destruction of blood cells; the light areas of their skin takes on a yellowish cast (jaundice). But cats can have such minor symptoms the owner may never realize the cat is infected.

The primary form of the disease develops without other disease being present. About one third of infected cats will die from the results of severe anemia if they are not treated.

The more common secondary form occurs when other illnesses like feline infectious peritonitis or feline leukemia virus have compromised the cat's immune system. Fewer cats survive this secondary form of the disease.

Infectious blood must be introduced into a healthy cat to transfer the disease. The mycoplasma bacteria is transmitted mainly by ticks and fleas that have fed off of other infected animals. It is also spread to kittens through an infected mother, or from body fluid exchange when during fights. Rarely, the disease can be transmitted inadvertently during blood transfusions of infected blood to an uninfected animal.

HEMOTROPHIC MYCOPLASMAS

SYMPTOMS: Sudden high fever; depression; weakness; loss of appetite; pale lips or gums; sometimes yellowish cast to tissue
HOME CARE: None
VET CARE: Tetracycline-like antibiotic
PREVENTION: Flea control

Anemia is caused a couple of different ways. Parasites that colonize the surface of the cat's red blood cells may cause the cells to rupture and die. Also, the body's immune system marks the infested cells for the spleen to filter them out of circulation. These blood cells are then either destroyed by the spleen, or are cleansed and returned to circulation. The parasites are scooped out like a cherry being pitted, but even these cleansed cells are damaged and die more quickly than normal cells. The bone marrow usually remains active making new blood cells to replace those being lost, but when production can't keep up with demand, anemia occurs.

The disease can affect all cats of any age or breed, but occurs most often in male cats between four to eight years old. Diagnosis is based on actually finding the parasite on the blood cell, so blood samples are examined with a microscope to find the tiny bugs. The blood smear will be stained to identify the mycoplasmas in the blood. A polymerase chain reaction (PCR) test, or a Coombs' test, may help identify the mycoplasmas.

The parasite is most likely to be found in the tiny capillaries where the blood doesn't move quite so quickly. A drop of this so-called "sludged blood" is collected by piercing the cat's ear with a needle, and collecting the tiny drop that appears. Cats typically don't tend to mind this type of sample collection nearly as much as drawing blood from a larger vein in the leg or neck.

But cats with suspicious signs are treated whether the parasite is found or not. The disease is primarily treated for ten days to two weeks with an antibiotic that kills the parasite. Left untreated, thirty percent of cats will die from complications of the infection.

Cats diagnosed or suspected of having been infected with this bacteria should never be used in blood donor programs. Be sure to provide effective flea and tick preventive measures to protect your cat from this infection.

HERBS

Herbs may be considered old fashioned in today's cutting-edge world of medicine, but holistic veterinarians continue to use herbs. Many of these plants are the foundation of modern drugs and medications, but don't cause the same side effects as the modern drugs. That's because the chemicals derived from herbs have been isolated to a single ingredient that works quickly but can sometimes be too harsh.

The original plant, though, has other components that buffer these effects. For instance, willow bark contains a chemical that works similarly to aspirin. But while aspirin can predispose to gastric ulcers, willow bark protects against them.

Most herbs contain active ingredients within their bark, seeds, roots, and leaves so a single plant could be effective in multiple conditions.

For example, slippery elm not only can ease diarrhea, it also will soothe a sore throat. Because they have many active ingredients, but are relatively safe, herbs may be effective even when the veterinarian hasn't been able to pinpoint what's causing the problems.

Herbs are rarely used by themselves. They work well alongside conventional treatments. Care must be taken, though, because the chemical components of the herb may interact with the medications your cat already takes. It's always best to check with your veterinarian about any herbal products before giving them to your pets.

One reason is that herbs are not as regulated as drugs. The strength of a given herb may vary and be much weaker—or even triple the strength—of the exact same herb from another company.

Here's another dangerous scenario. A common drug given for heart problems is digitalis. The herbal remedy for heart problems is hawthorn (*Crataegus laevigata*). If the two are given together they can amplify the effects of both the drug and the herb and create an overdose that could potentially kill your pet.

The U.S. Department of Agriculture has cataloged more than 80,000 herbs and choosing them can be confusing. Think of herbs as medicines, and the best person to prescribe medicines is your veterinarian after diagnosing a health concern.

Herbs also come in many forms—fresh, dried, concentrated, or packed into capsules—and the form may be chosen based on the best way to administer to your pet. Even when the active ingredients are the same, herbs have different effects depending on how they're prepared and packaged.

Apothecaries sell bulk herbs as fresh green plants, as dried or as powdered. Bulk herbs are usually prepared by steeping them in boiling water to make teas and tonics quickly absorbed by the body. This can be pretty easy to administer as liquids.

Fresh and dried herbs don't last forever. Look for expiration or harvest dates on the label and give them the sniff test. If they smell dry or musty, they've probably given up their essential oils and won't be as effective. Store herbs in a cool dark place or they lose strength when they're exposed to light and heat. Some herbs will react with chemicals in plastic containers, so it's better to store them in glass, instead.

Extracts and tinctures are concentrated liquid forms of herbs and work very quickly. They can be mixed in a glass of water and poured on your pet's food or administered directly into the cat's mouth. Some tinctures are made by soaking herbs in alcohol making them taste bad and some can be potentially dangerous (especially for cats!) because of the alcohol so only a vet should prescribe these.

Herbal capsules and tablets are just as effective as fresh herbs but are absorbed less quickly by the body. When speedy action isn't an issue they may be recommended for convenience of administration when it's easier to simply pill your pet.

The strength of herbs varies from batch to batch due to differences in climate, soil conditions, and which fertilizers were used. The only way to be sure you're getting the best quality every time is to rely on a reputable supplier. Ask your vet for a recommendation or purchase directly from the veterinarian.

CAT FACTS

HIGH RISE SYNDROME (HRS)
The term "high-rise syndrome" was coined to describe cats that fall from tall buildings. The syndrome is most common during warmer summer months when apartment windows are left open or loosely screened, or cats are allowed access to high terraces and balconies. All cats are at risk, but young cats seem to fall most often.

The problem increased as cats became ever more popular big city apartment pets. And whether the cat rolls off a windowsill in his sleep, misjudges a leap, or simply loses his balance and falls, the end result is severe injury at best, and often death.

Survival rate and the extent of injuries depend on the height from which the cat falls. Terminal velocity, the highest speed a cat will reach when falling, is sixty miles per hour and is achieved from falls greater than five stories.

255

CAT FACTS

Falls from the fifth through ninth floor are the most dangerous and result in the worst injuries. The cat's sense of balance prompts him to turn in the air and land on his feet (see BALANCE). The cat falls with his legs braced in front of him, and lands rigid. His legs hit first, then his head, and both can suffer terrible bone-shattering injury (see FRACTURE).

Surprisingly, cats survive falls from higher than nine stories with fewer injuries. Falls from these heights apparently allow the cat time to relax and "parachute" the legs outward so that the wind catches the loose skin in the thighs and armpits and slows the fall. Landing spread-eagle allows the chest and abdomen to absorb most of the shock, rather than the head and legs. Falls from the first through fourth floor aren't as likely to cause serious injuries, perhaps because the cat doesn't have time to reach tremendous speeds.

Injuries from falls can include any combination of fractures of the legs, pelvis, ribs, back (with resulting spinal cord implications), jaw, teeth and palate. Internal injuries that aren't necessarily visible are common.

Watch for stopped breathing, and be prepared to give artificial respiration. Control bleeding with pressure pads. Cover open wounds and keep your cat as still as possible. Any blood in the eyes, nose or mouth could mean a possible head injury. Slide the cat onto a flat rigid object like a cookie sheet or board, and then place a towel over top to keep him warm and safely in place for transport to the veterinarian. A cat that suffers a fall from any height needs immediate veterinary evaluation.

Protect your cat by keeping windows closed, screens secure, and access to balconies or terraces restricted.

HIP DYSPLASIA

The pelvis cradles the head of the femur (thigh bone) in a cup-like socket of bone that forms the hip. As a young pet grows, if the alignment isn't just right, a progressive, degenerative abnormality of the fit of these bones, or hip dysplasia, can develop. The misalignment causes wear and tear on the joint that promotes osteoarthritis (see ARTHRITIS).

Hip dysplasia is frequently seen in a number of pedigreed as well as mixed breed cats. The number has likely been under-reported due to the stoic nature of felines.

Severe disease may be seen as early as four months of age, but usually develops in nine to twelve-month-old pets. They tend to have trouble getting up, difficulty jumping, limp after exercise, or display a classic wavery or bunny-hop gait.

Pets with HD are not bred in an effort to avoid passing on the trait to offspring. Outward signs may point to a problem, but for a conclusive diagnosis, X-rays are performed while the pet is under anesthesia. The pet is placed on his back and the veterinarian looks for the typical arthritic changes and subluxation (laxness) of the bone fit (see X-RAY).

There are typically three levels of treatment. The vast majority of cats do well with medical management to control discomfort. Weight control and moderate exercise can help keep pets flexible. Cartilage-enhancing medications like chondroitin sulfate and glucosamineglycan, used at a very high dose early on, and for the rest of the pet's life, can slow the development of hip dysplasia.

Holistic veterinarians may recommend herbal relief such as boswellia to help relieve joint discomfort. Providing heat lamps or heat pads under the cat's bed also can provide relief, as well as regular gentle massage to keep the cat active (see PAIN).

Once arthritis has developed, other surgical options offer better results. A femoral head ostectomy (FHO) removes the femoral head, or "ball" of the joint, and prompts the pet's body to create a new "false" joint from fibrous scar tissue. This procedure works best for pets that weigh less than 40 pounds, and is the treatment of choice for cats when medical management fails. Total hip replacement surgery, long an option for dogs, has been available for cats since 2005 but is not often performed, since most cats do very well with the less expensive FHO.

HIP DYSPLASIA

SYMPTOMS: Reluctance to exercise; difficulty rising, running, or jumping; wavery gait, or bunny hops when running
HOME CARE: Encourage moderate exercise; provide good nutrition
HOLISTIC HELP: Supplements; heat treatment; herbal remedies; massage
VET CARE: Sometimes surgery
PREVENTION: None; provide good nutrition and keep cats lean to delay progression of disease

CAT FACTS

HOLISTIC MEDICINE While traditional "western" medicine can't be beat for addressing emergencies like broken legs and acute or critical health issues, holistic medical approaches may work better to prevent and treat chronic health challenges. The word *holistic* refers to a whole-body approach that addresses the health of the pet's physical and emotional being. This type of treatment may also be called "natural" or "alternative" medicine.

Rather that treating the "symptom" of disease, the holistic practitioner looks at the entire animal: diet, exercise, behavior, emotions, and even the environment. Conventional "western" medicine tends to focus on the disease, while holistic medicine focuses on the patient. Holistic veterinarians would rather try to prevent problems and to support the body's immune system to keep pets healthy rather than scramble to fix diseases or conditions after they happen. They believe once chronic problems develop they continue to get worse even with ongoing conventional treatment.

Veterinary holistic therapies encompass a wide range of old fashioned to cutting edge modalities. Some of these, like massage and acupuncture, have been successfully used in human medicine for centuries. Although veterinary supporters believe treatments like homeopathic remedies work exceedingly well, the way they work cannot always be satisfactorily explained by science. Holistic modalities also may include herbal remedies, flower essences, magnetic and light therapy, chiropractic care, nutritional supplements, and home prepared foods.

An integrated approach offers your cats the ideal care specific to his needs. Alternative/holistic veterinary medicine works great alongside much of mainstream medicine.

Conventional medicine can't be beat when it comes to diagnosing problems, so X-rays or blood analysis can reveal a tumor or fracture before the veterinary chiropractor provides a treatment. If your cat chews through an electrical cord and stops breathing, acupuncture resuscitation can start his heartbeat again until you can reach conventional trauma medicine help. Homeopathy can't perform surgery, but may help a traumatized pet survive surgery and heal more quickly afterwards.

Be sure to evaluate the claims of different holistic treatments before rushing into therapy. Sadly, when the term "natural" became very popular, some companies simply slapped on the label to increase sales. Just because something is "natural" doesn't mean it's safe or effective—poisonous mushrooms and a venomous snake bite are natural, too.

It's difficult sometimes to figure out odd-sounding therapies that work from quackery, so ask questions and do your research. Look for studies that back up the claims of a treatment's effectiveness. Your holistic vet will provide proven science when it's available. In fact, the National Institutes of Health (NIH) studies alternative care options for people and many of these apply to pets as well. Veterinary journals also publish studies and measure the effects of different techniques.

When a technique or product is very new there may not be scientific studies available. Because some of these therapies are "natural" there's not much money to be made and so costly evaluations may not be embraced by drug companies. In these cases, testimonials from other pet owners and veterinarians may provide convincing "anecdotal" evidence. Just take some claims with a grain of salt depending on who makes the claims—someone with a monetary gain could be suspect. But other pet owners and animal health professionals able to recognize true health improvements are more credible.

When choosing a holistic veterinarian, look for doctors that have training in natural and alternative treatments. Professional veterinary associations or holistic organizations offer study and accreditation (see APPENDIX B).

HOMEOPATHY

Homeopathy is a holistic modality embraced by some alternative medicine veterinarians. It is based on the concept that "like cures like." This sounds similar to the way that vaccinations are made using a part of the disease they are intended to cure, in order to "teach" the immune system to recognize and defend against the dangerous intruder—be that a virus or other pathogen.

Homeopathic remedies have become quite popular because giving the "wrong" remedy generally causes no harm, and owners like to try to treat cat problems at home. Homeopathic veterinarians, though, are in the best position to recommend homeopathic remedies.

Rather than using viruses, though, homeopathy treatment gives a pet miniscule amounts of substances that in larger doses would cause the same symptoms as the disease. For instance, the homeopathic treatment for vomiting would be to use a tiny amount of a substance that in its full strength would cause vomiting. Theoretically, this amplifies the original symptom and "wakes up" the body's defenses, causing the immune system to recognize the problem and gear up for the attack.

In order to identify substances that can cause certain symptoms, homeopathic practitioners test—or "prove"—the substances in healthy people. These folks are given the substance and describe what symptoms they feel. Pets aren't used in provings because they can't describe their symptoms. As a result, more than 2,000 homeopathic remedies have been proven, and homeopathic veterinarians say they work just as well in pets as in people.

Not everyone believes homeopathy works, and some attribute cures to the placebo effect. In other words, doubters suggest that the patient expects to get well by taking medicine so that even sugar pills work to a degree. Pets also can have a sort of placebo effect when the owner believes so strongly in the treatment they react differently around the pet and that influences symptoms and behavior.

But advocates argue that studies support the effectiveness of homeopathy. When researchers from the University of Washington and the University of Guadalajara looked at 81 children with diarrhea, children treated with homeopathy got better 20 percent faster than those given a placebo drug. Scientists in the Netherlands reviewed 107 smaller studies and found that 75 percent of the studies showed homeopathy to be effective. It may sound like magic, but something happens to get pets well.

Homeopathic remedies are labeled according to strength. A designation of "1X" means the remedy contains one part of the active ingredient and 10 parts distilled water or alcohol. A dose of 3X means a 1X solution has been diluted three times—a pretty concentrated dose. Many remedies are "1C" and have been diluted 100 times, or "1M" and diluted 1,000 times. It's not uncommon in homeopathy for a remedy to be diluted so much that not a single molecule of the active ingredient remains. That's yet another reason homeopathy seems like magic.

The remedies are prepared in a process of diluting and shaking, termed "sucussion." They are prepared in the same way flower remedies are diluted and succussed (see FLOWER ESSENCES). Sucussion is thought to encode the liquid with a "memory," or "vibrational energy" of the original substance, and the more it's diluted and succussed, the more powerful it becomes.

How can this be? We are used to thinking in terms of dilutions becoming weaker, but the opposite is true with homeopathy. The homeopathic X potencies (10-times dilutions) are weaker than the M potencies (1,000-times dilutions). Homeopathic remedies made for home use usually contain the lower potency X-strength remedies, while C- and M-strength remedies are typically prescribed by veterinarians.

Nobody knows how homeopathy works. Some researchers speculate the active ingredients become so minute they pass through the body's blood-brain barrier and influence the nervous system in ways we can't measure.

It takes great skill to properly prescribe the appropriate homeopathic remedy. They work best when matched to the individual pet's situation, and a one-size-fits-all approach may not work. While a conventional drug given to two cats to address the same problem generally work the same way, the homeopathic veterinarian must figure out the cause of the symptom, too. For instance, the remedy Nux vomica treats diarrhea due to eating rich food (maybe the pet raided the garbage). But if the diarrhea was caused by something else, a different homeopathic diarrhea remedy might work better. So there can be some frustrating trial and error before you find the proper remedy.

Homeopathic medicines don't always work quickly, either, and the longer the condition has been a problem, the longer the treatment may be required. Acute conditions like diarrhea tend to get better more quickly, though. For simple problems, homeopathic veterinarians say it's fine to try homeopathy at home, because giving the wrong remedy won't cause any problems.

Health food stores and pet supply companies often carry homeopathic remedies. The size of the patient makes no difference so you can use human products for your pets. It's the frequency of dosing that influences how strong the remedy becomes.

The remedies last nearly forever, so even though they can be expensive, it's a good investment. Sometimes you can find a pre-packaged home kit with a variety of remedies for the most common issues your cat may face.

Because they're energetic medicines, homeopathic remedies can lose their power when they're exposed to electromagnetic fields. TV sets or contact with your body's natural energy can reduce potency of a remedy. You might even absorb the effect through your hands.

That's why it can be tricky to administer homeopathic remedies to pets. You don't want to hide homeopathic remedies inside treats, either. They'll often come with dispensers able to shake out single tiny pills without you needing to touch them—so just open up the pet's mouth and shake one in, without touching. Don't feed your pet within 15 minutes of giving a remedy.

Homeopathic remedies also lose their effectiveness when they're exposed to heat or sunlight, or if they're stored near strong-smelling substances like coffee or perfume. When stored carefully—preferably in a dark, cool place—they'll last just about forever.

Be selective and try only one remedy at a time. Too many at once can interfere with healing. While homeopathy won't interfere with other medications or cause overdoses, the other conventional treatments may interfere with the effectiveness of the remedy. So check with your vet before mixing and matching.

Most acute problems like diarrhea or a swollen paw go away quickly. But if you don't see results in three days, you've likely picked the wrong remedy, so try a different one. While drugs work to eliminate symptoms altogether, homeopathic remedies just jump-start the body to heal itself—and that can take some time. Usually holistic vets suggest you give the remedy for a couple of days and then stop, and watch to see if it works.

ND# Hookworms

HOOKWORMS Hookworms (*Ancyclostoma* and *Uncinaria*) are intestinal parasites common to dogs and less common in cats. They are tiny thin worms less than a half inch long that take bites out of the wall of the small intestine, and live on the host's blood.

Several kinds of hookworms affect pets. The parasite is found more often in southern states where higher humidity and temperature make the parasite feel more at home. The adult females lay eggs, which are passed with the stool. When conditions are right, these eggs hatch and develop into infective larvae.

Hookworms prefer sandy soil, but may crawl onto vegetation seeking a host. Cats get hookworms by eating an infected mouse or cockroach, by swallowing larvae found in the soil or feces, or when larvae simply penetrate the skin, usually of the footpads. The immature worms migrate through the body until they reach the intestines, where they mature. Although puppies can become infected before they are born or through ingesting infected milk from their mother, this may occur but has not been definitively proven to happen with cats

HOOKWORMS

SYMPTOMS: Diarrhea and anemia; sometimes blood in the stool; weight loss; low energy
HOME CARE: None
VET CARE: Hookworm medication; supportive care when cat is anemic or dehydrated
PREVENTION: Keep litter box clean; avoid outdoor exposure

NOTE: Infective hookworm larvae are capable of penetrating human skin and causing a condition called Cutaneous Larva Migrans in which migrating larvae in the skin cause small, red itchy trails.

Hookworms cause blood loss (see DIARRHEA and ANEMIA). A large amount of blood in the stool may turn the feces black and tarry, but this is uncommon in cats. In young kittens, weak or malnourished cats, hookworms can cause sudden collapse and death. Hospitalization to address the anemia and shock may be necessary in severe infections. Adult cats with chronic infections typically suffer weight loss, diarrhea, anemia, and a general lack of energy.

Diagnosis is made by identifying eggs during microscopic examination of the stool. An oral medication typically is given to kill the adult worms in the intestinal tract or expel them. However, immature forms of the parasite may be retained in the cat's body, then cause a new outbreak when they migrate to the intestines during times of stress.

Preventing hookworm infection can be difficult. The best way is to practice good hygiene, and keep the litter box immaculate. Outdoor exposure is the greatest risk, so confining the cat indoors also helps. Sometimes of heartworm or flea preventive medications can also address hookworms.

HOUSEPLANTS, HAZARDS FROM see POISON.

HUMAN-ANIMAL BOND

Many ethical questions about pets would never be raised if not for the strong bond we share with our dogs and cats. Once a cat becomes a "family member," she is no longer a nameless, faceless piece of property that can be easily replaced if care becomes too expensive or time-consuming.

Studies on the human-animal bond have shown that children who learn empathy toward animals tend to feel it toward people, too. They recognize that "different" isn't "wrong." Learning to treat a dog like a dog and a cat like a cat, recognizing each species has its own physical and behavioral needs and are not little fur-covered humanoids, goes a long way toward developing a recognition and tolerance for all creatures that are different, including different people.

Behaviorists speculate that just as kittens have a socialization period during which they "learn" to accept other species, humans also have a similar window of opportunity. The pathways in the brain for various functions are forged early in life. Exposure to music, for instance, prompts the biochemical connections that embrace mathematical concepts, and hearing builds the routes necessary to develop language skills. Early positive contact with pets forms the necessary brain circuitry to "turn on" the switch that makes it possible for a special connection with an animal. Miss that window of opportunity, and the door doesn't open.

The "pet potential" probably exists in everyone, but not everybody develops the ability to connect with animals. In domestic cats the prime socialization period is two to seven weeks, and it's likely very early in children, too. People who miss that opportunity as young children can learn as they grow older, but may never quite understand the process or have that deep sense of "one-ness" with the animals in their lives.

Dr. Leo K. Bustad was one of the earliest to recognize the benefits of the human-animal bond. More than 20 years ago, he helped establish the Delta Society, an organization dedicated to celebrating and promoting pet-people partnerships, including training and certification of a variety of service animals that benefit human health.

Due in large part to these efforts, federal laws have been passed protecting the relationship between pets and their elderly or disabled owners or families residing in public housing. Additionally, state regulations barring animals from health-care facilities are being loosened to allow animal- assisted activity and therapy programs. Cats have always worked for people in a wide range of capacities, from hunters to protectors of grain. But modern pet partnerships go beyond traditional ones because to be effective, the "job" requires an emotional attachment between the animal and human.

For example, modern cats learn to "alert" their owners—that is, give a warning of impending medical events such as seizures and migraines—so they have time to seek help. Pets can detect changes in their owner's breathing or heart rate, so they can help head off blackouts, and even heart attacks. In the past decade, medicine has acknowledged the benefits that a positive pet relationship can have on our health, especially for stress-related conditions such as blood pressure.

Petting a cat or simply having them in the same room, lowers blood pressure. People living with pets visit the doctor less often, and recover more quickly when they are ill. Heart attack victims living with pets statistically survive longer than those without pets. Senior citizens living with cats, and children suffering from a variety of problems who have a pet all benefit both physically and mentally from this "pet effect."

Pets help people connect with other people. An elderly person stays more connected to life in order to care for a beloved pet, when she might not make the effort for herself. Pets help normalize relationships—disabled children who withdraw from peers interact with others when a "social" pet becomes the focus and bridge between them and other kids. Injury victims reluctant to endure painful rehabilitation will push themselves, when it means, for instance, twirling a ribbon toy for a cat. For many people, a connection with pets is vital. It's what we need to feel whole.

Hunting Behavior

The cat is by nature a predator, and is born with innate behaviors specific to hunting prey. This applies whether the cat is a free-living feral animal that relies on these behaviors to eat, or a pampered housecat that never wants for food. Many play behaviors use the same techniques as those used for hunting (see PLAY and FERAL).

However, instinct does not make every cat a successful hunter. Although all cats have the ability to hunt, skill and technique is learned only through practice. Kittens hone technical skills through play with their littermates, and by their mother's example. But even cats never exposed to prey as youngsters can learn to become successful hunters as adults.

Cats do not necessarily hunt to eat. Hunger does not trigger the behavior, it is the sound and sight of moving prey that provides the stimulus. Even well fed housecats react to a fluttering moth, leaping cricket or scampering mouse. The reaction to chase and capture is as natural to the cat as purring.

Feline hunting behavior relies heavily on sight and hearing to locate prey. Cats use a couple of hunting strategies, depending on the prey they seek. Sometimes Kitty prefers ambush, and will crouch in a likely spot—perhaps with eyes glued to the mouse hole—and wait with infinite patience for prey to appear. Cats may return time after time to areas where their hunts have been successful.

Fishing requires patience, too. Typically the cat waits in a likely spot on the bank for a suitable candidate to appear, then uses a paw to scoop and flip the fish from the water. In shallow water, Kitty may wade in and use both paws by pouncing and grasping the fish. Not all cats are able to perfect fishing technique, probably because of the visual perception difficulty regarding the water.

The stalk-and-pounce method is often favored. The cat walks slowly, pausing to stare about until prey is located. When the target is some distance away, Kitty quickly moves closer while staying low to the ground and using ground cover to shield her presence. When the distance is judged right, the cat abruptly stops and assumes the classic lying-in-wait pose: head and neck extend forward, body crouched closed to the ground, rear legs primed to spring forward. The cat may freeze in this position for endless minutes, patiently watching her prey. If the target moves farther away, the cat adjusts by ever-so-slowly creeping forward one paw-step at a time, even freezing with a foot in mid-air to avoid revealing herself. Again, she'll pose in the lying-in-wait stance, then readies herself for the grand finale.

CAT FACTS

The cat gathers her rear legs beneath her, preparing for a forward thrusting take-off, and without warning she springs toward the target. It may take several darting leaps before she's near enough for the final pounce.

Rarely is the quarry dispatched right away. Often, it escapes and Kitty must attempt to chase it down for recapture. Cats often indulge in a great deal of pouncing and tossing of prey into the air, allowing escape only to recapture small game.

But the action of playing with live prey is not intentionally cruel. It's a way for the cat to practice her skills, and also tests just how dangerous that rat or snake might be. Properly socialized felines have learned to inhibit their bite through play with owners and other cats, and toying with the quarry helps them build up the necessary excitement for the coup-de-grace.

Cats kill by biting the neck where the skull joins the spine, severing the vertebrae with the dagger-like canine teeth. They grasp the neck and use a "chattering" movement to position their bite accurately. In fact, cats frustrated in the hunt (i.e., watching from a window as squirrels play outside) often exhibit this chattering behavior which is actually the killing bite, in reaction to seeing out-of-reach prey.

CAT FACTS

Once the prize is dead and stops moving, the cat typically seems to lose interest for a short time. After the thrill of the hunt, the chase, and the kill, the cat needs time to return to an emotional equilibrium, and she may groom herself before claiming the prize. Then, she'll carry the prey to a well-sheltered area to eat.

For housecats, it's natural to bring prey home. Some behaviorist theorize that cats may look on humans as inept cat-children unable to hunt for themselves, so cats present food gifts with seeming pride to the chief care-giver in the home. More likely, the cat returns the prize to her nest—the house—with every intention of eating it later.

Eating wild game exposes cats to the risk of parasites (see TAPEWORMS and HOOKWORMS), as well as becoming nuisance bird-killers. Cats often learn to stalk without ringing preventative warning bells attached to their collars. The only way to prevent unacceptable hunting is by keeping the cat indoors. To keep the cat happy, provide indoor environmental enrichment and legal alternative outlets for hunting behavior.

HYPERESTHESIA SYNDROME

Hyperesthesia is defined as excessive sensitivity to touch. First described in the 1970s, the syndrome in cats refers to several specific obsessive/compulsive behaviors that have no recognizable stimulus.

All cats can be affected at any time in their life, but typically first appears in cats one to four years old. Hyperesthesia syndrome has been reported more frequently in Siamese, Burmese, Himalayans and Abyssinians.

The true incidence isn't known, perhaps because not all cases are being properly identified. The syndrome isn't diagnosed very often. Some feline practitioners who specialize in problem behaviors estimate about four percent of the cats they see suffer from this syndrome. However, the incidence in the general cat population would probably be much lower.

Hyperesthesia syndrome has three primary behavior patterns. The most common is called hyper-motor activity, characterized by excessive grooming. Typically, the pupils of the cat's eyes dilate followed by rippling of the skin on the back. It seems as if an increasingly intense sensation is felt by the cat on his tail and lower back. When Kitty can't stand the feeling any longer, he begins frantically licking and grooming the area over his spine and down to his tail. Some cats become so aroused they actually attack and mutilate themselves.

Inexplicable aggression is the second pattern of behavior. Cats seem friendly, and even beg for attention, then furiously attack when the owner attempts to pet them. The final pattern reported by the veterinary literature is seizure.

HYPERESTHESIA

SYMPTOMS: Rippling skin on the back; excessive self-licking or self-mutilation of tail; inexplicable aggression; seizure
HOME CARE: Interrupt behavior
VET CARE: Anticonvulsive; anti-anxiety or antidepressant drugs
PREVENTION: None

Experts disagree how to characterize the syndrome. The condition has been considered a type of epilepsy, and some behaviorists believe the strange behaviors are caused by psychomotor seizures triggered by stress. Other researchers believe the syndrome parallels human panic attacks and obsessive/compulsive disorders that occur due to the individual cat's personality in combination with the pressures of his environment, frustrations and stress levels.

Diagnosis involves eliminating other conditions that could prompt similar behavior, such as itchy skin, back pain, or simply high-energy play (see ALLERGY and PAIN). A behavior specialist is probably the best choice to make a definitive diagnosis (see APPENDIX B, VETERINARY RESOURCES).

Special equipment such as MRI or a SPECT Scan may be used to take pictures of the cat's brain. If the stress factors that seem to trigger incidents can be identified, it's hoped the syndrome can be eliminated. But even when problems can be identified, they often can't be fixed.

Some cats can be distracted from the behavior by an unexpected spritz of water from a squirt gun, or a sudden noise like clapping your hands, or slapping a newspaper against a table. Cats also respond to human anti-anxiety drugs and antidepressants. Drugs like Prozac and others act on the cat's brain to put a brake on the behavior, and are helpful in certain cases.

HYPERTHERMIA (HEATSTROKE)

Hyperthermia, also referred to as heatstroke, is body temperature elevated above normal. Hyperthermia results when the body's cooling mechanism is unable to adequately relieve excessive body temperature. Poor ventilation, direct sunlight and high humidity are predisposing factors. The condition most commonly affects cats during warm summer months.

Cats are not well equipped to deal with the heat and do not tolerate high temperatures well as people. What is warm to you may be unbearable to your cat. Whenever the environment reaches cat body temperature or above, unless steps are taken to protect the cat, hyperthermia will occur.

Most cases of heatstroke in pets are due to being left in a poorly ventilated car parked in the hot sun. Cats also suffer the condition when confined to cat carriers without adequate drinking water, or if unable to escape direct sunlight. Hot rooms or apartments that have poor circulation can be dangerous for cats. Curious felines that seek the warmth of the clothes drier may suffer hyperthermia, not to mention a possibly lethal battering. And cats may develop problems after extremes of exercise even if environmental temperature is comfortable. Cats with respiratory problems like asthma, obese cats, and short-nose cats like Persians and Himalayans are highly susceptible to the condition.

A rectal temperature over 106 degrees is diagnostic, but anything above normal should be addressed. Your cat needs help if she suddenly begins panting or breathing quickly, drooling or vomiting. The cat suffering heatstroke has a rapid pulse, staring or glazed eyes, and may develop diarrhea. In severe cases, the cat's gums become bright red and she may develop a bloody nose. In the final stages, panting turns to gasping, the cat becomes comatose and ultimately dies.

HEATSTROKE

SYMPTOMS: Panting; drooling; vomiting; temperature to 106; rapid pulse; staring; diarrhea; bright red gums; bloody nose; severe weakness; coma
FIRST AID: Wrap cat in cool wet towel; immerse cat in cool water; get to veterinarian
VET CARE: Cool water enemas; oxygen therapy; fluid therapy
PREVENTION: Keep cool water available at all times; provide good ventilation; never shut cat in closed car; keep fur well-groomed; restrict exercise during hottest times of the day

Treatment involves rapidly cooling the cat. If your cat is conscious or if you live farther than five minutes away from the clinic, try to lower the body temperature before rushing to the vet. Either wrap the cat in a towel soaked with cold water, or immerse the cat in a cool bath. Check Kitty's temperature every ten minutes, and continue cooling until her temperature drops to at least 103 degrees. You can also apply a cold, wet washcloth on the back of the cat's neck and then place a bag of frozen peas on top of the washcloth. That cools the cat and reduces the heat inside the brain to help prevent brain swelling.

Cats that show signs of severe weakness or that lose consciousness require immediate veterinary attention. Cool water enemas may be necessary to rapidly reduce the cat's temperature from the inside out. Cats suffering severe hyperthermia may need treatment for shock, including fluid therapy to combat dehydration. Oxygen therapy helps prevent brain damage (see SHOCK).

Prevent heatstroke by providing fresh drinking water at all times to your cat, along with proper ventilation and access to adequate shade. Avoid leaving any pet in parked, closed cars; even in the shade, the temperature in a closed car can reach 120 degrees in less than ten minutes.

A matted coat keeps heat from escaping; keep your longhaired cats properly groomed and mat-free, or clip the coat short during summer months. Restrict exercise during the hottest times of the day, particularly in high-risk cats.

Hyperthyroidism

The term hyperthyroidism refers to overactivity of the thyroid gland which produces excessive amounts of the active thyroid hormones thyroxine (T4) and triiodothyronine (T3). The condition is common in middle aged and older cats, particularly those 12 years or older (see GERIATRIC CAT).

In a majority cases, hyperthyroid in cats is due to a benign tumor (adenoma) of the thyroid gland. The remaining causes are due to thyroid carcinoma. Sarcomas (see CANCER) of the thyroid gland were previously thought to account for approximately only two to three percent of cases but a recent study indicated the figure might actually be much higher, approaching 25 percent.

Hyperthyroidism is considered the most commonly diagnosed disease of the endocrine system in cats. In some urban areas the disease is diagnosed in one of every 300 cats.

The double-lobed thyroid gland, located in the neck, secretes hormones that regulate the pet's metabolism, or how quickly the body uses nutrients. In cats, one or both lobes of the gland simply enlarge, producing a toxic nodular goiter in the neck. The abnormal condition causes overproduction of hormones that shifts the metabolism into overdrive.

A cat with hyperthyroidism typically have a ravenous appetite, hyperactivity, and a behavior change like a short temper or increased aggression. He is always hungry, but no matter how much he eats, he loses weight. He may act agitated, and pace a great deal. Some cats have upset stomachs and vomit, and often the stool and urine volume increases with the stool usually being soft. Cats suffering from hyperthyroidism may develop an oily coat, and typically exhibit very rapid nail growth (see CLAWS).

HYPERTHYROIDISM

SYMPTOMS: Ravenous appetite; weight loss; increased drinking and urination; seeks cool places to rest; hair loss; diarrhea; vomiting; hyperactivity; oily coat; rapid claw growth
HOME CARE: None
VET CARE: Drug therapy; surgery; radioactive iodine therapy
PREVENTION: None

A veterinarian may be able to feel the enlargement of the thyroid gland in the neck, or detect an increased heart rate. Because these signs may occur singly or in any combination, and can also point to a number of problem conditions, diagnosis often requires blood evaluation, microscopic examination of thyroid tissue, or other screening tests.

One study indicated 87 percent of hyperthyroid cats also have high blood pressure, and they may also have renal insufficiency (see KIDNEY DISEASE). Therefore, veterinarians look for these diseases if one of the three is diagnosed.

Most commercial laboratories measure thyroid levels as a routine part of blood test in cats. However, the thyroid level can be artificially suppressed by other health conditions. That's where the scintigraphy confirms and defines the problem.

Also called a thyroid scan, scintigraphy employs a radioactive particle that seeks out and attaches to thyroid tissue, which is then revealed on a gamma camera. It tells you if all the thyroid tissue is only in the neck right at the thyroid site, or other places. Scintigraphy defines the extent of the disease, and helps the veterinarian choose the best treatment options. For instance, if the scan shows the thyroid tissue is limited to the glands in the neck, surgery to remove affected tissue may be a good option.

A tiny dose of a mildly radioactive but inert metal called technesium is injected into the cat's vein, travels throughout the body, and within about 20 minutes it is preferentially taken up by thyroid tissue, salivary tissue, and the gastric mucosa. After 20 minutes, the cat is gently placed on the flat-faced camera, and the inch-thick crystal inside the camera picks up the X-rays emitted from the cat's body and glows in response.

With cancer, the radioactivity is scattered all up and down the neck, versus a localized benign process that's sharp and well defined and in one spot in the neck. Removing part or all of the affected thyroid may be the best choice. Daily thyroid supplements take the place of the missing gland after removal. Methimazole (Tapazole) is the drug of choice. This anti-thyroid drug doesn't cure, but does control, feline hyperthyroidism.

Transdermal medication has been successfully used for years in human medicine, and has been used for some time in veterinary medicine especially for pain control (fentanyl patches) and in hyperthyroid cats. The struggle and stress of medicating cats can make them even sicker, so ask your veterinarian about less stressful medication options.

Injecting radioactive iodine that selectively destroys thyroid tissue is another option, and that has a 98 percent cure rate for cats. Only specialized referral hospitals like university teaching hospitals offer this treatment, though. The government regulates the use of radioactive iodine, and a treated cat must be quarantined for one to four weeks, and his urine and feces monitored for radioactivity before he is released. All material removed from the cage must be handled as radioactive waste.

HYPOTHERMIA

Hypothermia is body temperature that falls below normal. Cats have several built in protective mechanisms to keep warm. Insulating fur traps a layer of air next to the skin, and heat is conserved by curling up in protected, sheltered areas. The action of shivering generates heat, and in cold weather cats keep themselves warm by burning more calories at the cellular level. In extremes of cold, the cat's body diverts circulation from the ears, toes, and tail and shunts blood to the trunk. Failure of these protective mechanisms can result in hypothermia. The action that protects vital internal organs from the cold actually promotes damage to the extremities (see FROSTBITE).

Outdoor cats are in the high risk category for hypothermia (see FERAL). Very young kittens unable to regulate their own body temperature are prone to hypothermia. Internal heat production relies on muscle and fat reserves; these are less available in young kittens and geriatric cats, and makes them more vulnerable to the cold. But any cat exposed to extreme cold, that becomes wet, or that suffers shock from other injuries risks hypothermia.

The condition is designated as mild, moderate, or severe according to the cat's body temperature. The cat suffering from mild hypothermia will act lethargic and shiver, and perhaps suffer muscle tremors. The body temperature will be 90 to 99 degrees F. If the cat is wet, a warm bath will help rewarm him. Dry him thoroughly with towels, but avoid using hair blowers which can burn the cat. Simply wrapping him in a warm blanket allows the cat's own body to rewarm itself and in mild cases is all that's required.

Cats experience moderate hypothermia when body temperature falls between 82 to 90 degrees; the shivering response will stop. Severe hypothermia occurs at body temperatures below 82 degrees, and is characterized by the cat losing consciousness with a severe slowing of heart and breathing rate. The cat may look dead.

Veterinarians have special thermometers able to record these low body temperatures, but standard rectal thermometers only measure as low as 93 degrees. If the cat has stopped shivering, and/or loses consciousness, veterinary attention is necessary if the cat is to survive.

HYPOTHERMIA

SYMPTOMS: Lethargy; shivering stops; temperature below 98 degrees; loss of consciousness; slowed body function; cat appears dead

FIRST AID: Wrap in blanket; give warm bath; get to veterinarian immediately

VET CARE: Aggressive core rewarming; heating pads; water bottles; warm water enemas; heated intravenous fluids

PREVENTION: Confine cats indoors during cold weather; provide shelter from wind and wet

CAT FACTS

Treatment is aimed at rewarming the cat, preventing further heat loss, and keeping vital organs working. Passive warming—wrapping in a blanket—is not sufficient in moderate and severe hypothermia.

Moderate hypothermia requires active external rewarming, which is the use of hot water bottles, electric blankets, recirculating water blankets, heating pads, or other heat sources. Heat is applied only to the body, keeping the extremities cool to prevent shock which may kill the cat. The cat must be protected from direct contact with the heat source, though, because hypothermia prevents the body from conducting excessive heat away, so cats can be easily burned.

Severe hypothermia requires core warming, which basically is heating the cat from the inside out. This can involve warm water enemas, warm intravenous fluid therapy, airway rewarming with oxygen, even heart/lung bypass machines to warm the blood. Fluids may be repeatedly flushed into the abdomen to warm the organs and tissues, then drawn back out until body temperature returns to normal. The prognosis for full recovery from severe hypothermia is guarded; organs and tissues are often damaged beyond repair.

If you believe your cat is suffering from moderate to severe hypothermia but are unable to reach veterinary help, treat the cat yourself using external warming techniques described above. The temperature of water bottles should be about 100 degrees, warm to the touch but not burning, and buffer with towels or blankets. Placement should be concentrated on the chest and abdomen, and in the armpit areas beneath the cat's legs. Take the cat's temperature every ten minutes until it reaches 100 degrees. When Kitty begins to revive and move, give her one to two tablespoons of honey or Karo syrup. Take her for veterinary evaluation as soon as possible.

Hypothermia can and should be prevented. Most cases of hypothermia occur in severe weather, but even moderately cold temperatures can be dangerous when wind chill raises the risk of hypothermia. Wet fur compounds the effects of cold, and wind strips away the protective warm air layer caught in the cat's fur.

Outdoor cats must have access to shelter from the wet, wind, and the cold. Loose bedding like straw or several blankets helps trap and hold pockets of warmer air when the cat builds a nest or burrows into it. An infrared lamp or warming pad is also helpful, but should be positioned so the cat can escape direct warmth to avoid burns.

Feed outdoor cats a higher energy-dense food during cold temperatures. The body must use more energy to maintain optimum temperature, so increase the frequency and the amount fed. Check with your veterinarian for a recommendation; a super-premium adult ration or a high calorie kitten food are appropriate. The best way to prevent hypothermia in cats is to keep the cat inside. (see FROSTBITE and OUTDOOR SHELTER).

279

280
CAT FACTS

281

IBUPROFEN Ibuprofen (propionic acid) is a common human pain reliever found in products like Motrin and Advil, and is one of a group of nonsteroidal anti-inflammatory drugs (NSAIDs) that includes naproxen (Aleve). A cat's body metabolizes, or breaks down, NSAIDs at a different rate than humans.

Vomiting is the most frequent sign, with the digested blood making the vomitus look like old coffee grounds; occasionally, bright red fresh blood is seen. The drug prevents oxygen from being absorbed into the blood, which may result in your cat's gums turning blue from lack of oxygen, and the cat having difficulty breathing.

IBUPROFEN

SYMPTOMS: Vomiting bloody or coffee-ground-like material; blue gums; difficulty breathing
HOME CARE: EMERGENCY! SEE VET IMMEDIATELY; stop administering the NSAID medication immediately
VET CARE: Stop administration of the NSAID drug; sometimes fluids or oxygen therapy or other support
PREVENTION: Don't give your cat medication without a vet's advice

Diagnosis is based on history of the drug used, X-ray evaluation, and/or by gastroscopy—visual examination of the gastrointestinal tract using a special instrument called an endoscope that's fed down the cat's throat (see ENDOSCOPE). Treatment includes stopping use of the NSAID, and prescribing ulcer medication similar to what is used in humans. Veterinary supervision is necessary.

If you suspect that your cat has ingested Ibuprofen, induce vomiting (see ADMINISTER MEDICATIONS) using three percent hydrogen peroxide, one tablespoon per 10 pounds of pet, and immediate contact your veterinarian (see POISON).

IDENTIFICATION

Outdoor cats in particular but also indoor pets should wear some form of easily recognizable identification to protect them from being stolen, and ensure their safe return if they stray from home. Up to 70 percent of animals that arrive at shelters have no identification, and a great percentage of these are euthanized.

One of the best precautions an owner can take to protect their cat is to record the cat's appearance with photographs. These should include a close up of the face, as well as full body shots from both sides and the back. Document any distinguishing marks; there are many gray and white cats, but yours may be the only one with three gray freckles in a triangular pattern on a white tummy. Should the worst happen and your cat becomes lost, have these photos in file, make posters and advertise Kitty's loss, and even leave copies at area shelters to alert them.

Other identification is even more important. A number of pet identification systems are available. The most common and simplest is a metal or plastic tag containing the owner's contact information which is attached to the cat's collar. Rabies tags documenting vaccination that are attached to collars are also a means of identification. They usually include the contact information of the veterinary clinic, and a serial number that identifies the cat and its owners. Cats may lose collars, though, and strays often are wearing no easily visible identification.

Tattoos are used more often in pet dogs than in cats, and provide a permanent identification on the animal's body. The owner's social security number or the animal's registration number is commonly tattooed onto the skin, often on the inside of the thigh. The tattoo number can then be registered in a local or national database that can retrieve the owner's contact information should that animal become lost. The drawback of tattoos is that whoever finds the

CAT FACTS

cat must know to look for the telltale mark, as well as what to do with that information. Also, tattoos may be obscured by fur or fade over time.

A very effective identification is the microchip. A tiny silicon chip similar to what is used in computer technology is programmed with an identification code, encased in surgical glass the size of a grain of rice, and implanted beneath the cat's skin between his shoulders. Special scanning equipment is designed to read the microchip information in much the same way that food item prices are scanned at the grocery store. A database keeps track of the owner and pet information, and matches the identifying code to the animal so the owner can be contacted. Many veterinary clinics and most animal shelters are now equipped with microchip technology (see APPENDIX B, PET SERVICES).

IMAGING, CT and MRI In neurology and neurosurgery, which involves the brain, spinal cord, and nervous system, the biggest advances in the past several years have all stemmed from using computed tomography (CT) and magnetic resonance imaging (MRI) to better "see" the brain. CT and MRI are more sensitive than X-rays for identifying abnormalities in complex parts of the body. The main advantage is the ability to remove bones from the picture, which otherwise obscure a clear view of the target.

Brain studies using CT are done with or without contrast, while spinal contrast and thoracic (chest) and abdominal CT usually use contrast medium—that is, injecting a dye like iodine to help tell different structures apart. Iodine has a high atomic number, so it absorbs lots of radiation, which shows up in the test by making the vessels opaque.

In small animals, CT or MRI are most commonly used to diagnose diseases of the brain, spine, nasal and sinus cavities, and middle ear. Less commonly, they are used to detect muscle or skeletal diseases, respiratory problems, and masses on the heart.

CT and MRI imaging are mostly available in veterinary schools and secondary private referral centers. CT uses an X-ray source and detector to take pictures of an object's internal structure from 180 to 360 different directions, and then "reconstructs" that object through computer projections. Because it takes only two seconds to scan each "slice," CT offers a more accurate picture of moving portions of the anatomy (i.e., in the chest/abdomen region moved by breathing and heartbeats) than MRI.

Magnetic Resonance Imaging (MRI) was first used to scan a human wrist in 1977, and the first human brain MRI followed in 1979. Veterinary MRIs weren't used experimentally until the late 1980s. Today, the technology has become increasingly available, and more and more applications are being discovered. MRI images are similar to CT, but unlike using X-rays, no radiation is involved. The image comes from recording radio-frequency signals given off by the tissue.

While CT and X-ray imaging refer to "density" of tissues—bone shows up white on the images because it's denser than muscle tissue—that does not apply with MRI. Instead, body structures are defined by degrees of signal intensity. Each part of the body, from bone to skin or lungs, gives off a different amount of radio- frequency. On a MRI image, areas that are bright or white have increased signal intensity, and those that are dark or black have decreased intensity. The MRI offers unsurpassed soft-tissue detail. However, while CT takes seconds to scan a "slice," the MRI takes three to seven minutes per imaging sequence, and may take a total of 45 to 60 minutes for a complete scan (see X-RAY).

286
CAT FACTS

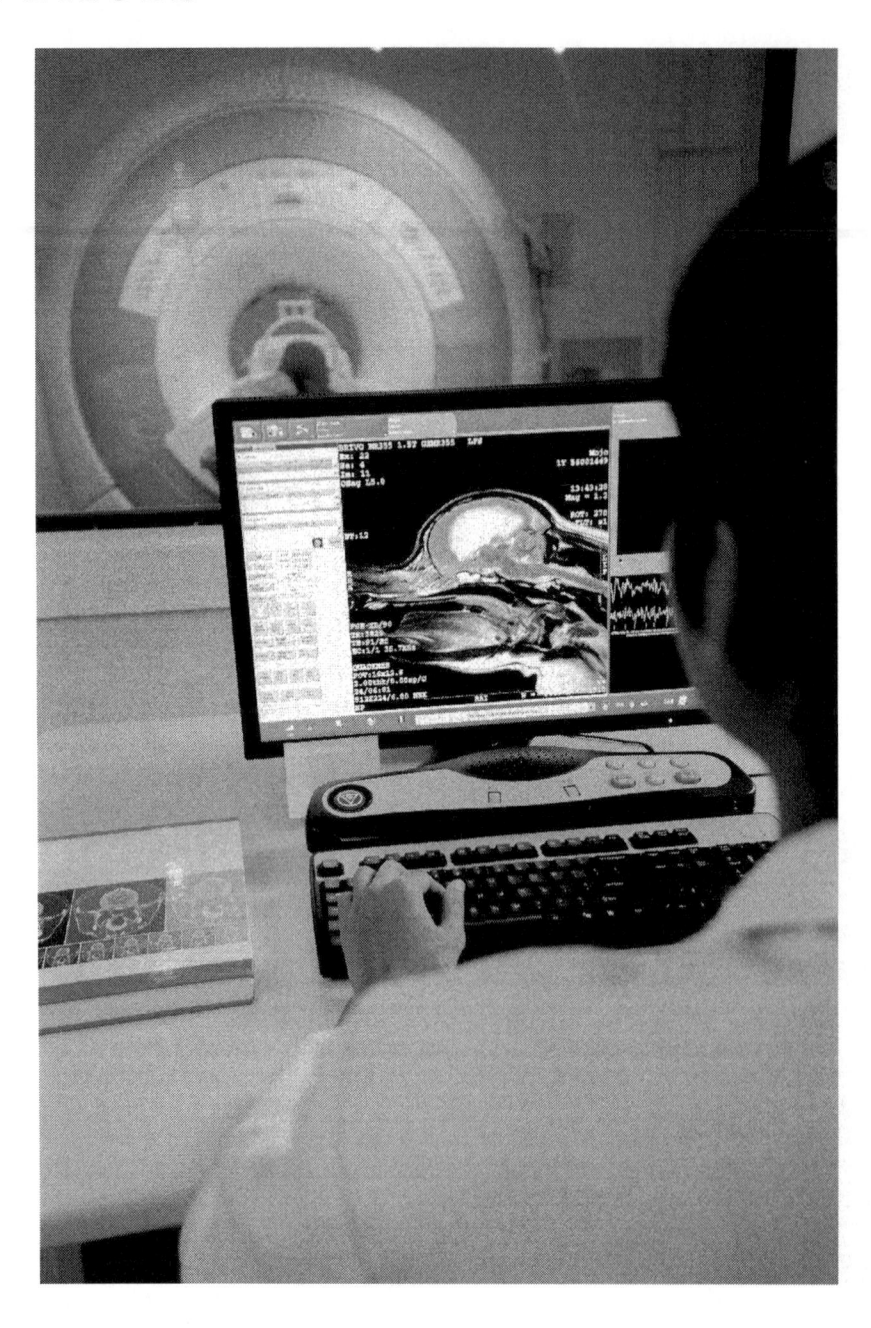

IMMUNE SYSTEM

The immune system is a complex defense mechanism that protects the cat from invading substances capable of causing injury or disease. The immune system targets foreign invaders, called antigens, and attempts to either neutralize or destroy them. Antigens include viruses, bacteria, toxins, and abnormal cells like cancer.

The primary immune system is composed of organs like the bone marrow and thymus which produce protective disease-fighting cells and molecules. These components of the immune system patrol the blood and lymphatic system for anything that doesn't belong. The secondary immune system's lymph nodes and spleen are a part of an intricate body-wide filter that removes antigens from circulation.

The immune system manufactures a kind of protein called an antibody in response to the presence of an antigen; this mechanism is referred to as a humoral immune response. Each antibody is a custom-creation that reacts only to one specific kind of antigen. Antibodies are not killers; they don't destroy the antigen directly. They're more like tattletales. Antibodies simply attach themselves to the antigen, marking it as foreign material so that other specialized cells can destroy it.

Sometimes specialized cells like macrophages and lymphocytes attack and destroy virus-infected cells or tumor cells without the aid of antibodies. This is called a cell-mediated immune response.

The combination of humoral and cell-mediated immune response doubles the body's protection. It's a type of insurance policy; what one system fails to neutralize, the other kills.

In addition, the body has a built-in memory for immunity. Even after the antigen has been destroyed, antibodies that "remember" the disease continue to circulate. They immediately recognize and react to the disease should it ever return, and this provides a kind of early warning system that prompts an immune response before damage can be done. This memory for danger is referred to as active immunity.

Active immunity lasts for a variable length of time, depending on the particular antigen involved. Active immunity can be artificially created by stimulating the cat's immune system to protect him from disease by using vaccinations. Passive immunity is what kittens receive from their mother when they nurse her antibody-rich first milk, called colostrum. A kitten's passive immunity lasts about four months at most (see VACCINATIONS).

INCONTINENCE see SOILING.

INFLAMMATORY BOWEL DISEASE (IBD)

Inflammatory bowel disease (IBD) refers to the chronic inflammation of the small intestine and occasionally the stomach. The cause isn't known, but it's suspected that something prompts the immune system to misfire and attack its own cells. The inflammatory response plugs up the tiny microscopic filaments that line the surface of the intestinal tract and transfer nutrients into the bloodstream.

Chronic vomiting is the most common sign of IBD. Episodes may be sporadic and occur during times of stress, or vomiting can be continuous. The cat also may frequently strain to defecate but pass only small amounts of feces which may be blood streaked. The homeopathic remedies Nux vomica and Arsenicum are helpful to stop both diarrhea and vomiting.

IBD

SYMPTOMS: Chronic vomiting; straining to defecate with minimal results
HOME CARE: Adjust diet
HOLISTIC HELP: Digestive enzymes; herbal therapy; supplements; homeopathy
VET CARE: Treating cause; sometimes antibiotics or immune suppressing drugs
PREVENTION: None

Diagnosis usually is made only after ruling out other causes for vomiting, such as giardia, trichomoniasis, heartworms, or a swallowed object. Conclusive evidence requires a biopsy of the intestine in which a sample of tissue is removed surgically from the anesthetized cat for microscopic evaluation. Sometimes a special instrument called a colonoscopy is inserted into the cat's rectum to view the tissue. But because only portions of the tissue may exhibit inflammation, even then diagnosis may not be definitive. The disease over the long term can result in scarring.

Some research supports the notion that a food allergy may be at fault, and in some cases a limited antigen diet may help the cat. Inflammatory bowel disease includes the damage or malfunction of the normal barrier protection in the gut. Damage can allow a kind of leakage of large protein particles, and give them contact with the immune system (see ALLERGY).

Holistic veterinarians recommend dietary changes based on the individual cat. In one Morris Animal Foundation funded study, veterinarians at Colorado State University reported that probiotics improved/reduced diarrhea in up to 70 percent of cats. Digestive enzymes to help may also be recommended. Milk thistle, an herb that supports the liver, may also be beneficial. Because inflammatory bowel disease often damages cells in the intestine, supplements containing glutamine are thought to help rebuild the intestinal lining and aid in its function.

Medical marijuana (or cannabis) today is also available for pets, but must be formulated so that pets receive the medical benefits of the cannabis (hemp) plant while reducing potential toxic concentrations of the herb. Hemp can be used to control pain and inflammation. Ask your veterinarian if this supplement may benefit your pet.

Drugs to treat bacterial overgrowth or parasite infection may be prescribed (see GIARDIA and TRICHOMONIASIS). Immune-suppressing drugs may also be beneficial.

INSECT BITES and STINGS

Cats are bugged by the same insects that afflict their owners. Bites cause allergic reactions and spread disease. Stinging insects more often result in local irritation, but can cause life-threatening reactions.

Cats are often tempted to chase and pounce upon fluttering insects. While moths or grasshoppers are harmless, catching a wasp or bee can have severe consequences. Fur protects the cat from body injuries, but stings often occur on the lips or inside the mouth when Kitty tries to catch the bug. Fire ants most often affect kittens that inadvertently stumble into their mound; they typically bite in swarms on the kitten's tender tummy and inside the flanks.

Stings and bites are painful and usually result in swelling and sometimes itching. A sore mouth can cause drooling and difficulty eating. Bees leave behind stingers, which are visible; if the stinger can be seen, remove it with tweezers or scrape it free with a credit card.

Sparsely furred areas like the belly and inside the thighs can be treated with a paste of baking soda and water, but this is messy to apply when the sting is surrounded by fur. Dabbing ammonia directly on the bites with a cotton ball or cotton swab helps soothe the pain, and ice packs will reduce the swelling of stings.

Stings inside the mouth are more difficult to treat. If your cat will allow it, flush the area with a teaspoon of baking soda mixed in a pint of water. Use a turkey baster to squirt the fluid onto the area, but take care the cat doesn't inhale the liquid.

While one or two stings can be painful, they are rarely dangerous. However, should the cat stumble into a hive or nest and receive multiple stings or bites, the situation can become lethal.

Black tea contains ingredients that help draw out toxins. Dip the tea bag in warm water, squeeze it out, and hold against the sting for 10 to 15 minutes. Chamomile tea will reduce the irritation and help prevent potential infection. Soak a cotton ball in room temperature tea and apply to the sting as a compress for 15 to 30 minutes. Do this three times on the first day, and for a few minutes three times a day for the next two days.

INSECT BITES & STINGS

SYMPTOMS: Local irritation; swelling or itching at site; drooling or difficulty eating; difficulty breathing; incoordination; collapse
FIRST AID: Ice packs; dab ammonia on spots; apply baking soda paste or flush with baking soda and water; breathing difficulties require immediate veterinary intervention
HOLISTIC HELP: Herbal therapy; aromatherapy
VET CARE: Epinephrine (adrenaline) counteracts life-threatening reaction
PREVENTION: Avoid contact with dangerous insects

A homeopathic remedy can help prevent swelling by giving two or three tablets of Ledum 30C immediately after the sting. The essential oils lavender or thyme also relieve irritation and itching. Mix three drops of either oil in a teaspoon of apple cider vinegar and dab on the bites (but NOT inside the mouth).

When swelling in the mouth, nose or throat area is severe, it makes breathing difficult. Cats occasionally suffer an allergic reaction called anaphylactic shock in which the airways become so constricted the cat cannot breathe. The cat will also drool, become uncoordinated, and collapse. These signs appear almost immediately following the bite or sting. Anaphylactic shock is an emergency that must be immediately addressed by a veterinarian if the cat's life is to be saved.

If you hear gurgling as his lungs fill with fluid, pick him up by his hind legs and hold the cat upside down for 10 seconds to help drain the fluid. Wrap your cat in a blanket to keep him warm. Give him a drop or two of honey or Karo syrup on the gums to help him maintain consciousness. Be prepared to perform artificial respiration.

CAT FACTS

INTRODUCING PETS It has long been thought that lions were the only truly social cats that voluntarily lived together. More recent studies have uncovered a parallel in our domestic cats. When food is abundant, cats do tend to live in close proximity and get along well together in extended social groups (see FERAL). In pet cats, this acceptance includes family members who are not feline.

However, cats prefer status quo, and for a cat the unexpected is cause for alarm. Therefore, the introduction of a new pet into the household must be done gradually, with attention to the resident cat's sensibilities.

Some cats are more accepting than others. How well the cat adapts to other cats, dogs, or other family members depends a great deal on the cat's own personality and sense of self, and on the finesse of initial introductions. Dominant cats may turn aggressive, while fearful cats become stressed and depressed if the proper preparations are not made.

Kittens generally accept new family members more readily, and usually adult cats are more accepting of kittens or puppies which aren't a threat to the resident cat's status. Introducing an adult resident cat to a new adult cat or dog can be done, too, but expect that the pair must sort out who is to be head honcho.

If possible, introduce the scent of the new pet to your resident cat before a true nose to nose meeting. This can be done by petting the new animal with a sock or handkerchief, then leaving the scented item in your house for Resident Cat (R.C.) to find, sniff and investigate.

Make one room of your house temporarily off-limits to R.C. and make this the new pet's home base. If you can manage, have a friend bring the new pet to your home and set her up in the room, while you play or feed R.C. to distract him. That way, R.C. doesn't immediately feel the entire house has been invaded by the interloper, and the new pet has some privacy to become acquainted with the new surroundings.

R.C. and the new pet should first get to know each other by sniffing under the door. Some cats will posture, hiss and growl; others will ignore the entire venture until they think you're not watching. Either behavior is normal. Be encouraged if the pair begin poking and playing with each other's paws under the door.

Try not to make a big deal over the new pet, it should be business as usual. Be sure to make time for R.C. If he's a shy, retiring cat, he may feel threatened and begin to withdraw if he feels he's losing your attention.

After two or three days—whenever R.C. stops growling at the door—have the pair switch places for half an hour or so. That offers each pet a chance to investigate the other critter's smells up close, and allows the new pet an opportunity to become comfortable with the rest of the house.

For introducing a new cat, you simply open the door, and allow them to meet at their own speed, on their own terms. Perhaps they'll ignore each other, or they may immediately become fast friends. Every case is different. Typically, cats begin introductions by sniffing each other's necks, then sniff the anal region. They may turn circles trying to sniff the other while preventing themselves being sniffed.

The resident cat usually has the upper "paw," but that's not always the case. There may be some hissing or growling, and unless the situation escalates to imminent attack, let the cats sort things out (see AGGRESSION). Interrupting too soon may actually delay the determination of who's to be top cat, and force a replay of the display at a later date.

CAT FACTS

There should be an escape route handy—a table top, or cat carrier—for either pet to get away when they've had enough. Until the pair have accepted each other, keep them separated when you are not there to supervise.

If the new pet is a puppy or older dog, he should be introduced in a carrier or on a leash, and under your direct control. Most adult cats can deal with a puppy and will soon teach the pup what a hiss and claws mean. Use caution when introducing your cat to an adult dog that has never met cats before. Dogs typically want to please their owner, so if the dog knows you want him to like Kitty, you'll be on the right tract. Obedience training the dog is a big help.

A dog gate will keep Poochie in one part of the house, while allowing R.C. to get to know him through the grillwork. Once you are satisfied the dog understands the cat is a part of his family, put him on a leash and take down the gate. If the dog is well behaved, remove the leash; the cat should always have a safe retreat the dog cannot reach. Don't leave them alone together until you are convinced the dog knows Kitty is off limits. Often, the dog is quite content to let Kitty be the boss.

Many of the same principles apply when introducing new human family members to your resident cat. If you have a kitten, do yourself and the pet a favor by introducing him as a youngster to a variety of people of all ages. An adult cat that has never before been around men can exhibit behavior problems when his single female owner decides to marry. And a new baby in the house can turn the most complacent cat into a jittering ball of furry nerves.

Allow R.C. to familiarize himself with the scent of the new family member ahead of time by bringing home the scented sock, just the same as with a new pet. Record the sound of your fiancé's voice and play it while you pet your cat, or have the fiancé bring special treats or new toys. The new family member's presence should be associated with only good things for your cat.

CAT FACTS

When you are expecting a baby, tape the sound of a baby crying and let Kitty listen. As you prepare the nursery, let the cat investigate the new scents (you should wear baby powder) and sights in the room. Make change gradually; you've got nine months to paint, change wallpaper, put up the bed and mobile, so don't do it all at once, or the change could throw Kitty into a tizzy.

Don't shut out the cat. Set up a baby gate if you don't want R.C. in the room, so he can at least watch and understand what's happening. Excluding your cat from this happy occasion in your life only makes the cat feel left out, confused, and even scared when he's cut off from the mysterious doings in that forbidden room.

Cats are typically very good with babies and children. When you bring home your new baby, act like it's no big deal, even though it is. Remember, you want R.C. to react like this is an expected part of cat life. Don't force an introduction, but if Kitty is interested and calm, let him sniff the baby's foot or hand. Let the cat see what smells so different and sounds so interesting, so he knows it's nothing to fear.

And praise the cat when he acts well. When R.C. knows that treating the new baby like one of the family is to his advantage, there should be no problem. If you like, R.C. can be allowed in the nursery when you are there to supervise. Letting the cat be a part of things takes away the mystery and the threat, so that Kitty associates your baby with good things for himself.

As your baby grows, be sure that she understands R.C. is not a toy. Cats learn to put up with a lot from young children, yet it's the cat's home, too. Children can and should be taught to respect pets from an early age. Teach your baby how to pet and hold the cat, and how to care for R.C. In that way, a mutual respect will grow into love that can last a lifetime for them both (see APPENDIX C, RESOURCES).

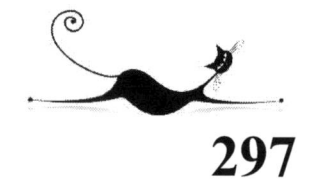

JACOBSON'S ORGAN

JACOBSON'S ORGAN The cat has a second scenting mechanism, called Jacobson's organs or vomeronasal organs. The organs are located between the hard palate of the mouth, and the septum of the nose. Each connects to an incisive duct, tiny conduits that open behind the cat's upper incisor teeth in the mouth and pass up into the nasal cavity. The ducts allow air to travel from the mouth into the nasal cavity.

The cat uses her tongue to trap scent particles and flick-transfer them to the ducts behind these upper teeth. Cats displaying this behavior, called by the German term flehmen, seem to grimace with distaste with their lips curled back and mouth open.

Although all cats have and use these specialized scent organs, it appears that intact male cats exhibit flehmen behavior most often. The behavior occurs primarily when Tom contacts the urine of a female cat that's in heat. The vomeronasal organs are linked to the hypothalamus, an area of the brain that acts as a kind of switchboard to direct information to higher centers. The hypothalamus integrates taste and smell, motivates appetite, and triggers certain sexual and aggressive behavior patterns. It's believed that vomeronasal organs mostly detect chemical substances, called pheromones, which are produced by animals to stimulate specific behavioral responses, especially sexual activities (see NOSE).

K

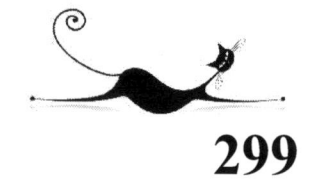

300 CAT FACTS

KIDNEY DISEASE
Kidney disease refers to a number of conditions that damage the organs and result in impaired kidney function. Normally, kidneys work as an organic filtering system that screens waste products from the bloodstream and excretes them into the urine. Kidneys also regulate the body's fluid composition and the nutrient content of the blood, as well as producing hormones that control red blood cell production and blood pressure.

Kidney disease is characterized as acute (of recent origination) or chronic (of long duration). The acute form can affect any cat at any age, and results from disease or poison that damages the kidney. Polycystic kidney disease (PKD) in Persians and Exotics, and amyloidosis in Abyssinians, is inherited.

The most common causes of acute kidney disease are periods of inadequate blood flow to the kidneys, toxicity from chemical agents such as antifreeze, Tylenol or certain antibiotics, and infectious agents. Some families of Abyssinian cats suffer from inherited amyloidosis, a rare condition in which protein is deposited in the kidneys, leading ultimately to organ failure.

Chronic kidney disease is considered a common condition of geriatric cats. Studies estimate 49 percent of elderly cats over 15 years old have some degree of kidney disease. However, the cause is rarely diagnosed. It isn't known why nearly all elderly cats suffer kidney damage, but it's thought to be the result of a lifetime of work.

Signs of acute disease are severe and appear all at once, while signs of chronic kidney disease develop very slowly over time. Kidneys are able to work quite well even when severely damaged, and cats typically show few symptoms until 75 percent of kidney function is gone. Consequently, owners rarely notice anything is wrong until the disease is quite advanced. Untreated kidney failure results in death.

One of the earliest signs is increased thirst and urination. This happens because when the kidneys lose their ability to concentrate urine, the cat must drink more and more water to compensate for excessive water loss. Cats in kidney failure may seek water in unusual locations, like the toilet bowl, fish tank or sinks. Owners also often notice a refusal to eat, weight loss, depression and weakness, or even dehydration.

As kidney disease progresses, the cat may develop a brownish discoloration on the tongue, and sores in the mouth. The breath may smell like ammonia. Finally, the cat falls into a coma, and then dies.

Diagnosis is based on signs of disease, along with blood tests that measure levels of creatinine and BUN (blood urea/nitrogen) and analysis of the urine. X-rays, ultrasound or other specialized examinations of the kidneys may be required. Creatinine levels are influenced by lean body mass, though, and a lean or underweight cat in kidney failure may have normal creatinine levels, so the diagnosis may be missed in these cases.

A new test from IDEXX Laboratories screens for symmetric dimethylarginine (SDMA), which is a new biomarker for kidney function. SDMA is a methylated form of the amino acid arginine, which is produced in every cell and released into the body's circulation during protein degradation. SDMA is excreted almost exclusively by the kidneys. This test offers a good estimate of glomerular filtration rate (GFR), an indicator of how well the kidneys are working. SDMA is not influenced by muscle mass. Research has shown that SDMA can identify chronic kidney disease an average of nine months earlier in dogs and 17 months sooner in cats. The SDMA biomarker test is recommended as a screening test for cats age six and older.

The prognosis depends on how far the disease has advanced. Some cats live with kidney disease for several years if the condition is mild to moderate.

KIDNEY DISEASE

SYMPTOMS: Increased thirst and urination; loss of appetite; weight loss; depression and weakness; dehydration; brown-colored tongue; sores in the mouth; ammonia breath
HOME CARE: Supportive care; good nutrition
VET CARE: Supportive care; drugs to normalize blood; therapeutic diets; sometimes kidney transplant
PREVENTION: None

Many cats have kidney disease, hypertension, and hyperthyroidism at the same time. About one in four cats with chronic renal failure or hyperthyroidism also develop hypertension. Hypertension as a result of kidney failure can cause a stroke at worst, and erratic behavior and yowling at night at best. In fact, increased blood pressure is one of the major factors causing the disease to progress. The Doppler blood-pressure monitor is currently considered the most accurate machine for use on cats. An inflatable cuff is placed on the cat's foreleg, and a transducer reads reflected ultrasound signals bouncing off moving red blood cells.

Getting an accurate reading can be tough, though. Normal systolic blood pressure (during heart contraction) is about 110 to 125. Stress from going to the hospital can make the cat's blood pressure go higher and cause an inaccurate reading. Sedation also interferes with accuracy. Often, multiple readings over several days must be averaged to get the best picture of the cat's situation.

Compromised kidney function in extremely advanced kidney failure makes it difficult for the cat to filter the waste produced from protein metabolism. For that reason, traditional therapy includes changing the cat's diet to a high quality but lower protein ration.

Cats with kidney failure also are unable to get rid of extra phosphorus, and the excess can result in a number of secondary problems. Special diets for kidney disease typically reduce phosphorus levels. Some diets also adjust the amount of dietary salt. Your veterinarian can recommend an appropriate diet for your individual cat's needs. Most cats with renal failure lose their appetite, and these diets may not be palatable to your cat. If your cat refuses to eat the therapeutic diet, offer other brands and try to find a kidney diet your cat will accept. In many cases, though, you must give in to the cat's preferences, and let him eat something rather than let him starve.

Drugs like sodium bicarbonate help normalize the blood if it becomes too acidic, and potassium supplementation can help even out the blood potassium level. Lots of fresh water should be available to the cat at all times.

Hemodialysis has long been available for human patients, but the machines that cleanse the blood have not been available for use in cats and dogs until the past few years. In the past, peritoneal dialysis offered an interim solution for pets with acute kidney failure. The procedure pumps fluid into the pet's abdominal cavity, where it absorbs waste products, then is drawn back out mechanically via a large needle inserted through the abdominal wall. The dialysis allows the kidneys time to heal and keeps the body from being poisoned, while the underlying cause for the problem can be treated and hopefully cured.

In 1998, Dr. Larry Cowgill, a professor at the University of California at Davis, developed the world's first companion animal hemodialysis program. This was finally possible when the technology used in human dialysis became sophisticated enough to be adapted to cats and dogs. His program has served as a model for several other veterinary dialysis programs.

Dialysis is used primarily to treat pets suffering from antifreeze poisoning, kidney infections, and systemic illnesses that secondarily affect the kidneys. Less frequently, pets are placed on dialysis until a kidney transplant operation can be done. Animals that are not able to maintain their body weight or become anemic despite treatment may be helped with getting a new kidney.

Depending on the specific case, kidney transplant may be an option. The best candidates are cats in the earliest stages of the disease that don't have other health problems.

The ideal candidate is negative for feline leukemia, feline immunosuppressive virus, heart disease, diabetes or inflammatory bowel conditions. Blood work and urine tests are done, along with an EKG, X-rays and ultrasound. If there's a suspicion the anti-rejection drugs required after the surgery could bring on dormant health problems like a urinary tract infection, a two-week trial of the drugs may be done prior to the surgery. Age doesn't matter—successful transplants have been done for cats as young as two or as old as 18.

Once the cat has been approved for transplantation, a blood cross match pairs the cat to the best donor. The donor cat must be a young, healthy adult. Ideally, this cat is the same size or slightly larger than the recipient cat. An animal needs only one working kidney to remain healthy. Part of the "deal" includes adopting the cat that donated the kidney. The donors usually go home two days after the surgery.

Recipient cats remain hospitalized for a week before the surgery for preoperative tests, and a week after, to ensure the new kidney works. The recipient cat is fed a protein-restricted diet, and anemia is addressed either with a whole-blood transfusion or erythropoietin, a hormone that stimulates red cell production.

The procedure requires two surgical teams working on both cats at the same time. The left kidney usually is donated because it has a slightly longer vein. Then the recipient cat is surgically opened and prepared to receive the new kidney. The old organs are left in place as a backup in case the donated kidney fails.

The transplanted kidney is sutured to the nearby abdominal wall, and the ureter sutured to the bladder, in order to prevent any future twisting of the organ. Most transplanted kidneys are functioning well within 72 hours of the transplant.

The donor cat tends to recover very quickly. The recipient cat typically receives intravenous fluids, and is fed and medicated through a tube. After the transplant, the cat must be on anti-rejection medicine and be pilled twice a day for the rest of his life. The same medicines used in human transplant patients, cyclosporine and prednisone, work for feline patients.

Many cat owners have become accustomed to giving fluid therapy and other medicines and have no problem with lifelong program. But for cats that hate pills that can be a quality of life issue.

Only a handful of private practices and universities are performing kidney transplants. As of this writing, a list of facilities currently performing the surgery is available at the website http://www.felinecrf.com/transb.htm. The costs is several thousands of dollars.

Early detection is the single best way to identify kidney problems before they become severe. A blood test may catch the disease in your older cat before signs become apparent. All middle aged and older cats should undergo periodic examinations (see GERIATRIC CAT).

KITTEN

A kitten is an immature cat. Generally speaking, a cat is designated a kitten from birth to about one year of age.

Every cat develops differently, and some breeds of cats do not reach full maturity before they are two or even three years old. However, in the show ring, the kitten class encompasses pedigreed kittens between the ages of four to eight months. More specifically, a cat should be considered a kitten as long as he continues to grow.

Newborn kittens are about four to six inches long and two to four ounces in weight. They are born blind, deaf and toothless, and totally dependent on their mother. Unable to regulate body temperature, or even urinate or defecate on their own, kittens will die without prompt attention from the queen.

A kitten's first impulse is to find warmth. The blunt kitten faces act as heat-seeking sensors that direct the babies toward the queen's warm breasts. Kittens depend on the queen and their littermates for warmth. Littermates nest together in furry piles to warm each other. A kitten that is separated from his siblings or mother is in grave danger of dying from the cold. Whenever a kitten finds itself alone or starts to feel cold, he begins to cry loudly for Mom to rescue him.

One of the first sensations the newborn kitten feels is being washed by his mother. The queen grooms her babies not only to keep them and the nest clean, but to stimulate them to defecate and urinate. The vibration of her contented purr is a beacon that tells the babies where she is, and calls them to her.

From the beginning, scent helps identify life for the kitten. Kittens leave their own personal smell upon the queen's breast when they first nurse, and from that time forward preferentially seek that particular nipple. The kittens push against the mother's breasts rhythmically with their forepaws, kneading to stimulate the flow of milk. The first milk the kittens drink, called colostrum, is rich in maternal antibodies that provide passive immunity and help protect the babies from disease during these early weeks of life (see IMMUNITY).

The first week is spent eating, sleeping, and growing. Birth weight doubles by the end of the first week. The weak legs provide only limited locomotion and the newborns drag themselves on their bellies using their front legs. Soon the young kittens exercise their muscles by crawling over and around each other.

Great changes take place during the second week of life. Eyelids which have been sealed shut since birth begin to open between the ninth and twelfth day, and the kittens begin to see their world for the first time. It is at this point that the furry babies learn specifically what their mother looks like. This optical imprinting helps define for the kittens what they and other cats should look like. All kittens' eyes are blue at this point; their adult eye color develops usually by the age of 12 weeks.

About the same time, the kitten's ears unseal, and sound sense begins to develop. Kitten teeth also begin to erupt until all the baby teeth are in by about seven to eight weeks of age. Kittens are also standing for the first time on wobbly legs, and trying to imitate Mom by walking.

By the third week, they're beginning to play with their littermates. The kittens follow the queen to the litter box, watch and learn and soon are imitating her bathroom etiquette. They learn how to retract their claws, which to this point have been continually extended. And, they begin grooming themselves (see GROOMING).

By four weeks of age, kittens will have doubled their weight again. Between four to six weeks of age, the queen's milk production slows down just as the babies' energy needs increase. The mother begins weaning the kittens from nursing, and they start sampling solid food. They'll be able to do without Mom's milk by the time they're eight weeks old.

Kittens spend a great deal of time playing with each other. Play is fun for the babies. It's also great exercise that helps kittens learn how to use their bodies properly to do all the important cat things, like leaping, pouncing, running and climbing. Social skills are also learned by interacting with littermates and Mom. The kittens learn to inhibit the use of their claws and teeth when they are bitten or clawed by each other. By playing with a variety of objects, like leaves, bugs or string, the kitten learns what can and cannot be done with that object. A nine week old kitten spends up to an hour playing each day. Everything is filed away in the feline memory, and applied to life.

KITTEN SOCIALIZATION: Socialization refers to the sensitive period in your kitten's development when he learns from positive and negative events. The *prime* socialization period for kittens falls between two to seven weeks of age; however, socialization continues through 12 to 16 weeks and also has an impact.

Early experiences during this window teach him to tell the difference between safe and positive events, or scary and dangerous ones. Kittens that are well socialized to other pets, people, and places—that is, exposed to positive interactions with them—learn that people, pets, and new places are nothing to fear. Socialized kittens become more confident, well-adjusted babies who grow into well-adjusted adults. Because stress impacts health, well socialized kittens will be healthier, too.

Conversely, kittens that experience negative, scary interactions—or no contact at all—with humans and other animals have a more difficult time adjusting to them. For instance, if Mom-cat fears dogs and teaches her babies by example, or a kitten is frightened by a dog during this period, the baby will be reluctant to accept dogs when he grows up. Feral kittens that never interact with humans during this important period become terrified of people. Kittens handled daily by people during the first month of their life have an improved learning ability (see FERAL).

Kittens are ready to go to new homes by the time they are 12 weeks old. By waiting until this age, the babies receive full benefit of playing and learning from their siblings, which helps them be better adjusted to other cats as adults.

A healthy kitten has bright, clear eyes and clean, soft fur. The baby has clean clear ears, eyes, nose and anus with no discharge. Well socialized kittens are curious and friendly, and are easily engaged in a game. Proper health care includes preventative vaccinations, screening for intestinal parasites, and a nutritionally complete and balanced kitten diet.

Kneading

The term refers to the cat's habit of treading with her front paws as though "kneading" dough. Cats flex each of their front paws rhythmically in turn against usually soft surfaces like carpet or an owner's lap. Kneading may or may not be performed with claws extended.

The action is used by kittens against their mother's breast to prompt the flow of her milk. The behavior in adult cats is thought to hearken back to kittenhood, and appears to be an expression of contentment.

310
CAT FACTS

311

LASER TECHNOLOGY

Medical lasers have been commonly used only since the early 1980s. The laser advantage, basically, is that it will seal blood vessels, lymphatics and nerve endings, so you don't have as much hemorrhage or as much inflammation or pain. However, because surgical lasers use photothermal energy—heat—healing takes longer than an incision with a scalpel. But lasers are able to vaporize tissue in a very controlled and gentle way that offers a strong advantage.

Lasers are often used in dermatology and skin cancer therapies. Veterinary ophthalmologists have developed ways to treat glaucoma, or to use lasers to spot-weld retinal detachments back in place. In addition, laser energy can be shot through special fibers to reach deep within the body without requiring invasive surgery.

Although the carbon dioxide laser is quite common, a variety of special lasers such as the diode laser and the Nd:YAG laser (neodidium yutridium aluminum garnet laser) are available. Each type uses a different wave length of energy, which is absorbed by tissue in different ways and offers specific benefits. Today, the price has come down, and the lasers themselves are better suited to veterinary practice.

LICE

SYMPTOMS: Scaling or scabby skin; itchiness; visible bugs or eggs stuck to hairs
HOME CARE: Treat weekly with cat-safe topical flea product; discard infected bedding; thoroughly vacuum premises
VET CARE: Same
PREVENTION: Keep cat well groomed; avoid contact with other cats

LICE Lice are parasites that lives on the skin. The tiny insects are wingless flat creatures equipped either with sucking or biting mouth parts. There are a number of types that affect animals, but each species prefers a specific host. Cats are parasitized by *Felicola subrostrata*, a biting louse that feeds on sloughed skin debris.

Louse infestation, called pediculosis, is not common in cats, but all cats are at risk. The condition is often associated with poor sanitary conditions or neglect, and usually affects malnourished debilitated cats unable to groom themselves. Cats are generally infected by direct contact with another infested animal.

Lice seem to thrive during cold winter months. Seeing the parasite or the eggs glued to the individual hairs of the fur coat is diagnostic. Signs vary from cat to cat, but may include scaling skin, itchiness, or scabby skin (see MILIARY DERMATITIS).

Treatment consists of a weekly topical treatment of a cat-safe flea product applied either as powder, shampoo or dip for up to five weeks. Lice can't survive for long when off the host. Destroying the cat's infected bedding and thorough vacuuming of carpets is usually sufficient to eliminate the parasite from the environment.

LICK GRANULOMAS see EOSINOPHILIC GRANULOMA COMPLEX.

LIFESPAN see GERIATRIC CAT.

LITTER When a multiple birth occurs in animals, the offspring are collectively called a litter. A mother cat's babies are referred to as a litter of kittens.

CAT FACTS

Litter also describes the absorbent substance, often clay, which owners provide for their cat's indoor toilet. Commercial litter products are a relatively new innovation, and changed the lives of cats for the better. The convenience of the first dried ground clay product, introduced as "Kitty Litter" in 1947, paved the way for cats to move permanently indoors.

The best litters are absorbent products that help control odor and that cats will accept. A wide variety of innovative products are made of everything from recycled newspaper to cedar shavings or processed grass.

However, clay-based litters remain the most popular choice for cats and owners alike. Clays that clump, the "scoopable" innovation introduced in the late 1980s, are a favorite with some owners because they make cleanup simpler. These products absorb urine into a ball, which can be easily removed while leaving the rest of the litter clean so the cat's toilet doesn't need to be changed as often. Such products often incorporate sodium bentonite, a kind of swelling clay, to enhance clump-ability. Because it also clogs plumbing pipes, it's not recommended that litters containing sodium bentonite be flushed.

LITTER BOX

A litter box is a shallow pan, usually plastic, that holds absorbent litter material and is designed to serve as the cat's toilet. A wide variety of commercial litter boxes are available, from fancy to plain.

The basic box should be large enough so that the cat has no trouble maneuvering inside. Most are about five inches deep, which is adequate for holding the preferred depth of two inches of litter without spilling when Kitty begins serious digging.

Standard pans are about 12-inches by 18-inches but are available in larger dimensions for big cats, or for multi-cat use. Covered boxes are available that help contain odor, offer the cat privacy, and keep litter in the box. "Automatic" litter boxes self-clean in various ways, by raking, flushing or other means of removing the waste.

Kittens begin to mimic their mother's litter box habits as soon as they're able to follow her from the nest. Bathroom etiquette varies slightly from cat to cat, but most cover their waste, which means the litter should be good for digging. The average cat eliminates three to five times a day, and waste should be cleaned at least daily.

Cats may be enthusiastic diggers who end up showering litter out of the box, or they may simply go through the motions and leave most of their bathroom deposit visible. Big cats, particularly males, may need larger boxes to keep from hanging over the edge of the box and missing the target when they eliminate. Some cats consent to share toilet facilities, but if you have more than two cats, multiple facilities are better.

You'll need at least two litter pans. The rule of thumb is to have one pan per cat, plus one. That's because often cats don't want to share bathroom facilities, or may prefer to use one for urine and the other for feces. Also, tiny kittens as well as arthritic senior cats need extra help to reach a distant box, so two located in both ends of the house helps prevent accidents.

Clay-based litter products remain the most popular and economical choice, but there's a huge variety available to fit preference. You can find everything you need at most local grocery stores, but pet specialty stores and online venues may offer more choice. Once you've found a product Kitty likes, *don't change it*! That might turn him off to the litter box.

Plain clay litters work very well, and often include odor-control technology that helps keep the bathroom smelling fresh to both you and the kitten. They absorb moisture and help contain the waste by drying it out. You'll need to clean out solid waste (and liquid, as much as possible) at least once a day, and once a week change out the entire contents with fresh litter.

Clumping litters are composed of finer granules that are less abrasive on tender paws. They congeal liquid waste into a solid ball for easy removal. That prolongs the life of the rest of the litter. Clumping litters are one of the most convenient, popular products available. Clay-based clumping litters were the first to appear, and they are recommended for the automatic litter pans.

Other products are made of crystals, paper, wheat, cedar shavings, pine pellets, and all sorts of environmentally friendly ingredients. Those that are biodegradable may be flushable, too—but that will vary depending on your septic system.

Cats can be taught to toilet in the human commode. However, that does not always allow owners to adequately monitor the eliminations for health purposes.

Many cats have distinct preferences regarding their litter boxes. A few simple guidelines will keep the cat happy.

First of all, locate the toilet away from sleeping and eating areas. Once the toilet location is determined, don't move the box. After finding litter that Kitty likes, don't change it. Switching brands can confuse the cat and may cause elimination problems.

Most importantly, keep the box clean. Feces and wet spots should be removed daily, and the entire box emptied and disinfected weekly. Proper hygiene not only reduces the risk of health problems, but also prevents many potential behavior problems. Cats often refuse to use a dirty box (see SOILING).

LIVER DISEASE

Liver disease is any condition which impairs that organ's normal function. The liver is the body's metabolic headquarters. It serves a dual role both as a kind of factory, and as a filter.

Food absorbed by the intestines is carried by the blood directly to the liver. There, the liver processes sugars and fats, stores vitamins and minerals, and makes necessary proteins and enzymes. The liver also manufactures hormones and important blood-clotting substances, as well as the bile that's necessary for absorption of fats. The processed material is either stored or delivered throughout the body as needed by the blood.

Blood is also filtered as it passes through the liver. Substances like drugs that are carried by the blood are metabolized, or altered, into other forms. Bacteria, toxins, even viruses are shifted out of the blood system by the liver. Consequently, the liver is exposed to infection and injury more than any other part of the cat's body. Parasites, birth defects and cancer may also interfere with normal function. Liver disease is serious and often life-threatening to the cat, and is estimated to affect about three to five percent of sick cats seen by veterinarians.

Fortunately, the liver has quite a bit of built-in redundancy, and only a small portion of the organ needs to function to maintain the cat's health. After some insults, it's fully capable of regenerating to its original size. But some diseases damage the liver so badly it isn't able to recover.

Signs can be confusing because liver disease mimics other illnesses, and often the sick cat has problems in other body systems at the same time with symptoms that overlap. Cats that have liver disease can also suffer from diseases of their intestinal tract and pancreas, a triaditis where all three are inflamed at once.

LIVER DISEASE

SYMPTOMS: Anorexia; vomiting; diarrhea; weight loss; lethargy; sometimes yellow cast (jaundice) to inside of the ears, whites of eyes or gums
HOME CARE: Nutritional support
HOLISTIC HELP: Herbal therapy; massage; supplements; aromatherapy
VET CARE: supportive care; placement of feeding tube; force feeding
PREVENTION: keep cats trim; keep poisons out of reach of the cat

The signs of various kinds of liver diseases are remarkably similar, and typically include loss of appetite, vomiting, diarrhea, weight loss and lethargy. Some conditions will cause the pale areas of the cat's skin to turn yellow, or jaundiced. This is most often apparent on the inside of the ears, the whites of the eyes or the gums. Because signs are so vague and resemble other feline health problems, the cat owner may not realize the cat's in trouble until the disease is quite advanced.

Treatment depends on the specific cause of the disease. A biochemical profile of the blood is the first step toward diagnosis. Liver enzymes may be elevated for a number of reasons, though, and elevated enzyme values does not automatically mean the cat has liver disease. Blood tests, imaging techniques and symptoms can point to liver disease. But a definitive diagnosis can only be made examining tissue beneath the microscope. An ultrasound-guided needle allows cells to be collected through the abdominal wall, often without invasive surgery. This biopsy generally is done by anesthetizing the cat. Cells may be collected using a fine needle inserted into the liver through the abdominal wall, or the procedure may require surgery.

Fatty liver disease is the most common liver ailment in cats (see FELINE HEPATIC LIPIDOSIS). Overweight cats are at highest risk for this condition, and the definitive sign is when an obese cat suddenly stops eating. For reasons not completely understood, fat is moved into the liver and becomes trapped, resulting in compromised function. For cats that are acutely ill and refuse to eat for days and even weeks, a feeding tube may be placed to allow the cat to be fed a soft diet, either while in the hospital or after going home. It may take weeks of tube feeding before the cat's appetite returns to normal. Cats tolerate these tubes quite well, though, and most owners become adept at feeding the cat in this way. Once the cat's appetite returns, the right diet helps them recover.

Treatment depends on the cause of the problem and how early it's caught. Once the liver scars from the inflammation, the damage is hard to reverse. Inflammation of the liver—the various hepatitis diseases—is treated with drugs to suppress the inflammation. Of course, the liver processes many drugs, yet is compromised. So when drug therapy is needed in these cats, veterinarians try to select drugs that rely primarily on the kidneys to process.

Hepatitis, or inflammation of the liver, usually is the result of exposure to a toxin like chemical insecticides, or drugs like aspirin or Tylenol. Treatment consists primarily of supportive care, and removal of the poison. In certain toxicity cases, early intervention allows the liver to recover with little or no damage to the organ. Prednisone isn't a cure but reduces inflammation in some kinds of liver diseases and cats improve without many side effects.

Cholangiohepatitis is an inflammatory condition of the bile tract that interferes with the excretion of bile, and is considered the second most common feline liver disease. Cure is rare; therapy is designed to control the disease. When caused by bacteria, long term antibacterial therapy is prescribed. Conditions that result from over-reaction of the immune system require immune suppressing drugs like corticosteroids.

Holistic veterinarians recommend a number of herbs and supplements to help cleanse and support the liver. Dandelion helps remove toxins, and milk thistle has been shown to help the liver generate new cells and protect it from toxins. Nutritional supplements such as raw beets contain natural chemicals that also work very well to support the liver. Cats shouldn't have more than a few slivers of raw beet, as it's quite powerful, so offer once a day for five days, and then give the body a rest.

When cats refuse to eat anything else, some holistic vets recommend creating a raw liver formula by combining raw egg yolk, raw sheep or beef liver, a teaspoon of honey, two tablespoons of plain yogurt and a cup of water in a blender. Offer the cat as much as he wants every hour or two for up to a week or so, until his appetite for regular food returns.

The nutraceutical SAMe (S-Adenosylmethionine) increases antioxidant levels in liver cells to protect them from toxins and death and often is used to treat liver ailments. An oral medication, brand name Actigall or Ursodiol, is a naturally occurring bile acid that also can help protect the liver from further damage.

LOWER URINARY TRACT DISEASE (LUTD)

Lower urinary tract disease, in the past called feline urologic syndrome or FUS, refers to a complex of disease conditions that affect the urethra, urinary bladder and/or ureters. Cats are prone to urological disorders because many normally urinate only once a day, and some only once every two or three days.

LUTD is associated with a wide range of conditions, including the formation of urinary stones, the obstruction of the urethra, and cystitis (see CYSTITIS). The syndrome affects male and female cats equally, although the narrow structure of the male cat urethra makes them more prone to suffer from blockage.

LUTD is a major health concern of pet cat owners, probably due in great part to effective veterinary client education. The true incidence is not known, but the condition is estimated to affect about ten percent of pet cats seen by veterinarians, with new cases each year reported to be less than one percent of the total cat population.

A variety of conditions, alone or working in combination, appear to be responsible for LUTD. However, the majority of cases are idiopathic which means nobody knows why the cat has problems. A major contributing factor appears to be stress. Treatment depends on the specific symptoms, and the cause when it can be determined.

Inflammation of the urinary bladder affects some cats and results in cystitis. Bacteria may be involved in cases that recur, but often the initial cause is unknown. When infection is present, it can spread up the ureters into the kidneys. Without treatment, the kidneys may be damaged (see KIDNEY DISEASE).

New research points to striking similarities between interstitial cystitis in women and idiopathic LUTD in cats. The symptoms seem to be identical in both. Both feline and human sufferers can go for long periods without problems, and then experience painful flare ups of recurrence. Stress appears to trigger the condition and/or make it worse.

The formation of mineral crystals in the cat's urinary tract is called urolithiasis. These crystals or stones were once thought to be the major cause of LUTD, but more recent findings suggest urinary tract stones account for only a small percentage of cases.

LUTD

SYMPTOMS: Dribbling urine; urinating in unusual locations; frequent voiding of small quantities of urine; bloody urine; urine with a strong ammonia odor; squatting or straining at the end of urination; listlessness; poor appetite; excessive thirst. COMA AND DEATH WITHIN 72 HOURS FOLLOWING COMPLETE OBSTRUCTION.
HOME CARE: After diagnosis; feed prescription diet; monitor toilet habits
VET CARE: Hospitalization; catheterization; fluid therapy; sometimes surgery
PREVENTION: None

The mineral deposits range from microscopic to sand or even golf ball sized stones. Crystals irritate the lining of the lower urinary tract, and cause life-threatening problems if they cannot be passed through the system and block the flow of urine.

Blockage usually results from the formation of soft, paste-like urethral plugs that may contain a combination of minerals and a mucus-like substances referred to as matrix. No one is certain exactly what causes development of plugs; however, because some urethral plugs are composed of blood protein components, there is speculation they may result from leakage of blood from inflamed bladder walls commonly found in idiopathic LUTD.

The blockage of urine flow may develop slowly over a period of weeks, or quite suddenly. In either case, the condition is extremely painful. Picture the bladder filling and expanding like a balloon with no outlet. Urine may be forced up into the ureters, in which case the kidneys stop working and poisons build up in the blood. Reversible damage may occur within 24 hours, and irreversible kidney damage within five days. Coma followed by death occurs within 72 hours following complete obstruction.

Blockage is a veterinary emergency. Plugs often lodge near the urethral opening, and may be moved by massaging the cat's penis. Other times, the cat must be anesthetized and a catheter passed into the urethra. Gentle pressure with fluids moves the plug, then flushes the crystal-laden urine from the cat's system. Fluid therapy increases urine output and rehydrates the cat. If a catheter is unable to unblock the cat, a needle is passed through the cat's abdomen directly into the bladder to empty the urine.

Cats suffering an episode of LUTD often require hospitalization for up to a week. Upon returning home, a management program designed to eliminate existing crystals and keep them from returning must be instituted. Up to 70 percent of cats with LUTD relapse one or more times.

The mineral content of the cat's urine and the urine's acid/base balance have an influence over whether or not crystals will form. Infrequent urination concentrates minerals in the cat's urine, and reduced exercise and reduced water intake also contribute; however, the content of the cat's diet may be the deciding factor. One common type of crystal, called struvite, is composed of a combination of minerals including magnesium. This led to the belief that dietary magnesium caused struvite formation, but further research has shown it's not that simple.

Cats normally produce an acidic urine, but the composition of the diet can affect urine acidity. Some kinds of magnesium, like magnesium oxide, may foster struvite formation by decreasing the acidity of the urine, while types like magnesium chloride help to acidify the urine and don't contribute to struvite formation. Neither of these magnesium sources are used in commercial cat foods; adequate amounts are obtained naturally from other ingredients. Today's cat foods are typically formulated to promote a cat's natural urine pH, or to help produce an acidic urine, and such commercial diets are usually considered appropriate for cats that have never before suffered an episode of LUTD.

There's been speculation that dry foods cause LUTD, but research has been unable to show a consistent connection between incidence of the condition and the form of the cat's food. Because the causes of LUTD are multifactorial and often unknown, preventing the condition in cats that have never before suffered from LUTD isn't possible. When a cat has previously experienced problems, your veterinarian may prescribe special diets as a treatment or management, depending on the problems.

Cat owners should be aware that about half of LUTD cats suffer from calcium oxalate crystals rather than struvite. Signs are the same, but the treatment is different. Commercial cat diets formulated to "promote urinary tract health" are designed to prevent struvite. But these same diets can increase the risk for calcium oxalate crystals by changing the acid/base balance of the cat's urine. While struvite crystals are most common in young and middle aged cats, it appears that calcium oxalate develop more frequently in geriatric cats.

Unlike struvite crystals, which can be dissolved by feeding the cat a special diet, calcium oxalate stones that can't pass out of the body when the cat urinates must be removed surgically. Sometimes the veterinarian recommends lithotripsy, a procedure that uses ultrasonic shock waves to pulverize the stones into tiny pieces in the hopes the cat can pass the fragments through urination. After removal, there is a 30 to 40 percent chance they'll recur.

Increasing the cat's water intake helps keep calcium oxalate stones from reforming by keeping the urine as diluted as possible. Some researchers recommend feeding the cat an alkalinizing diet such as prescription diets designed for cats with kidney failure to help reduce the chance of calcium oxalate stone recurrence.

LUNGWORMS

Lungworms are a slender, hair like worm *Aelurostrongylus abstrusus* that parasitize the cat's lungs. Cats contract the worm by eating rodents, birds or frogs that harbor the parasite.

Adult worms live in the lung tissue. The eggs they lay hatch into larvae that migrate up the windpipe to the throat, and then are swallowed and reach the digestive tract. Immature worms are excreted with the feces. Finding larvae in a stool sample is diagnostic.

The larvae must be eaten by and spend developmental time in a snail or slug to become infective. When a bird, frog or rodent eats this infective snail or slug, the cycle is complete.

Most cats infected with lungworms exhibit respiratory signs that are so mild they often aren't even noticed. Others may suffer from a dry, hacking cough as a result of secondary infections like bronchitis or pneumonia. In severe cases, the cat's breathing is noticeably labored, sometimes to the point of death.

Bronchitis or pneumonia are treated with antibiotics, and require a veterinarian's care. Worm medications such as fenbendazole and levamisole, though not approved for use in cats, are generally effective against lungworms. The possibility of lungworm infection can be avoided if the cat is prevented from hunting and eating small game (see HUNTING BEHAVIOR).

LUNG WORMS

SYMPTOMS: Dry cough; labored breathing
HOME CARE: None
VET CARE: Medication to kill parasite
PREVENTION: Prevent cat from hunting and eating prey

LYMPHOSARCOMA see CANCER.

326
CAT FACTS

327

CAT FACTS

MAMMARY GLANDS

The mammary glands are modified sebaceous glands that in female mammals secrete milk through nipples. Both male and female cats usually have eight breasts located in four pairs along the abdomen.

In male cats and in female cats that are not producing milk, the breasts are relatively flush with the abdomen, and are apparent only by slightly elevated light pink nipples. When milk is produced, the breasts slightly swell, the nipples darken, and the fur on the abdomen surrounding the nipples may thin. The breasts nearest the flanks tend to be most favored by kittens because they produce the most milk.

A lump, bump or swelling of the breast not associated with nursing kittens should be seen immediately by a veterinarian to rule out cancer. The mother cat exhibiting a high fever during nursing can also be an indication of trouble; stop the kittens from nursing and see a veterinarian (see ECLAMPSIA and MASTITIS).

MANGE

SYMPTOMS: Intense itching of face, head and neck; red scaly sore; yellowish crusting on skin; thinning hair and thickening skin; mousy smell

HOME CARE: Warm water soaks; mild grooming shampoos; lime sulfur or benzoyl peroxide products; wash bedding; vacuum carpet and throw away bag

VET CARE: Skin scraping to diagnose; sometimes antibiotics or anti-inflammatory medication

PREVENTION: Avoid contact with infected animals

MANGE

Mange refers to a skin condition resulting from microscopic parasites, called mites, which burrow into the skin. Mites are similar to insects, but are actually more closely related to spiders. Mange is not common in cats, but there are several kinds that can potentially cause problems.

The most common mite affecting cats is *Otodectes cynotis*, the ear mite. **Otodectic mange** is uncommon. The mite more frequently affects the skin of the ears (see EAR MITES).

Notoedric mange, also called head mange or feline scabies, is caused by the mite *Notoedres cati* which deposits eggs in burrows it makes in the outer surface of the cat's skin. Diagnosis is made by scraping the skin to collect mites that are present, and examining the material microscopically.

Notoedric mange is extremely contagious. It is considered uncommon, but appears to be a problem in some geographic regions. The mite completes its life cycle in a two week period spent entirely on the cat, and can't survive long in the environment. Signs of disease are intense itching on the head, face and neck. The cat typically scratches and shakes his head trying to get relief. Red scaly sores develop with yellowish thick crusting, and as the hair thins, the skin thickens and becomes leathery and wrinkled. The affected skin smells musty or mousy.

Cats and dogs in contact with the infected animal should also be considered infected and treated. Gentle soaking with warm water and mild soaps help loosen the crust, while antibiotics and steroid therapy treat secondary infections and relieves itchy skin. A 2.5 percent lime sulfur dip used weekly will kill the mites. Pets showing signs should be dipped two weeks beyond apparent cure, while exposed pets should be dipped at least twice. Thoroughly wash the cat's bedding, clean all surfaces, and vacuum carpeted areas and throw away the bag.

Sarcoptic mange and **demodectic mange**, both common afflictions in dogs, are extremely rare in cats. The signs, diagnosis and treatment of sarcoptic mange in cats is similar to that of feline scabies. Itchiness and red scaly sores with hair loss are the signs of sarcoptic mange. Demodectic mange may not itch, but results in patchy hair loss or over-all thinning of the hair coat, with or without pus-filled lesions and crusty sores.

The demodex mite isn't contagious, and is a normal inhabitant of cat skin. It occasionally causes problems in immune-suppressed cats that have other health problems. Most often, affected cats are youngsters.

Initial signs included localized areas of hair loss, usually on the face and especially surrounding the eyes and ears. These eventually develop itchy, crusty sores that can become infected. A generalized form of demodectic mange affects the whole body. The mite can also infest the ears.

A skin scraping is used to diagnose the condition, but often the mite is hard to find. For unknown reasons, many times the condition goes away without treatment.

The localized form may be treated topically with benzoyl peroxide-containing products that exfoliate, or strip away layers of the skin along with the mite. For generalized demodectic mange, aggressive veterinary treatment is necessary (see WALKING DANDRUFF).

MARKING

Marking is a behavior cats use to identify territory. Cats spray urine and defecate, scratch, and rub against objects to leave visual and scent cues. These signals not only indicate ownership, but also tell other cats who has been there before them, how long ago the mark was left, the sexual status of that cat, and other important information. In this way, cats can avoid confrontations by anticipating how fresh or old the mark is, and adjusting their paths accordingly. And, because the pungent scent tends to fade as soon as it contacts the air, markings must be constantly freshened with new markings on top or nearby the original.

Cats, both males and females, normally urinate in a crouching position and release the urine over a flat surface such as the litter in a litter pan. Marking with urine, called territorial spraying, is done by using a slightly different technique. Rather than releasing urine downward while squatting, the cat stands erect and urine is sprayed outward against vertical surfaces such as walls or trees. The cat backs up to the target, tail held straight up with the tip quivering, and releases short bursts against the item.

Territorial spraying is a sign of dominance, and is a normal behavior for sexually intact cats, particularly males. Spraying marks the boundaries of the cat's territory, as well as suppressing the sexual behavior of other less dominant cats that venture into that territory. Intact female cats that spray do so more often during breeding season to announce their availability to male Romeos.

This normal spraying behavior is a nuisance to humans particularly when the cat is an indoor pet. The unaltered male cat's urine has a particularly strong odor that is difficult to eliminate from household furnishings. Neutering the cat stops territorial spraying in 80 to 90 percent of cases.

Altered cats of either sex that spray are usually experiencing stress. When feeling insecure, a cat attempts to assert control over his or her environment by aggressively marking territory with the comforting familiarity of personal scent.

Middening is the deposition of feces most often in strategic and conspicuous open areas of the cat's territory, as a way to mark the area as owned. Middening is the least common form of feline marking. The cats' habit of covering waste is often attributed to instinctive behavior left over from a wild existence, and designed to protect cats living in the wild from a predator's detection. But not all cats cover their feces. Cat owners have often experienced a cat using a bathroom deposit to express dissatisfaction with a situation.

CAT FACTS

Aggressive cats tend to leave their droppings uncovered and prominently displayed as a sign of their dominance and ownership of a particular territory. Cats less self-assured or who are "trespassing" in another cat's "owned" territory cover their waste to avoid detection and, perhaps, as a sign of deference to the cat in control. It's probable that housecats cover their waste in deference to living within a territory "owned" by a more dominant, potent creature—the human owner.

Cats that leave their waste uncovered may be expressing a dominant behavior and signaling that territory belongs to them. And, when something happens that ruffles Kitty's whiskers, a bathroom deposit left in the middle of the floor or on the bed may be a way of saying, "I own this joint, get with the program!" However, inappropriate elimination also can be caused by health problems or emotional issues, and should never be ignored (see SOILING).

Marking behavior also includes a combination of visual and scent cues left by scratching an object. Claw care requires that the cat scratch objects to shed old growth and keep new nails healthy. Scratching also scars the object with visible claw marks as well as leaving behind scent from special glands located in the cat's paw pads. Scratching is a normal behavior for the cat, and cannot and should not be eliminated. Objectionable scratching can usually be addressed by redirecting the behavior to more acceptable objects (see SCRATCHING).

Bunting refers to the cat's habit of bumping and rubbing her head and body against people, other animals or objects. Cat owners typically consider the action to be a sign of affection, but it is more than that. Special glands in the skin of the chin, lips, forehead and tail secrete the cat's identifying scent. Other cats, objects and people are paid the highest compliment when they are bunted by a cat, or the cat rubs and twines about them. The scent that's transferred identifies that person or other animal as "family," a sharing of scent that is comforting and familiar to the cat. Social grooming is thought to also figure in this mechanism of sharing scent. In effect, an owner so marked becomes a part of the cat's territory, perhaps the most important part of all.

MASSAGE Massage is a hands-on therapy that addresses the tendons, muscles and other soft tissues by gently manipulating these areas with your hands and flexing the joints. Massage increases blood flow to sore spots and removes lactic acid that collects in tissues and makes the cat stiff and painful. That helps speed recovery from muscle pain or strain, and can also loosen tight tendons and scar tissue from old injuries.

Massage is a good way to relax with your cat after high energy play. Adolescent cats and kittens can be hard to contain and sometimes get sore just from growing so fast. A massage can ease the discomfort, and get the kitty ready to rumble all over again.

The hands-on treatment has added benefits, too. It reduces stress and even helps strengthen the immune system. Since contact with pets also benefits human health, massaging your cat has benefits for you both.

Range of motion exercises where the cat's joints are moved probably are best left in the hands of a professional--or have your veterinarian show you how to safely do this. But simple massage techniques can be safely done by you at home and your cat will tell you where he wants the attention most, by backing his butt-end near your hands, or purring when you rub his shoulders. Here are some massage techniques for you to try. Your cat will just think it's a petting session.

Effleurage is a gentle long, slow strokes with your palm, starting at the pet's head and continuing down to the tail and feet. This technique helps move the blood through the body but also is a stroke that encourages relaxation. Start with a soft touch, and then slowly increase the pressure of your palms.

Fingertip massage uses the tips of your fingers in small, circular patterns to move the muscles beneath the skin. Don't press directly over the bone. Instead, use fingertip massage on each side of the spine, for example, to ease stiff muscles and tissues.

Petrissage is sort of a combination of effleurage and fingertip massage, and uses a kneading technique. Your cat may not need this intense type of massage, or may object since it can be a bit painful on sore areas. But petrissage done correctly can move waste products out of the sore muscles.

TTouch ("tee-touch") is a specialized massage developed by Linda Tellington-Jones that works particularly well to address fear and aggression issues in pets. Tests show that TTouch changes the electrical activity in pets' brains. This helps them relax so they're open to learning new ways of coping, rather than just reacting out of fear. TTouch uses very specific circular stroke patterns on the surface of the skin all over the pet's body, with extra attention paid to the ears. The basic circle technique is called the Clouded Leopard TTouch because the strokes follow the circle shape of leopard spots. For cats, use one or two fingers to push the skin in a clockwise direction by "drawing" a complete circle with your fingers. Completing the circle changes the brain waves. After completing each circle, slide your hand on the pet's body an inch or two, and form another circle. Never lose contact with the body. Continue making "chains" of circles all over, as long as the pet allows. A ten-to-twenty-minute session is a good target. Let your cat be your guide, whether he wants a light touch or stronger pressure.

Many of the same touch rehab techniques created for human athletes have been adapted to dogs, and in some cases, also benefit cats. Massage and muscle stretching, muscle stimulation with E-Stim (electrostimulation), or treadmills and whirlpools are available. Swimming is a great low-impact way to rehab after surgery or injury, but cats are not fans of water. It's scary for them to get their face wet or be "dunked" in a body of water.

One of the newer developments in rehab is the underwater treadmill, where you just open up the door, and they walk into an empty holding tank that looks kind of like an aquarium. The door seals, and the warm water is pumped into the chamber very slowly, underneath their paws, so they don't get as scared. These specialized treadmills gives enough buoyancy so the cat can use his legs and move the joints without painful weight bearing issues.

The water, warmed to 85 to 90 degrees, soothes sore muscles, and walking on the underwater treadmill doesn't force them to stay afloat. The walking in water offers lower impact exercise compared to swimming, and the cat slowly builds up speed and stamina over time. The therapist controls the amount of water and the speed at which the treadmill runs.

The University of Tennessee unit, the first of its kind, was based on a human unit used by the U.T. football team. There are windows on all sides so the therapist can watch the pet's body in action—and so the cat can see where he's going. For some animals, the underwater treadmill treatment may reduce the need for pain medication or surgery, and helps pets recover more quickly after surgery

MASTITIS
Mastitis refers to an inflammation of one or more of the glands of the breast. Infection usually is caused by bacteria that is introduced by a scratch or puncture wound. Keeping the kittens' nails clipped may help prevent some cases.

Both the tissue and the milk it produces is affected; kittens that drink this toxic milk become ill and can die. Signs of toxic milk syndrome in kittens may include depression and lethargy, diarrhea, fever, and bloating. Kittens should be prevented from nursing from infected milk.

Instead, bottle feed the babies using a canned commercial kitten milk replacer available from your veterinarian (see MILK, AS FOOD.)

Cats suffering from mastitis typically have a high fever and refused to eat. The affected breast appears swollen, pink-to-blue in color, and is usually extremely tender to the touch. The milk may appear normal, but often is tinged with blood or a yellowish cast, or is thick or stringy.

Get the queen to a veterinarian immediately. The infected milk will be cultured to determine the type of bacteria involved, so the appropriate antibiotic may be administered. If an abscess has developed, treatment may involve surgical drainage of infected glands. Gentle massage of the affected breasts several times a day, and application of moist warm towels may be helpful (see ABSCESS).

MASTITIS

SYMPTOMS: Nursing cat with high fever; loss of appetite; swollen tender breast with bluish color; yellow or blood streaked milk; milk that's stringy or thick

HOME CARE: Once diagnosed, gently massage breast several times daily and apply warm wet compresses

VET CARE: Culture milk to diagnose; administer antibiotics; sometimes surgical drainage is required

PREVENTION: Clip kitten's claws

MATING see REPRODUCTION

MEGA COLON

Mega colon describes a greatly enlarged and flaccid colon that has lost the ability to move fecal material out of the body. The cause of the condition remains a mystery. It is suspected that a poor nerve supply to the organ results in the inability to properly contract.

The colon is the end portion of the large intestine that connects to the rectum, where waste leaves the body. Affected cats won't pass fecal material for days or even weeks when smooth muscle movement stops.

MEGA COLON

SYMPTOMS: Constipation
HOME CARE: Veterinary prescribed laxatives; enemas; special diets
VET CARE: Anesthetize cat to clean out colon; drugs to promote colon motility; sometimes surgical removal of disease colon
PREVENTION: None

The condition can be congenital and cause problems from birth, or may develop later in life as a result of tumors, strictures within the tissue that narrow the passageway, or foreign bodies that block the passage or injure the organ. A poor nerve supply to the colon may prevent proper contraction. In most cats, the cause remains a mystery.

The lining of the colon pulls moisture from the waste material. So when feces remains too long in the colon, the dry fecal material becomes harder and even more difficult to move causing constipation. The colon soon fills up with dry fecal balls, stretching and expanding the colon to gigantic proportions until waste cannot be passed naturally.

Fecal balls too large to pass through the cat's pelvis must be mechanically removed by the veterinarian after the cat has been sedated. Medical management helps many cats and prevents repeated bouts of fecal impaction. Laxatives, enemas, therapeutic diets, and motility drugs that help the colon to contract help some cats.

Surgery that removes the sick portion of the large intestine has been used to treat megacolon. The rectum is left intact and reattached to the small intestine to create a functional bowel. The surgery, called a subtotal colectomy, is complicated and used mostly as a last resort in severe cases, but can restore near normal bowel function.

Cats are usually somewhat depressed and refuse to eat for 48 hours after the surgery, and sometimes have a mild fever. Most cats maintain their normal body weight or even gain a little.

For the first three to four days following the surgery, cats typically pass a dark, tarry liquid stool. Feces remain liquid and poorly formed for two to six weeks until the ileum, the last section of the small intestine, increases its ability to absorb liquids. Then the feces usually become soft and poorly formed (cow pie consistency) and remain that way for the rest of the cat's life. Cats usually use the litter box two to three times a day, but the total amount of water loss in the feces equals that of normal cats.

MICROFILARIA see HEARTWORM DISEASE.

MILIARY DERMATITIS

Miliary dermatitis, also called scabby cat disease, is a skin reaction that is a symptom of disease rather than a separate disease itself. It's characterized by rash-like scabby bumps. The condition is quite common, and cats develop miliary dermatitis in response to a number of things.

The crusty sores are easily felt beneath the fur when the cat is stroked. The condition may have been named "miliary" because it feels similar to millet seeds. Miliary dermatitis may be concentrated in one isolated area, or scattered over the entire body.

Cats develop the rash in response to allergic reactions to any number of things, most typically flea hypersensitivity, atopy, and food allergies. Symptoms also may arise from ringworm or skin parasites like lice or mange. Bacteria, immune mediated conditions, drug reactions, and nutrition problems can also cause this condition.

MILIARY DERMATITIS

SYMPTOMS: Scabby rash
HOME CARE: Flea control
VET CARE: Treat underlying cause
PREVENTION: Avoid contact with allergy component

Successful treatment requires diagnosing the underlying cause, and addressing it specifically. For instance, if miliary dermatitis is due to an allergic reaction to fleas, then when the bugs are eliminated the rash should go away. Unfortunately, about one in six cases of miliary dermatitis are idiopathic, which means a cause cannot be determined. Cortisone may help control severe itching associated with some cases, and antibiotics may be prescribed to control secondary infections.

MILK, AS FOOD

From birth, kittens thrive on their mother's milk. If a kitten loses its mother or she is unable to feed the baby, milk is the obvious substitute.

However, the composition of cat's milk and cow's milk is quite different. Among other things, the calcium and phosphorous levels in cow's milk are much higher than that of queen's milk, which makes it inappropriate as a substitute for kittens. Human baby formula is similar in composition to cow's milk, and provides less than half of the protein and fat a kitten needs. It can be used in a short-term emergency situation by mixing it at twice the recommended concentration.

340
CAT FACTS

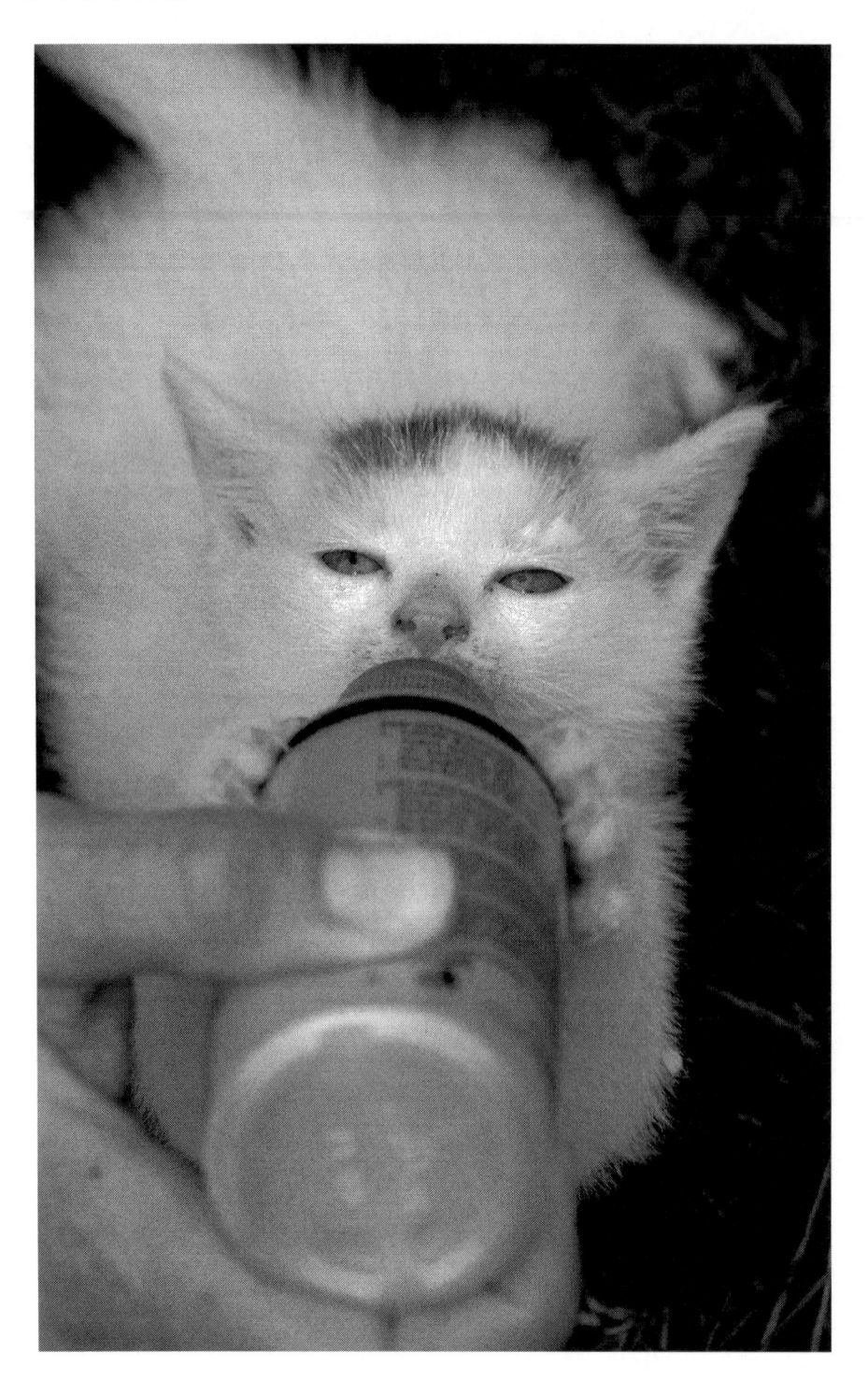

A better choice for long term supplemental or replacement feeding of kittens is commercial feline formulas. These are formulated to closely resemble the nutrient composition of queen's milk. Havolac, KMR and other brands are available from your veterinarian and pet product store.

Although a number of adult cats may relish milk, remember that it should never replace water in your cat's dish, nor be considered a complete food. Many cats and kittens aren't able to properly digest lactose, the sugar found in cow's milk.

Lactase is the enzyme required to break down lactose. If the cat's intestinal tract doesn't contain the right amounts of this enzyme, drinking milk will result in a nasty bout of diarrhea. A few commercial lactose-free milk drinks are available for owners who want to treat their cat without risking upset tummies.

MILK FEVER see ECLAMPSIA.

MONORCHID see CRYPTORCHID.

MUSIC THERAPY
Music therapy can help solve cat behavior problems as well as offer physical therapeutic benefits. Our pet cats are attuned to sound and are incredibly sensitive to noises, including music. Pleasant music can mask scary noises like thunder, or upsetting sounds like a trespassing cat's vocalizations that put your pet's tail in a twist. But more than that, the cadence of certain sounds influences the body's natural rhythms and can speed them up and energize the listener, or slow them down to calm him.

For instance, a fearful cat can be soothed with music or distracted with nature sounds like water running from a fountain. Lethargic pets that need to exercise can be energized with chirping bird sounds or fast music to get up and boogie to the beat.

Sound causes physical changes in the body. Brain waves change with different kinds of sounds—music with a pulse of about 60 beats per minute slows the brain waves so the listener feels more relaxed and peaceful and shifts the consciousness into a more alert state. This rhythm also slows breathing, which calms the mind and improves the metabolism. It works for humans, and also for our pets.

Even the heart wants to follow the pulse of the music—faster rhythms energize the listener as his heartbeat increases and blood pressure rises, while slower tempos calm. Listening to music releases endorphins—natural painkillers that are produced by the brain—and reduces the levels of "stress hormones" in the blood.

Sound therapy is still considered pretty new. One of the best known applications is ultrasound that uses the "echo" of high frequency sound waves to take diagnostic pictures inside the body—doctors even use it to break up kidney stones with vibration instead of surgery. Over the last 20 years, music therapy has become a staple of the human mental health profession, and is often used with troubled children and brain-disordered patients.

Today, harp music is used to relieve pain that drugs don't help, soothes emotional upset, and has become of particular help in hospice situations for human patients. The sound of harp music calms fractious cats and offers almost a natural sedative effect so that the upset animals become quiet, and go to sleep.

The simplest way to treat cats with music is to put on a CD or turn on the radio. Choose music you like—pets seem to respond best to music their owners enjoy because of the bond you share. If you have favorite music you often play, your pet will associate the sound with your presence, so playing that same music when he's alone will remind him of you and help ease problems like separation anxiety.

Soft music with a slow, steady rhythm helps calm agitated pets. It can help arthritic cats relax their muscles and increase their range of motion. It takes about 10 or 15 minutes for the music to take effect. Many pets enjoy Mozart or other classical music. New Age, soft jazz, southwest music with flutes and nature sounds, or even ballad-type Country can be soothing. The music should be melodic (not dissonant) and the tempo even and slow. You can play calming music anytime your pet feels stressed, or all day long as a background to help keep him calm.

Turn up the volume to energize your pet. Moderate to loud music with a more driving beat energizes the emotions and can encourage lethargic pets to exercise and lift depression or grief. Rock music, even the driving energy of Rap may get a pet's tail moving, but any up-tempo music from classical to contemporary has the power to energize. Again, play the music for at least 10 to 15 minutes at a time to get your pet in the right mood.

343

CAT FACTS

NAIL CLIPPING see GROOMING.

NAVIGATION Navigation refers to the cat's seeming innate ability to find his way home. Free-ranging cats often frequent territory of half a square mile or more. The homing mechanism for feral or free-roaming cats is a skill necessary for survival if the cat is to successfully range further away to hunt and return home to feed offspring.

Visual landmarks, scented signposts and familiar sounds are left behind or noted along the way, just as Hansel and Gretel scattered bread crumbs. These signals essentially map the cat's territory so that he can easily retrace his steps.

Cats that somehow move beyond familiar territory seem to somehow "know" the direction they should go, and set out straight for home. There is some speculation that, like birds, cats may use the position of the sun or setting stars to point them in the right direction to get them within scent- or hearing-range of their own or a neighboring animal's territory. From there, they can find their way directly.

Microscopic deposits of iron have been found in the front part of the brain of cats and some other animals, like homing pigeons. Scientist believe this acts as a kind of neurological compass that partially relies on geomagnetic sensitivity to the earth's magnetic field. This mysterious compass seems the best explanation for the extraordinary homing ability of the rare cat able to travel dozens or even hundreds of miles to get home.

NEUTERING Neutering, also called altering or sterilizing, is the surgical removal of an animal's reproductive organs. In pets, neutering commonly refers to the male, while spaying refers to the female (see SPAY). A gonadectomy, also called castration, is the surgical procedure that removes the male cat's testicles.

Neutering not only prevents the births of unwanted kittens, it reduces and in some cases eliminates certain health and behavioral problems. Excessive aggression that can result in abscesses, and marking behavior like urine spraying are greatly reduced in neutered cats, making the cat a better pet.

The greatest benefits are obtained when cats are altered before reaching sexual maturity. The exact timing varies from cat to cat and from breed to breed, but most male cats are able to reproduce by five to six months of age. Healthy males may be castrated at any time.

Prepubertal gonadectomy is defined as surgical sterilization of sexually immature animals six to 14 weeks of age. The American Association of Feline Practitioners supports neutering early in life as a safe and effective method of decreasing cat overpopulation, and one which confers long-term medical and behavioral benefits to the individual cat.

Neutering is done while the cat is under general anesthesia. Because the procedure is done quickly, often a relatively short-acting injectable drug is used. Other times, inhalant anesthetics may be used, or a combination of drugs. Depending on the cat, preanesthetic blood work may determine which anesthetic is best for the animal.

It's important that the cat's stomach be empty during the procedure so that if the cat vomits while asleep, the danger of inhaling the material into the lungs is reduced. Called aspiration, inhaling foreign material can cause life-threatening complications, including pneumonia. Generally, the cat should not eat or drink for a period of time prior to the surgery. If the cat sneaks an unauthorized snack, tell the veterinarian so that appropriate precautions can be made or the surgery can be delayed.

Once the cat is comfortably anesthetized, the surgical site is prepared by removing the hair and disinfecting the area with solutions like betadine and alcohol, or chlorhexidine and alcohol. The cat is placed on a towel or heating pad positioned on the surgical table to keep the cat's temperature constant. The surgeon wears sterile gloves and uses sterile surgical instruments, and the cat is draped with sterile cloth or towels to keep the site clean.

The two fur-covered spheres seen between the male cat's rear legs are the scrotum, skin sacs which contain the sperm-producing testicles. Each testicle is joined to a spermatic cord that contains an artery and the spermatic duct.

Testicles are expressed, one after another, through incisions made in each scrotal sac. The attached spermatic cords are tied with suture material to prevent bleeding, then the testicles are cut free. The stub of the spermatic cord recedes back into the surgical opening, leaving the scrotal sac empty. An antibiotic may be sprayed into the cavity, but scrotal incisions are usually left open to heal without benefit of stitches. Feline castrations rarely take longer than a few minutes to perform.

In rare cases, there's a failure of one or both testicles to descend into the scrotal sac as the cat matures (see CRYPTORCHID). However, both testicles must be removed to prevent objectionable sexual behaviors, so the abdomen must be opened to find the hidden testicle when castrating a cryptorchid cat. Your veterinarian can determine if your cat has a retained testicle. Besides behavioral differences, the intact male cat's penis has prominent spines which disappear once the cat is neutered.

Following surgery, the cat may be held overnight, and kept warm and monitored by the veterinarian. Cats often act a bit disoriented or even drunk for a short time after anesthesia, depending on the type of agent used. Cats typically are up and about within an hour or so of the anesthetic wearing off. Kittens especially seem to bounce back very quickly from the procedure.

Limit your cat's exercise for two or three days following the surgery, and monitor the incision site. The neutered cat doesn't need to see the veterinarian again unless there's a problem.

Post-neutering difficulties are rare, but see the veterinarian if there is a discharge or puffiness at the surgery site. Most problems are minor and involve the cat licking the incision. This can be prevented by using a collar restraint to keep Kitty away from the incisions until they heal (see ELIZABETHAN COLLAR).

NICTITATING MEMBRANE see EYES.

NOSE

The nose is a sensory organ that provides the cat with olfaction, or sense of smell. Scent cues give the cat her sense of place in the world. Smells identify friend from foe, communicate sexual information, and even prompt feline hunger. In many ways, scent rules the cat's life.

The cat's external nose varies in size and shape from breed to breed. Oriental breeds like Siamese have long straight "Roman" noses and wedge shaped muzzles, while the flat-faced profiles of Persians have broad snub noses and an indentation (break) between the eyes. The length of kitty noses can vary as much as two inches from one type to the other.

In fact, the short skulls of certain snub-nosed breed cats can distort and narrow the nasal passages and airways. Called brachycephalic airway syndrome, affected cats work so hard to inhale they may develop breathing problems. Physical activity, excessive heat, or stress prompts wheezing and noisy breathing. In some cases, surgery to increase the size of air passages may be necessary.

In domestic cats, the hairless point of the nose is called the leather, and comes in a variety of colors that, in pedigreed cats, typically matches or coordinates with the coat color. The nose leather is ridged with a unique pattern that is like a feline finger print; no two are alike.

The nostrils, or nares, are situated in the leather. They are the outside opening to the internal nasal cavity that runs the length of the cat's muzzle, ending when it opens into the cat's throat behind the soft palate. The nasal cavity is enclosed in bone and cartilage. Open spaces in the bone, called sinuses, connect to the nasal cavity. Sinuses help shape the sounds the cat makes, and are why meows sound the way they do. The openings in the bone may also function to reduce the weight of the skull. Sinuses in kittens are small and grow larger as the animal matures.

The nasal septum is a vertical plate made of bone and cartilage that divides the nasal cavity into two passages, one for each nostril. A series of rolled, bony plates called turbinates are located inside the nasal cavity. They are covered by three to six square inches of a spongy thick membrane, called the olfactory mucosa, which contains the scent-detecting nerves and cells. How well the cat smells depends on how many of these cells the cat has, which in turn is decided by the size and shape of her muzzle. Longer-nosed cats have more scent-sensing equipment than flat-nosed cats.

However, the cat's small size still allows her to have many more of these cells than people. Humans typically have five to 20 million scent analyzing cells, compared to the cat's 67 million. The king of scenting animals, the Blood Hound, has 300 million olfactory cells.

Odor particles are carried in the air, and are captured and dissolved by a coating of mucus that keeps the nasal cavity moist. Millions of microscopic hair-like receptors set in the olfactory cells extend into this thin layer of moisture, and make contact with the odor particles. It is believed that each different odor has a specific molecular "shape" which decides how much stimulation the nerve cell receives. The stimulated nerves signal the olfactory bulbs, which send the information directly to the brain, where the smell is interpreted as mouse, or whatever. A second more specialized scenting mechanism is thought to be used primarily in sexually-related odors (see JACOBSON'S ORGAN).

The cat's nose not only is a scenting organ, but also helps protect the respiratory tract by warming and humidifying air as it's inhaled. A protective layer of moisture is produced by serous glands and mucus glands throughout the nasal cavity. The muco-ciliary blanket is composed of microscopic cells covered with hair-like filaments called cilia that move the moisture toward the nostrils and throat. This mucus coating protects the body against infection by trapping foreign material.

However, because cats typically sense their world by sniffing, they are often exposed to illnesses and infected through inhaling bacteria or virus. Nasal disorders such as discharge, sneezing, or bleeding from the nose can indicate a number of different conditions (see UPPER RESPIRATORY INFECTIONS).

Kitty may tilt her head to one side, or squint the eye on one side when a foreign body lodges in the nasal passages. Sudden symptoms include violent sneezing and pawing at one side of the nose. Foreign matter like grass, an insect, or dust may work its way out by itself; other times, a veterinarian's help is advisable. Don't try removing foreign bodies yourself, or you could injure the delicate structures of the cat's nose.

The biggest problem in nasal disorders is that the cat loses her appetite. The smell of food prompts hunger, and when a stopped up nose interferes with scent detection, the cat just won't get hungry, and stops eating. Illness typically becomes even worse when the cat loses her appetite (see ANOREXIA).

NUTRIGENOMICS

A new science called nutrigenomics promises to prevent, slow the progression of, treat, or even reverse disease in dogs and cats. Researchers have identified 240 genetic diseases in cats, so nutrigenomics potentially could have far reaching benefits.

Nutrigenomics studies how individual nutrients or combinations of nutrients affect health by altering the expression of genes. Nutrigenomics views nutrients or bioactive foods as "dietary signals" that can directly or indirectly alter genomic expression or function. The science combines information from genetics, nutrition, physiology, pathology, molecular biology, bioinformatics, biocomputation, sociology, ethics, and other disciplines.

Experts compare genetic traits to a hand of cards dealt to you by your parents, and notes that no two individuals play identical cards the same way. Environmental factors can change how those cards—genetic traits—get played. Nutrigenomics doesn't look at the cards you're dealt, but how those cards are played (expressed).

Environment influences how genes are turned on and off, or turned up or down—whether the pet suffers severe, slight or no signs of disease at all. Genes load the gun, but environment pulls the trigger, and how genes are expressed changes constantly, sometimes minute-to-minute or day-to-day, and even over longer periods of your lifespan. Genes are critical for determining predilections, while nutrition modifies the extent to which different genes are expressed.

Nutrients influence gene and protein expression, and metabolite production. Resulting patterns (dietary signatures) studied in healthy and diseased groups of animals identifies abnormal versus normal dietary signals so researchers can adjust nutrients to help sick pets.

Commercial pet food companies look toward nutrigenomics to design cutting edge foods for pets. Such foods can turn "fat storer" pets into leaner "fat burner" individuals, reduce the signs of arthritis by "switching off" an enzyme that causes cartilage degradation, "starve" cancer, reverse cognitive brain impairment, or address insulin-receptors in diabetic cats. Even though nutrigenomics may not be able to completely prevent or cure a disease, it could very likely delay the onset of a condition, or at least modulate disease severity so it's manageable.

350 CAT FACTS

NUTRITION Nutrition refers to the food your cat eats. Cats require a nutritionally complete and balanced diet to maintain their optimal health. "Complete" means all necessary components are in the diet, while "balanced" means the components are in the proper ratios as compared to each other.

Nutrients are the components of food that provide nourishment. They must be supplied not only in the correct amounts, but in the proper balance because they benefit the cat both individually as well as by interacting with each other. Cats need a combination of six different classes of nutrients for good health.

Water is the most important nutrient. In fact, 84 percent of a kitten's body weight is water, and up to 60 percent of an adult cat's body weight is water. Water lubricates the tissue and helps electrolytes like salt to be distributed throughout the body. Moisture is used in digestion and elimination, and helps regulate the body temperature. Even a 15 percent loss of body water results in death (see DEHYDRATION).

Protein helps build and maintain bone, blood, tissue and the immune system. Proteins are composed of 23 different chemical compounds called amino acids. Some amino acids cannot be produced by the body in sufficient amounts and are called essential because they must be supplied by the diet. Cats require dietary histidine, isoleucine, leucine, arginine, methionine, phenylalanine, threonine, tryptophan, valine, and lysine. Unlike dogs, cats also require dietary taurine. A deficiency of taurine in the cat may result in blindness or heart disease (see CARDIOMYOPATHY).

Cats require much higher levels of dietary protein than do dogs, and should never be allowed to eat dog food. Cats are carnivores and must have animal source nutrients—or synthetic replacements—in their diet. Neither meat alone, nor a totally vegetarian diet provides balanced nutrition for the cat. Signs of a protein deficiency may include loss of appetite, weight loss, poor haircoat, poor growth, and impaired reproductive performance.

Carbohydrates provide energy, and are obtained from starches and grains. Fiber gives minimal energy, but helps regulate the bowels, assists other nutrient absorption, and may give a full feeling for obese cats that are dieting.

Fats provide 2¼ times the available energy per unit of weight than carbohydrates or proteins, and are particularly important for cats with high energy requirements, like pregnant or nursing queens. Fat also helps make food taste good to the cat. Fats are the only source of essential fatty acids, and are necessary for fat-soluble vitamins to be used. Fatty acids and fats promote healthy skin and fur, and signs of a deficiency include greasy fur, dandruff, weight loss, and poor healing of wounds.

Minerals are needed in relatively tiny amounts but are essential for nerve conduction, muscle contraction, acid/base balance, fluid stability inside the cells, and many other things. The term ash is used to describe the total mineral content of a particular food. The measure is obtained by burning the food, and measuring the unburned ash portion (mineral) that is left.

Necessary minerals include calcium, phosphorus, magnesium, potassium, sodium, chloride, and the trace minerals cobalt, copper, iodine, iron, manganese, selenium, and zinc. Minerals work together, and the balance is as important as the amount. Too much can be as dangerous as too little. An imbalance can cause bone deformities, anemia, muscle weakness, heart or kidney disease, and countless other problems.

Vitamins are used in biochemical processes inside the cells, and very small amounts are sufficient. Vitamins are divided into two groups. The B-complex vitamins are water-soluble, are not stored in the body, and must be replaced every day. The fat-soluble vitamins A, D, E, and K are stored in the body. Vitamins must be in proper combinations and amounts, or severe problems may result. Over-supplementation can be toxic to the cat, while insufficiency can cause dangerous diseases. Too much or too little of certain vitamins may result in problems such as lameness, skin problems like yellow fat disease, or rickets, anemia, bleeding, and even neurological disorders.

Nutrient requirements for cats vary depending on several factors, including the animal's age, health status, activity level, and living conditions. Every cat is different, but most are able to obtain optimum nutrition by eating commercial cat foods that have been properly formulated. Owners who choose to offer home prepared foods also must ensure these diets provide complete and balanced nutrition.

"Staged feeding" refers to the cat's life stage, and generally is divided into three broad categories: growth (kittens), reproduction and lactation (mother cats bearing and nursing kittens), and maintenance (adult cats). Pregnant cats, those nursing kittens, and growing kittens require much higher levels of energy than do adult cats. Among other things, kittens need more protein, fat, and calcium than mature felines. Adult cats may gain too much weight if fed a high-calorie kitten ration.

Always offer a food that is appropriate to your cat's life stage. High-quality commercial pet foods clearly label their products for growth and reproduction (pregnant or nursing mothers and kittens); maintenance (adult cats); or all life stages (from kittenhood to motherhood and adult maintenance). Feed only products that have been tested and are proven to be complete and balanced (see READING FOOD LABELS).

Specialty diets are also available that address a number of nutrition-related concerns. Those that help control health problems generally are available only through a veterinarian, and should be used only as prescribed. Many are designed to relieve specific clinical signs of disease by manipulating nutrient profiles, and are not appropriate for routine maintenance in healthy cats.

353

OBESITY Obesity is defined as an excess of body fat 30 percent beyond the normal and more often affects middle-aged and older cats. Obesity is the cat's most common nutritional disorder. A recent survey of veterinarians indicates that half of the adult cats seen are overweight or obese. In the six-to-twelve-year-old group as many as 40 percent of the cats are overweight or obese. According to 2014 statistics published by the Association for Pet Obesity Prevention, 57.9 percent of U.S. cats are overweight or obese.

The condition seems more common today primarily because of differences in feline lifestyle and feeding. A large number of cats are exclusively indoor pets with limited opportunities for exercise. Palatable commercial foods prompt more feline attention to food when Kitty is bored and left with little else to do. And the higher the fat and calorie content of the food, the greater becomes the risk for obesity.

All cats can potentially become overweight, but the problem appears to be more prevalent in mixed breed cats. A number of risk factors are thought to be related to feline obesity. The highest incidence appears in neutered middle aged six to 11 year old male cats.

There are a number of theories why neutered cats are more prone to obesity than intact ones. The removal of reproductive organs alters the hormonal balance and causes changes in metabolism. Also, cats are usually neutered in kittenhood or early adulthood when energy requirements are declining, but owners may fail to make appropriate dietary adjustments. Finally, neutering tends to curb certain behaviors of cats, such as roaming and fighting; the resulting decline in activity contributes to weight gain when the diet isn't adjusted (see NEUTERING and SPAYING).

In fact, surveys of overweight cats show they tend to be very inactive and sleep up to 18 hours a day. Overweight and obese cats are more likely to be fed high fat nutrient dense rations such as certain super-premium or therapeutic diets. One study of overweight cats reported an increased risk for dying in middle age. Researchers suspect fat cats don't live as long as thin ones, so obesity becomes a longevity and quality of life issue.

Overweight cats are more likely to develop diabetes mellitus, skin problems, lameness due to arthritis, and feline hepatic lipidosis, but cats almost never develop atherosclerosis. Severely overweight cats may be at greater risk for surgical complications from bleeding or anesthesia, heat or exercise intolerance, and complications from cardiovascular diseases.

Weight alone isn't a good measure of the percentage of body fat compared to muscle/bone mass. A better method is evaluating Kitty's condition by looking at his profile, and feeling his body.

355

Some breeds call for slightly different conformations—for instance, the Oriental-type breeds such as Siamese and Oriental Shorthair cats tend to have longer, thinner bodies than the cobby-type Persian breeds. In all cats, though, generally you should be able to feel the ribs but not see them. From above, you should see a decided break at the waist, beginning at the back of the ribs to just before the hips.

In profile, cats should have a distinct tummy tuck beginning just behind the last ribs and going up into the hind legs. Many adult overweight cats tend to carry a "pouch" of fat low in the tummy, but seem of average size otherwise. If you can't feel the cat's ribs, and/or she carries a pouch on her tummy, the cat is overweight.

Crash diets for cats can be deadly. Overweight felines in particular are prone to liver problems (see FELINE HEPATIC LIPIDOSIS), and so care must be taken to ensure your cat loses weight in a safe, gradual way. Before beginning a diet, your veterinarian should examine the cat to rule out potential health complications. The veterinarian will calculate how much weight should be lost, and suggest a diet and exercise plan appropriate to your individual pet. Usually, the target is to lose about one to one and a half percent of her starting weight per week.

With some cats, simply eliminating the treats (see FOOD SUPPLEMENTS) and slightly reducing the amount of their regular ration is adequate. Canned food is less calorie dense than dry foods, so rather than free-feeding dry food, success may be obtained by meal feeding with canned. Divide the food into four or even five small meals a day to help keep Kitty from feeling deprived. Multiple small meals also tends to increase the body's metabolic rate, which can help the tubby tabby slim down.

In other cases, switching the cat to a lower calorie/fat diet is a better option. Special "lite" diets are designed to provide complete and balanced nutrition in a reduced calorie/fat formulation that also satisfies the cat's need to feel full. These diets typically replace fat with indigestible fiber, dilute calories with water, or "puff up" the product with air. But some feline nutritionists believe cats are metabolically programmed to eat a set amount of calories, and eat until this set-point is reached. If this is true, special reducing diets may not work when offered free choice, because the cat simply eats more of the reduced-calorie food to get the same number of calories he'd get from a more concentrated food. Some commercial diets now use nutrigenomic principles to change the body's gene expression that impacts the way the body uses food (see NUTRIGENOMICS).

The definition for reducing products historically has varied between pet food companies, so that one company's "lite" product actually might have more calories than the next company's "regular" food. Be sure to compare labels before choosing a "lite" diet for your cat.

In extremely obese cats, veterinary prescribed reducing diets in conjunction with a therapeutic weight loss program supervised by the veterinarian is the safest option. In all cases, increasing the cat's exercise through the use of interactive toys is encouraged.

To keep your Kitty in condition, feed a quality complete and balanced diet. Monitor the cat's body condition, and adjust the amount of food offered as needed. Try meal feeding your cats in "treat puzzle toys" so they must work for the food. And play interactive games with your cat to promote healthy exercise (see also NUTRITION and FOOD).

OTITIS

Otitis is an inflammation of the ear which may happen suddenly, or be ongoing. It is generally categorized as otitis externa, otitis media, or otitis interna, which refers to the area of the ear the inflammation affects.

Cats suffering from immune disorders or diseases like feline leukemia virus or feline immunodeficiency virus are more prone to developing otitis. Normal ear secretions being thrown out of balance predispose the cat to otitis. This can be caused by something as simple as getting water in the ears during a bath.

Cats most commonly suffer from otitis externa, which is confined to the external portion of the ear canal and/or the ear flap. Otitis externa occasionally advances into the middle ear (otitis media), and even more rarely into the inner ear (otitis interna).

Signs of otitis include itchy or painful ears that may be red, raw, or even bloody if the cat has scratched them. Excessive shaking or scratching may result in severe bruising and swelling of the ear flap (see HEMATOMA). A bad odor from the ear indicates infection, as does any sort of discharge. Normal wax is light amber; an abnormal discharge can vary from clear and thin to waxy and crumbly, or even thick and cloudy yellow or green.

When the middle or inner ear is affected, the cat can show signs of nerve involvement. Symptoms include a head tilt, droopy eyelids or a facial palsy on the affected side. Inner ear infections can interfere with the cat's sense of balance so the cat may circle and fall toward the affected side. Extreme damage from otitis may result in deafness.

Ear mites are the number one cause of otitis externa in cats. Allergies or foreign bodies like grass seeds also cause ear inflammation, and yeast or bacterial infections are also common causes of otitis externa. Otitis media is usually due to progression of infection from the external ear canal, or penetration of the ear drum by a foreign object. From there, the problem can progress into otitis interna, where the cat really gets in trouble.

358
CAT FACTS

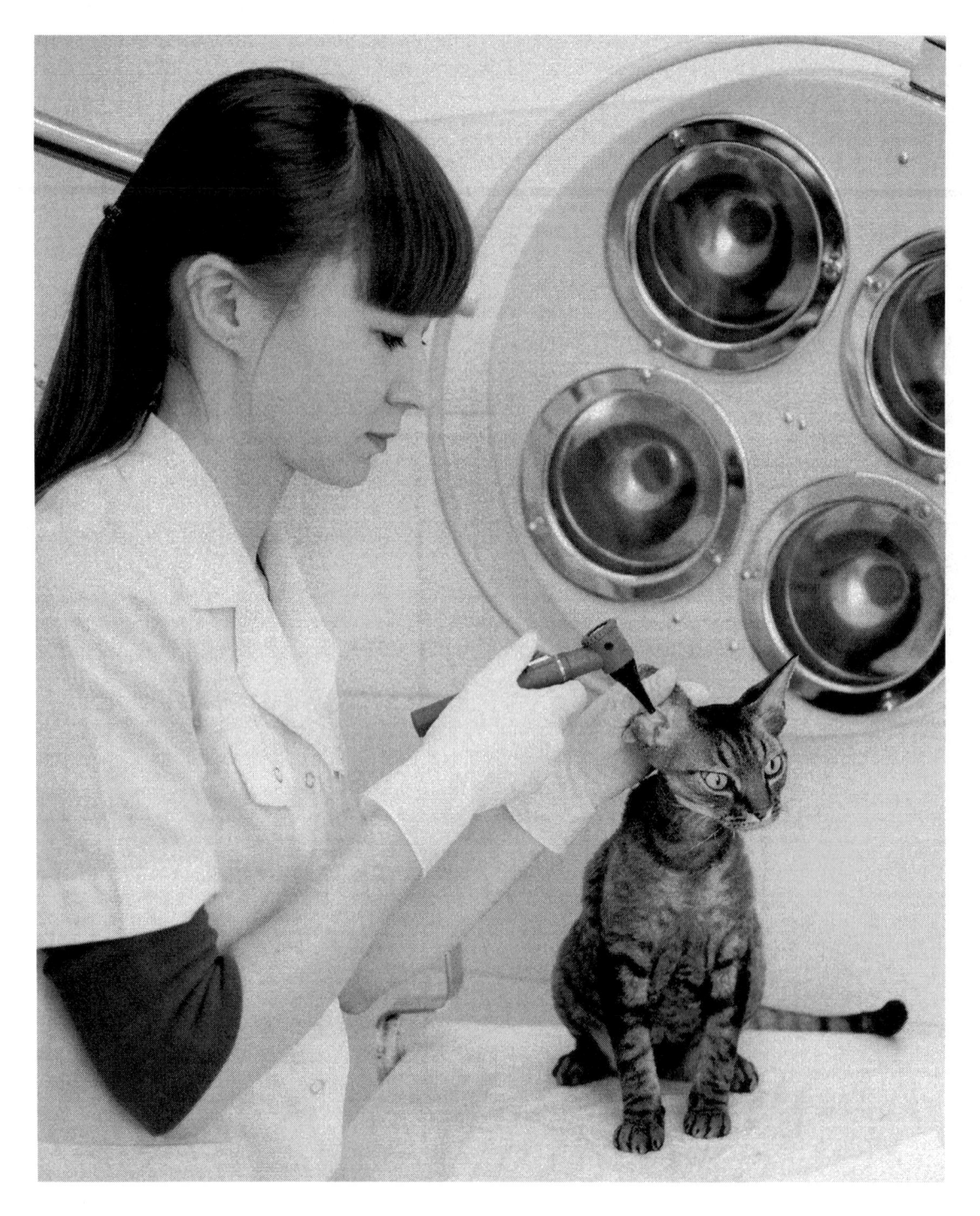

OTITIS

SYMPTOMS: Itchy ear; painful ear; red or raw ear; head shaking or scratching at ears; discharge; bad odor; sometimes head tilt; eye squinting or circling
HOME CARE: Gentle cleaning; treating with prescribed medication
HOLISTIC HELP: Herbal treatment
VET CARE: Antibiotics; steroids; antifungal creams; mite medications depending on cause
PREVENTION: Proper ear maintenance

Treatment depends on identifying and addressing the cause of the inflammation. Sedation or anesthesia may be necessary to thoroughly examine a cat's sore ears. An instrument called an otoscope that has a magnifying lens and light makes it possible for the veterinarian to examine the horizontal and vertical ear canal to see if the eardrum is intact.

The nature of the discharge can be evaluated, as well as the status of swelling or scaring of the ear canal. Foreign bodies may be visible during this examination as well. The veterinarian also collects a sample of the discharge and examines it under the microscope to identify if bacteria, yeast or ear mites are present.

The ears must be thoroughly cleaned and allowed to dry before treatment is effective, and general anesthesia may be required. The veterinarian should perform the initial cleaning to avoid further trauma to the ears. If the eardrum is ruptured, some ear cleaning solutions or medications can actually damage the middle ear, and make a bad situation even worse.

After the initial cleaning and flushing of the affected ears, most cases can be treated by owners at home (see ADMINISTER MEDICATION). Topical antibiotic ointments and drops, sometimes with steroids to reduce itchiness and inflammation, are generally prescribed for bacterial infections. Medicine is usually administered twice a day for two weeks. The herb pau d'arco, also called Inca Gold, is a natural antibiotic that quickly kills fungi and bacteria and may be recommended by your holistic veterinarian.

Yeast infections are treated with antifungal creams or drops twice daily for two weeks, then once a day for another week. If the infection is caused by more than one thing, an antifungal/antibacterial cream may be prescribed to address all issues. Diluted vinegar with water also can help clean the ears.

Acute otitis usually resolves within two or three days with treatment. But chronic problems take much longer to cure. Up to six weeks of treatment may be necessary when the eardrum is punctured in order to prevent permanent damage to hearing or balance. Occasionally the eardrum requires lancing to relieve the pressure of infection that has built up; usually, the eardrum heals quickly.

When infections are deep inside the ear, drops and ointments may not reach the source, and surgery may be necessary to clean out these pockets of infection. Long-term oral antibiotics are given to fight the infection, along with steroids to address inflammation and prevent nerve involvement. Still, neurologic signs may continue for the rest of the cat's life even after the infection is cured.

The best way to prevent otitis is to routinely check your cat's ears every week for parasites, and to keep them clean. Use a bit of baby oil or commercial ear cleaner on a cotton ball or cotton swab, and gently wipe clean the area you can see. Make ear maintenance a part of your cat's grooming regimen (see DEAFNESS, BALANCE and GROOMING).

OUTDOOR SHELTER In the United States, responsible cat lovers confine cats indoors to protect them from predators, disease, and accidental injury, while other countries may consider such confinement unnatural or even cruel. Without appropriate indoor enrichment, confined cats may suffer stress and associated health or behavior issues. Whatever your personal choice for your cats, it is vital that steps be taken to protect them.

Outdoor shelter is available for cats. Cat condos or homemade versions can be connected to pet doors or windows, to allow your cat indoor/outdoor access that's safe. You can find fence products that attach to existing structures, as well as unit systems that provide protected environments when cats spend time in the yard. *Cat containment systems* like Cat Fence-In (www.catfencein.com) attaches fine webbing to existing outdoor fences to keep cats safely inside while allowing them to enjoy the outdoors. Purr…fect Fence (www.purrfectfence.com) also offers a complete backyard fence enclosure. Affordable Cat Fence (www.catfence.com) receives positive marks as well. All three offer do-it-yourself kits.

Strays and feral cats you're unable to bring indoors also require outdoor shelter particularly when whether turns cold. A feeding station will help to keep food and water dry and will help with freezing weather.

If you are unable to build a shelter, you can use any type of strong box or crate, or buy a dog "igloo" from your pet supply company. Block off part of the larger opening to make it smaller and therefore warmer inside for the cats. Size should be approximately three feet by three feet and two feet high. Cats will cuddle together inside for warmth. Provide enough shelters so that about six cats can stay in each one.

It is safer to have two small openings for the cats to enter and be able to get away if danger presents itself. Put the openings on the side of the shelter that is protected from the wind. Two openings will give a chance at escape should a pesky raccoon for instance or any other animal try to enter the shelter. Raise the shelter off the ground by placing it securely on bricks or on a wooden pallet. If left on the ground it will retain moisture and will rot.

Insulate the shelter with thick plastic or other material to keep out wind and cold. Mylar insulation is made of polyester and aluminum that reflects radiant heat. It is used to keep houses

CAT FACTS

cooler in summer and warmer in winter. This type of insulation is normally used in attics and is a perfect material to use to insulate outdoor cat shelters. Or you can use straw for the bedding, not hay (it mildews) nor fabric. Blankets, sheets and towels retain moisture and remain damp and should not be used during winter. Bedding should be straw or made of a synthetic fleece material such as that used to make horse saddle covers. Clean shelters each spring and autumn by replacing the bedding with fresh hay (see FERAL and HYPOTHERMIA).

OVARIOHYSTERECTOMY see SPAYING.

363

CAT FACTS

PAIN Pain is extreme discomfort, usually in a specific part of the body, which is caused by illness or injury. Pain is a protective mechanism designed to prompt evasive action that stops the sensation, which in turn prevents further damage to the body. For example, a burn stimulates the paw or tail to recoil, while the pain of a broken bone motivates resting the area which helps speed the healing.

Before pain can be treated, the underlying cause for the discomfort must be determined. Pain can result from any number of things including arthritis, fractures, peritonitis, periodontal disease, or even systemic disease like feline infectious enteritis. Inflammatory pain develops from the body's immune response to infection or injury.

Common pain medications such as aspirin and Tylenol that people typically use to relieve pain are poisonous to the cat. Pain management is more difficult in cats because felines are much more sensitive to many of these drugs. When pain is due to inflammation, sometimes the veterinarian will prescribe steroid-type medications to make the cat feel more comfortable. If you suspect your cat is in pain, have the veterinarian examine Kitty to determine the underlying cause.

Response to pain travels through the nervous system, up the spinal cord to the cortex of the brain. Drugs and therapies can be used to control pain at any point along this pathway.

Agents that control pain, called analgesics, are matched to the type of pain. **Visceral pain** is dull, vague, and achy discomfort located inside the body and organs (i.e., intestines, heart, lungs). Visceral pain is caused by the tissue being crushed, torn or cut, by chemicals like drugs or poisons, or from a lack of blood to the area. **Somatic pain** is a sharp, localized pain in any tissue other than the viscera, such as the skin, muscle, joints, and bones. Somatic pain is caused by extremes of temperature, or by chemical or mechanical (i.e., crushing, cutting) injury. **Neuropathic pain** is a sharp, burning discomfort caused by direct damage to the nerves or spinal cord. This kind of pain often cannot be controlled with drug therapy. **Acute pain** results from a sudden stimulation—you hit your thumb with a hammer—and tend to be the most responsive to pain-relieving medication. **Chronic pain** is a dull, achy discomfort usually due to old injuries. **Cancer pain** falls into this category. Chronic pain tends to be hard to control.

Instead of a pill, medicines are being formulated in liquids that can be dripped into the pet's mouth or added to the food. Narcotic pain relievers such as morphine, codeine and Demerol are available by prescription only from the veterinarian. Codeine is preferred for cats because it's well absorbed in the digestive tract and provides effective relief for all but the most severe forms of pain such as cancer pain. Codeine can be compounded into fish paste to help cats accept it.

Buprenorphine is said to be twenty-five times more potent than morphine. It takes longer to work, but the effects last longer for pets that have severe or chronic pain.

Transdermal application means pain medication can be absorbed through the skin. Fentanyl (Duragesic) is an opioid drug that comes in a transdermal patch that provides prolonged narcotic relief for both dogs and cats. It comes in a variety of strengths and is particularly helpful for pets that are reluctant to take medicine orally. Today, Fentanyl is often used for post-operative pain.

The pluronic gel approach—a carrier substance that moves through the skin—allows combining all kinds of different analgesic drugs. For instance, DMSO (Dimethyl Sulfoxide) penetrates the skin within five minutes of application and carries other substances mixed with it into the body. Pain medicine mixed into the gel can be pasted on the skin, the gel carries the drug through the skin into the nerve tissue, and helps lessen the pain at the source.

Depending on the type of pain, acupuncture and nutraceuticals may be helpful in relieving the cat's discomfort. Environmental accommodation also is vital to help the cat maintain close to normal activities.

Veterinary anesthesia has traditionally been conservative because of fears about side effects and respiratory depression. For this reason, pets have been under-anesthetized as a rule. That's particularly important because of something called "pain memory."

Human anesthesiologists routinely administer general anesthesia, followed by a nerve block, which prevents pain in a particular region of the body, such as a leg being set or a joint that's being repaired. But until recently pets were simply given general anesthesia to keep them immobile, and oblivious to any pain during the treatment.

Your veterinarian may recommend PEMF therapy, which stimulate the electrical and chemical processes in the tissues to relieve inflammation and pain. Devices may be designed for whole body treatment or targeted areas of the body. Some of these devices have successfully completed efficacy studies and are FDA-approved. Therapeutic products may be available in mats, wraps or other devices from your veterinarian or over the counter (see PULSED ELECTROMAGNETIC FIELD).

Research has found that pain medication given before the pet undergoes a painful treatment can prevent the problem. Drugs given in advance of pain will reduce the amount of pain after the event. Doing this also decreases the total amount of pain medication needed. After surgery, continued pain control can be accomplished with drains that deliver the medicine into the chest and abdominal cavity, the joint, or even intravenously via a catheter.

366 CAT FACTS

Cats in pain don't act like themselves; retiring cats become demanding, friendly cats hide. It's hard to tell sometimes what Kitty's trying to say. Cats normally sleep curled up—he may be in pain if he sleeps hunched up, for example. Be alert for signs of pain (see chart), and have the cat checked by your veterinarian.

SIGNS OF PAIN

- **Hides,** remains very still and quiet
- **Becomes vocal,** meowing or crying
- **Acts agitated,** can't get comfortable
- **Pants** or drools
- **Refuses food**
- **Flinches,** hisses or strikes out when touched in tender place
- **Trembles**
- **Limps** or carries paw
- **Assumes hunched posture**
- **Squints** eyes, or has watering eyes

PANCREATITIS

Pancreatitis is the inflammation of the pancreas, an organ situated near the liver that provides digestive enzymes and insulin. The disease is commonly recognized in dogs, and although it was once thought to be rare in cats, we now know that acute pancreatitis is almost as frequent in cats as in dogs.

An inflamed pancreas releases digestive enzymes into the bloodstream and abdominal cavity rather than the small intestines. As a result, the enzymes digest the fat and tissues of the abdomen or even the pancreas itself.

The cause isn't clear in cats, but the condition is sometimes associated with diabetes (see DIABETES MELLITIS). Cats suffer chronic disease with vague signs that come and go. Most are lethargic, anorectic, dehydrated, and have low body temperature. Since the organ is linked to the intestines and also to the liver, cats suffering from pancreatitis may have concurrent liver or inflammatory bowel disease. It's possible that an inflammation can actually move from one organ to the other, making the disease even more difficult to diagnose and treat.

Acute pancreatitis can be completely reversed if the cause is identified and removed. However, more than 90 percent of all cases of feline pancreatitis are idiopathic—that is, they have no known cause.

The chronic form creates irreversible changes. Both forms can be mild or severe, and animals can recuperate from the mild form. The severe form causes extensive death of tissue, involves a number of organs, and means a poor prognosis.

Several new tests for diagnosing the canine disease have been modified for use in cats. Some tests like the feline trypsin-like immunoreactivity (TLI) are even more useful for cats than dogs.

Confirming the diagnosis relies on ultrasound. But a definitive diagnosis of feline pancreatitis should be made by a pancreatic biopsy. That requires exploratory surgery (laparotomy) that can be done less invasively with a scope (laparoscopy) (see ENDOSCOPE).

Cats typically don't vomit, and if they suffer liver complications—hepatic lipidosis—that makes fasting even more dangerous. Cats that do not also have a liver disease should have food withheld, though, for three to four days, and then have a carbohydrate-rich low-fat diet slowly introduced.

Currently there is no consensus on the best way to treat feline pancreatitis once it's diagnosed. Anecdotal reports indicate that cats with pancreatitis benefit from transfusion of fresh frozen plasma or fresh whole blood, which contain albumin and other components that help patients suffering from pancreatitis (see BLOOD). Other supportive care, such as fluid therapy, or drugs to control vomiting, is offered as needed.

Cats that have a mild form of chronic pancreatitis often benefit from a daily dose of pancreatic enzyme. A teaspoon of dried powdered extracts of beef or pig pancreas (Pancrezyme, or Viokase-V) can be mixed in the food given twice daily. If the cat refuses the treated food, the veterinarian may have other alternatives such as raw beef pancreas or a fish-based liquid supplement.

Parenteral nutrition—intravenous nutrition—does not stimulate the pancreas as much, but it requires constant monitoring. If you overfeed calories—in particular, fat—to cats intravenously, you can predispose to lipidosis, so you're back to making the situation worse. In most cases, she says veterinarians will place a tube device either down the throat or directly into the stomach through the cat's side. That is combined with fluid therapy to keep the cat well hydrated.

Cats that recover from acute pancreatitis may develop the chronic form of the disease where there is a lack of digestive enzymes. Food can't be digested or absorbed properly, and results in soft, pale, voluminous stools, weight loss, and greasy hair around the rectum or the entire hair coat. Diabetes often develops. Treatment includes diet changes, supplemental pancreatic enzymes, and vitamin and antibiotic therapy.

PANCREATITIS

SYMPTOMS: Lethargy; anorexia; dehydration; low body temperature.
HOME CARE: None
VET CARE: Therapeutic diet
PREVENTION: None

Panleukopenia see FELINE PANLEUKOPENIA VIRUS.

Parasites see EAR MITES, COCCIDIOSIS, CUTEREBRA, FLEAS, GIARDIA, HEMOTROPHIC MYCOPLASMAS, HEARTWORM DISEASE, HOOKWORMS, LICE, LUNGWORMS, MANGE, ROUNDWORMS, TAPEWORMS, TICKS and TRICHOMONIASIS.

Periodontal Disease

Periodontal disease refers to disorders that affect the teeth and gums. Cats develop dental disease no matter what form of food they are fed. In fact, all animals commonly suffer from periodontal disease, or problems of the mouth, teeth and gums. Seventy-five percent of cats develop some form of the disease by the time they reach two years old. As the cat ages, the risk becomes greater. The risks for periodontal disease increase 20 percent each year of a pet's life.

Unlike people, cats don't rely on chewing to process their food. They are more likely to bite off or pick up mouth-size portions and swallow them whole. That means they don't benefit from the scrubbing or detergent action of chewing food the way people do. Also, wet diets stick to the teeth more readily than dry foods.

Food that sticks to the surface of the cat's teeth as he eats is the perfect environment for bacterial growth. As the bacteria grows, a couple of things happen. A soft material called plaque accumulates and sticks to the tooth surface. Left unchecked, the plaque turns to a chalk-like material that mineralizes and forms hard deposits called calculus or tartar. Tartar is a buildup of yellow to brown crusty material on the teeth. This increase in bacterial activity in the mouth can produce odor which is an early warning sign of dental disease (see BAD BREATH).

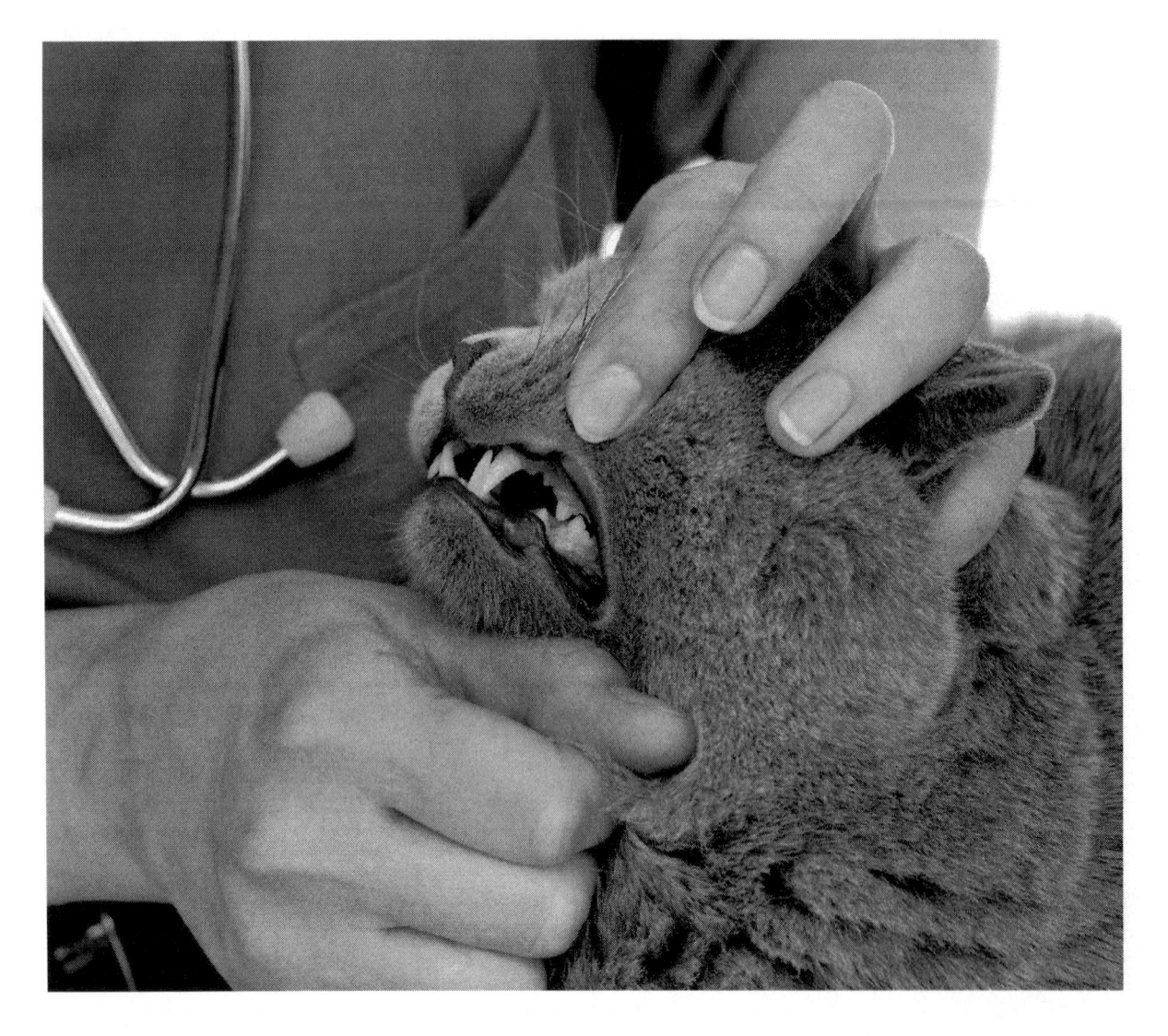

Enzymes released by the bacteria attack the surrounding tissue, causing inflammation. Called gingivitis, this inflammation of the gums is another early sign of periodontal disease. The gums at the tooth line will appear red and swollen, and tissue will be tender and may easily bleed.

The cat's immune system attempts to fight the bacteria, but instead causes even more inflammation and tissue destruction. The gums begin to recede from the teeth, and bone destruction loosens them until teeth simply fall out. Loose teeth or exposed roots are signs of gum recession due to chronic infection.

PERIODONTAL DISEASE

SYMPTOMS: Bad breath; yellow to brown debris on teeth; red swollen or bleeding gums; loose teeth; receding gums; reluctance to eat
HOME CARE: None
HOLISTIC HELP: Supplements
VET CARE: Anesthetize cat to clean and/or extract decayed teeth; antibiotics
PREVENTION: Clean cat's teeth weekly; avoid feeding exclusively soft diets

Cats are also prone to a condition called Feline Tooth Resorption (TRs), odontoclastic destruction of feline teeth classified as either type 1 or type 2. With type 1 lesions, there is no replacement by bone, whereas with type 2 there is replacement of the lost root structure by bone. There are five types of resorptive lesions. Type 1 or 2 can potentially be treated, but Types 3 and 4 and 5 are usually past doing anything for them other than extraction.

Defects develop at the gum line, or "neck" of the tooth, and form a tiny entry hole (or may start from the inside) to ultimately erode the tooth from the inside out. That leaves a hollow, fragile shell of tooth that can easily fracture, and cause severe dental pain. Lesions occur with a frequency of up to two-thirds of cats seen for dental problems.

Mouth infections are not only painful, but also impact the cat's overall health. Chewing can pump bacteria into the cat's bloodstream, which in turn spreads infection throughout the body. Periodontal disease has the potential to damage lungs, heart, liver and/or kidneys and can cause either sudden disease, or a slow, progressive deterioration that shortens the cat's life.

Today, veterinary dentistry is a growing specialty. Depending on the extent of the problems, a veterinary dentist can provide many of the same services available to people, including teeth cleaning, fillings, crowns, root canals, and even orthodontia work.

CAT FACTS

To treat periodontal disease, a thorough cleaning is required. Animal patients must undergo general anesthesia for this procedure because tartar must be scaled from the teeth even below the tender gum line. An ultrasonic cleaner removes the deposits, then the teeth are polished to smooth irregularities in the enamel that collect plaque. A fluoride treatment to help protect the teeth completes the cleaning.

When infection is present, antibiotics are prescribed. Feline cavities are difficult to fill because they leave teeth so fragile that often the tartar is all that holds them in place. Usually, decayed teeth are extracted. But simply removing the painful tooth often so relieves the cat so much that he begins acting like a kitten again.

Cats can develop a severe inflammation of the gingival tissues, called gingival stomatitis. Maine Coons are prone to the condition, but it appears to be more common in Oriental-type cats such as Siamese, Burmese and Abyssinians. Stomatitis resulting from an *excessive* immune response often is associated with food allergies or with early infections of calicivirus (see UPPER RESPIRATORY INFECTION). Infection with *Bartonella* (a blood parasite) as well as bacteria produced by dental plaque also is implicated.

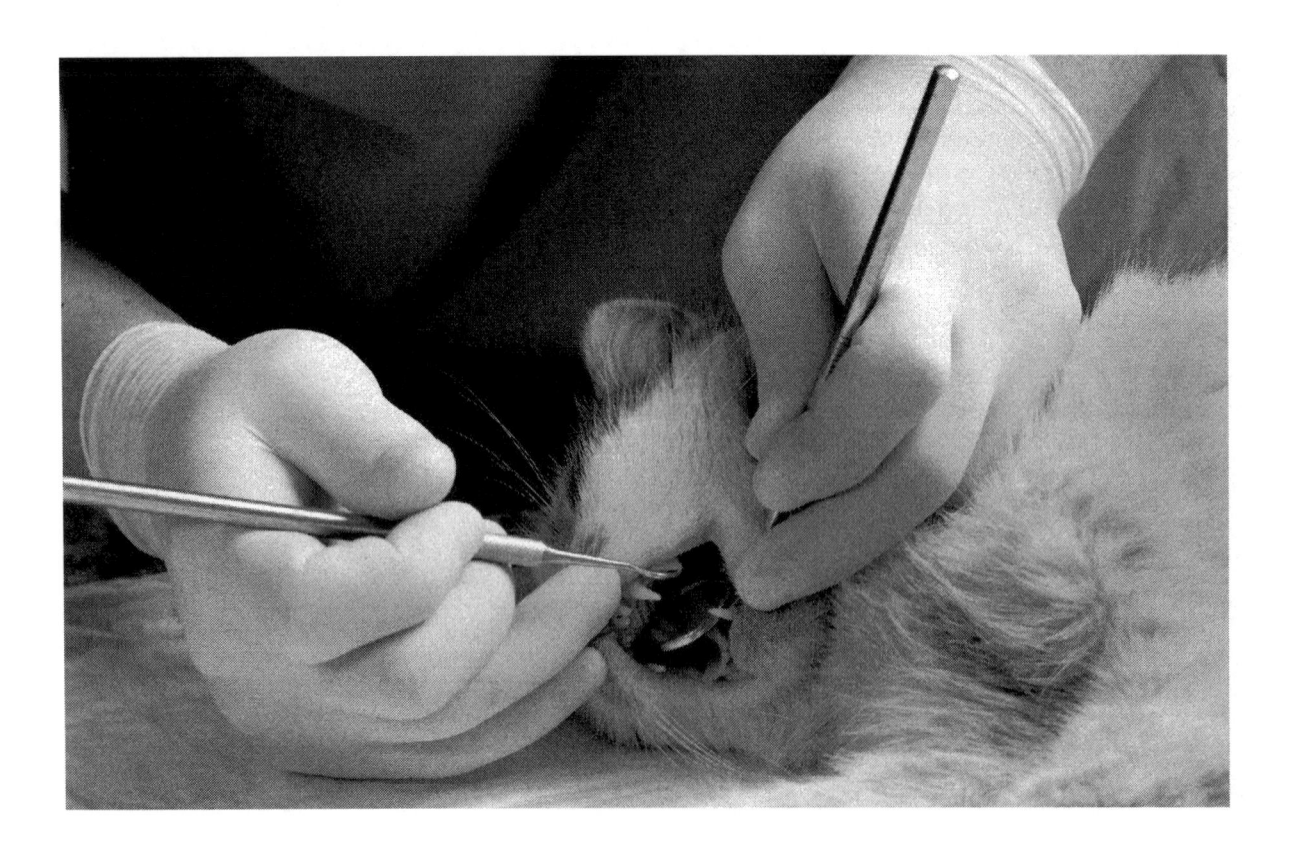

Stomatitis associated with *Bartonella* in otherwise healthy cats may be treated effectively with antibiotics. For cases of chronic gingival stomatitis in which antibiotics don't help, removal of all the teeth will be necessary. This condition probably results from calicivirus infection that prompts a malfunction of the immune system, which attacks the gums and teeth.

Sixty to 80 percent of cats do much better once all their teeth are removed. The pain is gone, and because cats don't tend to chew food much anyway, they typically do very well. A lot of times they don't even have to have a special diet. Whenever possible, veterinary dentists try to keep the canines (fang teeth) and carnassial teeth (big molars), which do most of the chewing. Without these teeth, the cat may have trouble keeping his tongue in his mouth.

For stomatitis, a variety of treatments may be offered after the cat's teeth have been thoroughly examined and cleaned. Treatment often includes combinations of antibiotics, a hydrolyzed protein allergy diet trial, antihistamines, lactoferrin, and interferon. Curcumin, zinc and lysine also may help. Some of these act as immune stimulants and/or simply help cats feel better. Prednisolone is said to work better than prednisone, but will require three months before seeing improvement.

Some holistic veterinarians recommend giving cats a naturally occurring enzyme called coenzyme Q10 to help gums heal. For cats, you can give up to 10 milligrams of coenzyme Q10 a day. It's available in health food stores.

Just like with owners, periodontal disease can be prevented by routine dental hygiene. How quickly plaque and tartar develop is influenced by a number of things, particularly food. The raw diets that cats in the wild eat tend to keep teeth clean; tearing through fur, skin and raw flesh naturally abrades the teeth. The processed foods that provide pet cats with complete and balanced nutrition often fall short on adequate dental abrasion, so extra help from the cat's owner is necessary.

Veterinary dentists recommend that cats have their teeth professionally cleaned as routine prevention just as often as people have their teeth professionally cleaned. Once or twice a year for cats younger than five years old is recommended, but more frequent cleanings are beneficial as the cat ages. Feed a "dental diet" and/or treats that include the VOHC (Veterinary Oral Health Council) seal of acceptance that shows these products have been proven to benefit dental health.

Commercial cat toothpastes in seafood, poultry and malt flavors are safe for animals to swallow. These pastes may include the enzymes glucose oxidase and lactoperoxidase, which have antimicrobial activity and aid in plaque control. Put the paste on the brush, let them lick the brush three or four times a day without making any effort to brush the teeth for several weeks, until the pet's coming to you to beg for treat time. Gradually progress to handling the cat's mouth until he's more comfortable. Finally, put a toy or a pencil in his mouth to prop it open, put your hand around his muzzle to hold him steady and keep the object in place, and then brush the teeth.

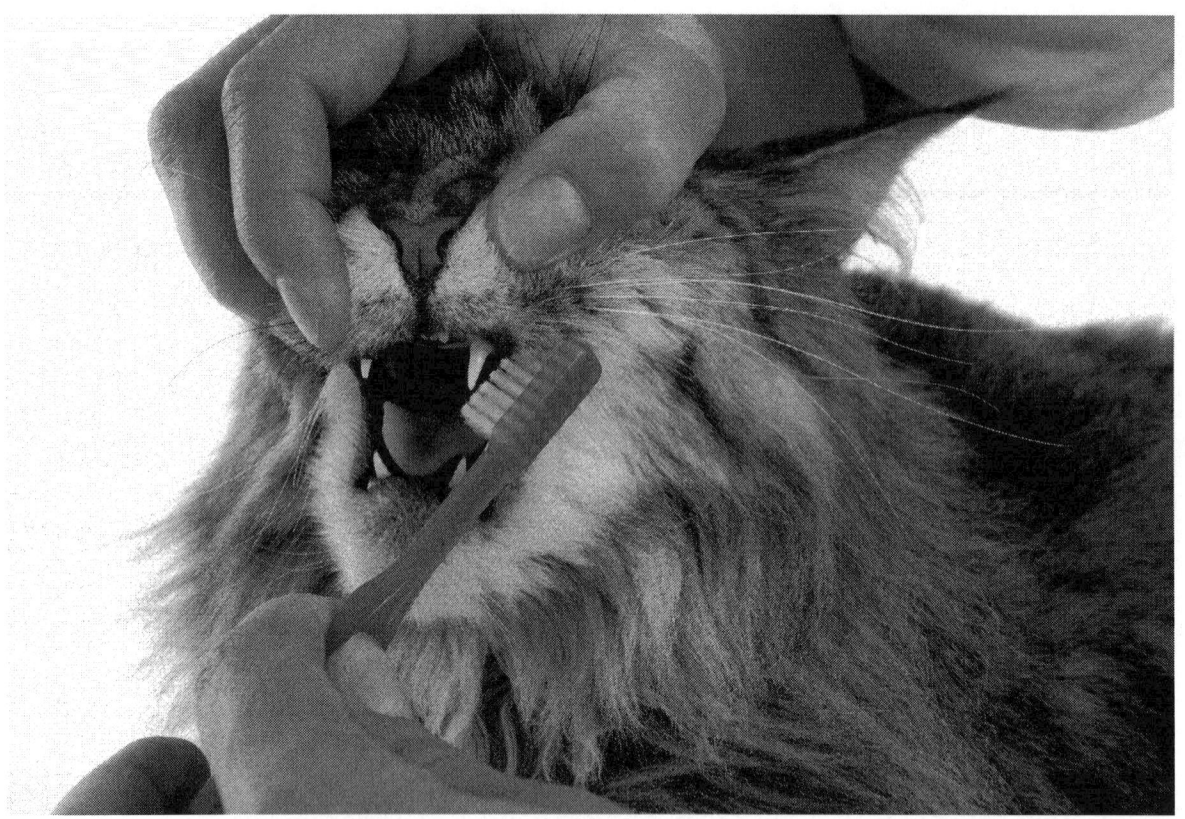

Ideally, you should brush your cat's teeth as frequently as your own—after each meal. Two to three times a week is often adequate, though, and once a week is better than nothing. Never use human products. Our toothbrushes generally are too large and stiff for the cat's tender mouth. Also, the levels of fluoride in human toothpaste are excessive for cats and may potentially result in kidney damage when the cat swallows the toothpaste. Cats aren't able to spit, and swallowing human toothpaste can upset their stomachs. Kittens often tolerate brushing well, but all cats and especially adults will probably need coaxing. Don't expect success the first time you attempt to clean Kitty's teeth. You'll need patience to get your cat to accept the procedure, but don't give up; the rewards may extend the cat's life.

PERITONITIS

SYMPTOMS: Extreme abdominal pain; hunching posture; stiff-legged walk or refusal to move; loss of appetite; depression; fever; distended abdomen
HOME CARE: None
VET CARE: Emergency surgery to repair damage; antimicrobial therapy to fight infection
PREVENTION: Keep swallowable objects away from the cat

PERITONITIS Peritonitis is an inflammation and sometimes infection of the abdominal cavity. It should not to be confused with feline infectious peritonitis caused by a virus.

Peritonitis results from contamination of the area usually from perforation of an abdominal organ like the stomach, intestines, or uterus. This can happen due to infections like pyometra, or from swallowed objects that puncture or cut.

The cat experiences abdominal pain, and assumes a hunched posture to protect the stomach area, a stiff-legged gait when walking, or may refuse to move at all. High fever is common, as is loss of appetite and depression. Sometimes the abdomen swells.

Prognosis for cats suffering peritonitis is not good, and the survival rate is poor. Treatment includes supportive care and massive antimicrobial therapy to fight infection and try to stabilize the cat. Surgery is necessary to repair the damage and flush out the infection.

CAT FACTS

PLAGUE Plague is a deadly bacterial disease historically associated with humans and wild rodents. Plague is considered a disease of antiquity, but despite advances in modern medicine that make cures possible, pockets of disease still exist. Today we know that plague not only affects traditional victims, but also causes disease in cats.

Epidemics so vast they were called pandemics began in the Mediterranean centuries ago. The pandemic of 541 AD killed 40 million people before it was through. Plague was named "the black death" when it returned during the 14th century when it killed 25 million people in Europe alone. China suffered an outbreak in 1855; about that same time Dr. Alexandre Yersin from the Institut Pasteur of France identified the bacterial organism that caused the disease, and named it *Yersinia pestis*.

Plague is a disease of rodents and fleas, and historically rats were the main reservoir for disease. Today in the United States, ground living rodents like prairie dogs and ground squirrels are the primary reservoirs. According to the Centers for Disease Control, most cases take place in Northern New Mexico, northern Arizona, and southern Colorado; California, southern Oregon, and far western Nevada. On average, seven human plague cases are reported each year in the United States. Cats are very susceptible to the disease, and an infected cat can spread the disease to humans.

Rodents that become infected may get sick with massive die offs of the population. Other times, the organism causes no problems and the rodents are simply carriers. As they feed on the infected animal, fleas swallow the organism in such massive quantities the bacteria literally blocks the flea's gut. The flea regurgitates and actually injects the organisms into new hosts with subsequent feedings.

Human infection usually results from bites of infected rodent fleas, which are different than the fleas that typically affect cats. Although plague fleas prefers the rat, squirrel or prairie dog, they'll make do with an available dog, cat or human.

Cats allowed outdoors in endemic regions, particularly those who hunt, are at highest risk (see HUNTING BEHAVIOR). Dogs rarely get sick the way cats do, but any roaming pet can become infested with infected rodent fleas and bring them home where they can potentially infect people. Cats commonly contract plague by eating infected animals. Prevalence appears to be cyclic in wild rodent populations, and spills over accordingly into cat and human populations. Plague can occur all year long, but the incidence seems to rise during the summer months of flea season.

Signs vary between bubonic, pneumonic, and systemic forms of the disease; each form involves a different part of the body. High fever and lethargy are the earliest signs in all three forms, but are often overlooked.

Cats typically suffer from bubonic plague, which incubates only two to six days. Lymph nodes that filter the organism from the blood are infected first, and become swollen by the second or third day after exposure. The painful swelling, typically in the groin area or armpits for people, is the "bubo" that gives this disease its name.

Cats usually develop a bubo beneath the chin on one side or the other. The feline bubo looks like a typical abscess, particularly when it ruptures and drains highly infectious material (see ABSCESS). Extreme caution is necessary when handling or treating cats with plague to prevent humans from catching the disease. Use gloves or wrap Kitty in a towel before transporting to the hospital. Alert the veterinarian of your suspicions so appropriate precautions may be taken.

PLAGUE

SYMPTOMS: High fever; lethargy; abscess-like swelling
HOME CARE: NONE—HIGHLY CONTAGIOUS TO PEOPLE
VET CARE: Tetracycline-type antibiotics
PREVENTION: Prevent cats from hunting

Septicemic plague is much less common in cats. It circulates throughout the blood and causes a more generalized illness. Pneumonic plague is the deadliest and most contagious form, and infects the lungs. Incubation takes only two to three days, and signs are similar to pneumonia. The pneumonic form is spread by inhaling infective droplets spread through coughing. Thankfully, this form of plague is rare in cats, for it is virtually always fatal.

Plague is most often diagnosed from clinical signs, but blood tests sent to specialized laboratories for analysis confirm the disease. Because plague is a human health risk (see ZOONOSIS), suspect cases are required to be reported to public health officials.

Plague can be cured when caught in time. Untreated or extremely late treatment of bubonic plague has a 50 percent mortality rate, untreated systemic plague has a 70 to 90 percent mortality rate, and pneumonic plague is 100 percent fatal when left untreated. The organism is susceptible to antibiotics such as streptomycin (preferred) or tetracycline, which may also be used as a preventative for cats and/or people who may have been exposed to plague.

Prevention involves avoiding exposure by confining cats indoors, using flea control, and evicting rodents that may be reservoirs of the disease. Avoid rodent extermination, or you'll end up with fleas with nothing to bite but you. Instead, clean out brush and wood piles, barns and sheds and make them inhospitable to flea-carrying varmints.

PLAY Play refers to behaviors in cats perceived by humans to be recreational in nature. Historically, many experts have theorized that play activities in kittens was instinctive behavior designed to hone adult hunting skills necessary for life in the wild. It follows that the domestic cat, as an adult, would continue play behaviors as a replacement for frustrated hunting activities.

However, some experts aren't convinced this is true, since many wild animals continue to play even as adults. In fact, even domestic cats that regularly hunt continue to indulge in play behavior. In any event, play is great fun for cats, whether kitten or adult.

Play behavior can be divided into three categories: locomotory, social and object play. Locomotory play involves running, jumping, rolling and climbing. Such activities may involve two or more cats, but kittens often engage in this type of play all by themselves. Social play is interactive, and may include wrestling and biting, pouncing, episodes of play-fighting, and even games of tag. Object play is just that; the kitten or cat plays with some interesting object such as a ball or feather.

Kittens begin social play as early as four weeks of age. The intensity escalates, peaks between nine and 14 weeks of age, and declines as the cat matures. Adult cats may enjoy playing with kittens, and introducing a youngster into the household may give a stick-in-the-mud adult cat a new lease on life. Social play isn't as common between adult cats, though, probably because unless they know each other very well, the play easily escalates into real fights (see AGGRESSION). However, in multi-cat homes, adult cats may wrestle, play-stalk each other, or engage in other forms of social play. Cats that know each other are able to communicate to each other their intention to play; they read the cues and understand it's a game.

Object play is often carried into adulthood. Cats enjoy pawing, stalking, biting and "capturing" objects, and seem to react as though they are dealing with something alive. Some cats, particularly kittens, engage in object play with objects that are invisible to the owner.

Play behavior can be an expression of emotion or of an individual cat's personality, and styles vary somewhat across breeds. Abyssinian and Rex breeds are athletic cats that tend to enjoy games of chase, Siamese like to fetch, Turkish Vans are fascinated by water, and Persians are sedate and tend to play more quietly.

380
CAT FACTS

 Commercial fishing pole style toys that prompt the cat to stalk, pounce and leap are one of the best interactive cat games available. However, toys don't need to be expensive to be successful. A peacock feather is popular with cats, and Kitty may also relish an empty paper bag in which to hide. A Ping Pong ball or crumpled piece of aluminum foil tossed into the bathtub provides lots of fun. Take care that the toys you choose for your cat are safe. Feathers and string toys or anything that can be swallowed should only be used when you can supervise to prevent Kitty from swallowing an inappropriate object (see SWALLOWED OBJECTS).

Playing together serves to reinforce social bonds between group members. And because an owner is perceived by the cat to be almost a surrogate mother-figure, playing with your cat brings you closer together. Play is often used as a particularly effective therapeutic tool in cats with health or behavior problems.

Interactive play encourages a tubby tabby to exercise and stimulates healthy weight loss (see OBESITY). Aggressive cats may benefit from play, which allows them to release their energy in a more productive way. And play can boost the confidence of a shy cat, distract the fearful cat, and help relieve stress (see FEAR).

PNEUMONIA

Pneumonia is an inflammation or infection of the lungs, and can be caused by viruses, bacteria, or parasites. Occasionally pneumonia develops as a result of aspiration, which means something that should have been swallowed was instead inhaled into the lungs. Aspiration of vomit may occur while the cat is under anesthesia, or suffers a seizure. Administering liquid medications incorrectly may also be a cause.

Most commonly, pneumonia affects very young kittens as a result of upper respiratory infection. Mortality rate can be as high as 50 percent in these instances. Old cats, those suffering poor nutrition, and cats with suppressed immune systems are also at higher risk for pneumonia.

Signs generally include a high fever with rapid or strained breathing. Cats that aren't able to get enough oxygen may have blue-colored gums. Coughing helps clear the lungs, but cats with pneumonia may have bubbly wheezing sounds when they breathe. Humidifying the air may help ease the breathing until veterinary attention is available. Diagnosis is based on examination of the lung secretions and chest X-rays.

Pneumonia requires prompt veterinary intervention, so get your cat to a hospital as soon as possible. Treatment usually consists of antibiotic therapy (see UPPER RESPIRATORY INFECTION).

PNEUMONIA

SYMPTOMS: High fever; rapid or strained breathing; wheezing; blue-tinged gums; coughing
HOME CARE: Get cat to vet ASAP; humidifier helps breathing
VET CARE: Antibiotics; supportive care
PREVENTION: Vaccinate for upper respiratory disease

POISON Poison as it applies to cats refers to any substance that through chemical reaction impairs, injures or kills the cat. Poisoning is a life-threatening emergency that should be addressed immediately by a veterinarian. The sooner the cat is treated, the better are his chances of survival.

If you suspect your cat has been poisoned, call your animal emergency center immediately and provide them with as much information as possible, then rush the cat to the hospital. When the veterinarian knows the kind of poison involved (check the label), how much was ingested, time elapsed from exposure, and the symptoms the cat is showing, better preparations can be made for your cat's swift treatment upon arrival. Take the package with you to help identify the poison, and if the cat has vomited, bring a sample.

Signs of poisoning vary depending on the chemical agent, the amount of exposure, and the individual cat. Treatment and/or antidote is often specific to the poison involved as well. The wrong treatment may cause more harm than good, which is why your veterinarian should address poisonings.

If the cat is unconscious or experiencing seizures (see EPILEPSY), first aid will not help; however, certain home treatments may in some instances improve the cat's chances for survival, particularly if veterinary help is unavailable. Treatment is aimed at getting rid of or neutralizing the poison, and may involve supportive care of the cat to combat shock and systemic signs.

Do not attempt to give medications by mouth unless the cat is fully conscious and remains in complete control of his body. Attempting to administer oral treatments to an unconscious cat risks aspiration of the medication into the lungs, and possible suffocation. Treatment for a specific poison attempts to do one or a combination of the following: decontamination, neutralization, dilution/absorption.

With contact poisons on the skin surface, treatment usually begins by flushing with plain water to decontaminate the cat. Wash or rinse the entire cat (for whole body poisoning) or the affected area for at least ten minutes. Cats exposed to natural gas, smoke, or carbon monoxide should be exposed to fresh air as soon as possible.

If the poison was swallowed within the past two hours, vomiting may help get rid of as much toxin as possible. However, vomiting is not appropriate for caustic poisons, which can do as much damage coming back up as they did going down. DO NOT USE SYRUP OF IPECAC to induce vomiting; it can be toxic for cats. Instead, one tablespoon of three percent household hydrogen peroxide that foams when squirted to the back of the tongue may induce vomiting within about five minutes. However, cats are notoriously difficult to make vomit, even for veterinarians; you may try a second dose if the first one fails, but stop there and get the cat to the veterinarian.

For caustic poisons like drain cleaner or bleach, DO NOT INDUCE VOMITING; not only will the poison burn on its way back up, but retching could cause the already damaged stomach to rupture. A half and half solution of lemon juice and water, or vinegar and water helps neutralize the effects of caustic alkaline poisons such as drain cleaner. Give the cat a total of about six tablespoons of the liquid (water/lemon juice or water/vinegar). Acids like bleach can be neutralized by giving the cat about two teaspoons of milk of magnesia.

Encouraging the cat to drink lots of water or milk helps dilute the poison. Milk also helps coat and soothe the injured stomach, and may also prevent certain poisons from being absorbed. Activated charcoal also helps absorb toxin. It's available as tablets or a powder that's mixed with water.

Here is specific advice on how to identify and handle some of the most common poison types. Please also refer to the poison treatment charts for further specifics.

Poisonous Flea Treatments: The most common poison affecting cats involves owner misapplication of insecticides, especially flea products. Toxicities often result from using dog flea products on cats, or misreading label applications and using too much of the substance. Some so-called "natural" products containing citrus oil ingredients like citronella can be poisonous to cats.

A wide variety of behavior changes can develop, from subtle to obvious. Cats poisoned with flea products may simply act lethargic, drool a lot with bouts of vomiting and diarrhea. Shivering, incoordination, or even staggering gait may be seen.

Usually the exposure is dermal, meaning the cat absorbs the toxin through the skin when the dip, spray or shampoo is applied. Signs may be delayed for several hours after exposure. However, as soon as you realize what has happened, decontaminate the cat by giving him another bath in plain lukewarm water, whether Kitty is showing symptoms or not. See a veterinarian to be sure follow up care is provided.

Home Medications: The second most common feline poisoning involves the misuse of medications, especially human pain relievers like Tylenol, aspirin, ibuprofen and neproxin (Aleve). The cat metabolizes these drugs more slowly than people, which means smaller doses remain in the cat's system for much longer periods. Giving a five pound cat a single five-grain aspirin tablet is like you taking 30 tablets. One extra strength Tylenol can kill a ten pound cat. Signs of aspirin toxicity include excitability or depression, vomiting, diarrhea, and incoordination. Tylenol acts primarily on the blood and can interfere with oxygen transportation so that cats turn blue (look at their gums) and have difficulty breathing.

Cats may also get into other medication and inadvertently overdose. The signs and treatments depend on the type of medication, and how much was taken. Induce vomiting or give activated charcoal, then get the cat to the veterinarian.

Houseplants: A number of plants contain toxins that are harmful to pets. These substances may be limited to certain parts of the plant, such as the leaves, bulb or seed, or may be throughout the plant. Contact with the plant delivers the toxin in some cases, but the most dangerous require chewing or swallowing. And while cats typically don't chew and eat plants nearly as often as dogs do, Kitty may shred the plant with his claws, and then become poisoned when he licks and cleans his claws.

The symptoms of poisoning can be as varied as the number of plants involved. Signs range from localized contact irritations and rashes, to systemic poisonings that result in drooling, vomiting and diarrhea, to hallucinations, convulsions and even death. In addition, individual cats appear to have varied tolerances for certain toxins; what causes severe mouth irritations in one cat may be eaten without problems by another. Therapy is aimed at counteracting or preventing the effects of the poison. Depending on the individual plant, the toxin may be addressed either by flushing the area of irritation, inducing vomiting, or dilution or neutralization of the poison.

Household Products: Cats may suffer toxicities from cleaning agents like bleach, drain cleaner, or phenol preparations like Lysol disinfectant or coal-tar products. Usually poisoning occurs when the product is splashed on the cat, or Kitty walks through a spill. Flush the area with lukewarm water to remove the toxin from the skin, and get the cat to a veterinarian. Other common household poisons cats may willingly eat or drink (see ANTIFREEZE and CHOCOLATE).

Pest Poisons: Cats that catch small game may be exposed if they eat a rodent that's ingested poison. Strychnine can result in seizures, arsenic can kill before signs develop (the cat's breath may smell like garlic), and anticoagulants such as warfarin results in bleeding from the rectum, nose, and the skin. Induce vomiting immediately if you see the cat swallow the poison, then get the cat to a veterinarian who administers specific antidotes for each.

If you are unable to reach a veterinarian, call the Animal Poison Control Center located online at the ASPCA.org website. They can walk you through emergency home remedies appropriate to your circumstance. Call (888) 426-4435. A $65 consultation fee may be applied to your credit card.

CAT FACTS

PLANT TOXIN	SIGN/SYMPTOMS	TREATMENT
APPLE SEEDS, APRICOT PITS, CHERRY PITS, HYDRANGEA, PEACH PITS	difficulty breathing, muscle tremors, convulsion, death	SEE YOUR VETERINARIAN IMMEDIATELY. Induce vomiting if ingested recently. These contain cyanide, which acts to suffocate the cat. A chemical antidote administered by the veterinarian is usually required to save the cat's life.
AZALEA	salivation, vomiting and diarrhea, muscle weakness, seizures, coma and death	administer lots of water to wash out the stomach, along with activated charcoal to absorb toxin, then see your veterinarian.
BELLADONNA, DATURA, HENBANE, JESSAMINE, JIMPSON WEED	dry mucous membranes, excessive thirst, rapid heartbeat, dilated pupils; can lead to coma or convulsions, and death	SEE A VETERINARIAN IMMEDIATELY. Supportive care along with chemical antidotes are required if the cat is to survive
BIRD OF PARADISE, BOX, CROWN OF THORNS, DAPHNE, ENGLISH IVY, HONEYSUCKLE, IRIS, SNOW-ON-THE-MOUNTAIN	intestinal irritation with nausea and vomiting. Cat exhibits stomach pain, suffers diarrhea immediately upon ingestion	induce vomiting, administer lots of water to dilute toxin, or several tablespoons milk to coat the stomach; giving activated charcoal helps absorb the poison. See a veterinarian as soon as possible.
BLACK LOCUST, CASTOR BEAN, ROSARY PEA	signs can be delayed up to 24 hours after ingestion, then abdominal pain, bloody diarrhea and vomiting. Cats may suffer fever, act depressed; signs can progress to coma, seizures and death.	HIGHLY POISONOUS: eating a single pea or bean can kill a cat. Induce vomiting, then get the cat to a veterinarian immediately.
CALADIUM, DIEFENBACHIA (DUMB CANE), JACK IN THE PULPIT, PHILODENDRON (HEART-LEAF & SPLIT-LEAF), SKUNK CABBAGE	irritation of the mouth, tongue and throat, increased salivation, with possible ulcers and swelling which may interfere with breathing	DO NOT INDUCE VOMITING. Offer water or milk to cleanse the cat's oral cavity. Rarely fatal; should see veterinarian if breathing becomes difficult or severe oral irritation develops.
CHINABERRY, MARIJUANA, MORNING GLORY, PERIWINKLE,	bizarre or odd behavior, trembling, convulsions	induce vomiting, and get to the veterinarian.

Plant	Symptoms	Treatment
CREEPING FIG, CHRYSANTHEMUM, WEEPING FIG	contact rash affecting skin surrounding and inside the mouth	wash area with cool water to sooth rash, see veterinarian
DAFFODIL, TULIP, WISTERIA (especially the bulbs)	gastric irritation, violent vomiting, possible depression -- death in severe cases	induce vomiting. Administer lots of water to dilute toxin, or several tablespoons milk to coat the stomach; giving activated charcoal helps absorb the poison. See a veterinarian as soon as possible.
ENGLISH HOLLY, EUROPEAN HOLLY	abdominal pain, vomiting and diarrhea when two or more berries are eaten; death reported rarely	SEE YOUR VETERINARIAN IMMEDIATELY. Supportive care is necessary to treat the digitalislike toxin
FOXGLOVE, LARKSPUR, LILY OF THE VALLEY, MONKSHOOD, OLEANDER	slowed heartbeat (this plant contains digitalis) followed by severe abdominal pain and vomiting. Finally, signs of agitation are exhibited, followed shortly by coma and death.	SEE YOUR VETERINARIAN IMMEDIATELY. Induce vomiting if ingested recently. This plant's toxicity can stop your cat's heart.
GOLDEN CHAIN, INDIAN TOBACCO, MESCAL BEAN, POISON HEMLOCK, TOBACCO	salivation, incoordination, muscle twitches, rapid heartbeat; breathing becomes labored and the cat can collapse in minutes to hours following ingestion	SEE YOUR VETERINARIAN IMMEDIATELY. This plant contains nicotine, and requires a chemical antidote to save the cat.
JERUSALEM CHERRY, POTATO (GREEN PARTS & EYES)	signs may not appear until 18-24 hours following ingestion; then the cat exhibits a painful abdomen, bloody diarrhea, vomiting, and dry mouth. Severe cases may proceed to tremors, paralysis, and cardiac arrest.	DO NOT INDUCE VOMITING as this may further damage the gastrointestinal tract. Immediate veterinary attention is imperative.
MOTHER-IN-LAW PLANT	vomiting, salivation, mouth irritation, diarrhea, occasionally staggering or collapse	DO NOT INDUCE VOMITING. Offer water or milk to cleanse the cat's oral cavity. Rarely fatal; should see veterinarian if cat loses coordination or collapses
POINSETTIA	irritates mucous membranes of mouth, may cause excessive salivation or vomiting but not death	Offer water or milk to cleanse the cat's oral cavity. Consult your veterinarian
RHUBARB (upper stem and leaves)	vomiting, excessive salivation, abdominal pain, staggers followed by convulsions	induce vomiting, then get your cat to the veterinarian. Without treatment, the toxin causes extensive damage to the cat's kidneys
YEW (American Yew, English Yew, Japanese Yew, etc.)	irregular heartbeat, dilation of the pupils, shivering, nausea, abdominal pain; but death often occurs without warning signs	SEE VETERINARIAN IMMEDIATELY. Induce vomiting if possible

CAT FACTS

OTHER TOXINS	SIGN/SYMPTOMS	TREATMENT
ACID POISONS (bleach)	when swallowed, drooling, pawing at mouth, painful abdomen; when spilled on skin, vocalizations, signs of distress, rolling, licking area	DO NOT INDUCE VOMITING! flush the area of contact with plain water for at least ten minutes; if substance was swallowed, administer two teaspoons of milk of magnesia; see a veterinarian ASAP
ALKALINE POISONS (drain cleaner)	when swallowed, drooling, pawing at mouth, painful abdomen; when spilled, vocalizations, signs of distress, rolling, licking area	DO NOT INDUCE VOMITING! flush the area of contact with plain water for at least ten minutes; if substance was swallowed, administer six tablespoons of half water and half lemon juice or vinegar to neutralize, then get cat to veterinarian ASAP
ANTIFREEZE (ETHYLENE GLYCOL)	drunken behavior, excessive thirst, increased urination, diarrhea, vomiting, convulsions, loss of appetite, panting	EMERGENCY! seek veterinary help ASAP. If ingested in last two hours, induce vomiting and/or administer activated charcoal; veterinary treatment administers 100 proof alcohol
CHOCOLATE	drooling, vomiting and/or diarrhea, excessive urination, hyperactivity, muscle tremors, seizures, coma	EMERGENCY! seek veterinary help ASAP. if ingested in last two hours, induce vomiting
COAL-TAR POISONING (phenol disinfectants like Lysol, treated wood, tar paper, heavy oil)	depression, weakness, incoordination, coma, death	get cat to veterinarian ASAP. Lysol is absorbed through skin; wash cat immediately if exposed.
FLEA PRODUCTS (ORGANOPHOSPHATES, CARBAMATES & CHLORINATED HYDROCARBONS)	signs may be delayed due to skin absorption of toxin; a variety of signs possible, including: apprehension, muscle twitches, shivering, seizures, drooling, diarrhea, hyperactivity or depression	wash cat as soon as you realize poisoning has occurred, even if several hours have passed and no signs are yet seen; then get to veterinarian ASAP
LEAD POISONING (insecticides, paint, linoleum, roofing shingles, plumbing materials, solder, batteries, golf balls)	abdominal pain, vomiting, seizures, uncoordinated gait, excitation, continuous barking, hysteria, weakness, blindness, chewing fits	when ingestion is within past 2 hours, induce vomiting; see veterinarian for specific treatment ASAP
MEDICATIONS, ASPIRIN, IBUPROFEN, TYLENOL, NSAIDS	blood in vomit that looks like coffee grounds	stop the medication, see your vet; if ingested more than 1 tablet in past 2 hours, induce vomiting, see vet ASAP

MEDICATIONS	various signs dependent upon toxic agent	induce vomiting if ingested within last two hours; seek veterinary help ASAP
PETROLEUM PRODUCTS (gasoline, kerosene, turpentine)	vomiting, difficulty breathing, tremors, seizures, coma, respiratory failure and death	EMERGENCY! DO NOT INDUCE VOMITING; SEE VETERINARIAN IMMEDIATELY; if help is more than thirty minutes away, give the cat 1 to 2 ounces mineral oil, olive oil or vegetable oil by mouth; follow it in 30 minutes with Glauber's salt (sodium sulfate) to stimulate defecation; be prepared to perform artificial respiration
PEST BAITS, ANTICOAGULANT TYPES (warfarin, pindone, Dcon, Mouse Prufe II, Harvoc, Talan)	bleeding in stool and/or urine, from nose, ears, and beneath the skin and gums—symptoms first appear several days after ingestion	EMERGENCY! induce vomiting if ingested within past two hours, then see veterinarian ASAP; blood transfusions and treatment with intravenous vitamin K is a specific antidote
PEST BAITS, ARSENIC (slug/snail bait, ant poisons, weed killers, insecticides)	thirst, vomiting, staggers, drooling, abdominal pain and cramps, diarrhea, paralysis, strong garlic breath	EMERGENCY! induce vomiting if poisoning occurred within last two hours, then see veterinarian ASAP; a specific antidote is available
PEST BAITS, BROMETHALIN (Assault & Vengeance rodenticides)	muscle tremors, staggering gait, high fever, stupor, agitation, seizures	EMERGENCY! induce vomiting if ingested within past two hours, then see veterinarian ASAP
PEST BAITS, CHOLECALCIFEROL (Rampage, vitamin D3)	vomiting, diarrhea, seizures, heart/kidney failure	EMERGENCY! induce vomiting if ingested within past two hours, then see veterinarian ASAP
PEST BAITS, METALDEHYDE (rat, snail & slug bait)	drooling, incoordination, excitability, muscle tremors, progressive weakness	EMERGENCY! induce vomiting if ingested within past two hours, then see veterinary ASAP
PEST BAITS, PHOSPHORUS (rat & roach poisons, matches & matchboxes)	vomiting, diarrhea, garlic breath, sometimes symptom-free period, then return of signs with painful abdomen, seizures and coma	EMERGENCY! induce vomiting if ingested within past two hours, then see veterinarian ASAP
PEST BAITS, SODIUM FLUOROACETATE (rat poison)	vomiting, agitation, straining to defecate/urinate, seizures (not triggered by external stimuli), staggering gait, collapse	EMERGENCY! induce vomiting if ingested within past two hours, then get to a veterinary ASAP; a specific antidote is available
PEST BAITS, STRYCHNINE (rat,	agitation, apprehension, excitement, seizures prompted by noises like clapping hands,	EMERGENCY! Seek veterinary help ASAP; cover cat with towel to

mouse, mole, coyote poison)	drooling, muscle spasms, chewing, collapse	prevent stimulation of further seizures; if poisoned within two hours and cat remains alert, induce vomiting
PEST BAITS, ZINC PHOSPHIDE (rat poison)	depression, difficulty breathing, weakness, seizures, vomiting (with blood), seizures, coma	EMERGENCY! induce vomiting if ingested within past two hours, then see veterinarian ASAP
SNAKE BITE (copper head, cotton mouth, rattle snake, coral snake)	restlessness, drooling, panting, weakness, diarrhea, collapse, sometimes seizures, paralysis or coma	EMERGENCY! SEEK VETERINARY HELP ASAP. If help is more than 30 minutes away, apply tight bandages between bite and cat's heart and loosen for 5 minutes once an hour; keep cat quiet until help is available. <u>Don't wash bite, don't cut bite to suction out poison, and don't apply ice to bite</u>--all could increase venom absorption and/or damage tissue further
TOAD POISONING	slobbering or drooling, pawing at mouth, seizures, coma, collapse	EMERGENCY! flush cat's mouth with plain water for at least 10 minutes, induce vomiting; be prepared to perform artificial respiration; SEE VET ASAP
XYLITOL POIZONING	vomiting, incoordination/drunk behavior, lethargy, seizures, collapse	EMERGENCY! signs appear within 15 minutes so induce vomiting immediately, seek veterinary help ASAP

POLYDACTYL see CLAWS.

PORCUPINE QUILLS

Outdoor cats may inadvertently encounter a porcupine with devastating results. The needle-like quills are up to four inches long and barbed to penetrate flesh and continue moving inward. Dogs seem more prone to injury than the more cautious cat. When an animal is stuck with quills, they typically will lodge in the face or open mouth.

Porcupine quills are exceptionally painful and cause even the most tractable cat to lose control, roll with pain, and strike out at anything within reach, even you. Accessible quills may be plucked out using needle-nose pliers; grasp the quill near the skin, and pull straight out.

However, the barbed ends can break off. Once beneath the skin, they travel inward and may result in deep infections. Also, a cat's fur may hide small quills that you may miss.

PORCUPINE QUILLS

SYMPTOMS: Needlelike barbs protruding from body; crying with pain; rolling; pawing at injured area
FIRST AID: Remove quill; disinfect wound
HOLISTIC HELP: Herbal treatment; homeopathy; flower essences
VET CARE: Anesthetize; remove quills; swab each wound with disinfectant; possibly oral antibiotics
PREVENTION: Supervise outdoor excursions

Because a cat in pain is rarely able to hold still even for a beloved owner's ministrations, a veterinarian is usually better equipped to do the plucking. Once anesthetized, a search and seizure of quills hidden by fur—and particularly inside his mouth—is more easily accomplished. The wounds are then treated with a disinfectant. You can also give the cat the flower essence Rescue Remedy to help ease the fear and stress associated with porcupine quill injuries.

Holistic veterinarians may recommend an antiseptic wash of calendula and St. John's wort. Put two drops of each tincture in one-half cup of water and use the solution to gently bathe the wounds. Be sure the tinctures are alcohol-free because alcohol may be dangerous for your cat, especially when he tries to wash himself.

Homeopathic Hypericum addresses pain. Give three pellets of Hypericum 30C, and repeat the dose up to three times as needed.

392 CAT FACTS

The only way to prevent your cat from a prickly encounter is to your cat inside and/or supervise outside adventures.

PREDATORY BEHAVIOR see HUNTING and PLAY.

PREGNANCY see REPRODUCTION.

PULSE
The pulse is the rhythmic speed at which the cat's heart pumps blood. Each cat's pulse rate is different, but the normal range for an adult cat is 160 to 240 pulses each minute. Young kittens' pulse rate is 200 to 300 beats per minute.

Pulse should be strong and regular. A fast pulse may indicate anything from excitement, to blood loss, infection or heart disease; a slow pulse may also indicate illness.

Your cat's pulse is determined by counting the number of beats in a minute. With Kitty standing, place the flat of your fingers on his side above the ribs directly behind his left front elbow. The pulse can also be felt by pressing your fingers firmly against the inside of Kitty's thigh where the leg attaches to the body.

PULSED ELECTROMAGNETIC FIELD (PEMF)

Pulsed electromagnetic field therapy influences the body's natural bioelectromagnetic fields. Every organ in the body produces its own signature bioelectromagnetic field. Disruption of electromagnetic energy in the cells causes impaired cell function, and PEMFs seek to address this impaired chemistry to improve cell function and positively impact health.

Holistic veterinarians may advocate the use of magnets, for instance, thought to positively influence these fields to effect health benefits. As a general rule, magnets produce stationary or "static" nonvarying magnetic fields that have a fixed strength and only penetrate the tissue a shallow distance. Magnets may be fastened against one or more acupuncture points to stimulate the point in a gentle but prolonged way. More commonly, magnets are found in mats for the pet to sleep on, or wraps and patches to place on specific parts of the body.

Low frequency PEMFs work more effectively because they penetrate every cell, tissue, organ and even bone, and stimulate the electrical and chemical processes in the tissues. Therapeutic PEMFs are specifically designed to positively support cellular energy, and vary in frequency, waveform, strength, and types of stimulators. These resonating magnetic fields can create currents without heating to alter cell signaling, and studies now show that the proper frequency and intensity can relieve pain, stimulate bone and wound healing, and provide other health benefits.

Devices that produce these benefits may be designed for whole body treatment or targeted areas of the body. Some of these devices have successfully completed efficacy studies and are FDA-approved.

Today, mainstream veterinary medicine also uses PEMF technology to help pets heal, and relieve inflammatory responses responsible for pain, among other things. Therapeutic products may be available in mats, wraps or other devices from your veterinarian or over the counter.

For example, the Assisi Loop® is an FDA-cleared Non-Pharmaceutical Anti-Inflammatory Device (NPAID®) that has undergone clinical evaluation with results published in peer-reviewed journals. It's used as both a first-line and adjunct therapy for managing persistent pain and inflammatory conditions that impact feline health. The Assisi Loop® is a light weight battery powered non-invasive therapy that employ targeted EMFs to reduce inflammation, promote healing of wounds and surgical sites, reduce arthritis discomfort, and ameliorate pain as well as aid in stroke recovery. It comes in two sizes (10 cm and 20 cm diameter coil), and has an auto-shut off as well as a cycling therapy version. It is available from your veterinarian, or from the company (with a prescription from your vet) and is easy to use at home. Ask your vet if PEMF therapy may benefit your pet.

PURRING

Purring refers to the rumbling sound produced by cats and kittens. The true purpose of purring isn't known, but is thought to be a form of communication and is found in wild cat species as well as in pet cats. The queen's purr may signal her presence to newborn kittens, and when the babies begin purring as early as two days old, it may tell the mother her babies are warm, safe, and fed.

Experts believe purring in adult cats may be a carryover of kittenish behavior, and point to the kneading behavior that often accompanies it. Cats purr only when in the presence of another cat or person, and some behaviorists believe the purr may communicate submission. We tend to think of purring as a sign of contentment; however, cats often use deeper, louder purrs when they are in pain or upset, and may even purr as they die, perhaps in an effort to comfort themselves. Think of your cat's purr as a smile—which could mean he's happy, uncertain, or anything in between.

Studies of vibrational frequencies of purring have been compared to the known healing effects of vibration therapy for humans. Frequencies between 20 and 140 hertz encourage quicker bone, wound and tendon healing as well as relief of pain and breathing difficulties. Cats purr at a frequency of 50 and 150 hertz, ideal for bone growth and healing. This may be part of the explanation why cats purr, despite pain or illness.

Exactly how cats produce the purr has fascinated humans for eons. Some experts theorize that structures in the cat's throat, called vestibular folds or false vocal chords, make the sound by rubbing together when air passes through as the cat inhales and exhales. Another theory purports that purring is caused by a rapid contraction and relaxation of the muscles surrounding the voice box and diaphragm, which in turn produces a turbulent air flow through the trachea. Yet a third explanation points to a turbulent flow of blood through a large vein in the cat's chest, again caused by diaphragmatic muscle contractions; the resulting vibrations are transmitted through the windpipe to the sinus cavities, which amplify the sound. This last theory seems supported by cats that have lost their "voices" due to injury, and can no longer vocalize meows but are still able to purr. Some recent reports suggest that the brain controls purrs and that a repetitive neural oscillator sends messages to the laryngeal muscles, causing them to twitch at a rate of 25 to 150 vibrations per second. This causes the vocal cords to separate when the cat inhales and exhales, producing a purr (see COMMUNICATION).

PYOMETRA
Pyometra is an infection of the uterus. This is a life-threatening condition that must be addressed by a veterinarian as an emergency.

High levels of the hormones estrogen or progesterone over a long period of time can result in pyometra. Intact queens over five years old that infrequently or never produce kittens are at the highest risk. Therefore, queens that are not in a professional breeding program should be spayed.

Signs most commonly develop about a month after the cat goes out of heat. Symptoms include loss of appetite, lethargy, increased thirst and urination, and a swollen abdomen. There may be a cream to pink or brown colored discharge from the vagina. Diagnosis is based on the above signs, and confirmed with an X-ray or ultrasound. The treatment of choice is spaying the cat to remove the infected reproductive organs and prevent the condition from recurring.

PYOMETRA

SYMPTOMS: Loss of appetite; lethargy; increased thirst and urination; swollen abdomen; sometimes a cream to pink/brown discharge from vagina
HOME CARE: None
VET CARE: Spay surgery; antibiotic therapy
PREVENTION: Spay cats that aren't to be regularly bred

396
CAT FACTS

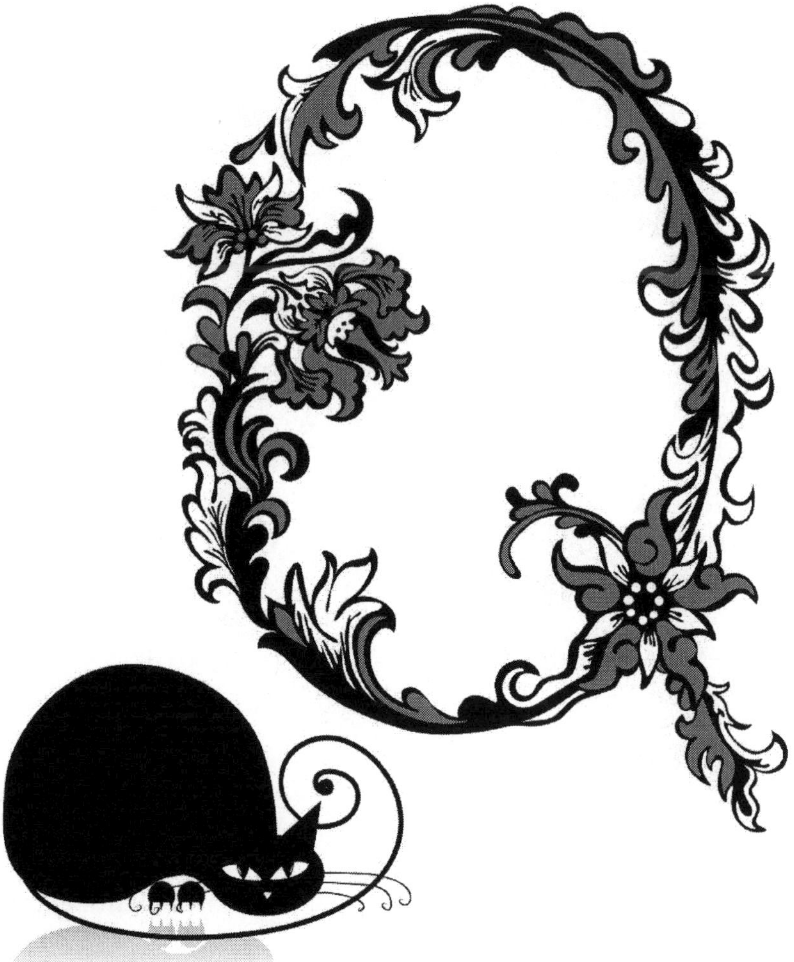
Q

CAT FACTS

QUARANTINE Quarantine refers to the isolation of cats that are ill or suspected to be ill, in order to prevent the potential spread of disease or pests to healthy pets or people. New cats should be evaluated and treated appropriately by a veterinarian prior to or very shortly after adoption. But even with a clean bill of health, quarantine is a prudent choice whenever a new cat or kitten is to be introduced into a home that already has pets.

It's obvious that a new cat or kitten showing signs of disease should be isolated from healthy animals. However, a cat can appear healthy and expose resident pets to disease before showing signs of illness himself. The amount of time between the cat being exposed to disease and then developing symptoms of illness is referred to as the incubation period. The length of time varies depending on the causative agent, with the incubation period for some viral diseases like rabies being months or even years (see RABIES). It is for this reason that rabies-free countries like the United Kingdom and states like Hawaii impose a quarantine on pets imported into these areas.

Usually, though, a cat incubating a highly contagious disease becomes sick within two to three weeks of exposure. Quarantine the new cat for a minimum of two weeks (a month is better) to reduce risk of exposure for your other pets. If the new cat does not become ill during the quarantine period, he can then be integrated into the household.

Prepare a special area, like a bedroom or enclosed porch, and furnish it with all the kitty necessities. The new cat and your resident pets should have no direct contact, not even sniffing noses through the screen. Use a disinfectant to keep the quarantine area and new cat accoutrements clean. Don't forget to disinfect yourself after interacting with the new cat to prevent you carrying something nasty out of the room on your shoes or hands, and infecting your other pets. One of the best and most economical disinfectants is Clorox at a dilution of one cup bleach mixed into two gallons of water.

QUEEN The term queen suggests royalty, and so is highly appropriate when used to speak of cats. The title is bestowed upon females of breeding age. It more specifically may refer to those female cats that produce kittens.

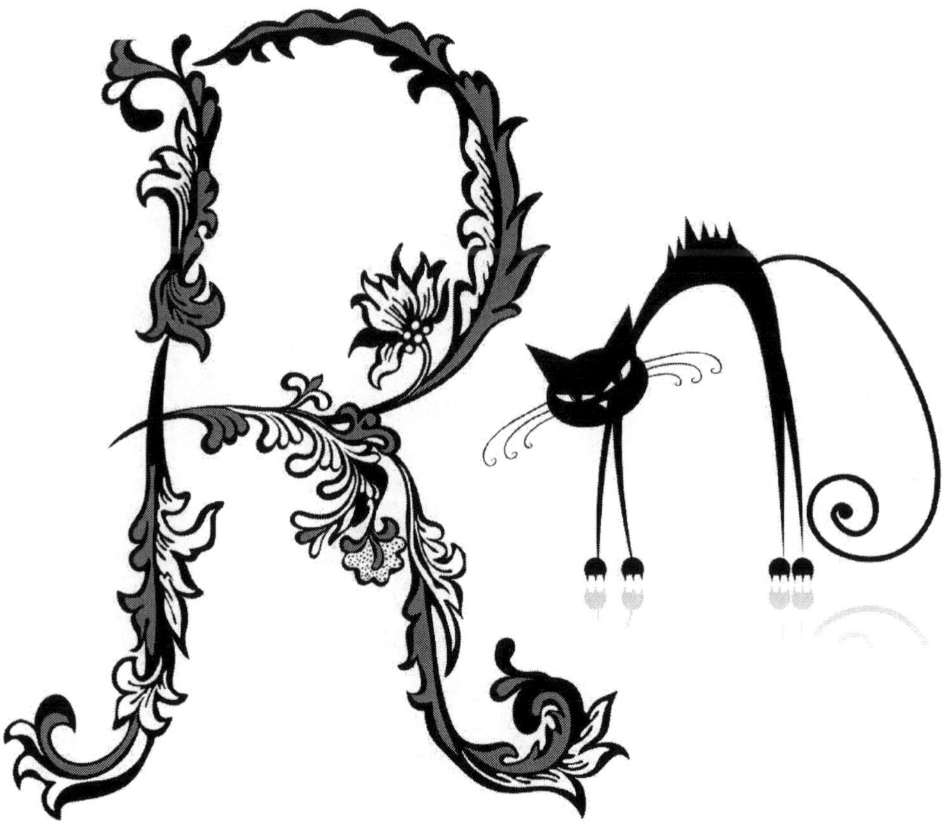
R

RABIES The rabies virus belongs to the family Rhabdoviridae and causes a viral disease that attacks the brain. Once the typical neurological signs appear, the disease is always fatal and victims suffer an agonizing death.

The disease has been recognized for centuries. Ancient Greeks dubbed it hydrophobia meaning "fear of water" because the throat paralysis often suffered by victims appeared to be an aversion to drinking. Rabies affects all mammals, including dogs, cats, and people.

Rabies has been found nearly everywhere in the world. After the first vaccine was developed by Louis Pasteur in 1884, rabies became preventable. Today a few places like Hawaii and Great Britain have eliminated the disease through enforcement of strict quarantine requirements.

RABIES

SYMPTOMS: Refusal to eat or drink; hiding; depression; drooling; throat paralysis and inability to swallow--or vicious; violent behavior; excessive vocalizing; spooky eyes; wobbly rear legs
HOME CARE: NONE—CONTAGIOUS TO PEOPLE
VET CARE: NONE—CONTAGIOUS TO PEOPLE; euthanasia; then testing of brain tissue to confirm disease
PREVENTION: Vaccinate cat, prevent contact with wild animals

However, rabies continues to be a presence in wild animal populations. Different strains of the virus affect specific kinds of animals, and there is a regional incidence associated with rabies. Animals most often associated with the disease include raccoons in the north eastern United States (New York, Connecticut, New Jersey, Maryland and spreading), coyotes in

Texas and the Southwest, foxes in Alaska and skunks in Kansas. Bats are also often associated with rabies. The disease can appear anywhere in any species.

There is a spillover from wild animal disease into domestic populations that parallels the incidence of rabies in feral reservoirs. Pets allowed to roam outdoors are at the highest risk for contracting rabies, because they are more likely to encounter a rabid animal and become exposed.

The incidence of rabies continues to be much higher in pet cats than in pet dogs, probably because fewer owned cats in the United States are vaccinated against rabies compared to owned dogs. According to the Centers for Disease Control, domestic species accounted for 8 percent of all rabid animals reported in the United States in 2013. Cats have remained the most frequently reported rabid domestic animal at 53 percent, followed by dogs at 19 percent. Close association with at-risk pets places owners at risk as well.

Rabies is spread by direct contact with an infected animal, usually through a bite that introduces virus-laden saliva into the wound. Following the bite, the virus multiplies in the tissue, then travels through the nerves to the spinal cord and on to the brain. The time it takes from the bite to symptoms varies from days to years. Signs appear once the virus reaches the brain, and in most cases, this incubation period happens within three to eight weeks of the bite. From the brain, the virus spreads to other tissues, like the salivary glands.

All infected animals exhibit behavior changes. Typically, the infected cat stops eating and drinking, and hides. The disease then progresses to one of two forms; paralytic or dumb rabies, and furious rabies.

In the dumb form cats act extremely depressed and sick, followed by paralysis of the throat and jaw muscles. Such cats drool excessively and can't swallow, and may appear to have something stuck in their throat. They are insensitive to pain. Cats with dumb rabies typically become comatose and die within three to ten days of initial signs.

Cats more commonly exhibit the furious form, and become extremely vicious and violent. They may roam for miles attacking real and imaginary objects in their path. These cats fear nothing, not even natural enemies, and often chew or swallow foreign objects. Such cats tend to exhibit a blank, spooky or anxious look. They vocalize a great deal, and owners of stricken cats have also described a wobbly or collapsing gait that affects the rear legs. Progressive paralysis results in death within four to seven days after onset of these signs.

There is no cure for rabies. Once signs appear, the animal or person will die. Therefore, all pets should be protected with a rabies vaccination. Even indoor cats are at risk because a rabid animal could enter the house through a pet door, chimney or open window, and cats can be exposed when they escape outside. Because of the human health risk (see ZOONOSIS), in some states rabies vaccination of cats and dogs is required by law.

CAT FACTS

Rabies diagnosis requires microscopic examination of the brain tissue of the suspect animal which cannot be done while the animal is alive. Wild animals that attack humans or pets should be euthanized immediately, and the brain examined for evidence of rabies. If your cat is bitten by a wild animal that cannot be tested for the disease, the cat should be considered exposed to rabies.

The rules regarding rabies exposure in pets vary from state to state. It's believed that animals are infectious only shortly before and during the time they show symptoms. If a biting animal was infective at the time of the bite, it usually exhibits signs of rabies within a ten day period, which is the recommended period of quarantine in such cases.

But handling potentially infected animals poses such a high human risk, it's usually recommended that unvaccinated dogs and cats exposed to rabies be euthanized and their brains examined for the disease. Depending on individual county and state laws, exposed pets may be allowed to live under stringent quarantine for six months and, if no signs develop, vaccinated prior to release. Recommendations for pets current on rabies vaccination that are exposed to the disease include immediate revaccination, and strict owner control/observation for no less than 45 days.

Avoid exposure for your cats and yourself by keeping cats indoors and providing proper protective vaccinations. Contact with wild animals exhibiting abnormal behavior, including stray or feral cats, puts you and your pet at risk.

Several states are conducting vaccination programs designed to immunize populations of wild animals to create "immune barriers" to slow or prevent the spread of the disease. Typically, vaccine-laced baits that the animal eats are seeded in rabies-prone areas.

The rabies virus can be killed by simple household detergents and soaps. Thoroughly wash bite wounds with soap and hot water as a first aid, then consult a doctor immediately. There is a post-exposure vaccine available for humans that is virtually 100 percent effective when administered in the right period of time.

READING FOOD LABELS

Pet foods are subject to national, state, and local regulations, including compliance with the Food and Drug Administration (FDA), the Federal Trade Commission (FTC), the United States Department of Agriculture (USDA) and State Feed Control Laws developed by the Association of American Feed Control Officials (AAFCO). These regulations cover everything from what goes into the food, to how it's distributed, sold, and even labeled. Reading and understanding food labels allows cat owners to choose the best product for their cat's needs.

All pet foods must disclose on their labels a guaranteed analysis, list of ingredients, and a statement and validation of adequacy. Research continues to refine the definition of exactly what the cat's nutritional needs are. After eight years of deliberation, the revised AAFCO Dog and Cat Food Nutrient Profiles were accepted by the full membership and the most recent incarnation will be published in the 2016 Official Publication. Reputable cat food manufacturers follow the AAFCO nutrient profiles or nutritional standards based on extensive nutrition research to formulate their foods.

The principle display panel of the label identifies the product by specifying the brand and product name. It may also include a "nutritional claim," and the total amount of food in the package must be stated. Finally, the words "cat food" or a similar designation must appear prominently on the label.

Even food names are regulated. Flavors are allowed in the name only if there's enough for the cat to actually recognize that flavor. Meat, poultry or fish must make up at least 25 percent of a product for that ingredient to become part of the product name, but a modifier, like beef "cakes" or liver "dinner" must also be used. A food called Kitty-Tom's Fish Dinner indicates that fish makes up at least 25 percent of the product. The same name without the modifier means the food must contain at least 95 percent of that ingredient. Kitty-Tom's Chicken Cat Food indicates that chicken comprises at least 95 percent of the product. "All" or "100 percent" means the product contains only the named ingredient with only water, preservatives, flavorings, vitamins and minerals added.

The information panel includes the guaranteed analysis statement, which lists the minimum levels of crude protein and crude fat, and maximum levels of crude fiber and moisture in the product. "Crude" refers to the amount measured by specific laboratory analysis, not the amount that can be used by the cat.

If the nutritional claim is not on the Display Panel, it's on the Informational Panel. Cat food manufacturers may label their products "complete and balanced" only if they meet the AAFCO standards, which must be validated by testing the food in one of two ways:

1. By laboratory chemical analysis or calculation of nutritional values. Products tested in this manner say, "(name of product) is formulated to meet the nutritional levels established by the AAFCO Cat Food Nutrient Profiles for (whatever life stage)."

However, with this validation, the food is not fed to cats to prove it's actually beneficial. Calculation does not determine digestibility or palatability, and is a less expensive way for the manufacturer to meet the requirements.

2. Feeding trials are done to show the food actually benefits the cat. The labels of products tested in this way will say, "Animal feeding tests using AAFCO procedures substantiate that (name of product) provides complete and balanced nutrition for (whatever life stage)."

CAT FACTS

Feeding trials are time consuming and quite expensive, but are the only way to truly determine the nutritional completeness of a given food. *The best foods are complete and balanced diets validated through feeding trials which determine palatability and whether the nutrients are actually usable by the cat's body.*

If the food does not say it is complete and balanced, choose another product. The so-called "gourmet" canned foods often are not complete and balanced and contain single-protein-source ingredients; they are intended to be used as supplements to a complete and balanced food, and shouldn't be fed exclusively.

Reputable pet-food manufacturers conduct long term feeding trials to assure nutritional adequacy. These tests may cover growth, adult maintenance, or reproduction. An "all life stages" claim is supported by testing through reproduction and growth.

Reproduction tests show the diet is able to maintain the queen through gestation and lactation, and the kittens until about six weeks of age. Growth tests begin with kittens at weaning and run for about ten weeks to see if a diet will support normal growth. And adult maintenance tests last at least six months with cats that are at least one year old.

Pet-food manufacturers also conduct short term tests to measure palatability and digestibility of diets. Palatability determines how good the food tastes to the cat by offering Kitty choices of food. Digestibility is the difference between what is eaten, and what comes out in the feces, and both input and output are measured to determine how the cat or kitten's body is able to use the food.

Labels may also provide a statement of caloric content of the food. Calorie refers to the measure of energy that can be acquired from eating a given food. Labeling calorie content isn't required (except in "lite" diets) but when it appears it must be stated as kilocalories per Kg of food. Usually it's also stated as "calories per cup of food" or "per can unit."

Dry rations generally contain 1400 to 2000 metabolized kilocalories per pound of diet (3080 to 4400 Kcal/Kg); semi-moist have 1200 to 1350 metabolized kilocalories per pound of diet (2640 to 2970 Kcal/Kg); and canned rations only provide 375 to 950 metabolized kilocalories per pound of diet (825 to 2090 Kcal/Kg). That's why cats must eat more canned foods than dry diets to obtain the same energy requirements.

The average adult cat needs about 35 kilocalories per pound of body weight each day. Kittens, pregnant or nursing queens, and cats under stress have much higher requirements; inactive cats need less. Feeding guidelines are on the label only as a starting point for the amount to feed your cat.

The food label must also include a list of all ingredients used in the food. The ingredients must be listed in decreasing order of the amount present by weight. Therefore, ingredients listed first are used in the greatest amounts, while smallest amounts are listed last. However, manufacturers aren't allowed to reference the quality of these ingredients.

In general, the ingredient list should have:

1. *One or more protein sources* listed as one of the first several ingredients;

2. *Carbohydrate source*, such as cereals;

3. *Fat source*; and

4. *Large numbers of trace minerals and vitamin supplements,* which will be toward the bottom of the list.

Water content varies depending on the form of food: dry foods contain 6 to 10 percent moisture, soft-moist foods contain 23 to 40 percent moisture, and canned foods contain 68 to 78 percent moisture.

Pet owners understandably are concerned about what goes into pet food, and AAFCO attempts to clear any misunderstanding with labeling definitions that manufacturers must meet. Definitions of terms can be very complicated, and may not mean exactly what everyone assumes. Some pet food terms have become associated with "good" compared to "bad" ingredients, so it's important to understand what exactly is meant by these terms.

Byproducts is one such label, and according to AAFCO definitions, a byproduct is what is left over after the intended product has been made. Those left-overs potentially are a great source of additional nutrients, depending on what they are. Here's an example: harvesting a common weed's flowers to make dandelion wine or an herbal remedy means the dandelion greens are byproducts. But harvesting that same plant for the greens only makes the bloom a byproduct. In fact, many "byproducts" do not include that term in the ingredient name at all.

Organic claims abound today, but these labels do not mean the food is any better than those not so labeled The organic label on pet foods mean the ingredients meet production and handling requirements of the USDA National Organic Program (NOP), which says these products are "produced through approved methods that integrate cultural, biological and mechanical practices that foster cycling of resources, promote ecological balance and conserve biodiversity. Synthetic fertilizers, sewage sludge, irradiation and genetic engineering may not be used." Certified organic foods display a USDA organic seal and must be made of at least 95 percent organic ingredients.

Natural is a descriptive term that until recently, was not even defined by AAFCO. It was used mostly by marketers to promote one type of food over another. In answer to consumer concerns, definitions have been created to create equal footing between any foods with this label claim. The current AAFCO definition says "natural" refers to "a feed or feed ingredient derived solely from plant, animal or mined sources, either in its unprocessed state or having been subject to physical processing, heat processing, rendering, purification, extraction, hydrolysis, enzymolysis or fermentation, but not having been produced by or subject to a chemically synthetic process and not containing any additives or processing aids that are chemically synthetic except in amounts as might occur in good manufacturing practices." Sound confusing? It is. This definition is very liberal and allows nearly all pet foods to carry some form of the "natural" label, because most pet food ingredients are 1) derived from plant, animal or mined sources; 2) can still undergo common manufacturing processes and retain the "natural" label; and 3) contain "trace" amounts of chemically synthetic compounds and still be called "natural."

Human-grade is a notable inclusion in the 2016 update. While the term "edible" is a standard in relation to food, "human-grade" is not, and the term isn't just about the ingredients. The U.S. Department of Agriculture (USDA) defines products fit for human consumption to be officially "edible" which requires them to have been processed, inspected and passed manufacturing regulations designed to assure safety for consumption by humans. This term's use has become so complicated and contentious that in the updated profiles, it will be left up to individual states to determine acceptability of "human grade" claims and whether they are properly substantiated.

Any questions concerning a cat food product should be directed to the manufacturer or distributor, whose name and address is required to be stated on the label.

The quality of a cat food isn't easy to determine, and the label will not tell you everything about the food. Feeding trials and quality ingredients cost more, which means more expensive foods tend to offer better nutrition than cheap foods. The reputation of the manufacturer and the manufacturer's history in nutritional research is important when judging the quality of a food. But even a quality diet is worthless if the cat refuses to eat it. Smell, texture and taste decide whether or not the food will be eaten. The best judge of palatability is your cat (see TONGUE).

REPRODUCTION

Reproduction refers to the process by which cats create offspring. The age at which a cat becomes sexually mature and able to reproduce varies depending on the cat's health, when they were born, and even the breed. Male cats typically reach puberty by nine months of age, and females between seven to 12 months. However, this varies a great deal from cat to cat, with some males not reaching sexual maturity before 16 months of age. Female cats may experience their first breeding cycle, called estrus or heat, as early as four months of age. But certain breeds like Persians mature later than other cats and may not experience their first estrus until they're nearly two years old. The reproductive life of a cat is quite long, with both males and females often able to produce offspring well into their teens. Females are able to produce litters of two to six kittens two to three times a year.

The estrus cycle is a period of time during which a female becomes sexually receptive to the male and breeding takes place. Again, the length of estrus is quite individual, but on average lasts five to eight days. This receptive period is followed by a "resting" period of three to 14 days when the cat is no longer receptive to breeding. Feline estrus occurs seasonally during specific time periods of the year, and is influenced by the amount of daylight. In the Northern Hemisphere, the feline breeding season generally is February through October. Cats that do not become pregnant continuously cycle in and out of heat during this time.

CAT FACTS

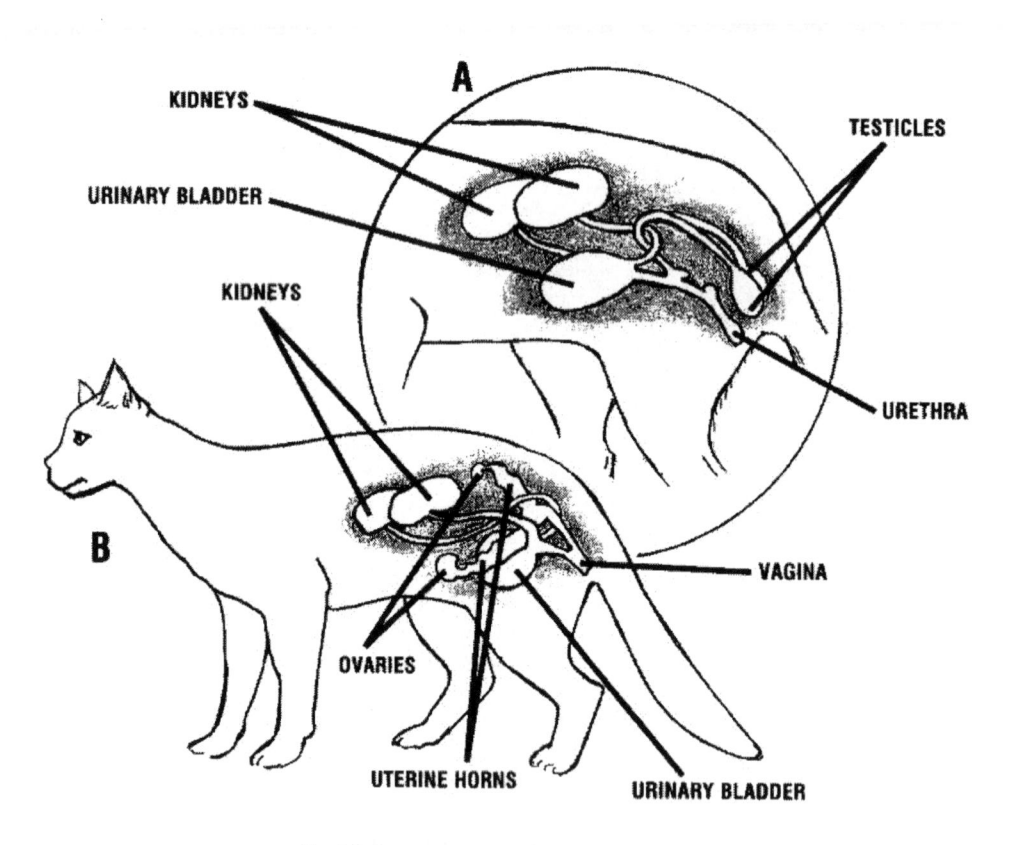

A: Male cat reproductive system
B: Female cat reproductive system

The period of estrus or heat is distinctive in cats. Cats show more behavioral than physical clues. The cycle begins with one to two days of proestrus during which time a female becomes more vocal, treads with her hind feet, and becomes excessively affectionate toward people and other cats of both sexes. With full estrus, she howls her readiness for a mate for minutes at a time, rolls about on the floor, and spends most of her time with her bottom in the air and tail held to one side. Male cats are alerted to her receptivity by her behavior and distinctive odor. They mark territory by spraying smelly urine that announces their status as breeding males, and defend that territory from other male cats in loud and often violent fights (see MARKING).

Breeding nearly always concludes with pregnancy. Sadly, the births of unwanted, unplanned kittens usually results in the untimely death of those kittens because there are not enough good homes to go around. Cat breeding involves much more than simply putting two pretty cats together. Feline matchmaking is a science, and proper selections of cat parents require a comprehensive knowledge of both feline health and genetics, as well as sufficient resources to defray the cost involved. Planned breeding should only be undertaken by experienced professional breeders. The vast majority of pet cats should be surgically sterilized (see NEUTERING and SPAYING). This removes the reproductive organs of male and female cats, and prevents accidental breeding.

Before planned breeding, both the male and female cat should be in optimal health. Medication, worming and vaccination should be avoided during pregnancy, and therefore must be addressed prior to breeding if possible. This not only protects the health of the queen, but also helps protect her kittens during and for a period after birth (see VACCINATIONS).

The female signals her readiness to mate by assuming the lordosis position; she crouches before the male cat, bottom in the air, and gives a distinctive cry that stimulates him to mount. He cautiously approaches her from one side, gently grasps the skin of her neck in his teeth, then straddles her as he treads with his rear feet. This prompts the female to arch her back, raising her rump and moving her tail to one side. Once the position is correct, the male begins thrusting, and ejaculates as soon as insertion takes place. Spines on the cat's penis stimulate the release of eggs from the ovaries when the male cat withdraws from the female's vagina.

As he withdraws, the female reacts with a cry or scream, and immediately rolls away from him. She may attack if he doesn't get out of her way quickly enough. The female typically engages in five to ten minutes of rolling, stretching and licking of her genitals following mating. A single breeding may last up to ten minutes, or be as short as 30 seconds. Another breeding may follow immediately, or be delayed for several hours. A single pair of cats may breed 20 or more times during the female's receptive period. It's also possible for a single litter to be fathered by more than one male. Ovulation usually occurs within 30 hours of breeding.

Gestation, the length of time between conception and birth, varies somewhat from cat to cat and from breed to breed. Feline pregnancy lasts about 63 to 69 days; Siamese cats typically carry their babies for 71 days.

Two to three weeks following conception, the first signs of pregnancy appear when the cat's nipples swell and change from light to rosy pink. Between day 17 and 25, a veterinarian can detect individual kittens by palpating, or feeling, the pregnant cat's abdomen. The mother cat's tummy won't noticeably thicken until about the fifth or sixth week of pregnancy.

410
CAT FACTS

Appropriate nutrition is particularly important for the pregnant cat if the unborn kittens are to mature correctly. Food intake typically increases, but overfeeding and excessive weight gain should be avoided. Provide a high quality commercial reproduction ration like an energy dense kitten food as recommended by your veterinarian. Food supplements are rarely required.

About two weeks before the birth of her kittens, the queen begins seeking an appropriate place to nest with her babies. A dry, warm, secluded area is preferred. Provide an easily cleaned nesting box for the prospective mother, but be prepared for her to make her own choices, like the sofa or the linen closet. During this time, queens typically rearrange the laundry basket or unmake the bed in an effort to create an appropriate nest.

Mammary glands begin to develop further a few days prior to queening, or giving birth. The fur on the breasts and genital region of longhaired mothers should be clipped in advance. During the first stage of labor, which lasts up to six hours, rectal temperature drops from the normal range to 98 or 99 degrees. During this time the queen pants and purrs and seeks an appropriate nest. Once the queen is settled in her nest, leave her alone; disturbing her may stop the labor. Healthy cats rarely have difficulty delivering kittens.

The second stage of labor usually lasts only ten to 30 minutes, and rarely longer than 90 minutes. A vaginal discharge signals imminent birth. Involuntary contractions begin, and soon the queen is fully involved and bearing down to deliver. If the first kitten isn't born within an hour following these strong contractions, take Mom to a veterinarian. Normally, a dark green-gray bubble which is the placental sack containing the kitten begins to emerge from the vagina, and should be fully passed within 30 minutes. Normal kitten presentation can be either tail or face first.

After a kitten is born, the queen cleans herself and consumes the placenta that follows the birth of each kitten, and bites through the umbilical cord. She licks her baby to clean it and to stimulate breathing. The queen may nurse the first born for a time before the next kitten birth. Kittens are usually born 15 to 30 minutes apart.

A veterinarian's assistance should be sought if no kittens appear after 90 minutes of labor, or if labor stops before all the kittens are born. After the birth, seek veterinary help if Mom appears restless or feverish, ignores her kittens, there's bleeding or a colored, white or foul-smelling discharge from the vulva.

The queen doesn't leave her newborns for 24 to 48 hours following the birth. During this time, she cleans and nurses them. The first milk, called colostrum, provides the kittens with important nutrients and protective antibodies (see IMMUNE SYSTEM). The mother licks their anal region to stimulate the newborns to eliminate, and the queen consumes the feces and urine.

A newborn kitten should actively squirm and cry. Kittens that feel cold to the touch and move or cry only weakly may be stimulated by massaging them with a dry, warm towel. Kittens that fail to breathe need immediate help. Wrap the baby in a dry, warm cloth, and cup him in both hands keeping his head secure as you swing him downward. This may help clear fluid from his lungs. When the baby begins breathing, give him back to the mother.

If for any reason the queen is unable to feed her babies, supplemental feeding may be necessary. Newborn kittens require feeding every two hours with an appropriate queen's milk replacer (see MILK, AS FOOD).

Nursing continues for up to eight weeks, and during this time the queen also protects and teaches her babies how to be cats. Depending on the time of year, estrus begins again a week or so following weaning.

RESPIRATION
Respiration is defined as breathing. Cats on average breathe at a rate of 20 to 30 respirations each minute, about twice as fast as people. The cat's respiratory system includes the nasal passages of the nose, the throat, voice box, windpipe, bronchial tubes and lungs.

Bronchial tubes are designed in a series of progressively smaller branches, like a tree. They culminate in tiny air sacs within the lung where the blood and oxygen exchange occurs. The diaphragm and other muscles of the chest pump air in and out of the lungs.

Normal breathing is even and unhurried. Changes in the respiration rate or breathing sounds can be an indication of a number of feline illnesses and should be addressed by a veterinarian (see ASTHMA and PANTING).

RESPIRATORY DISTRESS
Upper respiratory infections can cause obstruction of air and result in noisy breathing. Slowed respiration may indicate poison. Increased respiration, or panting, typically occurs after exertion and is a way for the cat to cool off. But prolonged labored panting can be a sign of heatstroke (see HYPERTHERMIA).

Wheezing is the sound air makes when forced through narrowed or constricted breathing tubes. This sound is typical of cats suffering from asthma, but may also indicate cancerous growths in the airways.

Painful breathing due to rib fracture or other painful conditions cause the cat to breathe in shallow, quick breaths to keep from moving too much. Fluid in the chest, called pleural effusion, also results in shallow breathing.

Cats rarely cough, and when they do it's usually a sign of a problem. Coughing may be the cat's attempt to clear swallowed hair or even a swallowed object like a needle from his throat. It can also be an indication of bronchitis or heartworm disease.

RESPIRATORY DISTRESS

SYMPTOMS: Gasping; panting; slowed breathing; pale or blue color to lips and gums; loss of consciousness
HOME CARE: Removing blockage from mouth and/or artificial respiration
VET CARE: Address cause; possible oxygen therapy
PREVENTION: Prevent poisoning, electrical shock, or other traumas that can cause breathing problems

RESTRAINT

Restraint involves restricting movement for the purpose of medication or transportation, while preventing injury to the cat or person handling the cat. Any cat that is in pain or frightened may become violent and cause injury to himself or the person attempting to help him. The amount of restraint depends on the individual circumstances, the competence of the cat handler, and the personality of the cat.

As a general rule, cats resent being forced to do anything. Restrict the cat only as much and as long as necessary to accomplish what needs to be done. Gentle, sure and firm movements are best.

Never swoop down on Kitty without warning. Sudden or rough handling tend to frighten the cat. Prepare in advance, gathering all necessary equipment and medication ahead of time so that you know what you're doing and are not rushed.

414
CAT FACTS

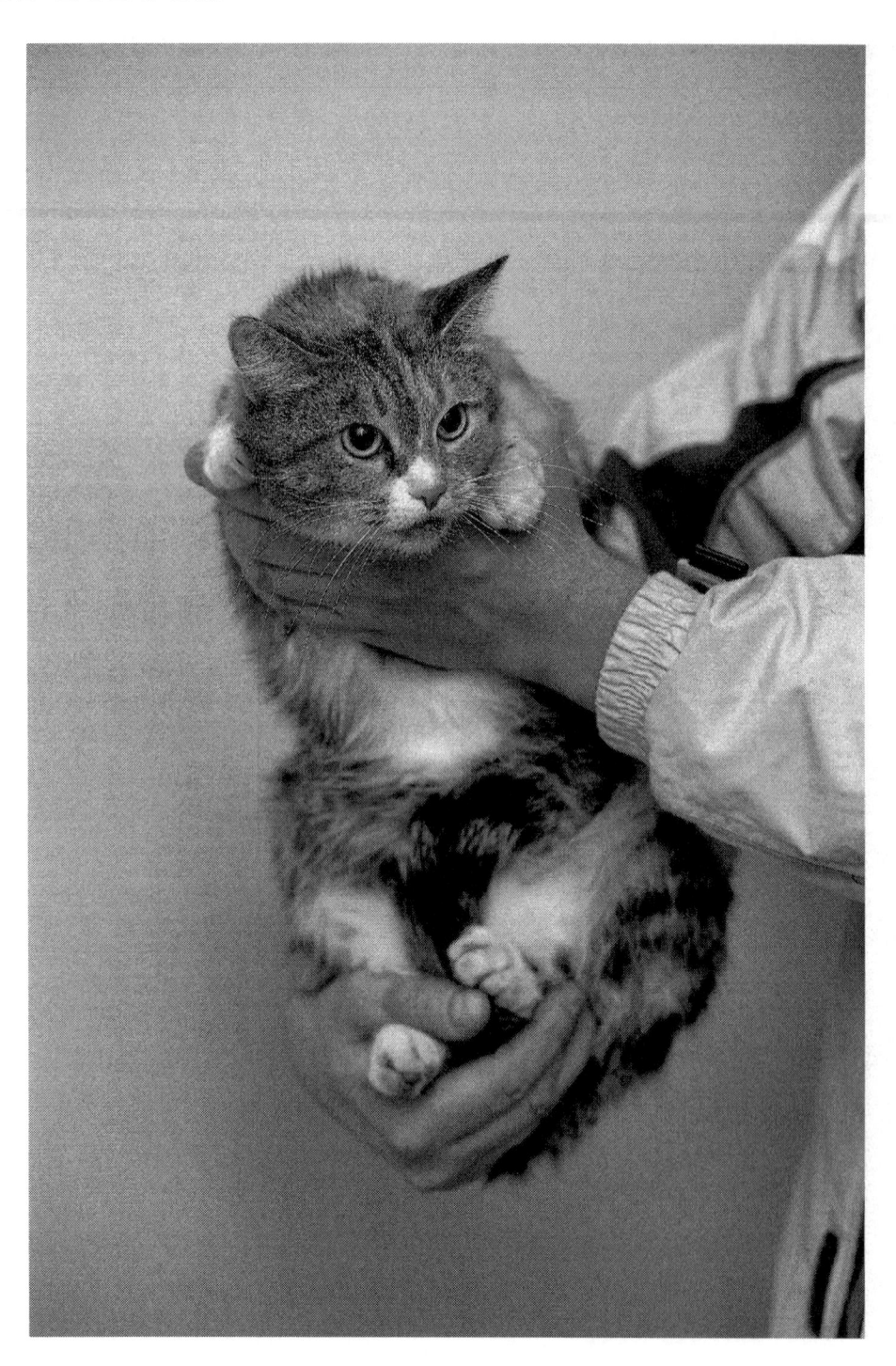

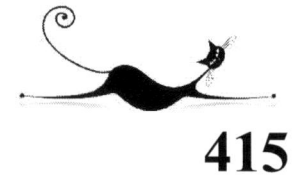

Your goal is to avoid the cat's teeth and claws. Two people work best; one restrains while the other attends the cat. Use one hand to firmly grasp the loose skin at the back of the cat's neck, called the scruff, and use the other hand to enclose both of Kitty's hind legs above the hock. Then gently stretch the cat out on his side.

Owners may often be required to restrain and medicate a cat all by themselves. Depending on the cat, simply grasping the cat's scruff and gently pressing Kitty flat to the table with one hand may be all that's needed while you medicate with the other. Commercial mesh cat bags or feline muzzles that cover the mouth and eyes are also helpful for immobilizing a cat for treatment. Unfortunately, it may be just as difficult to get the cat into the bag or muzzle as it is to perform the actual treatment. The more you fuss with the cat, the more agitated and difficult to handle he usually becomes.

Applying neck clips produced similar results to "scruffing." Called pinch-induced behavioral inhibition (PIBI) or "clipnosis," the response to the clipping is nearly identical to kittens picked up by the skin of their neck by their mother, and some cats even began to purr. Neurologic exams indicated that PIBI significantly decreased mentation but cats showed no signs of discomfort, pain, or fear—there were no significant changes in heart rate, blood pressure or temperature. However, the the clipping procedure won't work when the cat is already upset.

One of the simplest and best ways to restrain a cat is simply to wrap him in a blanket or large towel while leaving the treatment area on his body uncovered. Drop the fabric over the cat, covering his entire body, and wrap him up. Be sure to allow him breathing space. Many times, the cat calms down and stops struggling once his movement is restricted (see ADMINISTER MEDICATION).

RINGWORM
Ringworm is not a worm, it is a fungal infection of growing hair, dry skin, and sometimes the nails. There are many types, but about 95 percent of feline ringworm cases are caused by *Microsporum canis*. The condition also affects dogs and people (see ZOONOSIS).

The name comes from the ring-like lesions typically seen in human cases. Ringworm is a kind of biological contact dermatitis in which skin inflammation is caused by a substance produced by the fungus. The inflammation makes the skin inhospitable for the fungus, so it moves on to greener pastures. In people, the fungus grows outward away from the initial central inflammation in ever-widening rings, leaving the center to heal.

CAT FACTS

In cats, sores also grow outward from the infection, but rarely produce the ring pattern found in people. Ringworm in cats can look like a variety of other feline skin diseases, but hair loss is the most usual sign. Bald patches may develop in only one area, several spots, or cover the entire body. Ringworm is the most common cause of hair loss in kittens (see HAIR LOSS and SHEDDING).

The fungus, called a dermatophyte, lives only on hairs that are actively growing. Infected hairs eventually break off rather than fall out, leaving a stubby appearance to the coat. Mild to severe scaling or crusty sores typically develop with varying degrees of itchiness.

Cats are usually infected by coming in contact with infected hair, but ringworm can also be spread by contact with contaminated grooming equipment or from the environment. Contaminated hairs that are shed into the environment can remain infective for months, and provide a reservoir for reinfection of recovering cats.

All cats can get ringworm, and the length of haircoat has nothing to do with the risk. Both longhaired and shorthaired cats are equally affected. However, the most common victims are immune-compromised, young, and debilitated pets. Puppies and kittens are affected most frequently. Some cats carry the organism without showing signs themselves, and spread ringworm to other cats and pets. If one pet in the household is diagnosed, all should be treated whether they are showing signs or not.

RINGWORM

SYMPTOMS: Hair loss; skin inflammation
HOME CARE: Miconazole preparations or lime sulfur dips; vacuuming and cleaning surfaces daily with bleach and water solutions
VET CARE: Culture hairs to diagnose; antifungal medication; ringworm vaccination
PREVENTION: Avoid contact with contagious animals

Ringworm in cats is diagnosed by identifying the fungus. The veterinarian may use a Wood's Lamp to screen suspect cases; about half of *M. canis* cases will "glow" when exposed to its ultraviolet light. More cases are identified using a culture test which grows the ringworm fungus. A sample of debris brushed from the cat's skin and fur is placed in a special medium designed to grow certain ringworm species. It may take up to three weeks before the test indicates a positive result.

During treatment, infective animals should be quarantined from those not showing symptoms. Otherwise healthy cats tend to self-cure in nine months to a year, but during that time, can continually expose other animals (and people) to the fungus. People who are immune compromised, very young or very old are at highest risk.

Shaving ringworm-infected cats to aid treatment used to be routinely recommended but today is based more on the individual situation. Shorthair cats with fewer than five areas of infection may be effectively treated without a full body clipping.

Topical preparations of miconazole are helpful, but medicating the lesion before diagnosis may interfere with proper diagnosis. Miconazole alone or in combination with chlorhexidine is effective. Cats typically are bathed twice weekly, ensuring the product remains at least ten minutes on the cat's fur. Treat only after your veterinarian diagnoses the condition, and follow his or her recommendation.

Drugs that have been shown to be effective include griseofulvin, terbinafine, ketaconazole, and itraconazole. After ingestion, the drug is incorporated into the growing hair where it slows the growth of the fungus. Pills are usually given once daily for four to eight weeks, and should be continued two weeks beyond the time symptoms have disappeared. A vaccine is also available that may reduce the symptoms of the disease, when used in combination with other therapies.

Ringworm fungus can live in the environment for well over a year, where it can continuously reinfect cats. For that reason, this infected environment must also be treated; however, fungal spores are difficult to eliminate. Studies indicate that common disinfectants like chlorhexidine and water are not effective. Concentrated bleach or one percent formalin (a formaldehyde solution) have been shown to be effective, but neither are very practical in a home environment.

Daily cleaning of all surfaces using a diluted bleach solution (one part bleach to ten parts water), along with thorough vacuuming is the most effective and practical environmental treatment for most cat owners. Dispose of the vacuum bag by sealing in a plastic garbage sack and removing it from the house.

RODENT ULCER see EOSINOPHILIC GRANULOMA COMPLEX.

ROUNDWORMS

The roundworm is an intestinal parasite found in almost all kittens. Two types of roundworms infect cats. *Toxocara cati* most commonly affects kittens and can also be spread to people, while *Toxascara leonina* most frequently affects adult cats, and also dogs. Roundworms are commonly passed in the stool or vomited, and look like masses of spaghetti.

Kittens usually acquire roundworms from nursing the mother cat's milk. Cats also contract the parasite by swallowing infective larvae found in the environment, or by eating an infected host like a beetle or earthworm.

The *T. cati* larvae travel from the cat's stomach into the bloodstream, and on to the lungs. From there, they migrate into the windpipe, and may cause coughing. After again being swallowed, the parasites mature into one to three inch long adults that live in the intestines. Mature worms mate and lay eggs, which pass with the stool. These eggs develop into infective larvae, completing the cycle.

The other type of roundworm, *T. leonina* has a simpler lifecycle. Eggs are shed in the stool, and swallowing the eggs infects the host, where the worms mature in the intestines and eventually shed more eggs. Cats become infected most often by eating infected rodents.

Roundworms are rarely life-threatening, but massive infestations may result in intestinal damage or rarely in bowel obstruction. More typically, they interfere with digestion. Affected animals have a potbellied appearance, a dull coat, diarrhea, or mucus in the stool. Seeing the worms coiled in the feces or vomit is diagnostic, but usually diagnosis is made when the veterinarian identifies eggs during microscopic examination of a stool sample.

Liquid oral medication given in two doses two weeks apart is the standard treatment for roundworms. Pyrantel, fenbendazole and febantel are all quite effective, and are considered safe enough to use in three to four week old kittens as a preventative. Heartworm and/or flea preventive medications may also prevent roundworm infections.

ROUNDWORMS

SYMPTOMS: Potbellied appearance; a dull coat; diarrhea; mucus in the stool; seeing "spaghetti worms" in the stool or vomit
HOME CARE: None
VET CARE: Oral worm medication
PREVENTION: None

420
CAT FACTS

421

CAT FACTS

SALMONELLA *Salmonella* is a bacteria which can cause illness in people and pets, and can contaminate homemade as well as commercial pet foods, and lead to some pet food recalls. There are nearly 2000 kinds of salmonella bacteria. Most are found naturally in the environment, and can remain alive for months or years in manure or soil. Some types are normal inhabitants of animals, and don't cause problems. Others prompt a variety of illnesses from diarrheal disease to life-threatening illness that cause a variety of salmonella symptoms you need to watch for.

SALMONELLA

SYMPTOMS: Bloody diarrhea; foul-smelling diarrhea; fever; vomiting; loss of appetite; hunching posture from pain; depression
HOME CARE: None
VET CARE: Fluid therapy; antibiotics
PREVENTION: Avoid contaminated raw or undercooked meats; prevent cat from hunting

Kittens or young outdoor cats and those that are stressed by other illness or inadequate nutrition are most commonly affected. Cats contract the bacteria by drinking infected water, and eating raw or commercial food rations contaminated with infected droppings.

Most infected pets never show signs of illness, but may harbor the bacteria and spread the disease to other animals and people. When illness develops, signs include bloody, foul-smelling diarrhea; fever, vomiting; appetite loss; a hunching position due to stomach pain; and depression.

The bacteria may be carried in the bloodstream to the liver, lungs, kidneys or uterus. Signs of disease typically last four to ten days, but diarrhea may continue for a month or longer.

The condition is diagnosed from signs of illness, and from finding the bacteria in the blood or tissues of the affected cat. When enteritis is the primary problem, treatment usually consists of fluid therapy (see DEHYDRATION).

A culture of the stool sample will identify the strain of salmonella, so that the most effective antibiotic can be given. However, antibiotic therapy is only indicated in instances of severe systemic disease, to avoid the possibility of prompting the development of a drug-resistant strain of the bacteria.

Protect cats from salmonella by curtailing hunting. Cats that eat rodents or other wildlife are at much greater risk. If you choose to provide a raw food diet, take extra precautions to ensure the food is safe for your cats and humans handling the food.

Protect yourself by religiously washing your hands after dealing with feces or handling an ill cat. Use a dilute bleach and water solution (1 to 32 ratio) to disinfect your hands, cat bowls, toys, and areas where the cat sleeps.

SCENT see NOSE.

SCRATCHING

Scratching refers to scraping or scoring objects with the claws. Cats use both front and rear claws to scratch themselves in response to skin irritation or as a part of grooming, and use front claws to scratch objects. Animal behaviorists believe cats scratch objects primarily as a function of communication and secondarily to condition claws and tone muscles.

Recent studies have identified categories of scratching behavior. The first group are cats for which scratching is an inherent part of territorial behavior. Early separation from their mother at or before six weeks of age predisposes this group to display claw-behavior near their most important areas of activity; hiding places, litter box, hunting areas, sleeping spots. This basically posts a note to other cats saying the area is owned, and warns them away. When trained to avoid forbidden objects, these cats need a legal target near the original one.

The second group scratches during or after situations that worry them or cause stress. In particular, they claw in highly visible strategic locations, like the front door or sofa, when their environment is too big for them to keep under control, or the area is shared by other animals, especially other cats. For this group, scratching may be completely eliminated if the stressful events (a strange cat crossing their lawn) can be controlled.

Scratching is normal cat behavior. Typically, the cat stretches forward as far as he can reach, extends his claws, and repeatedly draws them through or against the object's surface back toward himself. This leaves visible scores on hard objects, and shreds or tatters softer materials. Scratching can become a destructive behavior when inappropriate objects in the home, such as the piano or sofa, are the cat's target.

Because scratching is innate, it's nearly impossible to prevent. In many cases, however, the behavior can be modified and redirected to more appropriate scratching surfaces. It is more difficult to alter established habits than to prevent them from developing in the first place.

Probably the best approach is to offer the cat a better scratching alternative while making forbidden objects less attractive. Cover forbidden horizontal surfaces with cat-repellent materials like heavy plastic runners, nub side up. For vertical objects like drapes or upholstered furniture backs, try plastic shelf paper that has adhesive on both sides. The plastic surface is a turn-off, but the sticky surface is singularly distasteful to the cat.

425

CAT FACTS

A variety of commercial scratching posts are available that give the cat adequate scratching opportunities. Cats are attracted to specific structures, surface textures, and locations. Observe your cat and take into account his past targets to determine his scratching tastes.

Most cats prefer scratching vertical objects, but some like horizontal surfaces. Whatever the choice, it must be tall enough or long enough to accommodate the cat's full-length stretch, and so stable it does not slide about the floor or tip over when the cat assaults it. Cats tend to prefer flat surfaces with corners that can also be scratched, rather than round posts without edges.

Texture preference varies from cat to cat, and is critical in determining whether the cat will scratch the item or not. Because the greatest purpose of scratching is to leave visible marks, cats seem to prefer easily shredded material like loosely woven cloth coverings. This may be why cats snub posts with nubby, tightly woven fabric that catches claws, and instead return time after time to the sofa back.

The covering on a well-scratched post shouldn't be changed too often. Leaving the tattered material in place will keep Kitty returning for more. If your cat is choosing a table leg or door frame, a harder surface such as tree bark may be more appropriate for that particular cat. Many cats like sisal coverings. Some commercial posts provide two or more surface types that satisfy both grooming and marking urges.

When locating the scratching object, again take your cue from the cat. Prime scratching times are after meals and naps, and some cats use scratching as a greeting ritual. Cats can often be enticed to scratch posts located near food bowls, a favorite sleeping area, or a doorway. Because these marks are visual signals meant to be seen, the cat prefers to scratch in high-traffic areas and will ignore a commercial scratching post that's hidden away in a back room.

When redirecting scratch behavior, situate the replacement object directly in front of the damaged area on the forbidden item. You can gradually move the new scratching object to a more convenient location once the cat has switched his scratching allegiance.

For some cats, making the forbidden object distasteful while providing an irresistible new alternative is enough to reduce or totally eliminate destructive scratching behavior. For instance, place double sided tape products over "forbidden" targets while offering an irresistible "legal" scratch post conveniently nearby.

Cats dislike being forced to do anything, and carrying Kitty to the object and physically rubbing his paws on it may not sit well with him. The most important and basic principle regarding cat training is this simple rule: let the cat think it's his idea. Always praise and reward appropriate scratching with verbal praise, treats, or favorite games.

How to Trim Cat's Nails

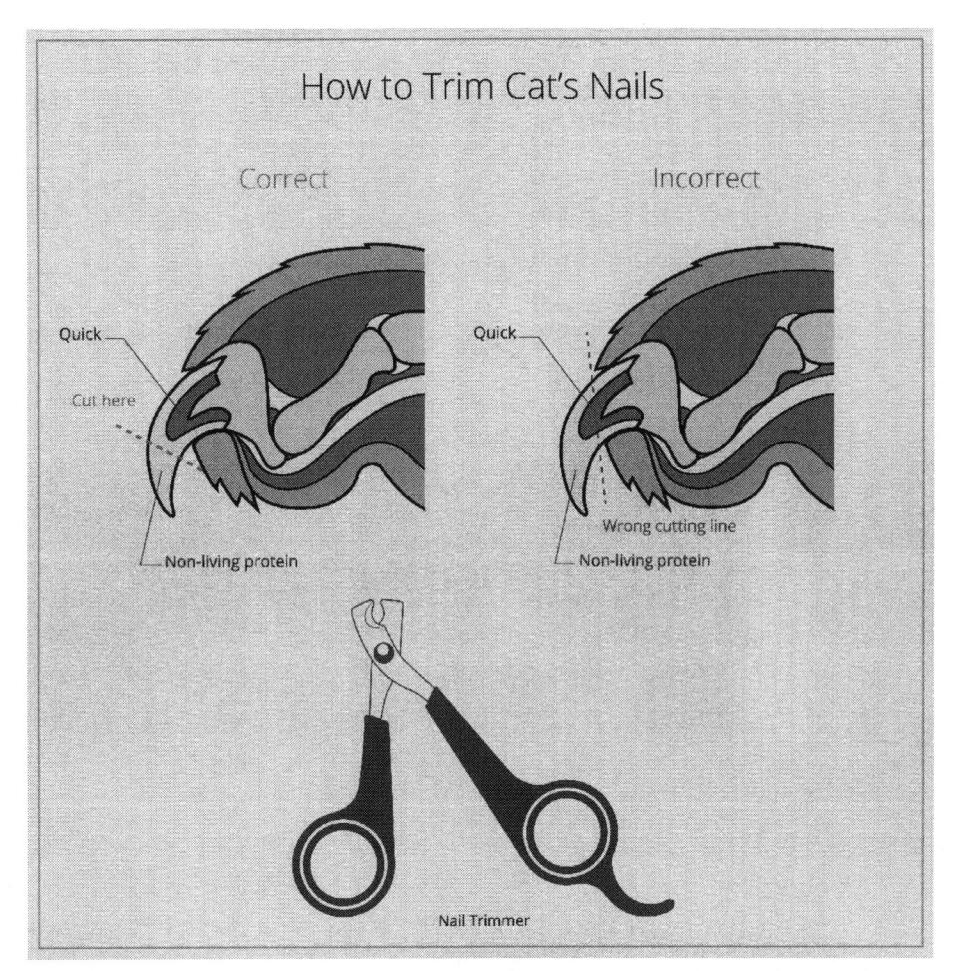

Correct — Quick; Cut here; Non-living protein

Incorrect — Quick; Wrong cutting line; Non-living protein

Nail Trimmer

Rubbing catnip over the new post entices some cats. Other times, draw Kitty's attention with a string or feather, drag it right up to and upon the scratching object, and let him sink in his claws when he captures the toy. Initially tipping a vertical post on its side and enticing the cat to climb aboard may get the message across when he feels the texture beneath his paws. The sound and sight of you scratching the surface with your own nails may also entice the cat to scratch. Reward spontaneous scratching with praise and petting.

Interrupt inappropriate scratching by remote correction techniques. Use these with care, however; some cats do stop scratching when an owner interrupts them, but this could result in the cat waiting until you're not watching to sneak-scratch the preferred yet inappropriate object. Physical punishment rarely if ever works, and instead can make the cat fearful of you, and further stress him when his natural urges to scratch are thwarted.

Trimming cats claws on a routine basis helps prevent damage should the cat target an inappropriate object. Products like soft plastic nail coverings are an option for some hard case cats. They are designed to attach to claws with a nontoxic adhesive. The plastic nail covers help reduce the damage claws otherwise inflict.

Most cats given adequate legal claw outlets can be persuaded to leave illegal targets alone. Declaw surgery has fallen out of favor to thwart this natural clawing behavior of cats, and is considered inhumane (or illegal) in many countries outside of the United States. Educate yourself about what's involved in this surgery, and potential consequences, before consulting with your veterinarian about such options.

SEPARATION ANXIETY

Separation anxiety is fear of being alone. Cats may go for years without issues, and then suddenly act out when your work schedule changes and keeps you away for long hours. Vacations also tend to trigger feline separation anxiety. Think of separation anxiety as a form of grief. Cats don't mean to "act bad," they just miss you so much they can't help themselves.

Like dogs with the same condition, cats may cry and become upset as you prepare to leave. More often, they don't react to your departure. They wait to "act out" once left alone, and urinate and defecate on owner-scented objects—most typically the bed.

The familiar scent of kitty's bathroom deposits actually comforts her, and *reduces* feelings of stress. Of course, these unwelcome "gifts" *increase* owner stress levels. And while angry reaction is understandable, your upset feelings increase the cat's anxiety even more.

Cats don't potty on the bed to get back at you because you left. Think of the cat's behavior as a backhanded compliment. Kitty wouldn't do this if she didn't love you so much!

Cats pay exquisite attention to the details of their lives. They'll often recognize subtle clues that you're preparing to leave long before you realize. A cat may figure out that you always freshen your lipstick just before you leave. Repeating these cues takes away their power.

Desensitize your cats to the presence of the overnight bag by leaving it out all the time. Put clothes in and out of the bag every day, but without leaving the house, so your cat no longer gets upset when she sees you pack.

Toss a catnip mouse inside the suitcase, and turn it into a kitty playground. That conditions her to identify the suitcase as a happy place, rather than associating it with your absence.

Use behavior modification techniques so the triggers lose their power. Pick up the car keys 50 times a day, and then set them down. Carry your purse over your arm for an hour or more.

When you repeat cues often enough, your cat stops caring about them and will remain calm when you do leave.

Fake your departure by opening the door and going in and out twenty or more times in a row until the cat ignores you altogether. Then extend your "outside" time to one minute, three minutes, five minutes and so on before returning inside. This gradual increase in absence helps build the cat's tolerance and desensitizes her to departures. It also teaches her that no matter how long you're gone, you always return.

Most problem behaviors take place within twenty minutes after you leave. The length of time you're absent doesn't seem to matter. Find ways to distract the cat during this critical twenty minutes so she won't dirty your bed.

SEPARATION ANXIETY

SYMPTOMS: Hides; cries when you leave; refuses to eat; eliminates on furniture, especially your bed
HOME CARE: Desensitize and counter condition to departures; distract with puzzle toys; treat with catnip
HOLISTIC HELP: Music therapy; flower essences; massage and TTouch
VET CARE: Antianxiety medications if severe
PREVENTION: None

Ask another family member to interact with the cat during this time. A fishing-pole lure toy or chasing the beam of a flashlight can take the cat's mind off her troubles. If she enjoys petting or grooming, indulge her in a touchy-feely marathon.

About 1/3rd of cats react strongly, another 1/3rd react mildly, and the last 1/3rd don't react at all to catnip. If your feline goes bonkers for this harmless herb, leave a catnip treat to keep her happy when you leave. Using catnip every day can reduce its effects, though, so use this judiciously (see CATNIP).

Food oriented cats can be distracted with a food-puzzle toy stuffed with a favorite treat. Make it extra smelly, irresistible and something totally different than her usual fare to be sure the treat makes the proper impression.

Cats that have been outside and seen the real thing often don't react, but homebody indoor-only cats enjoy watching videos of fluttering birds, squirrels and other critters. Find a nature television show such as on Animal Planet, and tune in for your cat's viewing pleasure.

Music may help. Playing familiar music that they associate with your presence can help ease the pain of you being gone. In addition, research has shown harp music works as a natural sedative, and actually puts cats to sleep (see MUSIC THERAPY).

Not all tips work with every cat, since every feline is an individual. But using these techniques alone or in combination can heal upset kitty feelings, and turn homecomings into joyful reunions.

SEXING

Determining a cat's gender is called sexing the cat, and is easily done in adult felines. Young kittens may be more difficult, particularly in longhaired varieties where fur tends to hide the clues.

To sex the kitten, simply lift the tail. By about eight to ten weeks of age, the male's testicles will be visible. Even before this, the genitals of male and female kittens are quite different upon examination. Lift the kitten's tail to examine the area. The male's urethra and rectum configuration resemble a colon (the urethral opening is round) while the female's looks more like an upside down exclamation mark (the urethral opening is a slit).

SHEDDING

Shedding is the normal loss of hair. The amount of the cat's exposure to artificial light or daylight, not the temperature, determines how much and when a cat will shed her coat.

The more exposure a cat has to light, the greater the amount she will shed. Indoor cats often shed year round, while outdoor cats living in the northeastern United States typically shed seasonally for many weeks when daylight increases during late spring.

A cat's fur grows between one quarter to one third inch each month, with the most activity occurring in the summer and the least during winter months. Growth rate is not continuous, though. Hair grows in cycles beginning with a period of rapid growth in the spring, followed by slower growth, and then ending in a resting stage. Mature hairs loosen in the follicles during this winter resting phase. In the spring, another cycle of hair growth begins, and new hair pushes the old loose ones out. This process is called shedding.

Cat hair is more easily pulled out during the winter resting period, and during this time, fright or stress may result in a sudden shed. That's because these emotions activate specialized muscles found along the cat's back and tail which are attached to the hair and cause it to stand on end when the cat is agitated. When the hair is already loose, the muscles literally pull the hair out.

The cat's hair grows and is shed in an irregular pattern. As the thick, wooly undercoat falls out, the cat may look moth-eaten. To help prevent skin problems and hairballs, groom the cat regularly paying particular attention during shedding season (see GROOMING).

SHOCK

Shock is the collapse of the circulatory system. Shock usually results from trauma associated with burns, crushing injuries, or profound dehydration. Common causes of shock include being hit by cars or falling (see HIGH RISE SYNDROME), hyperthermia, severe vomiting or diarrhea, dehydration, and excessive bleeding.

Due to decrease in blood volume or a collapse of the vessels, the heart can't adequately move the blood, and the tissues of the body become starved for oxygen. The body attempts to compensate by shutting down normal blood flow to non-vital areas. But as the organs become more and more oxygen starved, they start to fail. This creates a vicious cycle that intensifies the shock. Left untreated, the cat will die.

Signs include mental depression or loss of consciousness, a drop in temperature until the body feels cold to the touch, weakness, shivering, pale gums, shallow rapid breathing, and faint but rapid pulse greater than 240 beats per minute. Cases of shock must be treated as soon as possible by the veterinarian.

First aid includes keeping the cat warm by wrapping him in a blanket. If he's conscious, let him assume the most comfortable position. Speak calmly to soothe him. Rub the cat's gums with honey or Karo syrup to help raise blood sugar levels. When unconscious, keep the cat's head lower than his body to improve circulation to the brain. Check that the cat is breathing, and pull his tongue clear of the mouth to keep the airway open.

If he's not breathing or has no heartbeat, begin artificial respiration or cardiopulmonary resuscitation. Stabilize apparent fractures, address bleeding with pressure, then get the cat to the veterinarian as soon as possible. The ideal treatment is efficiently and quickly rehydrating the cat using intravenous fluids.

SHOCK

SYMPTOMS: Depression; loss of consciousness; cat feels cold; weakness; shivering; pale gums; shallow rapid breathing; faint rapid pulse
FIRST AID: Warm cat in blanket; if unconscious place head lower than body; artificial resuscitation
VET CARE: Intravenous fluid therapy
PREVENTION: Avoid trauma

SKIN

The skin is the largest organ of the body. Skin acts as a protective barrier between the cat and the outside world. Skin insulates from extremes of temperature, controls moisture loss, and shields the body from foreign agents like toxins or bacteria.

The outer layer, called the epidermis, provides external protection. It contains special pigment-producing cells that give your cat her distinctive color, and screens her from the harmful rays of the sun. The middle layer, called the dermis, is the thickest and gives the skin its shape. It also contains the elastic connective tissue that gives skin flexibility, along with nerves, and specialized cells of the immune system. Hair follicles which produce the root of each hair are found in this layer, along with sweat glands. Hair grows from the follicles, and each follicle is adjacent to a pressure-sensitive pad which responds to touch.

The furless paw pads and nose leather are the most sensitive surface areas of the cat's body. Therefore, the cat typically uses paw taps to test an object's relative safety.

The nose and muzzle area also are particularly sensitive to temperature, able to detect variations of only a degree or two. Newborn kittens use this ability to seek warmth, using their heat-seeking muzzles to find their mother or siblings (see KITTEN).

CAT FACTS

SKUNK ENCOUNTERS Cat allowed outdoors in rural areas may meet wildlife of the smelly kind: skunks. When bothered by a curious feline, the skunk does what comes naturally, and sprays its own brand of defense on the offending cat.

Skunks have musk glands on each side of the anus. These glands are equipped with retractable ducts. They can take aim and spray the stink a distance of 10 to 15 feet, so even standoffish pets are liable to get nailed.

Skunk spray contains thiols, an organic compound composed of a sulfur atom attached to a hydrogen atom attached to a carbon atom. The same types of compounds create bad breath or offensive odor of flatulence. Thiols have a lingering rotten egg odor, and the skunk's oily secretion makes it difficult to get rid of. Skunk spray is so pungent, a concentration of one in ten parts per billion can make humans gag.

The only thing you can do to eliminate the odor is bathe the skunked cat. It may take several sudsings and rinsings to be effective. A regular pet grooming shampoo may do the trick, but there are other more effective options.

Commercial products available from pet stores are designed to help neutralize skunk odor. A tried and true home remedy is a tomato juice soak; wash the cat first with pet shampoo, towel him dry, then douse him with the juice and let it soak for ten or 15 minutes. Then rinse him off and suds again with the regular shampoo. Alternate the tomato juice soak with the shampoo bath until he's less pungent.

Massengill brand douche is recommended by some professional groomers as an effective odor-absorbing soak. Mix two ounces of the douche to a gallon of water, pour over the washed cat, and let soak for at least 15 minutes. Then bathe with normal shampoo once more.

You can also use chemistry to neutralize the thiols. Mix one quart of 3 percent hydrogen peroxide with ¼ cup of baking soda, and one teaspoon of pet shampoo (any kind will work). Apply to the pet's wet fur, allow the mix to bubble for three or four minutes, then rinse thoroughly. This recipe, created by chemist Paul Krebaum, works better than anything on the market. You can't buy it, though, because the formula can't be bottled. It explodes if left in a closed container. So if your pet is skunked, mix only one application at a time. Otherwise you'll be cleaning up more than just the pet.

Avoid the problem altogether by preventing skunk encounters. Confine your cat inside, or supervise outdoor excursions. Skunks tend to be nocturnal, so try not to let your cat roam at night. If you want to have a pet door, provide those that only allow your cat access so that varmints don't come into your home.

SKUNK ENCOUNTERS

SYMPTOMS: Pungent odor
HOME CARE: Bathe
VET CARE: Same; sometimes ointment to soothe eyes
PREVENTION: Keep cats indoors at night; supervise outdoor treks; make pet doors inaccessible to wildlife

SLEEP

Cats spend 2/3rds of their life, 16 hours or more each day, sleeping. That's more than any other mammal, except for the opossum and some bats.

We don't know why cats sleep so much, but one theory is that predators that have few natural enemies can afford to sleep for longer periods of time. Others hypothesize the need for sleep increases in direct proportion to the amount of energy required. Being a predator, the cat's energy needs for hunting are extraordinary.

Sleep activity of cats, like people and many other mammals, is characterized by two patterns of brain activity. This activity has been measured experimentally with an electroencephalograph (EEG), a special instrument that records waves or pulses of activity on a graph.

CAT FACTS

When awake, the cat's brain broadcasts little bunched-together irregular peaks. The brain activity of the dozing cat, though, produces long, irregular waves called "slow-wave sleep" which usually lasts about 15 to 30 minutes.

Dozing cats generally lie with head raised and paws tucked beneath them. Sometimes the cat actually sleeps sitting up, in which case the muscles stiffen to hold Kitty upright. That way he's ready to spring into action, should it be necessary.

When Kitty moves from light to deeper sleep, his body relaxes, he stretches out and rolls onto his side. The brain patterns also change; they become smaller and closer together, in fact quite similar to waking patterns. However, the cat is fully relaxed and very difficult to awaken during deep sleep, which is referred to by experts as "rapid sleep" because of the quick movement of the brain waves. This phase typically lasts only about five minutes, then the cat returns to slow-wave sleep, and thereafter alternates between rapid and slow sleep until he wakes up. Rather than alternating types of sleep, kittens fall directly into deep rapid sleep until they are about a month old. Cat dreams are born during this rapid sleep (see DREAMING).

The cat's senses continue to record sounds and scents during up to 70 percent of sleep. This allows Kitty to awaken at the drop of a hat, or the squeak of a mouse.

More leisurely awakenings are followed by a nearly ritualistic program of blinking, yawning, and stretching. First the forelegs, then the back, and finally the rear legs each in turn are flexed. Most cats then spend a few minutes getting their fur back in proper shape (see GROOMING).

Unlike humans who sleep long hours at a stretch and usually at night, cats typically take short and long naps throughout the day. Individual sleeping habits vary, but very old and very young cats sleep more than healthy adults, and sleep time tends to increase on cold or rainy days. Conversely, when love is in the air, cats may sleep less in the pursuit of romance.

Cats tend to adapt to the people in their lives, sleeping when the owner is gone and spending awake time with you when you are home. Like their ancestors, cats are most active at daybreak and sundown.

437

S MOKE INHALATION see ARTIFICIAL RESPIRATION.

S OCIALIZATION see KITTEN.

S OCIAL STRUCTURE

Cat society defines how cats deal with each other. No longer thought of as antisocial loaners, today we know felines relate and interact with each other in dynamic and very fluid hierarchies.

Most cat behavior is designed to enable the cat to safely hunt and stay safe. Avoidance of threat by escape or hiding is a primary behavior used as a coping mechanism for stress, with fighting in defense or offense used primarily as a last resort when avoidance isn't possible.

When enough food and other resources are present, adult females associate in lineages, which are the building blocks of cat society. Similar to lions, domestic kitties in colony settings may suckle each other's babies, sever umbilical cords, move kittens to new locations, and otherwise communally raise the infants.

Large cat colonies may have several such lineages. Each usually consists of related adult females and successive generations of their offspring. Females relate within their lineage and to a lesser extent outside of it. These tend to be friendly, well-integrated groups of cats, with the eldest female holding the highest status. Juveniles and kittens automatically become socially integrated to their birth lineage and these ties usually last a lifetime if the cats remain in each other's company. Ties of adult females to their sons and daughters are stronger than to nephews and nieces.

Most observation of free-living cats suggests that adult males rarely are affiliated with any one lineage, usually only temporarily during mating. However, cats in feral situations often choose to sit together, establish feline friendships, and each individual favors company of some over others. The age, sex, social status and blood ties of the individuals involved govern these associations.

Toms also are said not to be involved in kitten rearing, but that's not always true. Intact toms have been seen helping queens defend kittens from invading toms, to groom babies, share food with juveniles, and to curl up around abandoned kittens. Males also sometimes disrupt intense wrestling play between juveniles, using a forelimb to separate them without using aggression against either.

Felines in any given family group—composed mostly of females with some immature males and the occasional Tom—offer a united front and show hostility toward strange cats that attempt to join the society. Non-group members are not allowed to casually approach and enter the group. If the unknown cat or kitten persists, they may eventually be integrated into the group but only over time that involves many interactions. Therefore, introducing a new cat into a resident cats' territory almost always proves challenging for owners. Introducing very young cats of the opposite sex into a resident adult's social group works best, as it offers the fewest social challenges to the dominant feline.

The feline social structure depends on a hierarchy of dominant and subordinate individuals. Rank of the individual cat decides which one gets the preferred access to valued resources: resting spots, food pans, water, toys, your attention, and so on.

Cats don't follow a clear linear hierarchy, though. There is usually an obvious top cat and one or two bottom cats (called pariahs because they get picked on by the others), but no number two, three, or four cats with stair-step ranking below the dominant feline. Instead, most cats share an equal "middle space." This more fluid social standing requires a decision about who eats first, crosses a path first, gets the best sleeping spot time after time, on a case-by-case basis. Sometimes the calico wins the day while the tabby gets her choice another time.

This time-share mentality allows every cat (even middle management) to feel like a King. Time-share means the cats don't need to fight over property. It may appear that one cat owns the second floor of your home, while another cat owns the family room. This makes perfect sense if you consider that people also bow to the whims of a boss while at work, but we call the shots in our own homes.

Subordinate cats signal deference by looking away, lowering ears slightly, turning the head away and leaning back when they encounter a cat dominant to them. Often close encounters are simply avoided by giving way spatially—the subordinate cat gets off the path, jumps off the chair, or otherwise acknowledges the other cat's right. Cat #1 may own the second floor, but when she's not around, Cat #2 lounges there with impunity—timeshares the area because the first cat wasn't using it. When the owner returns, the subordinate cat pretends not to care, looks the other way and relinquishes the territory when Cat #1 returns.

CAT FACTS

Dominant cats show their status with a direct stare, stiffening of the limbs, holding ears erect while turning them sideways, and elevating the base of the tail while the rest of it droops. The display usually prompts the subordinate cat to defer.

Fights occur most often during introductions of new cats into an existing feline society, or when a change in social status due to infirmity or maturing adolescent cats takes place. When rare valued resources must be shared, the potential for arguments escalates. Ownership of property rates very highly among cats, and providing an appropriate environment is vital to the cat's emotional and physical well-being. The American Association of Feline Practitioners (AAFP) and International Society of Feline Medicine (ISFM) suggest a healthy feline environment should contain five components: 1. A safe place; 2. Multiple separate resources (litter box, feeding stations, scratch areas, play/resting locations); 3. Opportunity for play/predatory behavior; 4. Positive, consistent and predictable human-cat interaction; and 5. Respects cat's sense of smell.

SOILING

Soiling refers to inappropriate elimination. Cats are normally fastidious in their bathroom habits, and refusing to use the litter box can generally be linked to some underlying cause.

The causes of soiling generally fall into four broad categories. **Medical causes** may be associated with FLUTD, kidney disease, diabetes mellitus, hyperthyroidism, arthritis or other orthopedic issues, or cancer. **Feline idiopathic cystitis (FIC)** may be another cause. Cats may lose litter box training because they physically can't control their bowels or urinary bladder, or because pain from a medical condition is associated with the litter box. Check with your veterinarian to rule out a medical cause.

Marking behavior, as well as **environmental and social factors** also may be involved. Soiling is often confused with territorial marking which a dominance display usually of intact male cats is. A change in the cat's normal routine, such as the addition of a pet, moving to a new home, or a change in the owner's work schedule may prompt marking behavior in cats that are stressed and are trying to bring their world back under control.

Cats also may snub their toilet if the litter material, the box itself, the location of the box, or its hygiene are not satisfactory. The cat's bathroom must be as attractive to the cat as possible or bathroom habits will become hit or miss at best (see LITTER and LITTER BOX).

Cats do not like to eliminate in the same area where they eat. Strong smelling deodorants used around the box or incorporated in the litter itself may cause cats to find another place. Remember, the cat's sense of smell is infinitely more sensitive than our own. A smelly toilet is the quickest way to train Kitty to ignore proper bathroom behavior. Avoid ammonia-containing cleaners, which tend to intensify the smell of urine (see NOSE).

Some cats require privacy when they use the bathroom, and placing the box in a high traffic area may prompt creative deposits in more hidden locations. Any change in the placement of the toilet, or of the type of litter itself can turn off the cat.

Be sure to thoroughly clean soiled areas of carpet with a commercial product designed for that purpose. If the scent is not eliminated, the cat may return to the scene of the crime and repeat the offense.

Simply mopping up the mess may satisfy your nose, but the smell lures your innocent cat back to the scene of the crime to repeat the dirty deed, time after time. Urine soaked into carpet proves particularly difficult to remove.

With fresh accidents, pick up the solids and blot up as much liquid as possible. Avoid using ammonia-based cleaning products. Since urine has ammonia in it, such products may mimic the smell and make the area even more attractive as a potty spot.

Once urine dries on carpet or walls your cat's "pee-mail" notes are even more difficult to locate and clean. Turn off all your lights and shine a high-quality black light on suspect areas—that makes urine glow in the dark. Don't forget to check vertical areas marking cats like to target (see MARKING). The best products don't just clean the area or cover up with perfumes, but actually neutralize the chemicals that smell bad.

Urine is composed of sticky urea, urochrome (the yellow color), and uric acid. The first two can be washed away, but uric acid is nearly impossible to dissolve and remove from surfaces.

That's why successful products not only clean away the urea and urochrome, they also neutralize the uric acid with enzymes or encapsulate the urine molecules to contain the odor.

Some targets, like your bedspread or the cat's bedding, benefit from being washed with the product in your washing machine. When the odor cannot be removed, it's best to discard the item if possible rather than fight the cat's instinctive urge to re-baptize the spot. For instance, bath mats often seem to be targeted, particularly those with rubberized backing, because to the cat the backing smells like cat urine. Some male cats also identify the strong smell of bleach as an invitation to spray, so using bleach to clean up soiled spots may in fact increase the problem.

442
CAT FACTS

You may need to confine the cat when unable to watch his every move. Unless ill, a cat will not soil the area where he sleeps, so placing him in a very small room or cage with the litter box should prompt him to do the right thing. Once he's regularly filling the box, you can gradually increase house privileges. When dealing with more than one cat, or a small cat in a large area, more than one litter box can be helpful.

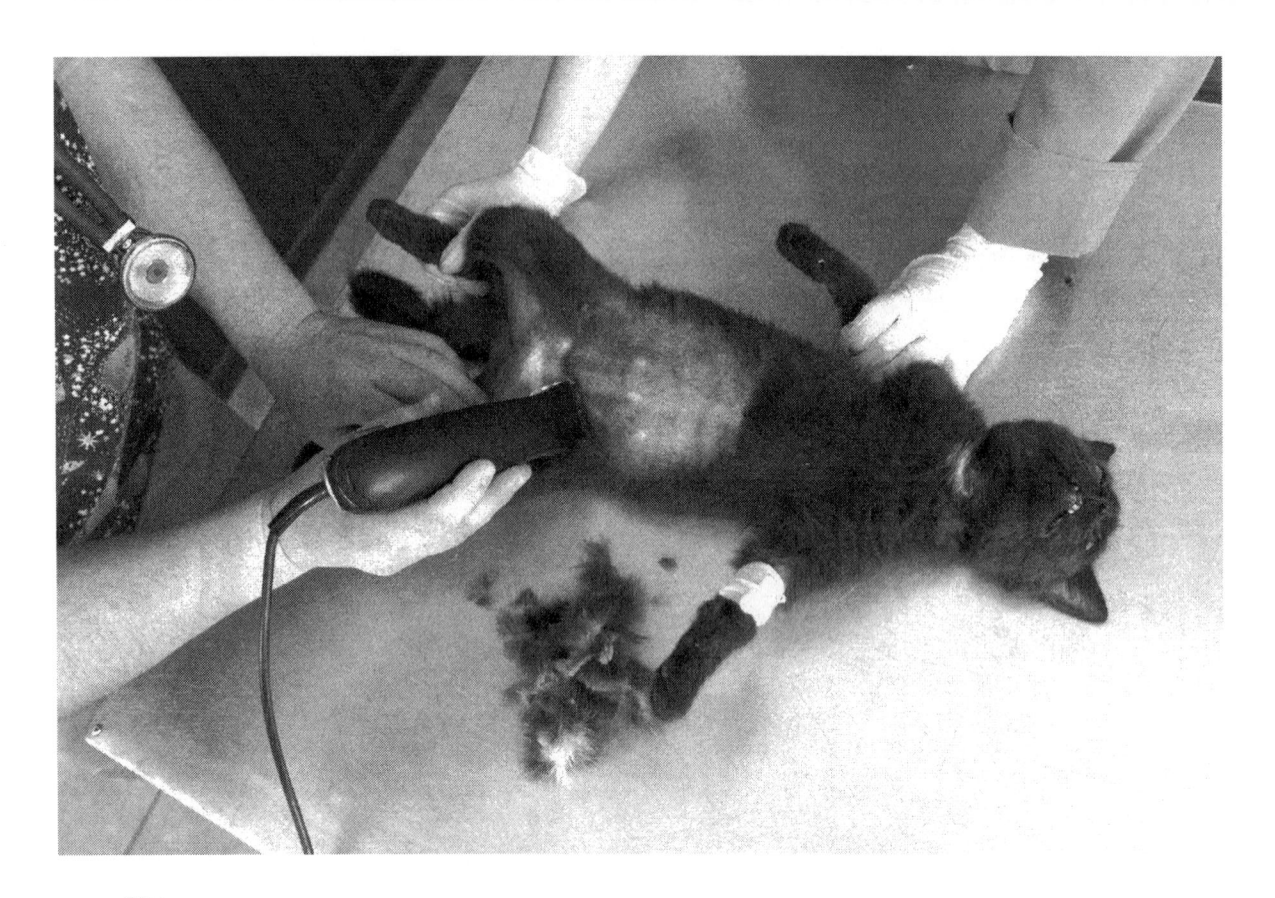

SPAYING Spaying is an ovariohysterectomy, a surgical procedure that removes the female cat's reproductive organs. Spaying prevents the births of unwanted kittens, eliminates or reduces the chances of health problems like pyometra and obnoxious heat behavior. Sexually intact female cats have seven times greater risk of mammary cancer than those that are spayed.

Cats should be spayed before reaching sexual maturity in order to reap the greatest health and behavior rewards. Individual cats and breeds mature at different rates, and even the time of year influences the timing, but many cats are able to reproduce by the age of six months or even younger.

Early age spaying and castration (neutering), more properly called prepubertal gonadectomy, is defined as surgical sterilization of sexually immature animals 6 to 14 weeks of age. The American Association of Feline Practitioners supports neutering early in life as a safe and effective method of decreasing cat overpopulation, and one which confers long-term medical and behavioral benefits to the individual cat.

Veterinarians prefer to perform the surgery when the cat is not in heat, because during estrus the reproductive organs engorge with blood, which slightly increases the risk of bleeding. But during breeding season it may be hard to avoid estrus, and postponement can result in unwanted kittens. If the cat is already bred, the procedure can still be done, but pregnancy slightly increases the cost and surgical risk. Surgery is also more complicated when the cat is nursing kittens. Consult with your veterinarian to determine the best schedule for your cat.

Surgery is performed while the cat is under general anesthesia. Most practitioners prefer for the cat to abstain from eating or drinking for a period prior to surgery to avoid the risk of inhaling vomit while asleep. Tell the veterinarian if Kitty eats something before the surgery, so that appropriate precautions can be made.

Both injectable and inhalant anesthetics may be used, alone or in combination, and many practices offer preanesthetic blood work that helps determine which anesthetic is best for the cat. Spaying a female cat is major abdominal surgery and is a longer procedure than castrating a male cat. Inhalant anesthetics are usually used. Gas anesthesia is administered either through a mask that fits over the cat's face, or through an endotracheal tube inserted into the cat's mouth and down the throat and into the lungs. The dosage for an inhalant anesthetic can be adjusted during surgery, so the cat awakens quickly after the anesthesia is stopped.

The sleeping cat is positioned on her back, usually on a towel or heating pad to keep her warm during the surgery. For the sterile procedure, the sleeping cat's stomach is shaved and then disinfected with antiseptic soap solutions. Depending on the individual case, respiratory and cardiac monitors or even EKG machines may be used.

A small slit in a sterile drape is positioned over the cat's tummy. The surgery is performed through this opening in the drape, which helps keep the surgery field sterile.

An inch-long incision is made in the skin of the cat's shaved abdomen, usually just below the belly button and along the midline. A surgical knife called a scalpel first cuts through surface skin, then a thin layer of fat, and finally through the abdominal wall. Special instruments hold the incision open so the surgeon can see into the cat's abdomen.

The cat's uterus is shaped like a "Y" with an ovary attached to the top of each "horn." An ovarian artery, vein and nerve are attached to each ovary. The spay hook, a long smooth metal instrument, is inserted into the abdomen to retrieve the uterus.

Each ovary is secured with stainless steel hemo-clips or an absorbable suture material to prevent bleeding, then is cut free in turn. The stumps containing the artery, vein and nerve fall back into the abdomen.

Next the uterus is ligated, or tied off, just ahead of the cervix, then cut free just beyond the tie. The uterus and ovaries are discarded. Once the surgeon inspects the area to ensure there is no bleeding, the uterine stump is allowed to fall back into the abdomen.

The incision is stitched closed in three layers. Internal stitches are often absorbable material the cat's body eventually dissolves, or they may be metal suture material or even staples. The last layer, the surface skin, is stitched using tiny individual loops that are separately knotted. A routine spay is completed in about 15 to 25 minutes.

Recovery time varies depending on the anesthetic used. Cats are moved from the surgery table to a recovery area where they're kept warm and monitored as they wake up. The drugs may cause the cat to appear a bit drunk for a time. Sometimes, the cat is kept overnight while other times the cat is up and ready to go home within a few hours.

Most cats don't bother their stitches, but you should monitor the area to be sure your cat isn't the exception. Try to keep the kitty calisthenics to a minimum for a couple of days following the procedure. Stitches are removed in a week to ten days following the surgery, and outdoor cats should remain inside until after the stitches are out.

Complications are rare, and usually a bit of inflammation at the incision site is the worst that happens. Bleeding or swelling of the incision line, loss of appetite for more than 24 hours, or prolonged listlessness should be addressed by the veterinarian.

SPRAYING see MARKING.

STEATITIS see YELLOW FAT DISEASE.

STOMATITIS Stomatitis is an inflammation and/or infection of the mouth. The condition can lead to dental problems. Stomatitis is often associated with infections of feline infectious peritonitis (FIP) (see PERIODONTAL DISEASE).

STRAY A stray is a once-owned cat separated from his home that must fend for himself. Stray cats exhibit a wide range of behaviors. Those treated well by owners in the past often seek human companionship. When there is a history of mistreatment or if the cat is injured, ill or emotionally traumatized, extreme shyness is usually the norm.

Cats become strays when they are somehow parted from their owners. Perhaps an indoor cat accidentally slips outside, and is chased far from home by a dog. Other times, an outdoor cat may learn he's fed by several homeowners when he wanders his rural territory making his "rounds." Because cats are strongly attuned to place and territory, when owners move to a new home, the cat may attempt to return to his old stomping grounds and become lost (see NAVIGATION).

Strays are even more tragically created when an unwanted cat is simply abandoned to make his own way. Most stray cats are adult cats, primarily because the "cute" factor of kittens tend to make them more desirable as pets. Therefore, kittens are generally more closely watched and prevented from straying. And, if they are abandoned to the street, a kitten rarely survives long enough to become an established stray.

Adult cats that have lived a sheltered life may not survive for long on their own; they tend to have an even shorter lifespan on the street than the feral cats. Strays are at high risk for disease and injury from other animals and lethal encounters with traffic.

CAT FACTS

Stray cats can and do make excellent pets. However, those that experienced mistreatment at human hands will not react in the same way as cats that have had strong positive relationships with previous owners. They may exhibit aggression, aloofness, or even fearful behavior.

If you already have pets, the resident animals' health and feelings must be addressed by providing safe quarantine and proper introductions. Strays that are ill or injured will need special veterinary attention.

When presented with a furry stepchild hiding in the back yard, before anything else try to establish if the cat is a former pet or a wild feline. Feral animals require special handling (see FERAL).

Friendly strays that beg for your attention are obviously the easiest to help, but remember that you don't really know this cat, so protect yourself. Wear long sleeves and padded gloves when handling any strange cat, and use a pet carrier to temporarily contain friendly ones to transport them to the veterinarian for a health evaluation.

Before catching the cat, decide your course of action once he's contained. Your options include relinquishing him to a shelter, temporarily holding him until you find his old owner or a new one, or adopting the cat yourself.

Shelters are warehouses for unwanted pets, and they strive to help animals the best way they can. When the stray is wearing identification, the animal will be held until every effort to find the owner is exhausted. Cats without identification are kept only a day or two, and if not adopted, they are put to sleep. Four cats in five meet this fate and are euthanized. It's sad to say, but a quick end to the suffering is infinitely preferable to a prolonged death on the street.

The other options mean taking responsibility for the stray's life yourself, and require you to bring the cat into your home (see QUARANTINE). Before you take this step, the cat requires a veterinary examination.

A recently lost pet is usually friendly and healthy. Tags on the collar, tattoos, microchip technology or other identification techniques help reunite pets with their lost owners, but it can take time and diligence to be successful.

To find a new owner for the stray, advertise the cat's availability, sing his praises; describe his looks and affectionate nature, and include he's a healthy neutered animal. Ask friends for names of people who may want a cat.

Don't give the cat to just anyone. After rescuing Kitty, you want a responsible, loving home for your adoptee, so don't hesitate to ask questions. Chances are you will fall in love with the stray before a new owner can be found, and will decide to keep the cat yourself.

FINDING LOST CATS or STRAY'S OWNER

- **Monitor** local lost-and-found advertisements for not less than a month
- **Contact** area shelters and give them a description of the cat; provide shelters a photo of the cat
- **Distribute** posters about the cat around the neighborhood (with or without photo)
- **Check** veterinary offices, pet stores, the post office, and community bulletin boards for "lost" notices; leave a "found" notice on each

STRESS

Stress refers to an emotional condition that results in physical or mental tension which impacts the health of the cat. The most common causes of stress in cats is other cats, and a change in the environment.

Moving to a new home, introduction of a new family member like a pet, baby or spouse, or conversely, the loss of a close family member, often result in stress. Cats in overcrowded conditions or with compromised health are subject to stress-related behaviors. Even a change in an owner's work schedule, a stray cat in the neighborhood, changing the carpet, or switching brands of cat food or litter may cause stress to some cats.

Some stress is good for cats and helps them learn to cope with changes in their routine. For instance, offering cats puzzle toys filled with food offers a challenge that engages the brain and gives cats confidence they can solve frustrating situations. Too much stress, though, impacts both the emotional and physical health of the cat.

One of the most common manifestations of stress is an increase in territorial marking and inappropriate elimination. Cats may become more demanding of attention, exhibit extremes of rubbing against owners and objects, and spray urine on and/or scratch objects to emphasize territorial boundaries. Sometimes stress will result in aggressive behaviors toward other pets or the owner (see MARKING, SOILING and AGGRESSION).

Insecure cats may react to stress by withdrawing. The affectionate cat suddenly ignores the owner, snubbing overtures almost like a spiteful person refusing to speak to the offending party. Other times, the cat simply hides (see FEAR) or becomes destructive.

The best way to address stress in cats is to remove the cause, if it can be identified. In addition, play therapy may help cats by giving aggressive cats an outlet and building the shy cat's self-confidence. Interactive games are best, such as fishing pole style toys. A great deal of gentle enticement may be necessary to engage the withdrawn cat into a game, so be patient.

450
CAT FACTS

A small percentage of cats try to relieve their stress by licking themselves excessively. Over grooming behaviors are seen most often in the Siamese, Burmese, Himalayan and Abyssinian breeds (see HAIR LOSS).

STROKE

SYMPTOMS: Seizure; depression; circling; dizziness; incoordination; any kind of behavior change.
HOME CARE: Provide nursing care
VET CARE: None
PREVENTION: Prevent parasites like cuterebra

STROKE Common causes of human strokes are smoking, primary high blood pressure, and atherosclerosis—deposits of cholesterol-rich plaques within the arteries. Strokes are not nearly as common in cats because they don't have those diseases.

A cerebral vascular accident—called a "stroke" in humans—is a disorder of the blood vessels in the brain that results from interference with the blood supply. Signs may include any one or combination of a seizure, depression, circling and/or dizziness, incoordination, or any kind of behavior change.

There is a specific syndrome called feline ischemic encephalopathy, and in most cases a cause can't be determined. But sometimes it's due to a parasite when it migrates into the cat's brain by mistake (see CUTEREBRA). More commonly, infectious diseases and endocarditis, an inflammation of the heart tissue, bring about strokes in cats. But by far, the major culprit in feline strokes is high blood pressure caused by kidney failure or heart disease. They may go blind, or have bleeding inside the eye.

Diagnosis can be difficult. Imaging diagnostics like MRIs reveal the vascular structure of the cat's brain. Cats get plaque development from thyroid changes, and blood clots from endocrine diseases, and quite a few cats get vascular accidents.

Even with an MRI, the changes caused by the brain damage may be hard to see, because if the stroke is big enough to see in the brain stem, the animal is probably not alive. A very small stroke is going to do a lot of damage. However, strokes that occur in the forebrain are easier to see on the MRI. Cats can suffer fairly good size strokes in the forebrain and survive.

Not much can be done once the injury has occurred. By the time the veterinarian sees the cat, the consequences are probably as bad as they'll get. Treatment aims at discovering the cause—high blood pressure, for instance—and treating that.

Your veterinarian may recommend PEMF therapy, which stimulate the electrical and chemical processes in the tissues to relieve inflammation and pain. Some cats recovering from strokes have benefited from this therapy. Devices may be designed for whole body treatment or targeted areas of the body. Some of these devices have successfully completed efficacy studies and are FDA-approved. Therapeutic products may be available in mats, wraps or other devices from your veterinarian or over the counter (see PULSED ELECTROMAGNETIC FIELD).

Cats often seem severely affected but then begin to slowly improve and recover more quickly and easily from strokes than people do. Cats usually suffer strokes in the forebrain, but they rely on their brain stem for their strength and function. Affected cats usually suffer only a few subtle deficits and won't be paralyzed on one side like the human.

The brain doesn't really feel pain the way that the rest of the body does. So a stroke isn't painful or progressive, and can resolve over time. Cats are very good at compensating for a weak leg, for example, and don't worry about needing to drive a car or that people might look at them funny if they wobble a bit. They're much more able to function and deal with their disabilities and adjust.

STUD TAIL Also referred to as tail gland hyperplasia, stud tail is a relatively uncommon condition affecting skin glands in the cat's tail. It's most common in sexually active Persian, Siamese and Rex male cats, or "stud" animals, but can affect intact or neutered male or female cats as well.

A group of modified sebaceous glands found along the top of the tail base where it joins the body are collectively called the preen gland, or supracaudal organ. These glands produce a semi-fluid substance called sebum that is composed of fat and other components. Sebum covers the hair coat to give the fur a protective luster. When these glands in the tail overproduce sebum, stud tail is the result.

Signs include blackheads in the skin and a waxy black to yellowish debris at the base of the tail that clutters the fur. The hair looks greasy and may become matted and fall out. Occasionally, a secondary infection of the hair follicles causes painful itching.

STUD TAIL

SYMPTOMS: Tail has blackheads and/or waxy debris; oily fur; hair loss; sometimes itchy
HOME CARE: Wash tail; apply benzoyl peroxide ointments
VET CARE: Antibiotics may be required
PREVENTION: Keep area clean; rub in corn starch or baby powder to dry oil

Treatment is simply keeping the area clean. A tar and sulfa shampoo formulated for cats is appropriate, but a non-medicated grooming shampoo may work as well.

Wash the area twice a day. Simply drape the cat's tail into the sink—you don't have to get the whole cat wet—but be sure to thoroughly rinse all the soap out. In between, rub baby powder or corn starch into the affected fur to absorb the oily material.

Some veterinarians recommend judicial use of benzoyl peroxide-containing ointments to dry the area. Avoid anything stronger than a five percent solution. If the area is very red or appears infected, or the area is itchy, see the veterinarian for appropriate treatment.

SUNBURN Sunburn, or solar dermatitis, is an inflammation of the skin that results from overexposure to the sun. Cats are intrepid sunbathers, but thinly furred and light colored cats are at risk for painful burns, just like fair skinned owners. Pets living in particularly sunny regions, or in the mountains at higher elevations tend to burn more quickly.

White cats with blue eyes, and those with white faces and ears are at highest risk because of their lack of protective pigment in the hair and skin. The tips of the ears, nose, eyelids and lips are commonly affected.

455

Initial signs are redness that progress to hair loss, crustiness and itching, and even curling of the edges of the ears. Typically, the problem goes away as the weather turns cooler, then returns once again during the hot summer months. Not only is sunburn uncomfortable for the cat, it can also lead to disfiguring loss of the ear tips, or dangerous sun-induce tumors (see CANCER).

Prevent sunburn by keeping the cat inside. If the cat must go out, avoid the most dangerous hours of the day from ten a.m. to four p.m. Topical sunscreens containing PABA and a high sun protector factor (SPF) of 15 or higher should be applied before sun exposure. Pet or play with the cat until the lotion is completely absorbed to keep him from licking it off.

To treat the burn, veterinarians may prescribe steroid creams or pills to control the inflammation. A cool, damp cloth or a moisturizing cream containing aloe vera or jojoba applied two or three time a day will help cool the burn.

If you have an aloe vera plant, break off one of the leaves and squeeze it near the broken end. The thick, translucent gel that emerges can be spread on the sunburn to ease the pain and speed healing. Vitamin E oil applied to sunburn can help the injury heal and prevent scarring. Witch hazel is an herbal extract that evaporates as quickly as rubbing alcohol but doesn't sting, so will cool the burn very effectively. Apply witch hazel with a cotton ball two or three times a day.

SUNBURN

SYMPTOMS: Redness or crusting of ear tips or nose; or curling of ear tips; hair loss; itchiness

HOME CARE: Apply cool, damp cloth; mist burns with water; apply moisturizing cream

HOLISTIC HELP: Herbal treatments; supplements

VET CARE: Amputation of damaged ears; topical steroids

PREVENTION: Keep cats inside during prime sunburn hours; draw the blinds; apply sunscreen with SPF 15 or higher

SWALLOWED OBJECTS Cats, like babies and young children, tend to put objects in their mouths. Anything that is small enough can be swallowed by the cat.

Whole toys or parts of toys, jewelry and coins are often swallowed. String type material is the most common culprit, and also causes the worst damage. String, thread with or without needles, yarn, fishing hooks and lines, and tinsel from Christmas trees hold particular risk for cats. Christmas trees are tempting to cats that are fascinated by the dangling, dancing ornaments. Breakable items, the hooks they are hung with, and even the needles from the tree cause problems when they are swallowed.

When the swallowed object is small enough, it may pass through the digestive system and be deposited in the litter box without causing the cat any problem. But objects, even tiny ones, can lodge in the intestinal tract, and cause severe complications for the cat.

The symptoms vary depending on the location of the blockage. Extreme caution must be used when investigating cases of swallowed objects, because the cat will be greatly distressed and may bite an inquisitive owner who tries to open his mouth. It can be even more dangerous for the cat when the owner tries to remove the object. Items like string should never be pulled, because often they are hooked to a needle or fishhook and attached to tissue further down the digestive tract. The veterinarian should evaluate and address the problem of swallowed objects.

Objects caught in the throat prompt a variety of signs, including pawing at the mouth when objects catch between the teeth or stick to the palate. Cats may also retch or gag, and possibly cough. An object caught in the stomach or intestines causes vomiting which may come and go for days or weeks if the blockage is not complete and food can pass around it.

If your cat can't breathe, she'll die within minutes. As long as you hear wheezing or noise from breathing, you have time to try and get rid of the obstruction. Use a cloth to grip and pull out her tongue, and use your fingers, tongs, tweezers, needle-nose pliers, or a hemostat to grip and pull out the object. Try once or twice—if you fail, attempt the Heimlich maneuver, and then seek immediate help.

To perform the Heimlich maneuver on your cat, hold her back against your stomach with her head up and feet hanging down. Fit your fist into the slight dip beneath her ribs, and pull in and up toward your belly and chin with a strong thrusting action. Repeat two or three times to see if it's dislodged the object. You can continue the maneuver while somebody else drives you both to the veterinary emergency room.

Complete blockage of the digestive track is also a medical emergency that results in sudden, constant vomiting. Cats refuse to eat, and any water they swallow is immediate thrown up. The stomach becomes bloated and painful.

Swallowed string is particularly deadly because of the way the intestines move. In up to half the cases of swallowed string, the end of the material wraps around the base of the cat's tongue while the rest goes down the throat. The body attempts to pass the string through the intestinal tract using muscle contractions called peristalsis that move through the entire length of the intestine to help push the contents through. But when the string is stopped at one end, the intestine "gathers" itself like fabric on a thread, resulting in a kind of accordion formation. This causes sudden severe vomiting and diarrhea, and rapid dehydration.

The veterinarian must determine exactly what to do in this circumstance. Pulling at the visible string can cut the intestines, which can kill the cat. Sometimes, cutting the thread from its anchor will allow the material to then be passed through the body without further problem. But other times, surgery is necessary to remove the obstruction.

SWALLOWED OBJECTS

SYMPTOMS: Pawing at mouth; choking or gagging; vomiting; diarrhea; bloated stomach
FIRST AID: Remove small objects caught in teeth or mouth; Heimlich maneuver; DON'T PULL STRING ITEMS or risk killing the cat
VET CARE: Diagnostic X-rays; surgery to remove object
PREVENTION: Supervise play with toys; keep swallowable objects out of cat's reach

Blockage that is ongoing may result in irreparable damage that can kill the cat. Sharp objects may slice or puncture, resulting in perforation of the bowel, and obstruction may interfere with blood flow to the organs and cause bowel tissue to die. Peritonitis is the end result in either case, and usually kills the cat.

Symptoms generally are diagnostic, particularly if the owner has seen the cat swallow the item. But X-rays are also required not only to definitively identify the object, but to determine the exact location and size of the blockage. Non-metal objects won't be visible on routine radiographs, though, in which case barium helps clear things up.

Barium is clearly visible in X-rays, and can provide a positive contrast that outlines the foreign object. Depending on the suspected location of the blockage, barium may be given to the cat either orally, or as an enema. Other times, an endoscope is able to locate and retrieve the object without surgery (see ENDOSCOPE).

Once the object is pinpointed, surgery clears the obstruction and repairs the damage, if possible. Most cats recover from these episodes as long as surgery is performed before peritonitis develops. When dead bowel syndrome is involved, the affected sections of tissue are removed and the living portions of bowel reattached; often, the cats so treated have a good prognosis.

Preventing swallowed objects should be done at all cost. It is up to the owner to choose cat-safe toys (remove tiny pieces) and to supervise during play. Anything a child would put in his mouth is fair game for cats. Feather and string-type toys should only be used as interactive toys; the cat should not be allowed to play with them unsupervised.

SWEAT GLANDS

Sweat glands are sac-like structures in the skin that open to the air, and secrete fluid. Cats have two kinds; the first type, called apocrine sweat glands, are found all over the body attached to most hair follicles, and aren't present in hairless areas. The largest are found in the cat's lips, face, scrotum, and upper surface of the tail. Apocrine sweat glands are coiled pockets that produce a milky scented fluid that's released into the hair follicle, and appear to influence sexual attraction.

The second type is the eccrine sweat glands, which are found only in the cat's foot pads. Eccrine glands appear to function the same as sweat glands in people. That is, high body temperatures, excitement or stress prompt a release of fluid on the foot pad surface which aids the cooling process by evaporation. That's why an excited or frightened cat may leave behind telltale damp kitty foot prints.

However, these eccrine glands are not nearly as efficient for cooling as are human sweat glands. Cats must rely on other means to cool themselves off (see GROOMING).

461

TAIL see COMMUNICATION.

TAPEWORMS Tapeworms (cestodes) are flat worms that look like ribbon or tape, and are the most common intestinal parasite affecting cats. There are several varieties, but *Dipylidium caninum* is seen most often in cats and dogs.

In order to infect a cat, the immature worm must spend developmental time inside an intermediary host. *D. caninum* is serviced by the flea. If the cat has fleas, statistically there is about a 45 percent chance Kitty will also have tapeworms. Consequently, outdoor cats are at highest risk for tapeworms, and the incidence closely parallels flea season.

Flea larvae eat tapeworm eggs found in the environment, and the larval worm develops as the flea itself matures. Cats are so clean, they often groom away and swallow nearly half of all the fleas that parasitize them. In fact, cat owners may be surprised to see tapeworms when they didn't realize Kitty had a flea problem. But swallowing even one infective flea is enough to give the cat tapeworms.

Young tapeworms attach themselves to the wall of the small intestine using hooks and suckers on the head end, called the scolex or holdfast. Tapeworms do not eat through mouthparts, and they have no digestive system. Instead, tapeworms absorb nutrients through their body surface. The body is made up of a chain of segments called proglottids that grow on the worm from the neck down. Adult worms continue to add segments as long as they live, and can reach two feet in length with hundreds of segments.

Both male and female reproductive organs are found in every segment, and when mature, eggs are produced. A single segment may contain up to 200 eggs. The proglottids furthest away from the head are most mature, and when fully "ripe" they break away and are passed in the cat's stool.

Proglottids can move independently, and they crawl about after leaving the cat's body. When they dry, segments look like grains of rice. Cats infested with tapeworms commonly have these segments stuck to the fur beneath their tail or surrounding the anal area. Owners may also see segments in the cat's stool in the litter box, or crawling about in the cat's favorite resting area. When dried segments rupture, they release eggs in packets into the cat's environment. The life cycle can be completed in two to four weeks.

Because egg-filled segments are passed sporadically, microscopic examination of the stool rarely diagnoses tapeworms. It's considered diagnostic to find the segments on the cat.

In most instances, tapeworms are more of a nasty nuisance than a medical problem. But left untreated, infestations can become massive and interfere with the cat's digestion and/or elimination. The worm's hook-like attachments can damage the intestinal wall. A large number of long worms may become suspended throughout the length of the intestinal tract, and in kittens this may cause blockage. Diarrhea with mucus and occasionally blood may be seen as a result of tapeworm infestation. Ongoing infestation can cause an unthrifty appearance, and reduced energy.

TAPEWORMS

SYMPTOMS: Rice-like debris; moving segments stuck to anal area or in cat's stool
HOME CARE: None
VET CARE: Anti-tapeworm medication
PREVENTION: Flea control

Although flea tapeworms are by far the most common kind, cats also contract other kinds of tapeworms by eating wild animals like mice or rabbits. In addition, there is a human health risk associated with two species of tapeworms, and cats may potentially carry disease to people if they eat the host animal. *Echinococcus granulosis* which has a sheep host is found in Utah, California, Arizona and New Mexico, and *Echinococcus multilocularis* which commonly affects foxes and rodents is found in Alaska, the Dakotas and surrounding North Central states. Both cause deadly cyst growths in the liver and lungs of infected people. The Centers for Disease Control recommend that pets living in these areas, particularly those with access to host animals, should be treated every month for tapeworms as a precaution.

Tapeworms are killed with a drug called Droncit (praziquantel), which can be given as a pill or injection. One dose is sufficient, unless the cat is under constant exposure for reinfection. Controlling fleas is the best way to prevent tapeworm infestation.

TARTAR see PERIODONTAL DISEASE.

TASTE see TONGUE.

TAURINE see CARDIOMYOPATHY and NUTRITION.

TEETH Teeth are bony growths on the jaw found inside the mouth used for capturing, killing and preparing food, and as tools for defense. Almost without exception, kittens are born without teeth, but by eight weeks of age, kittens will have 26 milk teeth referred to as deciduous teeth. By examining the teeth, you can tell the approximate age of a kitten.

The 12 incisors, six on the top and six across the bottom at the front of the mouth, are the first to appear at about two to three weeks of age. At four weeks, the dagger-like canines appear next to the incisors, one on each side, top and bottom. Between three to six weeks, the premolars grow behind the canines, three on the top and two on the bottom. The last deciduous premolar erupts by six to eight weeks of age. Kittens don't have molars.

Adult teeth replace the baby teeth beginning at about three to four months of age when permanent incisors appear. The roots of baby teeth are usually absorbed, so erupting adult teeth simply loosen and push out the baby teeth as they grow. The remaining permanent teeth make their appearance when the kitten is four to six months old. Permanent teeth replace baby ones tooth for tooth, and also add four molars, one on each side both top and bottom.

Molars are sharp, triangular teeth located on the side toward the rear of the cat's jaw, and are the "carnassial" teeth characteristic of meat eaters. They work like scissors to shear flesh and crush bone. A total of 30 adult teeth are present by seven months of age.

If the deciduous teeth fail to fall out, the cat may appear to have a double set of teeth. These extra baby teeth should be removed to allow room for the permanent ones to come in. Otherwise, the teeth can be pushed out of alignment and cause possible problems with eating or dental hygiene (see also PERIODONTAL DISEASE).

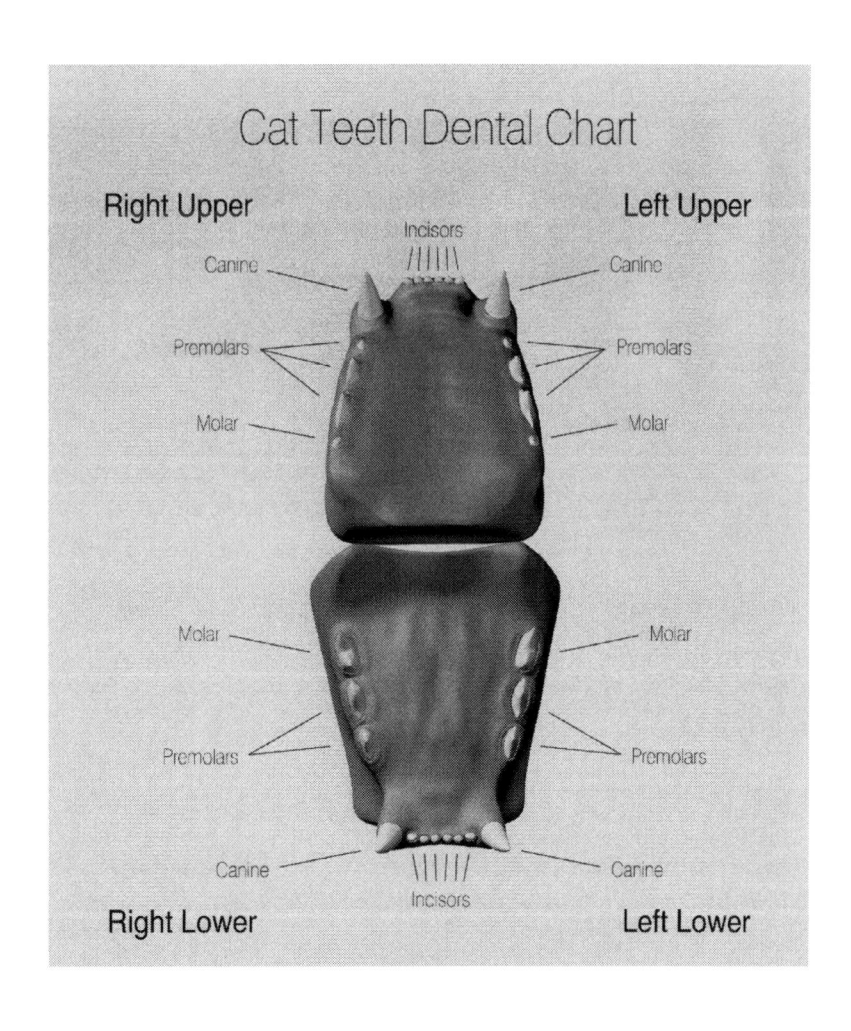

466
CAT FACTS

TEMPERAMENT see AGGRESSION, ALOOFNESS, FEAR and KITTEN

TEMPERATURE
Temperature is the measure of body warmth. An adult cat's normal body temperature ranges from 100 to 102.5 degrees Fahrenheit, while a newborn kitten's temperature may be considerably lower (see KITTENS). An abnormal temperature is an indication of illness.

Temperatures higher than normal are referred to as a fever, and can be a sign of infection related to a wide variety of illnesses, or of heatstroke (see HYPERTHERMIA). Those below normal can point to shock as a result of trauma, or loss of body heat from extreme cold (see HYPOTHERMIA). Treatment depends on the underlying cause.

A rectal thermometer, either digital or bulb, is used to measure the cat's temperature. Cats may need to be restrained to have their temperature taken, particularly if they're not feeling well. The key is to be gentle but firm.

Shake down the thermometer until it registers about 96 degrees, and lubricate the tip using baby oil, mineral oil or petroleum jelly. Kitty may either stand or recline on his side for the procedure, whichever is more comfortable for the cat.

With one hand, gently grasp his tail and lift, then insert the lubricated tip of the thermometer about an inch into the anus with your other hand. Hold the thermometer in place for at least three minutes, then remove and wipe clean, and read the cat's temperature. Thoroughly clean the thermometer after each use with alcohol or a comparable disinfectant.

TETANUS

SYMPTOMS: Muscle spasms, especially in face and jaw; rigid extension of rear legs; difficulty breathing
HOME CARE: None; emergency! See vet immediately
VET CARE: Tetanus antitoxin injection; antibiotics; fluid therapy; sedatives
PREVENTION: Remain vigilant to wounds and treat promptly; sometimes vaccination as recommended by vet

TETANUS Also referred to as "lockjaw," tetanus is caused by a bacterial neurotoxin. Almost all mammals are susceptible to tetanus but cats seem to have a natural resistance.

The bacterium is a common inhabitant of the soil. Also, many animals naturally harbor the bacteria in their intestines without it causing illness. In most cases, the infectious agent is introduced into tissue through a deep puncture wound.

Illness appears within two weeks. The bacterium grows best in low-oxygen locations, such as a sealed-over flesh wound (see ABSCESS). As the agent grows, it manufactures a toxin that affects the central nervous system. The animal dies in about 80 percent of cases.

Treatment includes tetanus antitoxin, antibiotics, fluid therapy to fight dehydration, and sedatives to control spasms. Recovery may take as long as six weeks. Prevent tetanus by reducing the opportunities for wounds. Keeping cats inside will virtually eliminated any chance for infection.

TICKS

Ticks are eight legged blood sucking skin parasites that are very common on dogs. They are found rather infrequently on cats that have healthy grooming habits and keep their fur and skin clean. These relatives of spiders are gray or brown with oval-shaped leathery or hard flat bodies that balloon with blood during feeding. There are a wide variety of ticks, ranging from pinhead size to as large as a lima bean when fully engorged.

Most ticks that affect cats spend 90 percent of their life cycle off the host. They usually have a three-host cycle, which means each stage of tick development feeds on a specific host. If the preferred host like a mouse or deer isn't available, ticks will feed upon anything that's available, including cats, dogs or people.

Tick eggs hatch into seed ticks, which are tiny six-legged larvae. The larvae crawl onto vegetation, and climb aboard animals as they pass by. Larvae feed for several days, then drop off and molt into eight-legged nymphs, which again seek an appropriate host. After another blood meal, nymphs drop off and molt into adults. Adults must again feed before mating, then they drop off the host, and females lay 1000 to 4000 eggs. The entire sequence may take as long as two years.

Ticks are a concern not only because their bites can develop into infected sores, but massive infections may result in anemia. Even more serious, ticks can carry and transmit a number of devastating illnesses that affect cats or even people.

The tick generally must feed for 12 to 24 hours before any organisms will be transmitted into the host; they don't tend to hop off one host then bite someone else. Although it's possible, people rarely get tick-borne diseases from their pets. You're much more likely to become infected by trimming the azaleas. However, removing ticks from your pet with your bare hands can, in some instances, expose you to infection.

TICKS

SYMPTOMS: Small bee bee to lima bean size bugs attached to skin on cat's head, neck, or between toes
HOME CARE: Wear gloves or use tweezers to remove ticks; treat wound
VET CARE: Same as home care
PREVENTION: Cat safe insecticides

Cytauxzoon felis is a protozoan parasite of the blood spread by ixodid ticks, and is considered a rare condition. It's currently most commonly found in the wooded areas of the southern United States. The natural host appears to be wild cats like bobcats and lynx, where it usually causes no problems. But in domestic cats, infection quickly causes a fatal disease. The organism attacks red blood cells. Signs include loss of appetite, depression, fever, labored breathing and dehydration or anemia. Diagnosis is made by examining a blood sample microscopically. More than 50 percent of cats die within a week of infection. Infected cats do not transmit the disease to people or to other cats (see CYTAUXZOON).

For people and dogs, Lyme disease is a blood borne illness caused by the bacteria *Borrelia burgdorferi*. It's transmitted by the tiny deer tick, *Ixodes scapularis* found most commonly in the north eastern, north central, and Pacific coast states. People and dogs are often affected with devastating signs, but cats rarely show signs of illness and experts can't agree whether cats can be infected or not. The most common sign in dogs is lameness. People typically suffer an initial red circular rash surrounding the tick bite, followed by a variety of signs including weakness, fatigue, chills, and arthritis-like joint pain. Left untreated, signs may disappear only to recur months to years later with ever worsening symptoms and possibly permanent damage.

Antibiotic therapy during early stages of the disease is usually quite effective in eliminating the organism.

Rocky Mountain spotted fever is an infectious disease caused by the microorganism Rickettsia rickettsii. It's transmitted by *Dermacentor andersoni,* the Rocky Mountain wood tick, and by *Dermacentor variabilis*, the American dog tick, both found throughout the western and northwestern United States and Canada. Cats don't get sick from this disease, but an infective tick hitchhiking on the cat could potentially expose the owner. Signs don't develop until several days after the bite. Early symptoms include fever up to 105 degrees, chills, headache, and muscle pain. About five days later, a spotted rash appears first on the backs of the hands, then spreads to cover the whole body. Early treatment with antibiotics is usually effective, but without treatment, the condition can be fatal.

Preventing ticks on your cats is the best away to avoid illness for you and your pets. Cats allowed outside are at the highest risk for ticks, and the best prevention is confining cats indoors.

Some flea preventative preparations are also effective against ticks; however, many designed to address ticks in dogs can be deadly for your cat, so be extremely careful using these preparations. Check with your veterinarian. If your cat is allowed outside, inspect him each time he comes inside and remove ticks before they have a chance to attach themselves and transmit disease.

Wear gloves to remove ticks from your pet. Ticks are usually found on the head, back of the neck or between the cat's toes where Kitty can't easily groom them away. If the head of the tick is buried, use tweezers to grasp the tick right at the skin level, and pull firmly straight out.

TOM

The term tom refers to male cats of breeding age (see REPRODUCTION). It more specifically may refer to intact male cats capable of producing kittens.

TONGUE

The tongue is a long, narrow, highly mobile organ rooted in the floor of the mouth. In cats, the tongue acts as a tool for grooming, eating and drinking, and contains the sensory organs responsible for taste.

Rows of horny, backward-hooked projections called papillae populate the center of the cat's tongue. These serve as rasps when licking food, a siphon to collect water, and as a comb when self-grooming. Newborn kittens only have a single row of papillae rimming the tongue which helps them grasp the nipple while nursing.

Taste buds are on the edges of the tongue and inside the mouth and lips. Cats detect sour in all areas, bitter at the back of the tongue, and salty only on the tip or front of the tongue. Cats can detect sweet, but unlike dogs, cats rarely respond to or seek out sweet tastes. When they do, sweet flavors can get them in trouble (see ANTIFREEZE and CHOCOLATE). Odors tend to be the determining factor in what Kitty likes to eat, but taste plays a role as well, particularly in differentiating meaty flavors (see EATING).

472 CAT FACTS

TOUCH Touch refers to contact with the skin, which contains a multitude of temperature and pressure sensitive nerve endings.

The skin is the largest organ in the body, and in cats is much thinner than in most other animals. The furless paw pads and nose leather are the most sensitive areas of the cat's body. Paw taps are typically used to test an object's relative safety (see SKIN).

The nose and muzzle area are particularly sensitive to temperature, and able to detect variations of only a degree or two. Newborn kittens use this ability to seek warmth, using their heat-seeking muzzles to find their mother or siblings.

Skin acts as a protective barrier that insulates the cat's body from extremes of temperature, prevents the escape of moisture, and the invasion of foreign agents like toxins or bacteria. The outer layer, called the epidermis, contains the pigment that screens the body from the harmful rays of the sun, and gives the cat his distinctive color. The second layer, called the dermis, contains the nerve tissues, sweat glands, and supports the hair follicles which generate the root of each hair.

Hair grows from the follicles, and each follicle is adjacent to a pressure-sensitive pad. Direct contact with the skin, therefore, is not necessary for the cat to detect touch; merely brushing the tips of the fur triggers a response. Whiskers are the most sensitive of all.

Touch not only protects the cat from injury, but is also a pleasurable sensation, and is one of the first things the cat experiences as a newborn when he is washed by his mother. Stroking parallels the sensation Kitty feels when groomed, and vice-versa. Touch provides an emotional link between the cat and other creatures, and may also be important in feline communication.

Cats crave warmth and are devoted sun worshipers. Cats can tolerate temperatures as high as 126 degrees Fahrenheit before feeling discomfort. This insensitivity to high temperatures may result in the cat's tail becoming singed or even burned before registering pain, particularly in cats that enjoy sleeping close to the fireplace.

TOXOPLASMOSIS

Toxoplasmosis is a disease caused by the single cell organism *Toxoplasma gondii,* a parasitic protozoan. Infection with toxoplasmosis in animals, including people, is quite common but disease caused by the parasite is considered relatively rare. Domestic and wild cats are the only animals in which toxoplasmosis can reproduce, and the chance of contracting toxoplasmosis from well-cared-for pet cats is extremely low. The most common source for people in the United States is undercooked or raw meat, especially pork.

Cats become infected either by swallowing the infective stage of the protozoan from the environment, by eating infected animals, or by eating raw meat. The protozoans multiply in the wall of the small intestine and produce egg-like oocysts. Infected cats are the only animals that pass on these immature forms of the organism; they are shed in the cat's stool.

Oocysts are passed in great numbers in the cat's feces for two to three weeks. However, once this stage is passed it's rare for the cat to ever again shed the eggs.

After two to five days, oocysts mature into infective forms of the organism. These organisms can survive in moist or shady soil or sand for many months. The disease is spread when an animal or a person swallows these infective organisms.

Once inside the bird, rodent, cat or person, the protozoan continues to mature, causing pockets of disease throughout the body. If the victim survives this stage of the illness, usually symptoms go away and the disease becomes dormant; the protozoan remains in certain muscle tissues and even the brain.

TOXOPLASMOSIS

SYMPTOMS: Transient lymph node enlargement
HOME CARE: None
VET CARE: Rarely needed
PREVENTION: Prevent cats from hunting; feed safe meat; keep litter box clean

Cats are diagnosed when a microscopic examination of their stool reveals oocysts, which means the cat is *at that time* capable of spreading disease. A blood test shows if the cat has ever been exposed. A positive test in an otherwise healthy cat means Kitty is actively immune, and is an unlikely source of disease.

Cats rarely show signs of the disease. The immune system of most cats interferes with the life cycle of the organism, so that toxoplasmosis in cats enters a dormant phase often for the remaining lifetime of the cat.

Healthy adult humans rarely get sick, either, even when infected. Toxoplasmosis may be found in any cell of any warm blooded animal. It's been estimated that half the people in the United States have been exposed, but never developed symptoms. Like cats, infected people may have brief signs and then their immune system sends the organism into a dormant stage. The most common sign is swollen lymph glands.

However, some cats' immune systems aren't able to stop the disease, particularly those infected with feline leukemia virus or other immune suppressing illnesses. In these cases, toxoplasmosis affects the lungs, eyes, lymph nodes and brain with symptoms of rapid breathing, loss of appetite, and lethargy. Often, pneumonia develops. Antibiotics are available to address the infection and help prevent the shedding of infective eggs.

The disease can cause life-threatening illness in immune suppressed people, too. In these cases the person is either unable to fight off initial infection, or dormant disease may reemerge. Toxoplasmosis also may severely damage or kill unborn babies if the mother first contracts the disease while she's pregnant; such mothers rarely show any symptoms themselves. A blood test can determine whether a person has ever been exposed to the disease. A positive test before pregnancy means exposure has already taken place, and the fetus will be protected against infection.

Common sense sanitation prevents the spread of the disease. Since several days are needed for the oocysts to become infective, simply cleaning the cat's litter box each day eliminates that route of infection. People in high risk groups, such as pregnant women or those with compromised immune systems should have someone else perform litter box duty.

The chance of contracting toxoplasmosis from a well-cared for pet cat is extremely low. To reduce risk even further, wash your hands after handling raw meat, and cook it thoroughly before eating. Don't feed your cat undercooked or raw foods, and prevent the cat from hunting. Wear gloves while working in the garden to prevent contracting the disease from the soil (see also ZOONOSIS).

TRAINING

Training is teaching. With cats, training most often refers to educating the cat to understand the differences between acceptable and unacceptable behavior.

Unlike dogs, cats rarely seem to enjoy learning simply to please their owner; they want to please themselves, too. Cats are highly intelligent animals, and most relish learning anything that piques their interest.

Physical punishment such as slapping or hitting with hands or objects has no place in training cats or any other animal. It won't work, and shouting isn't particularly effective either. Cats that are punished in this way may learn to hide the inappropriate behavior while continuing to practice it in private. The cat learns to associate hands with pain rather than petting; shy cats may become traumatized introverts and dominant cats may turn into aggressive attack animals.

Correcting (not punishing) inappropriate behavior, does have its place in cat training, but must be used judiciously. The most effective techniques either interrupt, distract or redirect the poor behavior, or makes the behavior unpleasant so Kitty stops on his own. Squirted water from a distance, clapping your hands, shaking a tin can with coins, hot tasting or foul smelling sprays judiciously applied to forbidden objects, or even a tossed toy all work as corrections when used appropriately.

Say "no" with a firm voice during corrections, and eventually the cat should learn to stop the behavior on the word alone. Some cats respond better to the owner hissing "SSSSST!" at them like another cat might do to show displeasure. Be aware, though, that dwelling too much on the negatives may teach the cat misbehavior is a great way to get your attention.

The best way to train a cat is through the use of positive reinforcement. That simply means rewarding the desired behavior. With dogs, verbal praise is often reward enough; cats tend to need a more tangible prize to motivate their interest, such as a tasty treat, or a special toy or game. Make the training session a game to engage your cat's interest and keep it.

Professionals who train cats for the movies often use a hand held clicker in conjunction with other incentives like tiny treats. The clicking sound reinforces the good behavior by signaling the cat he's done something right. Only click the clicker and give the treat or toy when the cat does what's expected. Soon, he'll associate the behavior with the reward.

Both negative and positive reinforcement only work when you catch the cat in the act. Pets aren't able to relate what happened 15 minutes ago with the reward or correction taking place this minute. Cats live in the here and now, and to get your message across, your reaction must be immediate. Don't give treats indiscriminately if that's what you're using for training rewards. Using interruptions of the behavior, followed by positive reinforcement, often works wonders.

Consistency is key. You can't be lenient one day and expect the cat to toe the line the next. That's confusing to the cat, and it's not fair to change the rules. (See also LITTER BOX and SCRATCHING).

TRAVELING

It is the rare cat that is not required to travel from home sometime during her life. All cats should make regular trips to the veterinarian. Some travel to a boarding facility or groomer, and show cats travel a great deal.

Cats should travel in the safety of a confined carrier, even for relatively short trips. Unless quite accustomed to the excitement, trips can upset digestion and tempers and result in messes or tantrums better handled in confined, easily cleaned spaces. Even a cat used to car rides may suddenly be startled by something out the window. This can potentially interfere with your driving and possibly cause an accident. Should a car accident happen, an unrestrained cat in the car becomes a furry projectile that may injure you, and most certainly will suffer severe trauma herself.

Commercial carriers, from elaborate to simple, are available for the comfort of the cat. The best cat carriers are large enough for your adult cat without being cramped. For quick trips, cardboard pet totes available from pet supply stores or the veterinarian's office are fine. Veterinarians (and cats) prefer top-loading carriers that open and fold down so the cat never feels forced into, or dragged out of the container. But if you'll be making a long trip or plan on several outings, invest in a more substantial carrier.

Hard plastic carriers must be airline approved if your cat is to be transported with the luggage. Only a few small animals at a time are allowed to be on airplanes as "carry on" luggage, so call ahead and reserve space if this is your intention. The sturdy airline carriers are usually box shaped with a grill opening in one side or the top. Canvas bags or duffle type carriers with zipper openings are also popular for cat transportation. When riding in the car, secure the carrier with a seat belt if possible. Situate carriers in back seats away from airbags, which can crush the carrier and injure the pet when deployed.

Traveling can be stressful for the cat that's not prepared. Plan trips ahead of time, and acclimate your cat to riding in the carrier. If possible, turn the cat carrier into a play area or even a bed for the cat, so a trip to the vet isn't the carrier's only association.

Toss a ping pong ball into a hard carrier, leaving the door wide open, and invite the cat to play. Put a favorite toy or blanket inside to make a snug nest. And take the cat for short car rides from kittenhood on, and make sure they don't all end up at the veterinarian's office. Then when you really need to get the cat into the carrier quickly, the mere sight of it won't make the cat run hissing from the room.

In some cases, your veterinarian may prescribe a tranquilizer for you to give to your cat (not to take yourself!) that will reduce Kitty's stress level during trips, and consequently your own.

TRICHOMONIASIS

Trichomoniasis is a disease caused by a type of protozoan called *Trichomonas foetus* (or by *Pentatrichomonas hominis*) that causes inflammation of the large bowel. Kittens are most commonly affected, but adult cats and some dogs may be affected.

The organism is quite fragile outside of the body, but can live for about 30 minutes outside the body, 60 minutes in water, and three times that long in cat urine or canned cat food. Much about the life cycle, transmission and parasite hosts (slugs have been implicated) remain unknown, but recent experimental infection of cats the *T. foetus* organisms were found in the feces beginning 15 days post-infection. It's probably spread to other pets that have access to the infected cat's litter box.

Some infected cats show no signs, but surveys indicate that up to one-third of all pedigreed cats are infected even if they do not show signs of illness. It's rarely tested for and may be implicated in many chronic diarrhea conditions (see INFLAMMATORY BOWEL DISEASE). The diarrhea may go away, only to return again months later.

Signs include an intermittent diarrhea and stools of cow pie consistency that may contain blood and mucus. Some cats continue to feel fine and have no other signs, but others become quite sore. The cat's anus can swell and become red, causing pain during defecation. In severe cases, the rectum may prolapse and protrude through the anus. The diagnosis can be tricky because the diarrheal symptoms can point to many other conditions. Also, the parasite looks very similar to giardia and may be misdiagnosed (see GIARDIA).

A standard fecal floatation only rarely finds the parasite. A fecal smear examined under the microscope can pinpoint the bug, and a fecal culture used to grow the parasite can confirm the diagnosis. The most accurate diagnoses is made using polymerase chain reaction test (PRC test) which is more sensitive and will show the presence of the genetic material that makes up the trichomonas organism.

Research has shown that most cats' diarrhea, colon inflammation and infection spontaneously resolves, but this can take up to two years. There is no approved treatment but several drugs appear to be effective against feline *T. foetus*.

TRICHOMONIASIS

SYMPTOMS: Intermittent diarrhea; cow pie soft stools with distinctive odor; diarrhea with blood and mucus; swelling and redness of the anus; pain in the anal area; prolapse rectum
HOME CARE: None
VET CARE: Specific drug therapy
PREVENTION: None

Ronidazole for 14 days is currently considered the treatment of choice, but causes reversible neurotoxicity in some cats with signs of lethargy, anorexia and neurological signs. Metronidazole and tinidazole have also been used in the past but are not as effective at clearing infections as with ronidazole. Resistance has also been reported to both metronidazole and ronidazole.

In research trials, a variety of home treatments often recommended for treating diarrhea such as slippery elm, pumpkin have not been consistently effective at impacting the diarrhea. However, cats do sometimes improve with careful dietary management. Keeping infected cats separated and providing different litter boxes can help control infection (see INFLAMMATORY BOWEL DISEASE).

TYLENOL see PAIN and POISON.

481

CAT FACTS

ULCER An ulcer is an open sore that is slow to heal and can result in tissue loss and sometimes infection. Cats may develop ulcers on their eyes as a result of injury, on the skin surface secondary to trauma or insect bites, or due to other problems like eosinophilic granuloma complex. Any slow to heal sore requires veterinary attention.

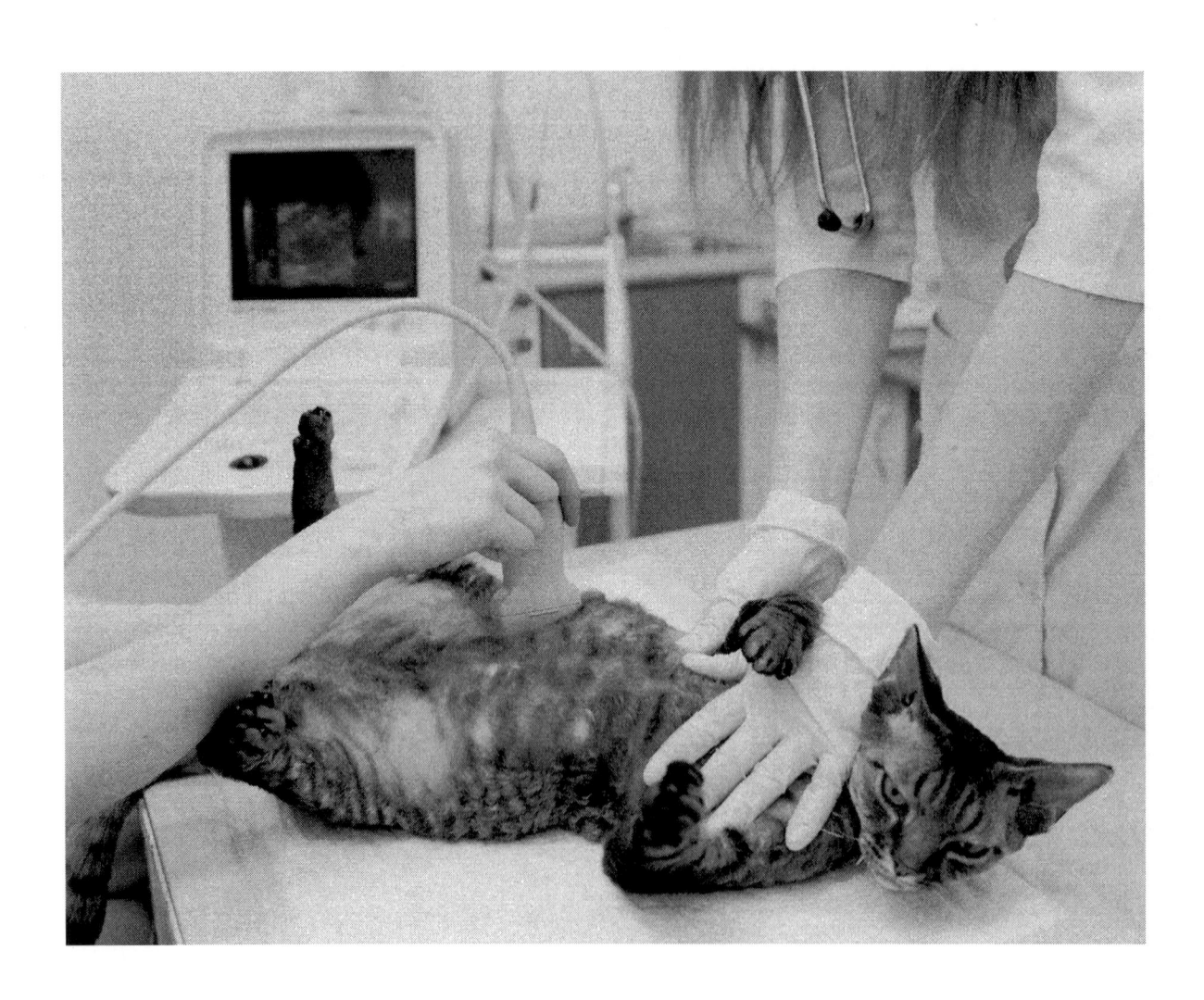

ULTRASOUND

An ultrasound is a diagnostic tool that uses high-frequency sound waves to penetrate body tissue. The waves pass through or over areas of varying density. The echo-reflection of these waves produces a two-dimensional image that offers the veterinarian an accurate picture of soft areas of the body not visible with X-rays.

M-mode (time motion) echocardiography, the oldest form of the procedure, was introduced to veterinary medicine in the late 1970s. It provides information about a very narrow target of tissue, and the two-dimensional echocardiography provides a wide overall view of the heart. It is ideal when assessing the relative size of the heart chambers and thickness of the cardiac walls.

Doppler echocardiography detects how blood flows throughout the heart. In echocardiography, sound waves are bounced off the heart muscle and surrounding tissues, the echoed signals are processed, and this information is then displayed in a visual or auditory format.

Ultrasound has largely replaced cardiac catheterization, which was used in the past. That procedure, which is very involved and invasive, requires anesthetizing the pet and placing catheters directly into the heart to inject dyes that show up on X-rays or angiocardiograms. Echocardiography gives veterinarians the capability to put a transducer on the chest, and look at cardiac anatomy and heart function noninvasively.

The technology, although expensive, has become more widely available. Nearly all veterinary cardiologists in the U.S. have fairly high- end level machines and do cardiac ultrasound.

UNTHRIFTY

The term "unthrifty" refers to a cat's general unhealthy appearance, and more specifically, to a poor coat condition. Rather than clean and shiny, and lying close to the body in soft layers, the fur of an unthrifty animal appears unkempt, and may be tangled or matted. Coat condition varies from dry and brittle to sticky, oily and greasy. An unthrifty appearance signals illness, because cats tend to neglect their own grooming when they don't feel well (see GROOMING).

UPPER RESPIRATORY INFECTION (URI)

Upper respiratory disease complex is caused by a variety of viral and bacterial agents, alone or in combination, resulting in illness similar to flu and colds in people. The cat's habit of being led by the nose makes him extremely susceptible to URI because along with interesting smells, cats also inhale viruses and bacteria.

The most common infectious respiratory diseases in cats are feline viral rhinotracheitis (FVR), also called the feline herpesvirus-1; feline calicivirus (FCV); and Chlamydia (also called feline pneumonitis), caused by a primitive bacteria called *Chlamydia psittaci.* Rhino and calicivirus cause up to 80 percent of all feline upper respiratory infections.

Disease is spread primarily through direct contact between cats. Infectious agents are in the sick cat's saliva, nasal, and eye discharges. Nose-to-nose greetings between cats, contact with contaminated cages, food bowls or litter boxes, and coughing or sneezing spread the infection. Virus can also be carried on human skin, and may be spread simply by petting one cat after another. Chlamydia and rhino agents don't survive long outside the cat, but calicivirus can survive one to two weeks at room temperature in the environment.

URI most often affects cats living in crowded conditions where the cats give it back and forth to each other. These infections are particularly devastating to cats with compromised immune systems suffering from feline leukemia virus or feline immunodeficiency virus. Some cats, though, may recover from URI yet continue to shed virus and infect other healthy cats. Stress may trigger a recurrence of disease in such cats.

In otherwise healthy adult cats, URI signs are often quite mild. Sneezing is the most common sign of rhino and calicivirus infections. Cats also typically develop a transient stuffy nose or watery eyes. Chlamydia infections occur less frequently, and signs include mild eye or nasal inflammation, and sometimes small, raised blisters may appear on the surface of the eye.

Other times, infections can become life-threatening, particularly in very young kittens or older cats. The symptoms are the same, just more severe. Plugged noses depress the cat's appetite, and fasting further debilitates the cat. Calicivirus can produce painful ulcers in the nose and mouth which also can make the cat refuse to eat food. Some kittens develop polyarthropathy/stomatitis as a result of calicivirus infection that causes arthritis in kittens.

URI

SYMPTOMS: Sneezing; stuffy nose or nasal discharge; runny eyes; mouth or eye ulcers; loss of appetite
HOME CARE: Nursing care including humidify air to help breathing, keep eyes and nose clean; nutritional support to keep cat eating
HOLISTIC HELP: Homeopathy; aromatherapy; herbal treatments
VET CARE: Supportive care; antibiotics
PREVENTION: Vaccination

Polyarthritis/stomatitis, also called "limping calicivirus," is a relatively common syndrome in young kittens believed to be an immune-mediated complication of the infection. Kittens usually have a transient fever and shifting leg lameness associated with pain on moving around, as well as mouth sores, and recover within three to four days. Soreness returns two weeks later (without the mouth lesions), and the veterinarian will be able to find immune-complex deposits in the joints. In many cases, this syndrome occurs in cats that have been vaccinated within the past month with caliciviral vaccines. Treatment for the joint soreness aims to relieve the discomfort with antibiotics and anti-inflammatory drugs (see PAIN).

Upper respiratory infections may progress into the lower respiratory tract and result in bronchial infection or even pneumonia. The overlap of symptoms makes it difficult to identify the specific disease a cat may be suffering, but unless the condition becomes chronic, identifying the specific virus or bacteria probably isn't important. When necessary, the agent can be identified with laboratory tests that include microscopic evaluations of mucus membrane tissue scrapings, blood tests, culture, and virus isolation techniques. Even then, a specific diagnosis may not be possible.

There is currently no effective systemic antiviral medication available. Cats suffering from URI are treated with supportive care that may include administering fluids, and therapy that softens nasal and eye discharge. If secondary infections are a problem, antibiotics may help relieve the signs and shorten the course of the infection. Tetracycline is helpful with Chlamydia infections, and medicated eye drops and ointments help soothe and heal painful corneal ulcers.

Simple nursing care the owner provides at home is the single most important therapy the cat receives. Nutrition must be maintained if the cat is to recover, and an owner nearly always is more successful in coaxing a reluctant eater at home. A food that's good to help reduce congestion is warm tomato juice, and many cats like it. Offering a couple of tablespoons of warm tomato juice each day may help boost the cat's appetite (see ANOREXIA).

Nasal and ocular secretions are sticky and can dry and crust, making the cat feel even worse and making breathing even more difficult. Cleaning the cat's nose and eyes is an important part of therapy. Use a soft cloth or cotton dampened with saline or warm water to gently soak crusts away.

A humidifier will also help the cat breathe. If you don't have a humidifier, simply run hot water in the shower or bathtub, and have the cat spend time in the steamy bathroom to ease congestion.

Holistic veterinarians suggest adding 10 pellets of Mecurius 30C to the humidifier water to help relieve the congestion. Or use the aromatherapy treatment called Immupower, a combination product that contains hyssop, mountain savory, cistus, camphor, frankincense, oregano, clove, cumin, and dorado azul. Dilute the oil 50/50 with pure vegetable oil, and rub a bit on the ear tip every four to six hours, to help your cat breathe more easily.

L-lysine is an amino acid that inhibits the synthesis of herpesviral proteins. Theoretically, this reduces the replication of the virus. A number of "lysine" products are available that may benefit cats suffering from chronic infection with herpesvirus.

Chronic infections of rhinotracheitis can actually invade and destroy tissue or bone within the nose, resulting in ever more frequent infections as well as compromising the cat's sense of smell. Even more rarely, these infections climb from the nose into the brain. Surgery that cleans out the infection may be an option in such extreme cases.

URI is more easily prevented than treated, and vaccinations are the best choice to avoid feline upper respiratory diseases. Be aware, though, that cats may be exposed to URI before they receive vaccinations, and become latent carriers. Also, because there are many strains of calicivirus, a vaccine that protects against one may have no effect on another; most vaccines include two or more strains for broader cross-protection (see VACCINATIONS).

In addition to a good vaccination program, reduce crowding to help prevent infection. Isolate new cats before introducing them to your pets to help prevent contagion (see QUARANTINE). And good ventilation may help reduce the incidence of aerosol infection caused by sneezing and coughing.

Because cats may appear healthy yet be carriers, some experts recommend that catteries wean kittens early at four to five weeks. This may help prevent a queen from transmitting the virus to her kittens during this critical period. The kittens are raised away from adults to break the line of transmission. However, this may negatively impact socialization, so consider all angles.

UVEITIS

Uveitis is an inflammation of the iris, which is the colored portion of the eye. It is a common condition in cats, and may affect only one or both eyes.

Signs of uveitis are striking. The eye color changes, and the surface of the eye roughens. This is a painful condition for the cat, and he typically squints and has watering eyes. The pupil may become quite small, and the inflammation results in a softening of the entire eyeball. Cats suffering from uveitis show sensitivity to light, and they may suffer from spasms in the eyelid. Loss of vision is also a symptom (see BLINDNESS).

The most common cause of uveitis is systemic disease such as feline leukemia virus, feline infectious peritonitis, feline immunodeficiency virus or toxoplasmosis. Injury to the eye may also result in iris inflammation.

UVEITIS

SYMPTOMS: Change of eye color; rough eye surface; squinting and watering eye; soft eyeball
HOME CARE: None
VET CARE: Treat cause if possible; steroids relieve inflammation; medication to relieve the pain
PREVENTION: Avoid exposure to feline leukemia virus, feline immunodeficiency virus or toxoplasmosis

488
CAT FACTS

Blood tests are done to determine whether the cause is infectious or not. The treatment addresses the inflammation, as well as the underlying cause. Steroids are often helpful for relieving the inflammation. Pills or injections, along with eye ointments and drops, are typically administered for two weeks. Eye drops that contain atropine help the pupil to dilate and relieve the pain. Veterinary supervision is required to treat uveitis.

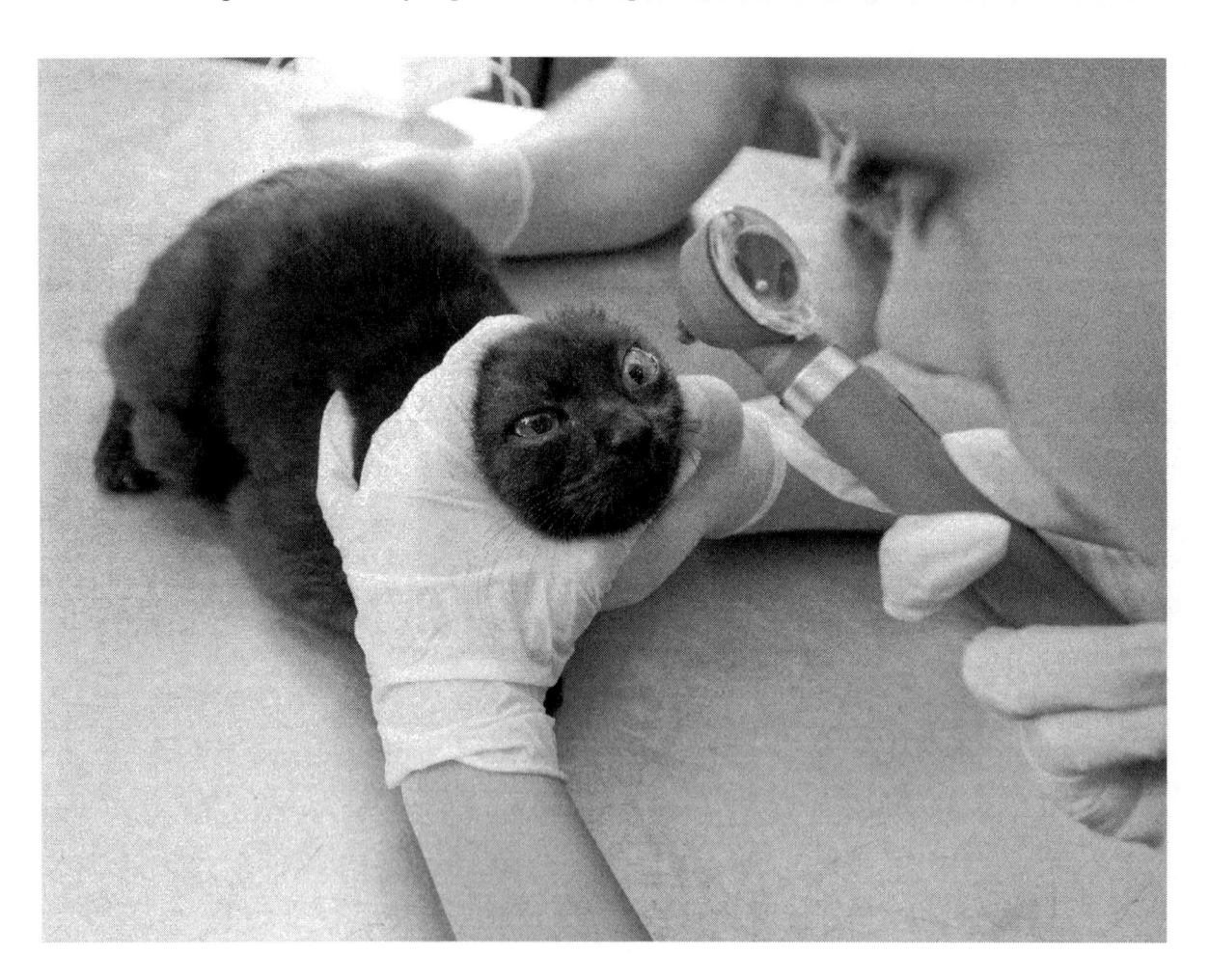

489

CAT FACTS

VACCINATIONS Vaccinations are medical treatments, often injections, designed to stimulate the immune system to mount a protective defense against disease. Vaccines literally program the cat's body to recognize disease-causing viruses and bacteria, and fight them off.

Vaccines stimulate immunity by exposing the cat to a non-disease-producing form of an infectious agent via injection or sometimes nose or eye drops. This causes the immune system to produce protective cells and antibodies. Acting like "smart bombs," these agents seek out and destroy dangerous pathogens hopefully before they are able to cause illness.

Kitten immunity isn't fully mature until they're at least eight weeks old—and every kitten is different, so it's hard to predict the timing. In addition, passive immunity received from nursing their mother's milk can neutralize vaccinations until the kitten is about 14 weeks old. For that reason, kittens (and never-before-vaccinated adult cats) receive a series of protective vaccinations over a period of time to better ensure the cat will be protected.

In the past, shots were given every single year as a matter of course, even though no studies had been conducted to show the duration of vaccination protection. Also, kittens and adult cats were often vaccinated against a wide range of illnesses, even when the risk for getting the disease was slim. The [2013 Feline Vaccine Advisory Panel Report from the American Association of Feline Practitioners (AAFP)](#) recommends that kittens and cats should be protected against those conditions for which they are at risk.

Generally, it is recommended that all cats receive protection with **core vaccinations**—that is, the most common and dangerous illnesses for which the kitten will likely have the greatest risk for exposure. Core vaccines include panleukopenia virus (FPV); feline herpesvirus-1 and feline calicivirus (FHV-1/FCV) collectively called upper respiratory infections, or URI. Oftentimes, these vaccinations are given in combination. The risk of your kitten getting deathly sick by skipping protective shots far outweighs the chance of a vaccine failure or problem reaction. All kittens need core vaccines to protect themselves—and you—from devastating illness.

Non-core vaccines are any other preventative shots that may benefit kittens and cats in specific risk categories for that particular disease. They may include vaccinations against rabies; Chlamydia and Bordetella, two respiratory agents; feline leukemia virus (FeLV); feline immunodeficiency virus (FIV); feline infectious peritonitis (FIP); and dermatophyte (ringworm) vaccines may fall into this category.

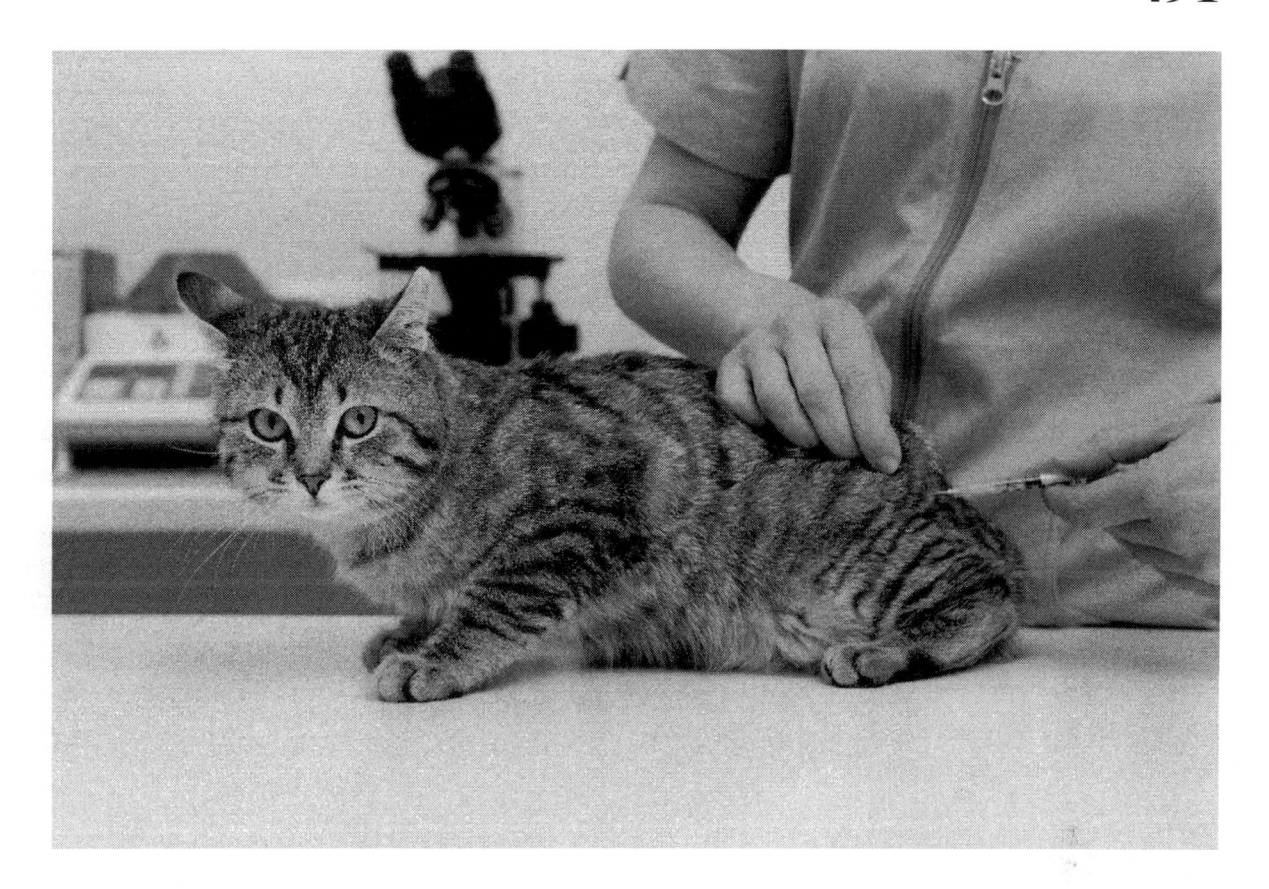

Because rabies is also a human health risk, vaccination of cats for rabies may be mandated by local and state laws. Bordetella might be indicated if kittens and cats are exposed in a shelter situation in which kennel cough has been diagnosed. FeLV and FIV vaccinations require tests that show your kitten is clear of these diseases before giving the vaccination. Kittens at low risk for FeLV and FIV—indoor, only-kitties never exposed to other cats—may not need this shot. However, FeLV is deadly and incurable, so discuss options with your veterinarian to offer the best protection for your situation.

Most kittens are inoculated with a series of protective shots as maternally derived antibodies (MDA) fade away. This protection last longer or shorter depending on the particular protective agent—for instance, MDA for herpes may only last until six to eight weeks, but for panleukopenia may last and interfere with protection for 14 to 15 weeks. Therefore, first vaccinations are typically given between six to nine weeks of age, with boosters repeated every three to four weeks until the kitten reaches about 16 weeks of age, to ensure the kitten has the best chance for protection. The exception is the rabies shot, which typically is given at 12 to 16 weeks for the first time, and then either yearly or every three years depending on local law.

Today, a number of veterinarians also recommend that after the initial vaccination series and first year booster, cats be re-vaccinated every three years rather than annually. Follow your own veterinarian's recommendation. She'll know best what will work for your individual situation. Vaccination reactions like lethargy or soreness are much more likely to occur when multiple shots are given at the same time. Ask your veterinarian about spreading the vaccinations out over several visits instead. Rather than the combination shot, for instance, separate inoculations with one or two at a time may be more appropriate.

Most vaccines are designed to prevent disease, but some will only reduce the severity of the illness but not keep Kitty from getting sick. The effectiveness of the shots depends on many things: age of the kitten, individual immune system, exposure risk, and other health problems. In the case of shelter adoptions and of back-door waifs, the kitten may look perfectly healthy but be incubating an illness he was exposed to before you found him. The stress of a visit to the veterinarian may prompt him to come down with something. It's rarely the shot that causes such a problem.

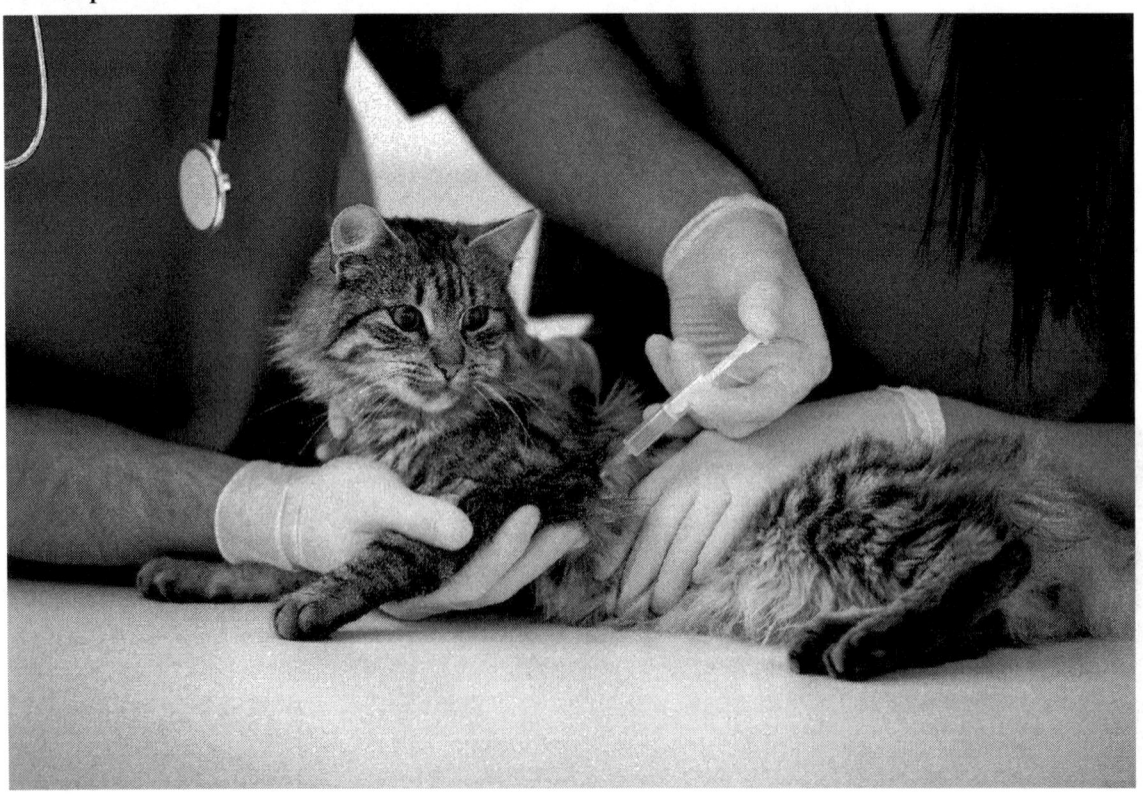

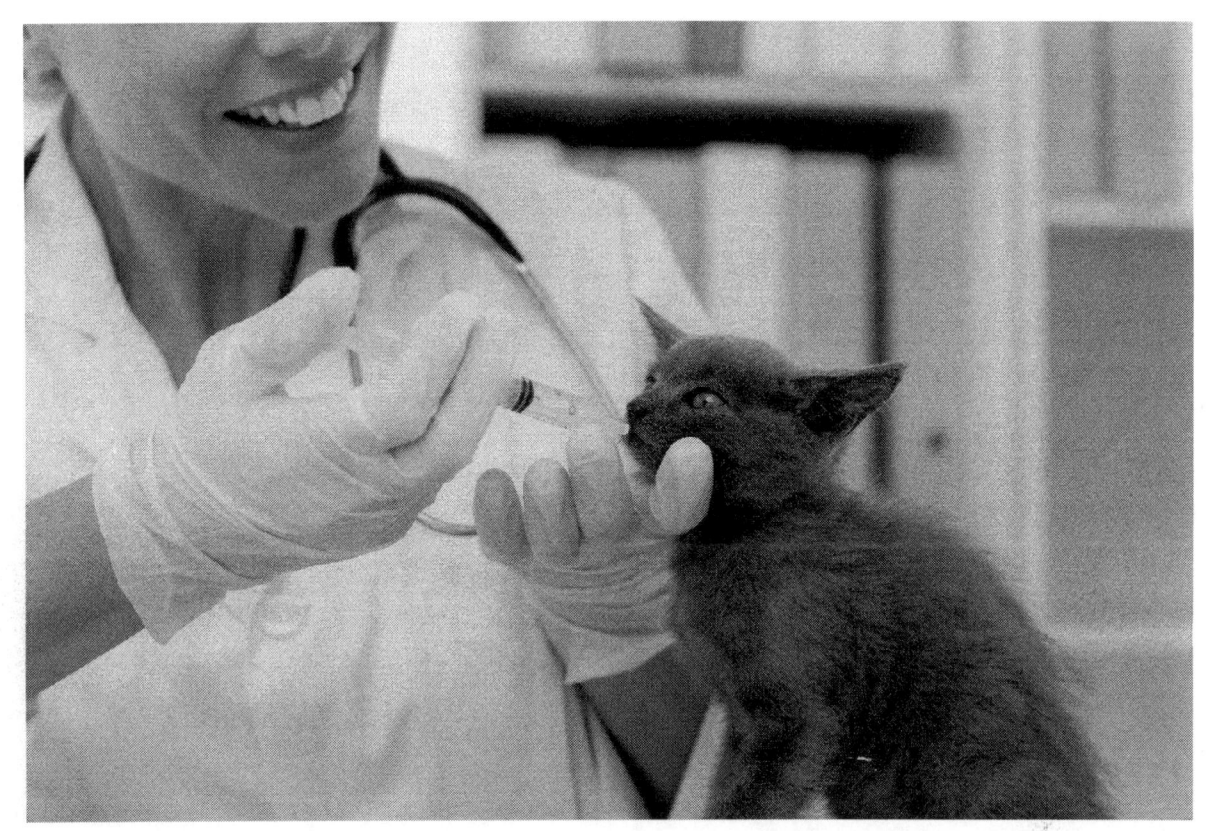

Most feline vaccinations are either modified live, or are "killed" vaccines. Vaccines can be modified so that their potential to cause disease is greatly reduced or eliminated, while retaining the ability to multiply inside the body the way a normal virus would. Because this more closely imitates a natural infection, the cat's immune system is better stimulated. Modified live vaccines also overcome maternal immunity more easily, and so provide a better and quicker protection for kittens than killed vaccines.

But with certain disease-causing agents like rabies and feline leukemia virus, it's not always possible to inactivate virus enough to ensure they won't cause the disease they are trying to prevent. Modified live vaccines may also cause problems in cats with suppressed immune systems, and can result in birth defects in unborn kittens when the vaccine is given to mother cats during pregnancy.

Killed vaccines offer a safer alternative. They are usually more expensive because they must also contain an additive called an adjuvant that stimulates the immune response. While a modified live vaccine may be effective after only one dose, a series of two vaccinations is generally required when using killed vaccines to ensure the best protection.

The most common type of vaccination reaction is moderate lethargy or a slight fever for 24 hours or so after the treatment. These signs generally clear up without treatment. Local reactions may include tenderness or swelling at the injection site, but this also usually fades away in a few days. Occasionally a cat will suffer an anaphylactic reaction (see ALLERGY) within ten to 15 minutes after the vaccination. Signs vary from relatively minor problems like facial swelling or hives, to severe breathing problems along with vomiting, diarrhea, and collapse. These are emergencies that require immediate veterinary help.

In rare cases, the swelling at the vaccination site develops into a tumor (see CANCER). If swelling persists for more than a week, see your veterinarian. Because of concern over injection-site tumors, today veterinarians keep track of what shot is given, and the body location of the injection. The standard procedure gives the panleukopenia and URI vaccinations on the cat's right shoulder; rabies as far down the right rear leg as possible; and FeLV as far down the left rear leg as possible. Some veterinarians now give the vaccinations in the cat's tail. That allows the affected area to be amputated should a tumor develop, without additional risk to the cat. Most of these tumors have been associated with the FeLV or rabies shots that contain adjuvants that help stimulate immune response, so pay particular attention to any bump or swelling after these vaccinations. Some veterinary studies indicate that the cat's tail works equally well as a vaccination site, and would also be advantageous if a tumor developed because the tumor could be effectively treated by amputating the tail—rather than a leg.

Immunity against viruses generally lasts longer than bacterial immunity, and some vaccinations like the modified live vaccine for panleukopenia provides virtually life-long protection. But killed vaccines don't protect nearly as long as modified live, and local immunity in the nose or eyes doesn't last as long as systemic protection that includes the whole body. In fact, some vaccinations offer protection for less than a year.

Studies are being conducted to determine the actual duration of vaccination protection and the optimum revaccination schedule. Titer tests (measuring the individual cat's blood for immunity levels) are also available and some veterinarians rely on titer tests to determine the frequency of vaccination. Rely on your local veterinarian's recommendation to best protect your cat. He or she has the most up to date medical information and best knows the disease incidence in your area, and your cat's individual situation.

VESTIBULAR SYNDROME

Middle age to senior cats sometimes suffer from sudden, unexplained balance problems referred to as vestibular syndrome. The pet commonly begins to suffer from dizzy behavior, head tilt, circling, and falling with difficult getting up. Oftentimes the pet's eyes will jerk back and forth from side to side. The head tilt, circling and falling will be in one direction, indicating which inner ear is affected. Usually the cat also vomits and/or refuses to eat, probably due to nausea from the associated signs.

VESTIBULAR SYNDROME

SYMPTOMS: Dizzy behavior; head tilt; circling; falling; eyes jerking; vomiting; anorexia
HOME CARE: None
VET CARE: Usually goes away without treatment
PREVENTION: None

There is no definitive diagnosis, and the signs may be confused with other conditions such as cancer, particularly since most victims are older, senior cats. The veterinarian makes the presumed diagnosed based on signs, and eliminating other causes, such as inner ear infection, which can be treated and result in resolution of the problems.

When neither an ear infection nor cancer is found, the condition is considered idiopathic (of no known cause). Unfortunately, there is no treatment for idiopathic vestibular syndrome. Most cases, however, gradually get better on their own over a period of a week to a month. The veterinarian may give your cat medications to abate the nausea and dizziness, or possibly fluids if the cat refuses to eat.

In most cases, the signs completely go away and never return. Other times, though, a few of the behaviors linger such as head tilt or circling. When the symptoms persist more than a month without abatement, the veterinarian may recommend further screening tests to look for a tumor.

VISION see EYES.

VITAMINS see NUTRITION.

VOCALIZATION see COMMUNICATION and PURRING

VOMERONASAL ORGAN see JACOBSON'S ORGANS

VOMITING
Vomiting refers to stomach contents being forcefully expelled up the throat and out of the mouth by strong muscle contractions. The process begins with salivation and repeated swallowing, and Kitty may seek attention during this time. Shortly thereafter, abrupt contractions of the stomach and abdomen begin, the cat extends his neck, opens his mouth and makes a strained gagging sound as the stomach empties. In certain

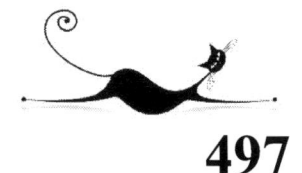

instances when the cat has eaten something he shouldn't, vomiting should be induced by the owner or veterinarian (see POISONING).

Gastric irritation is the most common cause of vomiting in cats. This is often due to swallowed hair resulting in hairballs, eating grass or too much food, or simply eating too fast. Cold canned food prompts some cats to regurgitate.

Vomiting differs from regurgitation, which is a passive process that doesn't involve strong muscle contractions. Regurgitation happens minutes to hours after eating, and the expelled material is undigested and may even be tube-shaped like the throat. Occasional regurgitation is quite common in cats, and probably isn't a cause for concern unless it interferes with nutrition. Chronic regurgitation typically is seen in a young cat that as a result grows very slowly. It can be caused by a birth defect that prevents the esophagus from properly coordinating the passage of food into the stomach.

Vomiting is probably not a cause for concern if it happens only once or twice and the cat acts normal before and after. Resting the digestive tract by withholding food and water for 12 hours or so will usually resolve the gastric irritation.

But when vomiting fails to bring up the anticipated hairball, is not associated with eating, and/or the cat acts like he feels bad before or after the event, vomiting may indicate serious illness. Vomiting can be one sign of panleukopenia, heartworms, swallowed objects, or liver or kidney disease. If there is blood in the vomit, if vomiting continues longer than 24 hours, or if other signs such as diarrhea accompany the vomiting, see your veterinarian.

498
CAT FACTS

499

500 CAT FACTS

WALKING DANDRUFF

Also called Cheyletiella dermatitis or "walking dandruff," this condition is caused by a mite called Cheyletiella yasguri. The mite lives on the surface of the skin, and causes a disorder that tends to be limited to scaling and crusting of the skin. This condition is more common in dogs and most commonly affects puppies.

The skin may be itchy or not, and occasionally the lymph nodes will also swell. It is contagious to other pets, and to people.

The mite is quite large and an infestation looks like white specks on the skin or fur; it can be seen with (sometimes without) the aid of a magnifying glass. The entire life cycle—egg, larva, nymph, adult—is completed on the host and takes about four to five weeks. However, adult female mites can survive for about two weeks off the host, increasing the risk of contagion to other victims.

WALKING DANDRUFF

SYMPTOMS: Scaling; crusty skin; dandrufflike flakes; itchy skin; swollen lymph nodes
HOME CARE: Flea treatment
VET CARE: Same as home care
PREVENTION: Routine flea prevention

Diagnosis is based on the signs, and by finding the mite during microscopic examination of skin debris. *Cheyletiella* mites are easily killed with flea treatments or lime sulfur dip, as recommended by your veterinarian. In fact, the condition is rarely a problem in areas where routine flea prevention is practiced. If your dog is diagnosed, you'll also need to treat the cats and all other pets in contact with a diagnosed animal, and environmental treatment is also recommended.

WEANING see KITTEN and REPRODUCTION

WHISKERS
Whiskers are a type of specialized hair referred to as vibrissae or sinus hairs that are found on the cat's muzzle, eyebrows, sometimes the cheeks and chin, and on the underside of the lower forelegs. Whiskers are very long and stiff, yet flexible, and serve a sensory function for the cat.

The hairs are seated deep in the skin, with the base of the hair surrounded by a forest of nerve endings. These nerves register the slightest vibration or contact with the hair. Whiskers are efficient antennae that detect everything from the measure of a narrow opening, to shifts in the wind and barometric pressure. Whiskers also protect the cat's eyes from injury, providing a startle reflex that shuts the eyes if anything touches them (see HAIR).

WOOL SUCKING

This behavior problem occurs most frequently in Siamese and Burmese cats, and is seen almost exclusively in adult cats. The cat chews cloth using the large molars at the side of his mouth. Loosely knitted or woven wool items are preferred, but other fabrics are also chewed when wool isn't available. Large holes can be made in sweaters, blankets or other items within minutes. The behavior is erratic and unpredictable.

WOOL SUCKING

SYMPTOMS: Chewing or sucking fabric, especially wool
HOME CARE: High fiber diet; feed greens or canned pumpkin
VET CARE: Same
PREVENTION: Put wool items out of reach; treat targets with cat repellent like bitter apple

Wool sucking or chewing is not due to a nutritional deficiency, but is believed to be related to eating. The behavior can be prompted by withholding food, and appears to abate when food or plants are made available. Experts believe wool sucking results from a craving for roughage or indigestible fiber.

A diet higher in fiber may help such cats. Try supplementing the diet with canned pumpkin, a leafy lettuce, crunchy green beans or another vegetable source. Many cats relish cat grass.

Some behaviorist recommend modifying the cat's behavior by treating a target item with something that smells or tastes bad to the cat. Commercial pet repellents are available, or use bitter apple. Keep tempting objects out of reach.

WORMS see PARASITES.

504
CAT FACTS

505

CAT FACTS

X-RAY

X-rays, also referred to as radiographs, are a type of invisible wave-like electromagnetic radiation similar to but shorter than visible light. This specialized radiation is able to penetrate with varying success the different structures of the body, and leaves a record on photographic film.

Radiation that is able to penetrate all the way through the body results in a negative image on the film. The more waves that pass through, the darker the image, while the fewer there are, the lighter the picture on the film.

Air allows the most penetration and these areas look black on the film. Fat is next, and is dark gray. Fluid or soft tissue will be recorded in varying degrees of medium to light gray. X-rays aren't able to penetrate extremely complex or dense portions of the body, like bones, which will appear white on the film.

X-rays are an important diagnostic tool in both human and veterinary medicine. They make it possible to see broken bones, bladder stones, or swallowed objects, and allow the doctor to identify many conditions without the invasiveness of exploratory surgery. This enables the patient to receive a diagnosis and treatment that otherwise might come too late.

The radiation level in diagnostic X-rays is carefully regulated so that it won't cause health problems. When used therapeutically as a treatment for cancer, the intensity of the radiation is increased and targeted to specific areas (see CANCER).

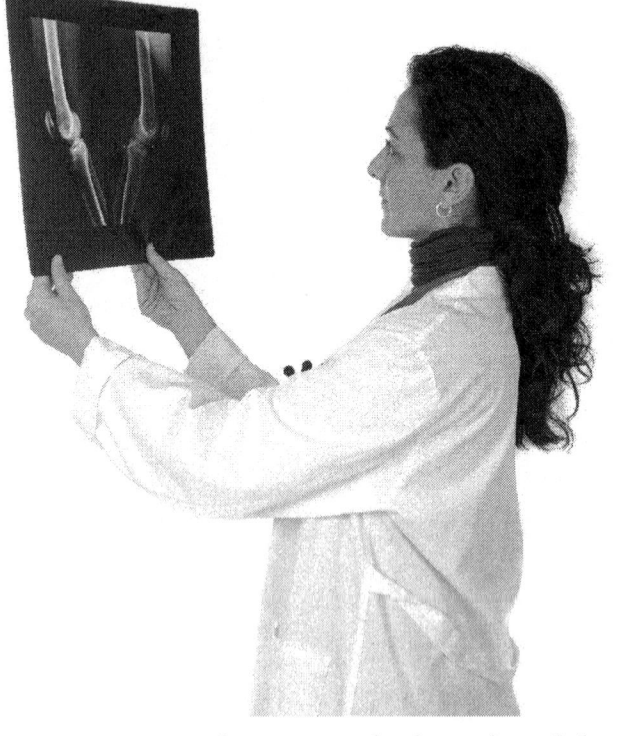

XYLITOL POISONING

SYMPTOMS: Vomiting; incoordination/drunk behavior; lethargy; seizures; collapse
FIRST AID: EMERGENCY! SEE VET IMMEDIATELY! If you witness the cat ingesting a product with xylitol, induce vomiting immediately and then see the vet.
VET CARE: Supportive care; fluid therapy; monitoring blood and enzyme values
PREVENTION: Keep xylitol-containing products out of cat's reach.

Xylitol Poisoning Xylitol is a naturally-occurring sugar alcohol used for sweetening in sugar-free products such chewing gum, candy, toothpaste and baked products. It also comes as a granulated powder. Both forms are highly toxic to cats. Xylitol ingestion causes a rapid release of insulin in the cat, which in turn results in a sudden decrease in blood glucose levels. Depending on the size of your cat, a single piece of sugar-free gum may cause symptoms that result in death.

Dogs are more susceptible than cats perhaps due to their sweet tooth, but it's assumed that cats may also be poisoned by ingestion of xylitol. The ingested substance may cause vomiting, incoordination, seizures, or even liver failure. Bleeding may develop in the cat's gastrointestinal track or abdomen, as well as dark red specks or splotches on his gums. Usually the symptoms happen quickly, within fifteen to thirty minutes of ingestion, but some kinds of sugar-free gum may not cause symptoms for up to twelve hours.

Diagnosis is based on blood screening tests and urinalysis, as well as coagulation and other tests to screen for bleeding disorders. By the time signs develop, it may be too late for vomiting to do any good. But if you see your cat eat something containing xylitol, induce vomiting immediately and then get to the vet.

CAT FACTS

The veterinary treatment consists of supportive care, which may include fluid therapy, and continued blood tests to monitor the progression of the poisoning for at least 24 hours. Cats suffering from low blood sugar alone tend to recover well. If the cat develops liver damage, the prognosis is guarded.

Protect your cat from xylitol poisoning by knowing the ingredients in your products, and keeping them out of reach. For kitty thieves that won't be deterred, be safe and keep xylitol products out of your house altogether.

509

CAT FACTS

YELLOW FAT DISEASE (STEATITIS) Steatitis means an inflammation of fat. In cats, it refers specifically to a condition in which fat is changed into hard, painful deposits beneath the skin.

No one is certain what causes the condition. It's thought to occur as a result of excessive dietary fish oil fatty acids without adequate amounts of preservatives like vitamin E.

Historically, cats that became sick with this condition were fed diets primarily consisting of tuna. The strong flavor of this diet is highly addictive to cats, and many refuse to eat anything else once exposed to the flavor. Tuna fish is already low in vitamin E, and problems in canning processes used in the past resulted in a further break down of this vitamin. The resulting tuna diets were extremely deficient in vitamin E, and cats that ate them exclusively developed yellow fat disease.

During the digestion of large amounts of unsaturated fatty acids, compounds called reactive peroxides are produced. This oxidation process destroys vitamin E. The body tries to make up the vitamin E deficit by substituting other fatty acids like arachidonic acid. But this throws the fatty acid ratio out of balance, and that can result in fat disposition. Consequently, enzymes in the body react with the fat in a process called saponification; the fat is turned into hard, soap-like deposits beneath the skin. Typically, these deposits range in color from a dirty white to a dark brownish mustard--which is how the condition came to be called yellow fat disease.

Steatitis is considered rare today, because the canning process has been improved, and because commercial cat food diets are much better. The condition is most often seen in pampered pets, typically young overweight cats with finicky eating habits. Changing a cat's diet regularly or offering highly palatable foods increases the odds of developing finicky feeding behaviors.

The first signs of vitamin E deficiency are a dull, greasy hair coat and flaky skin. The fat deposits are painful, and cats typically are reluctant to be touched. They flinch when petted, and walk stiffly or refuse to move at all. Eventually, the cat stops eating, even refusing tuna.

Fat deposits may appear anywhere on the body, but most often are located in the groin area. The skin feels lumpy or bumpy. Diagnosis is based on physical signs, and a history of the cat's diet. A microscopic examination of a sample of affected tissue shows inflammation or changes in the structure of the fat.

Treatment consists of feeding the cat a complete and balanced diet, along with vitamin E supplementation. Oftentimes, 100 IU of vitamin E twice daily resolves the condition within a few weeks. Steroid therapy may help to relieve inflammation and make the cat more comfortable during recovery. Fat deposits that become infected require antibiotic treatment, and surgical removal of severely infected tissue may be necessary.

It's much easier to prevent the problem from ever occurring simply by feeding an appropriate diet (see EATING, FOOD and NUTRITION).

YELLOW FAT DISEASE

SYMPTOMS: Dull greasy fur; flaky skin; painful skin; stiff gait or refusal to move; lumpy bumpy skin particularly in groin region

HOME CARE: Feed complete and balanced diet; eliminate fish especially tuna or tuna oil

VET CARE: High doses of vitamin E; steroids to reduce inflammation; antibiotics; sometimes surgical removal of infected areas

PREVENTION: Feed complete and balanced diet

512
CAT FACTS

513

CAT FACTS

ZOONOSIS A zoonosis is a disease that can be transmitted from an animal to a human under normal conditions. People are susceptible to a variety of viral and bacterial diseases, fungus, and parasitic disorders that more commonly afflict animals.

There are more than 200 known zoonoses, but only a handful are associated with pets. Most problems are transient and easily treated, and cases are relatively low. However, zoonoses should never be taken lightly because a small percentage can cause debilitating illness or even death.

Without exception, the most common zoonotic diseases associated with cats can be avoided. Basic hygiene and other common sense preventative measures will protect both you and your pet from illness (see CAT SCRATCH DISEASE, HOOKWORMS, TOXOPLASMOSIS, PLAGUE, RABIES, RINGWORM, TAPEWORMS, and TICKS).

CAT FACTS

APPENDIX A

CAT ASSOCIATIONS and BREEDS AT A GLANCE

A cat association is a national organization that registers cats, keeps records of their ancestry in pedigrees, publishes breed standards, sponsors cat shows, and determines who will judge them. Catteries are individual establishments that strive to produce the "ideal" cat of a given breed. These cats are then shown in contests sanctioned by the cat association in which that cat is registered. The goal is to determine which cat is closest to the breed standard of perfection.

Catteries often hold membership in local cat clubs, which in turn are members of one or more cat associations. There are a number of cat associations. Breed standards may vary from association to association, for not every cat association recognizes the same cat breeds. If you are interested in learning more about cat show opportunities for you and your cat, contact one or more of the following organizations.

America Association of Cat Enthusiasts (AACE)
http://www.aaceinc.org/

American Cat Association (ACA)
Ms Irene Gizzi
11482 Vanport Ave
Lake View Terr. CA 91342
818-896-6165
http://www.americancatassociation.com/

American Cat Fanciers' Association (ACFA)
P.O. Box 1949,
Nixa, MO 65714-1949
417-725-1530
http://www.acfacat.com/

Canadian Cat Association (CCA)

5045 Orbitor Drive
Building 12, Suite 102
Mississauga, ON L4W 4Y4
905-232-3481
http://www.cca-afc.com

Cat Fanciers' Association (CFA)
260 East Main Street
Alliance, OH 44601
330-680-4070
http://cfa.org/

Cat Fanciers' Federation (CFF)
CFFinc@live.com
937-787-9009
www.cffinc.org

Fédération Internationale Féline (FIFe)
http://fifeweb.org/wp/lnk/lnk_org.php

The International Cat Association (TICA)
PO Box 2684
Harlingen, Texas 78551
956-428-8046
www.tica.org

National Cat Fanciers' Association (NCFA)
10215 W. Mt. Morris Rd.
Flushing, MI 48433
810-659-9517

World Cat Federation (WCF)
http://www.wcf-online.de/WCF-EN/index.html

CAT FACTS

BREEDS AT A GLANCE Every cat is an individual and generalities may not apply to every feline a given breed—cats may be shy or good with kids due to socialization or circumstances apart from breed tendencies. And cats may never experience the listed health concerns or may develop others not mentioned.

BREEDS	BODY TYPE	COAT TYPE	COAT CARE	ATTITUDE	HEALTH CONCERNS
Abyssinian	semi-foreign	short	low	high activity, in-your-face, enjoys kids and other pets	anemia, kidney problems, over-grooming, cardiomyopathy, hyperesthesia syndrome
American Curl	semi-foreign	Medium-long	medium	average activity, curious, playful, enjoys kids and other pets	none mentioned
American Bobtail	domestic	Short to medium	low	loving, intelligent, devoted, extremely interactive	none mentioned
American Shorthair	domestic	short	low	average activity, athletic, affectionate, enjoys kids and other pets	none mentioned
American Wirehair	domestic	medium	low	average to low activity, quiet, retiring, prefers watching	immune system tends to develop late
Balinese	foreign	medium	low	high activity, talkative, protective, prefers people to pets	none mentioned
Bengal	semi-foreign	short	low	average to high activity, doglike, very trainable, enjoys kids and other pets	none mentioned
Birman	domestic	Medium to long	medium	low activity, quiet, enjoys kids and other pets	cataracts
Bombay	domestic	short	low	high activity, outgoing, enjoys kids and other pets	none mentioned
British Shorthair	domestic	short	low	low activity, calm, quiet, independent, can enjoy kids	rare blood type B, cranial deformities, cataracts
Burmese	cobby	short	low	high activity, in-your-face, demanding, prefers being only cat	cranial deformities, hyperesthesia syndrome, asthma, cardiomyopathy, wool sucking, overgrooming
Burmilla	cobby	Semi-longhair to short	low	sociable, playful, affectionate, kittenlike attitude	none mentioned
Chartreux	domestic	short	low	average activity, quiet, doglike, prefers dogs to other cats	none mentioned

Colorpoint Shorthair	foreign	short	low	high activity, talkative, devoted, good family pet	none mentioned
Cornish Rex	foreign	short	low	high activity, athletic, enjoys kids and other pets	may have type B blood, stud tail
Cymric	cobby	Medium-long	medium	average activity, affectionate, likes being center of attention	spinal problems, weak hips
Devon Rex	foreign	short	low	high activity, extreme energy, loves people	spasticity, stud tail, may have rare type B blood
Egyptian Mau	semi-foreign	short	low	high activity, quiet, affectionate, prefers being only cat	none mentioned
European Burmese	semi-foreign	short	low	Affectionate, intelligent, loyal, inquisitive, playful, enjoy lap sitting, likes other cats and dogs	none mentioned
Havana Brown	semi-foreign	sjprt	low	average activity, quiet, affectionate, enjoys kids and other pets	none mentioned
Himalayan	cobby	long	high	low activity, sweet, laid back, gets along with other cats	cataracts, over-grooming, hyperesthesia syndrome
Japanese Bobtail	semi-foreign	short	low	average activity, talkative, active, enjoys kids and other pets	none mentioned
Javanese	foreign	medium	low	high activity, extremely vocal, curious, wants to be in the middle of things	none mentioned
Korat	domestic	short	low	average activity, gentle, quiet, hates noise, devoted, prefers being only cat	none mentioned
La Perm	semi-foreign	Short to medium long	medium	gentle, affectionate, very active, but enjoy lap sitting	none mentioned
Maine Coon	domestic	long	medium	average activity, calm, loyal, enjoys kids and other pets	cardiomyopathy
Manx	cobby	short	low	average activity, calm, loves people, likes being center of attention	spinal problems, weak hips
Norwegian Forest Cat	domestic	long	medium	average activity, gentle, loves people, good family pet	none mentioned
Ocicat	domestic	short	low	average activity, devoted, easy to train, not shy, prefers multipet homes	none mentioned
Oriental Longhair	foreign	Short to med-long	low	high activity, talkative, in-your-face, one person cat	none mentioned

Persian	cobby	long	high	low activity, serene couch potato, good family pet	glaucoma, stud tail
RagaMuffin	domestic	medium-long	medium	Sweet, enjoys children, calm, patient	none mentioned
Ragdoll	domestic	long	high	low activity, sweet, gentle	none mentioned
Russian Blue	foreign	short	low	high activity, agile, playful, reserved, prefers being only cat	none mentioned
Scottish Fold	domestic	short or long	low or high	average activity, quiet, sweet-tempered, enjoys kids and other pets	inflexible tail, crippled hind limbs
Selkirk Rex	domestic	Short or long (curly)	low to medium	easy going, congenial	none mentioned
Siamese	foreign	short	low	high activity, extremely vocal, very trainable, loves people, great family pet	hyperesthesia syndrome, stud tail, asthma, glaucoma, wool sucking, breast cancer, cardiomyopathy
Siberian	domestic	long	medium	personable, calm, quiet, acrobatic, enjoy kids and other pets	none mentioned
Singapura	domestic	short	low	average activity, curious, friendly, enjoys kids and other pets	none mentioned
Snowshoe	semi-foreign	short	low	low activity, affectionate, lap cat, prefers being only cat	none mentioned
Somali	semi-foreign	Medium-long	medium	high activity, nonstop action, enjoys kids and other pets	hyperesthesia syndrome, anemia, kidney problems, overgrooming
Sphynx	semi-foreign	bald	low	average activity, gregarious, athletic, enjoys kids and other pets	oily skin, sometimes immune system problems
Tonkinese	semi-foreign	short	low	high activity, talkative, outgoing, loves people, enjoys kids and other pets	none mentioned
Turkish Angora	semi-foreign	Medium-long	low	average activity, intelligent, stubborn, hates noise, one person cat	none mentioned
Turkish Van	semi-foreign	Medium-long	medium	average activity, affectionate, a loner, prefers being only cat	none mentioned

APPENDIX B

RESOURCES

ANIMAL WELFARE & INFORMATION SOURCES

Alley Cat Allies
http://www.alleycat.org

Alley Cat Rescue
http://www.saveacat.org

American Humane Association
http://www.americanhumane.org

American Society for the Prevention of Cruelty to Animals
https://www.aspca.org

Barn Cats Inc.
http://barncats.org

Feral Cat Coalition
http://www.feralcat.com

Humane Society of the United States
http://www.humanesociety.org

522 CAT FACTS

National Animal Care and Control Association
http://www.nacanet.org

Pet Partners (formerly Delta Society)
https://petpartners.org/

FURTHER READING

Complete Kitten Care by Amy Shojai

ComPETability: Solving Behavior Problems in Your MultiCAT Houshold by Amy Shojai

ComPETability: Solving Behavior Problems in Your CAT-DOG Household by Amy Shojai

Complete Care for Your Aging Cat by Amy Shojai

New Choices in Natural Healing for Dogs and Cats by Amy Shojai

The First-Aid Companion for Dogs and Cats by Amy Shojai

PET SERVICES

International Boarding and Pet Services Association
http://www.ibpsa.com

National Association of Professional Pet Sitters
http://www.petsitters.org

National Animal Poison Control Center
https://www.aspca.org/pet-care/animal-poison-control

Pet Sitters International
https://www.petsit.com

Spay USA
http://www.spayusa.org

EXPERT RESOURCES

American Animal Hospital Association
https://www.aaha.org/pet_owner

Animal Behavior Society
http://www.animalbehaviorsociety.org/web/index.php

International Association of Animal Behavior Consultants
http://iaabc.org

American Holistic Veterinary Association
http://www.ahvma.org

American Veterinary Chiropractic Association
http://www.animalchiropractic.org

American Veterinary Medical Association
https://www.avma.org/Pages/home.aspx

CAT FACTS

The International Veterinary Acupuncture Society
https://www.ivas.org

American Board of Veterinary Practitioners
http://www.abvp.com

American Board of Veterinary Toxicology
http://www.abvt.org

American College of Theriogenologists
http://www.theriogenology.org/

American College of Veterinary Anesthesiologists
http://www.acva.org/

American College of Veterinary Behaviorists
http://www.dacvb.org/

American College of Veterinary Clinical Pharmacology
http://www.acvcp.org

American College of Veterinary Dermatology
http://www.acvd.org

American College of Veterinary Emergency and Critical Care
www.acvecc.org

American College of Veterinary Internal Medicine
http://www.acvim.org

American College of Veterinary Microbiologists
http://www.acvm.us

American College of Veterinary Nutrition
www.acvn.org

American College of Veterinary Ophthalmologists
http://www.acvo.org

American College of Veterinary Pathologists
http://www.acvp.org/

American College of Veterinary Preventive Medicine
http://www.acvpm.org

American College of Veterinary Radiology
http://www.acvr.org

American College of Veterinary Surgeons
http://www.acvs.org

American College of Zoological Medicine
http://www.aczm.org/aczmmain.html

American Veterinary Dental College
http://www.AVDC.org

FELINE RESEARCH ORGANIZATIONS AND FOUNDATIONS

CATalyst Council
http://www.catalystcouncil.org

526 CAT FACTS

Morris Animal Foundation
http://www.morrisanimalfoundation.org

Winn Feline Foundation for Cat Health
http://www.winnfelinefoundation.org

APPENDIX C

Symptoms at a Glance: The Quick Reference Guide for Home Diagnosis

The following correlates to an alphabetical list of the common signs and symptoms of illness with the troubling condition(s) that each may indicate. To use the chart, look up one or more of the problem signs your cat may be suffering. Then read the corresponding entry topic to learn more about a given disease or condition. This will help you identify what's troubling your cat and learn whether immediate veterinary care is necessary or a home remedy may suffice.

Whenever possible, the appropriate home treatment or first aid is listed in the text entry so that, if possible, you can tend to your cat yourself. However, this chart is only a *guide*. No book can ever replace the expertise of a veterinarian, who is in the best position to accurately diagnose and treat any troubling illness from which your cat may be suffering.

SIGNS AND SYMPTOMS	*DISEASE OR CONDITION*
Aggression, toward people/other pets	Dominance, fear, hyperesthesia syndrome, pain, rabies, stress
Aggression, toward self (mutilation)	Hyperesthesia syndrome
Appetite, increased	Diabetes mellitus, hyperthyroidism
Appetite, loss of (anorexia)	Abscess, anemia, aspirin poisoning, cancer, cystitis, dehydration, enteritis, feline hepatic Lipidosis and liver disease, FIV, feline panleukopenia, FIP, FeLV, fever, haemobartonellosis, hairballs, insect bites/stings, heart disease,

528 CAT FACTS

	kidney disease, LUTD, mastitis, pain, periodontal disease, peritonitis, pyometra, rabies, stomatitis, swallowed object, upper respiratory disease
Blackheads/pimples, on chin and mouth	Acne
Blackheads/pimples, at tail root	Stud tail
Bleeding	Cancer, poison, trauma
Blood, in queen's milk	Mastitis
Blood, in stool	Aspirin poisoning, Coccidiosis, colitis, hookworms, other poison
Blood, in urine	Cancer, cystitis, LUTD
Blood, in vomit	Aspirin poisoning, other poison
Bloody nose	Head trauma (falls), hyperthermia
Blindness	Cataract, epilepsy, FIP, FeLV, glaucoma, taurine deficiency, trauma
Breathing, choking/gagging	Hairballs, swallowed objects
Breathing, gasping, wheezing	Asthma, cancer, heartworms, pneumonia
Breathing, labored	Cardiomyopathy, electrical shock, FIV, heartworms, insect bites/stings, lungworms, pneumonia, vaccine or drug reaction
Breathing, panting	Antifreeze poisoning, pneumonia, pain
Breathing, rapid	Anemia, eclampsia, pneumonia, shock
Breathing, stopped	Drowning, electrical shock, hypothermia
Bumps	Abscess, cancer, cyst, plague, yellow fat disease, vaccination reaction
Chewing, fabric	Wool sucking
Chewing/grinding teeth	Seizure, rabies

Choking/gagging	Hairballs, swallowed objects
Circling	Head trauma, otitis
Claws, nail bed sores	FeLV, FIV
Claws, rapid growth	Hyperthyroidism
Coat condition, dry	Giardia, roundworms, tapeworms, yellow fat disease
Coat condition, oily	Hyperthyroidism, stud tail, yellow fat disease
Coat condition, ricelike debris	Tapeworms
collapse	Eclampsia, heartworms, insect bites/stings
constipation	Cancer, hairballs, inflammatory bowel disease, mega colon
coughing	Heartworms, lungworms, pneumonia
crying	Dominance display, estrus, pain
depression	Anemia, dehydration, fever, FeLV, feline panleukopenia, FIP, haemobartonellosis, kidney disease, peritonitis, rabies, shock, stress
diarrhea	Antifreeze poisoning, changing diet, chocolate poisoning, Coccidiosis, colitis, enteritis, feeding milk, feline panleukopenia, food allergy, giardia, hairballs, hookworms, hyperthermia, hyperthyroidism, liver disease, poisoning, roundworms, swallowed object, trichomoniasis
Drinking, difficulty/refusal	Cancer, rabies
Drinking, increased thirst	Antifreeze poisoning, cystitis, diabetes, mellitus, hyperthyroidism, kidney disease, LUTD, pyometra
Drooling	Aspirin poisoning, chocolate poisoning, eclampsia, foreign body, hyperthermia, insect bites/stings, pain, periodontal disease, poisoning, rabies, stomatitis
Drunk, incoordination	Antifreeze poisoning, aspirin poisoning, eclampsia, head trauma (high-rise syndrome), insect bites/stings, otitis, poisoning, xylitol poisoning
Ears, dark crumbly debris	Ear mites

530 CAT FACTS

Ears, discharge and/or odor	Otitis
Ears, red or raw	Allergy, otitis
Eyes, change of color	Uveitis
Eyes, cloudy	Cataract, glaucoma
Eyes, dilated	Glaucoma
Eyes, discharge/runny	FeLV, pain, upper respiratory infection
Eyes, glazed/staring	Hyperthermia, rabies
Eyes, hard	Glaucoma
Eyes, pawing at	Glaucoma, otitis, pain, uveitis
Eyes, rough surface	Uveitis
Eyes, soft	Uveitis
Eyes, sores/ulcers	Upper respiratory infection
Eyes, squinting	Glaucoma, otitis, pain, ulcer, uveitis
Eyes, swelling	Glaucoma
Flinching	Pain, fear
Hair loss	Eosinophilic granuloma complex, fleas, hyperthyroidism, mange, psychogenic alopecia, ringworm, shedding, stress, stud tail
Head tilt	Head trauma, otitis
Hiding	Fear, pain, stress
Hissing	Aggression, dominance, fear, pain, stress
Hunching (painful abdomen)	Cystitis, feline panleukopenia, peritonitis, swallowed object, trauma
Hyperactivity	Aspirin poisoning, chocolate poisoning, hyperthyroidism

Itching, of back and tail	Fleas
Itching, of chin	Acne
Itching, of ears	Ear mites, otitis
Itching, of face, mouth, head, and neck	Food allergy, mange
Itching, localized	Insect bites/stings
Itching, self-mutilation especially tail	Hyperesthesia syndrome
Lethargy	Abscess, cancer, cardiomyopathy, cystitis, fever, fleas, heartworms, hookworms, hypothermia, liver disease, LUTD, plague, xylitol poisoning
Licking, coat or skin	Abscess, allergy, fleas, insect bites/stings, lice, mange, ringworm
Licking, genitals	Anal gland problems, constipation, cystitis, labor, LUTD
Limping, lameness	Abscess, arthritis, cancer, fracture
Loss of consciousness	Asthma, chocolate poisoning, drowning, electrical shock, hyperthermia, hypothermia, shock, trauma
Lumps	Abscess, cancer, plague, vaccination reaction, yellow fat disease
Milk, yellow/blood streaked	mastitis
Mouth, blue-tinged tongue/gums	Pneumonia, respiratory distress, Tylenol poisoning
Mouth, bright red gums	Carbon monoxide poisoning, gingivitis, hyperthermia, hyperthyroidism
Mouth, brown tongue	Kidney disease
Mouth, burns	Caustic poison, electrical shock
Mouth, dry/tacky gums	Dehydration, kidney disease
Mouth, jaw paralysis	Abscess, fracture, rabies

Mouth, loose teeth	Gingivitis, periodontal disease, trauma
Mouth, pale	Anemia, eclampsia, fleas, haemobartonellosis, hookworms, shock, trauma
Mouth, pawing at	Swallowed object
Mouth, sores/ulcers	FIV, kidney disease, stomatitis, upper respiratory infection
Mouth, stringy saliva	dehydration
Mouth, swollen/bleeding	Gingivitis, insect bites/stings, periodontal disease, trauma
Mouth, yellow/brown tooth debris	Periodontal disease
Muscle tremors	Chocolate poisoning, dehydration, eclampsia, hyperesthesia syndrome
Nose, bloody	Cancer, hyperthermia, poisoning, shock, trauma
Nose, discharge/runny	FeLV, upper respiratory infection
Odor, anal area	Anal glands, flatulence, poor grooming
Odor, ammonia breath	Kidney disease
Odor, ammonia urine	Cystitis, LUTD
Odor, bad breath	Periodontal disease
Odor, of body	Cancer, mange
Odor, from ears	Otitis, cancer
Odor, mousy	Mange
Pacing	Eclampsia
Paddling, with feet	Dreaming, seizure (epilepsy)
Pale: ears, nose, toes, tail tip	Frostbite
Pulse, too fast	Anemia, hyperthermia, shock

Pulse, too slow	Hypothermia, poison
Rolling (female cats)	Estrus, play invitation
Rolling (male cats)	Play invitation
Scooting (on bottom)	Anal gland problems, tapeworms
Seizures	Antifreeze poisoning, chocolate poisoning, electrical shock, epilepsy, hyperesthesia syndrome, low blood sugar (diabetes), kidney disease, liver disease, poisoning, xylitol poisoning
Shivering	Hypothermia, shock, fear
Skin, loss of elasticity	Dehydration, kidney disease
Skin, lumpy/bumpy	Cancer, insect bites/stings, vaccination reaction, yellow fat disease
Skin, painful	Abscess, ulcer, yellow fat disease
Skin, pepperlike debris especially at tail	Fleas
Skin, red and peeling ears, toes, nose	Frostbite, sunburn
Skin, red and sores	Mange, ringworm
Skin, scabby	Fleas, lice, miliary dermatitis, ringworm
Skin, scaly	Lice, mange, yellow fat disease
Skin, thickened, especially around eyes and ears	Mange, sunburn
Skin, waxy debris at tail root	Stud tail
Skin, yellow crusting	Mange
Skin, yellow tinge (jaundice)	Haemobartonellosis, liver disease
Sleeping too much	Anemia, obesity

CAT FACTS

Sneezing	Upper respiratory infection
Sores, draining	Abscess, cuterebra, plague
Sores, slow healing	Cancer, ulcer
Stiffness, of joints	Arthritis, cancer
Stiffness, rear limb paralysis/pain	Cardiomyopathy, rabies
Stiffness, walking	Eclampsia, pain, peritonitis, yellow fat disease
Swelling, of abdomen (no pain)	FIP, giardia, obesity, pregnancy, roundworms
Swelling, of abdomen (painful)	Constipation, hairballs, LUTD (blockage), peritonitis, pyometra, swallowed object
Swelling, of breast	Cancer, mastitis
Swelling, of ear flap	Hematoma
Swelling, of ear tips, nose, tail, or toes	Frostbite
Swelling, of face/head	Abscess, insect bites/stings, tight collar, trauma
Swelling, of lymph nodes	FIV, plague, toxoplasmosis
Swelling, of skin	Abscess, acne, cuterebra, fracture, insect bites/stings, plague
Temperature, too cold	Anemia, antifreeze poisoning, dehydration, hypothermia, kidney disease, shock
Temperature, fever	Abscess, eclampsia, feline panleukopenia, FIP, FIV, haemobartonellosis, hyperthermia, mastitis, peritonitis, plague, pneumonia
Urination, blocked	LUTD
Urination, excessive	Antifreeze poisoning, chocolate poisoning, diabetes mellitus, hyperthyroidism, kidney disease, pyometra

Urination, frequent/small amounts	Cystitis, LUTD
Urination, in odd places	Cystitis, LUTD, stress
Urination, straining	Cancer, cystitis, LUTD, poison
Urination, with blood	Cancer, cystitis, LUTD, poison
Vaginal discharge	Imminent birth, pyometra
Vomiting	Antifreeze poisoning, aspirin poisoning, changing diet, chocolate poisoning, enteritis, feeding milk, food allergy, feline panleukopenia, FIV, hairballs, heartworms, hyperthermia, hyperthyroidism, inflammatory bowel disease, liver disease, roundworms, swallowed object, overeating, xylitol poisoning
Weakness	Anemia, cardiomyopathy, haemobartonellosis, hyperthermia, kidney disease, shock
Weight, unable to maintain	Giardia, poor nutrition, tapeworms
Weight gain	Diabetes mellitus, obesity
Weight loss	Anemia, cancer, diabetes mellitus, diarrhea, FeLV, FIV, FIP, heartworms, hyperthyroidism, kidney disease, liver disease, malnutrition, stomatitis

536 CAT FACTS

A

AAFCO, 398, 399, 401
About the author, 538
Abscess, 14, 118, 334, 375, 464
Acne, 17, 152
Acupoints, 19
Acupuncture, 19, 50, 138
Acupuncture resuscitation, 85
Additives, 204
Adequan, 50
Administer medication, 20, 44, 49, 98, 133, 357, 411
Adoption, of cat by human, 24
Adoption, of kittens (others) by cat, 25
Affection, 26, 115, 225, 331
Aggression, 27, 61, 134, 140, 170, 173, 191, 294, 330, 376, 379, 445, 462
Aging, 49, 104, 215
Allergens, 31
Allergies, 17, 19, 31, 33, 34, 35, 36, 53, 55, 137, 161, 229, 243, 336, 370
Allergies, of humans to cats, 36
Allergy, 36, 106, 133, 146, 160, 271, 289, 490
Aloofness, 37
Alter, 37
Amitriptyline, 120
Amputation, 38
Anal gland, 38
Anaphylaxis, 39
Anemia, 40
Anesthetic, 42
Anorexia, 43, 174, 346, 482
Antibodies, 31
Antifreeze, 44, 383, 467
Aromatherapy, 47
Arrhythmia, 47
Arthritis, 48, 129, 215, 256
Artificial respiration, 51, 84, 142, 155, 434
Aspirin toxicity, 52
Association Of American Feed Control Officials, 398
Asthma, 19, 36, 51, 53, 54, 55, 56, 246, 273, 408
Atopy or inhalant allergy, 32

B

Bach flowers, 198
Bad breath, 58, 367
Balance, 60, 145, 147, 170, 209, 256, 358
Bartonella henselae, 91
Bathing, 61, 233
Behavior modification, 29, 61, 130, 424
Biopsy, 124
Bites, 289
Bleeding, 40, 41, 52, 61, 62, 131, 132, 208, 233, 256, 343, 346, 350, 352, 383, 407, 428, 439, 440, 447, 503
Blindness, 64, 168, 221, 483
Blood, 15, 38, 40, 46, 52, 61, 64, 75, 80, 83, 85, 92, 100, 102, 103, 106, 117, 119, 121, 122, 123, 132, 133, 134, 135, 136, 138, 145, 162, 171, 177, 178, 180, 181, 182, 183, 184, 185, 186, 187, 188, 193, 194, 195, 205, 211, 244, 246, 248, 249, 250, 251, 252, 256, 258, 260, 262, 263, 264, 275, 276, 278, 282, 287, 288, 300, 301, 302, 303, 304, 310, 315, 316, 317, 320, 332, 334, 339, 343, 349, 362, 365, 370, 375, 376, 383, 389, 391, 408, 411, 419, 428, 434, 439, 447, 448, 455, 459, 464, 465, 470, 471, 475, 479, 481, 490, 493, 503, 504
Bone cancer, 75
Breed, 68
Breeding, 71
Brushing teeth, 371
Bubonic plague, 375, 376
Bunting, 331
Burns, 71
Byproducts, 401

C

Calorie, 176, 400
Cancer, 74, 124, 160, 184, 274, 323, 452, 490, 502
Car sickness, 86
Carbohydrates, 202, 203, 349
Carbon monoxide poisoning, 80

Carcinogen, 75
Cardiomyopathy, 81, 216, 244, 349, 460
Cardiopulmonary resuscitation (CPR), 52, 84, 142
Carnivore, 86
Cat associations, 90, 512
Cat scratch disease, 91
Cataract, 88, 168
Catnip, 90, 222, 423, 424, 425
Cesarean, 94
Chemotherapy, 77
Cherry eye, 95
Chiropractic, 96
Chlamydia, 97
Chocolate, 97, 383, 467
Choking, 98
Cholangiohepatitis, 317
Claws, 99, 233, 275, 388
Coccidiosis, 102
Cognitive dysfunction, 103
Colitis, 105, 106, 139
Communication, 16, 19, 30, 61, 104, 107, 109, 112, 115, 164, 170, 225, 334, 377, 391, 419, 458, 469, 492
Constipation, 115, 116, 241, 335
Coughing, 380, 409
Cross-match blood, 64
Cryosurgery, 79
Cryptorchid, 116, 117, 339, 343
CT-scans, 123
Cuterebra, 117, 184, 367, 447
Cyst, 117, 118, 217, 459
Cystitis, 119
Cytauxzoon, 121, 123, 465
Cytology, 76, 123, 124, 125

D

Deafness, 128
Declawing, 100, 129
Dehydration, 45, 46, 52, 103, 132, 133, 137, 179, 188, 274, 300, 349, 428, 419, 454, 464, 465
Demodectic mange, 327, 328
Dermatitis, 32, 133, 336, 337, 411, 450, 496
Dermis, 429, 469
Destructive behavior, 134
Diabetes, 58, 88, 132, 134, 135, 136, 203, 216, 303, 352, 364, 436

Diarrhea, 24, 34, 35, 43, 45, 48, 52, 97, 98, 102, 106, 132, 133, 137, 138, 152, 158, 159, 178, 185, 188, 206, 241, 242, 252, 260, 261, 263, 273, 288, 289, 316, 333, 339, 382, 383, 414, 418, 419, 428, 454, 475, 476, 490, 493
Diets, 35, 50, 81, 88, 106, 116, 134, 152, 153, 192, 200, 203, 204, 205, 216, 241, 302, 321, 322, 336, 350, 352, 354, 355, 367, 371, 400, 506
Dilated cardiomyopathy, 81
Displacement grooming, 225, 226, 229
Distemper, 139
Dominance, 139, 140
Dreaming, 141, 432
Drinking, 141
Drowning, 142

E

Ears, 61, 110, 129, 144, 145, 147, 238, 355
Ear mites, 21, 61, 128, 144, 237, 249, 327, 367
Eating, 61, 141, 149, 174, 221, 467, 507
Echocardiography, 83, 246, 479
Eclampsia, 153, 154, 326, 339
Electrical shock, 71, 155
Elizabethan collar, 16, 156, 157, 250, 344
Endoscope, 158, 282, 365, 455
Enteritis, 139, 158, 180
Eosinophilic granuloma complex, 36, 160, 311, 414
Epidermis, 429, 469
Epilepsy, 160, 162, 179, 184, 381
Estrus, 402, 403, 404, 408, 439
Euthanasia, 163, 164
Euthanasia, 163
Eyes, 32, 36, 37, 65, 88, 89, 93, 95, 109, 122, 124, 128, 141, 162, 164, 167, 168, 182, 186, 218, 224, 229, 231, 236, 237, 256, 266, 270, 273, 306, 308, 316, 327, 344, 411, 450, 471, 478, 480, 482, 483, 490, 491, 492, 498

F

Falling, 170
False pregnancy, 170
Fats, 349
Fatty liver disease, 43, 170
FDA, 35, 50, 79, 104, 147, 205, 210, 363, 390, 398, 448

Fear, 28, 61, 140, 170, 379, 445, 462
Fecal impaction, 336
Feeding, 174
Fel d1, 36
Feline aids, 174, 177
Feline calicivirus, 174
Feline enteric coronavirus, 174
Feline hepatic lipidosis, 43, 170, 174, 317, 354
Feline immunodeficiency virus, 41, 174, 177
Feline infectious anemia, 179
Feline infectious peritonitis, 41, 174, 180
Feline ischemic encephalopathy, 183
Feline leukemia virus, 41, 184
Feline panleukopenia, 137, 139, 160, 180, 187, 367
Feline rhinotracheitis, 189
Feline sarcoma virus, 75
Feline urologic syndrome, 189
FeLV, 74, 75, 76, 178, 179, 184, 185, 186, 189, 486, 487, 490
Feral, 37, 189, 190, 215, 265, 292, 308, 342, 359, 360, 397, 398, 434, 441, 443
Fever, 191
Fibrosarcoma, 75, 76, 79, 124
Fighting, 191
FIP, 180, 181, 182, 441, 486
FIV, 74, 177, 178, 179, 189, 486, 487
Flatulence, 192
Flea, 32, 193, 195, 197, 224, 367, 382, 458
Flea allergy, 17, 32
Flower essences, 18, 30, 198, 223
Food, 34, 43, 86, 137, 150, 153, 188, 192, 199, 204, 205, 206, 315, 334, 337, 350, 354, 355, 366, 367, 398, 399, 407, 408, 426, 507
Food allergy, 34
FPV, 187, 188, 486
Fracture, 207
Frostbite, 71, 211, 212
Fur, 15, 16, 17, 18, 28, 32, 33, 47, 49, 62, 68, 71, 76, 99, 109, 112, 115, 131, 149, 162, 170, 195, 199, 224, 225, 229, 231, 235, 236, 237, 240, 241, 242, 263, 276, 278, 283, 289, 290, 308, 311, 326, 336, 343, 349, 371, 388, 389, 407, 413, 426, 430, 432, 449, 458, 464, 469, 479, 496

G

Geriatric, 29, 64, 115, 164, 200, 215, 216, 274, 277, 300, 304, 311, 321
Gestation, 405
Giardia, 106, 137, 160, 217, 289, 367, 475
Gingivitis, 218
Glaucoma, 168, 218, 219
Glucosamine, 50
Glucose, 134, 135, 136, 137, 503
Grass, eating, 221
Grief, 164, 221, 222
Grooming, 17, 61, 100, 129, 132, 168, 216, 224, 225, 229, 241, 306, 342, 358, 427, 432, 456, 479

H

Haemobartonellosis, 250
Hair, 16, 17, 26, 36, 37, 68, 72, 77, 148, 193, 195, 197, 206, 217, 224, 225, 229, 231, 233, 240, 241, 242, 243, 277, 322, 327, 343, 345, 366, 409, 411, 412, 413, 426, 427, 429, 449, 450, 452, 456, 469, 493, 497, 498, 506
Hair loss, 133, 229, 242, 412, 446
Hairballs, 115, 137, 241
Heart disease, 244
Heart failure, 83
Heartbeat, 244
Heartworm, 123, 244, 246, 247, 263, 366, 367, 409
Heat stroke, 247
Hematoma, 62, 145, 248, 355
Hemodialysis, 302
Hemolytic anemia, 41
Hemotrophic mycoplasmas, 179, 250, 367
Hepatitis, 317
Herbs, 252
High rise syndrome, 61, 170, 210, 254, 428
Hip dysplasia, 256
Holistic, 19, 47, 55, 79, 96, 163, 193, 198, 206, 223, 252, 258, 259, 261, 318, 357, 371
Homeopathy, 39, 44, 84, 87, 116, 121, 138, 223, 258, 259, 260, 261, 288, 291
Hookworms, 106, 137, 160, 262, 263, 270, 367, 510
Houseplants, hazards from, 263, 383
Human-animal bond, 30, 263
Human-grade, 402

Hunting, 61, 149, 159, 164, 190, 265, 266, 269, 270, 322, 374, 342, 374, 376, 389, 434
Hyperesthesia syndrome, 161, 173, 270
Hyperthermia, 154, 247, 272, 408, 462
Hyperthyroidism, 48, 216, 274, 276, 301, 436
Hypertrophic cardiomyopathy, 82
Hypothermia, 142, 212, 276, 278, 360, 463

I

Ibuprofen, 282, 283
Identification, 30, 36, 76, 283, 443
Imaging, 285
Immune system, 185, 188, 215, 245, 287, 407
Immunotherapy, 34, 36
Inflammation, 39, 48, 49, 50, 54, 55, 64, 79, 88, 89, 105, 106, 115, 119, 120, 121, 123, 129, 133, 145, 146, 158, 181, 210, 218, 219, 221, 246, 288, 289, 310, 317, 333, 355, 357, 358, 362, 363, 364, 365, 368, 370, 373, 379, 390, 411, 440, 441, 447, 448, 450, 452, 475, 480, 483, 484, 506, 507
Incontinence, 288
Inflammatory bowel disease, 106, 139, 288, 289, 475, 476
Insect bites, 40, 289
Insulin,, 134, 136
Introductions, 24, 30, 292, 295, 444

J

Jacobson's organ, 298, 345

K

Kidney disease, 41, 44, 132, 215, 275, 300, 319
Kidney transplants, 304
Kitten, 26, 30, 37, 61, 63, 86, 92, 94, 152, 162, 171, 176, 204, 233, 278, 287, 289, 295, 304, 306, 307, 308, 313, 334, 337, 348, 350, 370, 376, 394, 400, 407, 426, 429, 434, 435, 441, 460, 462, 486, 487, 488, 497
Kitten socialization, 26, 308
Kneading, 306, 309, 332, 391

L

Labor, 94, 407
Language, 107, 109, 264
Lasers, 310
Lice, 32, 224, 311, 336, 367
Lick granulomas, 160, 311
Limited antigen diet, 35
Litter, 14, 24, 37, 53, 66, 103, 104, 115, 119, 123, 130, 131, 132, 150, 153, 159, 177, 185, 186, 187, 195, 200, 201, 215, 216, 217, 241, 263, 306, 311, 312, 313, 314, 315, 328, 336, 405, 419, 436, 437, 438, 444, 453, 458, 471, 475, 476, 480
Litter box, 131, 177, 313, 315, 436, 472, 476, 480
Liver disease, 315
Lower urinary tract disease, 119, 121, 189, 318, 320, 321
Lungworms, 322
Lymph gland cancers, 75
Lymphosarcoma, 323

M

Mammary glands, 326, 407
Mange, 32, 144, 146, 327, 336
Marking, 61, 107, 131, 140, 172, 328, 404, 437, 441, 445
Massage, 51, 96, 136, 146, 212, 223, 226, 257, 258, 332, 333, 334
Mastitis, 326, 333
Mating, 334
Medicate, 20
Mega colon, 335
Meridians, 20
Microfilaria, 336
Microsporum canis, 411
Middening, 329
Miliary dermatitis, 32, 336
Milk, 137, 153, 334, 337, 339, 408
Milk fever, 153
Minerals, 349
Monorchid, 339
MRI, 123, 271, 285, 448
Music therapy, 171, 339, 426

540 CAT FACTS

N

Nail clipping, 342
Natural food, 68, 204, 205, 401, 518
Navigation, 342
Neoplasms, 74
Nest, 270, 278, 290, 306, 313, 407, 474
Neuter, 24, 29, 37, 76, 117, 134, 328, 342, 343, 344, 352, 405, 443, 448
Nictitating membrane, 344
Nose, 22, 24, 36, 43, 44, 47, 52, 62, 74, 85, 117, 147, 156, 175, 186, 256, 273, 291, 293, 298, 308, 344, 345, 346, 383, 388, 408, 419, 429, 437, 450, 453, 468, 480, 482, 486, 490
Notoedric mange, 327
Nutraceuticals, 206
Nutrient, 62, 86, 176, 200, 204, 205, 241, 274, 288, 347, 348, 349, 350, 399, 400, 401, 407, 458
Nutrigenomics, 347, 354
Nutrition, 43, 81, 86, 88, 152, 153, 174, 179, 183, 200, 201, 202, 204, 205, 206, 215, 216, 241, 336, 347, 348, 349, 350, 354, 355, 365, 371, 380, 399, 402, 407, 418, 460, 492, 493, 507

O

Obese, 51, 174, 177, 203, 273, 317, 349, 352, 355, 379
Old, 9, 43, 51, 54, 74, 75, 88, 90, 91, 104, 130, 134, 148, 152, 160, 161, 180, 181, 186, 190, 192, 215, 233, 242, 246, 251, 252, 256, 258, 270, 282, 300, 303, 304, 307, 308, 328, 330, 332, 352, 362, 367, 371, 391, 392, 400, 403, 413, 414, 427, 432, 441, 443, 460, 486, 538
Olfaction, 344
Oral medications, 22
Oral tumors, 75
Organic food, 401
Otitis, 61, 128, 145, 237, 249, 355
Otodectic mange, 144, 327
Outdoor shelter, 212, 215, 278, 358
Ovariohysterectomy, 360

P

Pain, 19, 27, 38, 42, 43, 48, 49, 50, 52, 72, 79, 83, 119, 121, 123, 130, 132, 163, 168, 171, 188, 209, 210, 212, 215, 219, 221, 271, 276, 282, 289, 290, 310, 332, 333, 340, 362, 363, 364, 369, 371, 373, 382, 388, 389, 390, 391, 397, 409, 411, 418, 426, 436, 448, 452, 465, 466, 469, 471, 475, 481, 484
Pancreas, 134, 135, 136, 206, 316, 364, 365
Pancreatitis, 135, 206, 364
Panleukopenia, 367
Parasite, 102, 117, 118, 121, 122, 123, 146, 184, 193, 217, 233, 243, 245, 250, 251, 252, 262, 263, 289, 311, 322, 367, 370, 414, 447, 458, 465, 469, 475, 499
Pathologist, 123, 124
Pathologists, 124, 521
Periodontal disease, 58, 179, 203, 218, 238, 367, 441, 460, 461
Peritonitis, 373, 455
Pest poisons, 383
Pet foods, 204, 205, 350, 399, 401, 402, 418
Photodynamic therapy, 79
Pilling a cat, 22
Plague, 374, 376
Plasma, 62
Platelets, 62
Play, 61, 265, 376, 379, 389, 426
Play aggression, *29*
Plural effusion, 83
Pneumonia, 379, 380
Poison, 44, 47, 49, 71, 98, 137, 221, 263, 283, 381, 476
Polydactyl, 99
Porcupine, 388, 389
Predator, 190, 265, 329, 431
Predatory aggression, 29, 389
Pregnancy, 170, 177, 389, 405, 439, 471, 489
Protein, 32, 35, 36, 63, 88, 100, 115, 135, 193, 202, 206, 241, 287, 289, 300, 301, 302, 303, 320, 337, 347, 349, 350, 371, 399, 400, 401
Pulmonary edema, 83
Pulse, 244, 389
Pulsed electromagnetic field, 50, 79, 210, 363, 390, 448
Purr, 141, 231, 306, 391, 411
Pyometra, 392

Q

Qi, 19
Quarantine, 24, 186, 394, 443, 482
Queen, 63, 94, 119, 153, 154, 185, 305, 306, 307, 334, 337, 338, 391, 394, 400, 405, 407, 408, 483

R

Rabies, 76, 189, 394, 396, 397, 398, 486, 487, 488, 489, 490
Radiation, 77, 78
Reading food labels, 192, 204, 205, 350, 398
Redirected aggression, 28
Reproduction, 61, 71, 94, 117, 119, 170, 334, 389, 402, 466, 497
Respiration, 408
Respiratory distress, 51, 408
Restraint, 209, 233, 409
Restrictive cardiomyopathy, 82
Ringworm, 212, 243, 336, 411, 412, 413, 486, 510
Rodent ulcer, 414
Roundworm, 244, 414

S

Salmonella, 206, 418
Sarcoptic mange, 327
Scent, 419
Scratching, 61, 134, 330, 331, 419, 420, 472
Sedative, 42
Seizure, 161, 162, 163, 184, 270, 379, 389, 447
Separation anxiety, 173, 222, 424
Sexing, 426
Shedding, 241, 242, 412, 426
Shock, 71, 133, 156, 208, 274, 428
Skin, 429
Skin cancer, 75
Skunk, 430
Sleep, 18, 26, 40, 104, 115, 141, 163, 215, 216, 254, 340, 352, 364, 390, 426, 431, 432, 443
Smell, 43, 58, 90, 203, 253, 298, 300, 306, 344, 345, 346, 383, 436, 437, 482
Smoke inhalation, 434
Social structure, 434
Socialization, 171, 434
Soiling, 61, 134, 173, 288, 315, 330, 436, 445
Spaying, 24, 37, 352, 360, 405, 438
Spraying, 28, 172, 328, 342, 404
Spraying, 441
Stalking, 29, 30, 267, 270, 376, 378
Status-related aggression, 28
Steatitis, 441, 506
Stings, 39, 40, 289, 290
Stomatitis, 370, 371, 441
Stray, 37, 189, 441
Stress, 42, 43, 47, 51, 53, 55, 82, 115, 119, 120, 121, 133, 135, 136, 199, 207, 215, 229, 235, 243, 263, 264, 271, 276, 288, 308, 318, 328, 332, 339, 344, 358, 379, 389, 400, 420, 423, 424, 427, 434, 444, 445, 446, 456, 475, 488
Stroke, 118, 184, 247, 447
Stud tail, 448
Sunburn, 450
Supplements, 84, 137, 154, 192, 204, 205, 206, 241, 258, 276, 289, 317, 400, 401, 407
Swallowed objects, 51, 98, 115, 137, 158, 160, 241, 379, 453
Sweat, 132, 224, 429, 456, 469

T

Tail, 38, 51, 55, 62, 68, 69, 76, 97, 100, 112, 115, 141, 146, 149, 195, 197, 207, 209, 211, 225, 231, 236, 270, 276, 328, 331, 332, 339, 340, 362, 404, 405, 407, 426, 427, 436, 448, 449, 456, 458, 463, 469, 490
Tapeworms, 458, 460
Tartar, 460
Taste, 460
Taurine, 81, 460
Teeth, 150, 460
Temperature, 122, 154, 191, 462
Territorial aggression, 28
Tetanus, 463
Theobromine, 97
Thrombosis, 83
Ticks, 121, 224, 367, 464, 510
TNR, 189, 190
Toenail, 99
Tom, 466
Tongue, 150, 225, 402, 460, 466
Topical treatments, 21
Touch, 229, 468

Toxoplasmosis, 206, 469, 510
Training, 107, 471
Transfusion, 63
Trap-neuter-return, 189
Traveling, 472
Treading, 308
Trichomoniasis, 106, 139, 289, 367, 475
TTouch, 223, 332
Tumors, 74, 77, 124, 218
Tylenol, 476

U

Ulcer, 160, 282, 478
Ultrasound, 89, 124, 182, 301, 302, 303, 317, 340, 365, 392, 479
Unthrifty, 479
Upper respiratory infection, 43, 370, 380, 480
Upper respiratory infection, 43, 97, 174, 188, 189, 346, 370, 380, 480, 481, 482, 486, 490
USDA, 398, 401, 402
Uveitis, 64, 168, 218, 483

V

Vaccinations, 188, 287, 405, 482, 486, 489
Vaccine-associated fibrosarcomas, 75
Vestibular apparatus, 60
Vestibular syndrome, 491
Vision, 492
Vitamins, 34, 204, 206, 349, 492

Vocalization, 492
Vomeronasal organ, 298, 492
Vomiting, 35, 40, 43, 45, 48, 52, 64, 77, 81, 97, 98, 132, 133, 158, 177, 179, 188, 206, 221, 241, 246, 259, 273, 282, 283, 288, 289, 316, 365, 381, 382, 383, 418, 428, 453, 454, 490, 492, 493, 503

W

Walking dandruff, 496
Weaning, 307, 400, 408, 497
Wheezing, 408
Whiskers, 77, 78, 110, 141, 150, 225, 241, 330, 497
Wool sucking, 498
Worms, 499

X

X-rays, 49, 54, 77, 83, 96, 158, 209, 246, 257, 258, 276, 285, 301, 303, 380, 455, 479, 502
Xylitol poisoning, 503

Y

Yellow fat disease, 204, 441, 506

Z

Zoonosis, 94, 376, 397, 411, 471, 510

About the Author

Amy Shojai is a certified animal behavior consultant, and the award-winning author of more than 30 bestselling pet books that cover furry babies to old fogies, first aid to natural healing, and behavior/training to Chicken Soupicity. She has been featured as an expert in hundreds of print venues including the Wall Street Journal, the New York Times, Reader's Digest, and Family Circle, as well as television networks such as CNN, and Animal Planet's DOGS 101 and CATS 101. Amy brings her unique pet-centric viewpoint to public appearances. She is also a playwright and co-author of STRAYS, THE MUSICAL and the author of the critically acclaimed September Day pet-centric Suspense Series.

546
CAT FACTS

Printed in Great Britain
by Amazon

bb79336c-1922-4068-86fd-1f223b96fc0fR01